# The Subprime Virus

# The Subprime Virus

## Reckless Credit, Regulatory Failure, and Next Steps

KATHLEEN C. ENGEL
PATRICIA A. McCOY

OXFORD
UNIVERSITY PRESS

2011

# OXFORD
UNIVERSITY PRESS

Oxford University Press, Inc., publishes works that further
Oxford University's objective of excellence
in research, scholarship, and education.

Oxford   New York
Auckland   Cape Town   Dar es Salaam   Hong Kong   Karachi
Kuala Lumpur   Madrid   Melbourne   Mexico City   Nairobi
New Delhi   Shanghai   Taipei   Toronto

With offices in
Argentina   Austria   Brazil   Chile   Czech Republic   France   Greece
Guatemala   Hungary   Italy   Japan   Poland   Portugal   Singapore
South Korea   Switzerland   Thailand   Turkey   Ukraine   Vietnam

Published by Oxford University Press, Inc.
198 Madison Avenue, New York, NY 10016

www.oup.com

Oxford is a registered trademark of Oxford University Press.

Library of Congress Cataloging-in-Publication Data
Engel, Kathleen C.
The subprime virus : reckless credit, regulatory failure,
and next steps / by Kathleen C. Engel and Patricia A. McCoy.
p.   cm.
Includes bibliographical references and index.
ISBN 978-0-19-538882-4
1. Subprime mortgage loans—United States.  2. Financial crises—United States.
I. McCoy, Patricia A., 1954–  II. Title.
HG2040.5.U5E54 2010
332.7'20973—dc22   2010003614

9 8 7 6 5 4 3 2 1

Printed in the United States of America
on acid-free paper

*To the memory of Fred Rebitzer, who understood
and believed in this project.
(K.C.E.)*

*To Chris, for being there for me.
(P.A.M.)*

# Contents

## Part IV  Solutions

# Acknowledgments

In the late 1990s, we embarked on a journey to understand why high-risk loans were ravishing Cleveland's neighborhoods. Little did we know that our voyage would last for more than a decade and eventually pay witness to the greatest financial cataclysm in most Americans' lifetimes.

Along the way, countless people assisted us with their insights, critiques, and support. Readers should not assume that those we thank endorse all of our ideas; many of the people we consulted had different points of view. To anyone we inadvertently forgot to mention, please accept our apologies. Any mistakes in this book are ours alone.

We have worked with a number of immensely talented collaborators. We are especially grateful to our coauthor, Susan Wachter, who was one of the first economists to encourage our research. The knowledge and intellectual rigor of our other coauthors, Raphael Bostic, Souphala Chomsisengphet, and Anthony Pennington-Cross, enriched our understanding of subprime lending and, in turn, this book. Recently, we have also had the pleasure of coauthoring with a talented new scholar, Thomas Fitzpatrick. Amy Dunbar and Andrey Pavlov, who have written articles with Pat, shed valuable light on subprime accounting issues and the workings of credit default swaps.

Over the years, we have benefited from the ideas of many other academics, researchers, and advocates. At the top of the list are Elizabeth Renuart and Kathleen Keest, who understand credit regulation better than anyone we know and have always been willing to teach us and engage with our ideas. Many other valued colleagues advanced our work by sharing their knowledge, playing devil's advocate, and urging us to refine our analyses. They include Bill Apgar, Vicki Been, Eric Belsky, Mark Budnitz, Kevin Byers, Jim Campen, Jim Carr, Mark Cassell, Ruth Clevenger, Marcia Courchane, Prentiss Cox, Steve Davidoff, Andy Davidson, Kurt Eggert, Ingrid Ellen, Keith Ernst, Ren Essene, Allen Fishbein, Linda Fisher, Jim Follain, Anna Gelpern, Ira Goldstein, Cassandra Havard, Howell Jackson, Melissa Jacoby, Creola Johnson, Adam Levitin, Alan Mallach, Cathy Mansfield, Joe Mason, George McCarthy, Larry Mitchell, Kathy Newman, Gail Pearson, Vanessa Perry, Chris Peterson, Katie Porter, Roberto Quercia, Harry Rajak, David Reiss, Kris Rengert, Steve Ross, Julia Sass

Rubin, Mark Rukavina, Heidi Schooner, Steve Schwarcz, Peter Siegelman, Greg Squires, Eric Stein, Michael Stegman, Elizabeth Warren, Henry Weinstein, Alan White, Larry White, Lauren Willis, Elvin Wyly, and Peter Zorn.

Other colleagues nourished our work through their real-world insights and suggestions for creative solutions to the problems created by subprime lending. They include Erin Boggs, Bill Breetz, Jean-Stéphane Bron, Mike Calhoun, Alys Cohen, Josh Cohen, Nadine Cohen, Gabriel Davel, Thomas Fitzgibbon, Bruce Gottschall, Patty Hasson, Carole Heyward, Adrienne Hurt, Tom James, Kirsten Keefe, Erin Kemple, Kermit Lind, Ruhi Maker, Jonathan Miller, Mark Pearce, Mark Pinsky, Howard Pitkin, John Relman, Jim Rokakis, Joe Smith, Diane Thompson, Jim Tierney, Cathy Toth, Jim Vitarello, Mark Willis, and Mark Wiseman. The late Ned Gramlich deserves his own separate mention as a source of inspiration.

This book also draws on the exceptional work of the National Consumer Law Center, the Center for Responsible Lending, the National Association of Consumer Advocates, AARP and the International Association of Consumer Lawyers. We don't have the space to individually name the staff and members of these organizations, and hope they know that by naming their organizations we are thanking them.

Closer to home, students in our seminars and our research assistants, especially John McGrath, Marcello Phillips, and Matt Vogt, enriched our research. The two research assistants who deserve our greatest thanks are Moira Kearney-Marks and Emily Porter, whose dedication and compulsiveness made it possible for us to complete the book.

Faculty colleagues, both at our law schools and elsewhere, commented generously on our work in a series of faculty workshops and symposia. Participants at seminars from South Africa and Australia to China and Peru also helped us hone our ideas. The Cleveland-Marshall Fund, the Leon M. and Gloria Plevin Endowment, Suffolk University Law School, and the University of Connecticut Law School Foundation provided us with generous financial support. Without librarians, books like ours would not be possible, and so special thanks go to Cleveland-Marshall librarians Schuyler Cook, Laura Ray, and Jessica Mathewson, and Yan Hong and Lee Sims at the University of Connecticut.

We are grateful to our editors at Oxford University Press. Terry Vaughn's enthusiasm for this project buoyed us countless times when we thought the writing would never end. The gracious and efficient Catherine Rae ably managed the production process and Keith Faivre and Marc Schneider shepherded us through the editing process with aplomb.

*Kathleen's thanks:* My parents and siblings and all the Rebitzer-Eckstein clan have been steadfast in their support of my research on mortgage lending and housing discrimination. Special thanks go to my mother, Joan Kaler, my third mother, Magda Rebitzer, and sisters, Karen Kearns and Terri Spinney, who actually read some of the book when it was too rough to show anyone other than family. My dearest of friends, Barbara McQueen, Dena Davis, and Lynne Brill, were my emotional mainstays and heard more whining than any friends deserve.

More than twenty-five years ago, I met my husband, Jim Rebitzer, who taught me economics. Without his constant lessons, I would not have had the confidence or knowledge to venture into research on financial markets. Jim's other gift has been his inexhaustible curiosity. Anyone who knows Jim knows he asks more than a few questions when a topic grabs him. Thankfully, this book grabbed him and his probing forced me to sharpen my thinking and exposition. My final thanks are to my wonderful girls, Hannah and Eden, for being fun, for being interested in my work, and for forgiving my preoccupation with this book.

*Pat's thanks*: I owe a special debt of gratitude to John Day, Sophie Smyth, and Art Wilmarth, who gave unstintingly of their time, both as sounding boards and as friends. I can never repay them; I can only hope to return the favor in kind. Others also supported me professionally and personally during the long haul leading up to this book. Peter Diamond paved the way for my empirical subprime work by generously inviting me to spend a year at the MIT Economics Department as a visiting scholar. Jeremy Paul believed in this project from the start, pushed me to refine my ideas, and championed my work in tangible and intangible ways alike. Peter Lindseth was a repeated source of inspiration. And I could not have completed this book without Kunal Parker's keen intellect, friendship, and merriment.

A number of kind souls kept me afloat while I raced to finish the manuscript. Peter Kochenburger, Patricia Carbray, and Blanche Capilos were the mainstays of the Insurance Law Center throughout. Ronald Buonomano provided the gentle nudging I needed to live a balanced life. Thanks, too, to Rick Coffey for his infinite patience and for summoning so much beauty on earth.

While writing *The Subprime Virus*, we often delighted in memories of Kathleen's father-in-law, Fred Rebitzer, and Pat's mother, Vivian Rogers, who both offered tokens of their love by forwarding to us every news clipping on subprime loans they could find. Their spirits live on in us and in this book.

# The Subprime Virus

# 1

▷

# Prologue

Hope doesn't come easy in Cleveland. You can see that on Chester Avenue, a hard-luck street spanning the leafy East Side suburbs and downtown Cleveland. A drive down Chester goes through Hough, one of Cleveland's poor neighborhoods, then courses through a midtown corridor with nondescript office buildings and vacant lots before ending up downtown. Still, every time we drove down Chester Avenue in the late 1990s to teach at Cleveland State, we felt a sense of hope. New homes were rising in Hough on lots once scarred by riots. The furnaces of the old LTV steel plant were firing, and the river that had once caught on fire had returned to its natural state. It looked like Cleveland might be shedding its reputation as a postindustrial wasteland after all.

That hope turned out to be fragile. Around 1999, we started hearing the term *predatory lending*. Lawyers and community organizers related incidents of mortgage brokers and lenders who duped homeowners with exorbitantly costly loans. These stories multiplied and so did Cleveland foreclosures. Eventually, Cleveland became the epicenter of the subprime crisis and the poster child for all that went wrong in the home mortgage market.

During Cleveland's Gilded Age, Chester Avenue, with its elegant homes and churches, mirrored the city's wealth. It was an address to have. After World War II, however, Chester Avenue went into decline as whites fled to the quiet of the suburbs, spurred by "block busting" realtors. Landlords carved the grand Chester homes into cramped apartments that they rented—often at outrageous prices—to blacks, who had moved north in search of prosperity and jobs. Over time, Hough's residents came to struggle with unemployment, discrimination, poverty, and crime. In the summer of 1966, six nights of riots left Hough a burned-out shell.

By the early 1990s, Chester Avenue was a depressing sight. Hough was strewn with empty lots and boarded-up drug houses. Crime plagued the streets, and firefighters torched vacant apartment buildings to practice extinguishing fires. Over half of Hough's children dropped out of school, and unemployment soared to 83 percent. Banks shunned Hough, and the neighborhood languished from years of disinvestment and neglect. Chester, once the emblem of Cleveland's glory, had become a symbol of the city's hard luck.

But change was in the offing. In 1994, the Clinton administration injected millions of dollars into Cleveland for urban development, and the city started revitalizing Chester Avenue block by block. The city razed abandoned buildings, sold empty lots to urban homesteaders, and helped them secure construction loans to build. Police, firefighters, and other city workers bought homes in Hough, enticed by generous tax abatements. New townhouses sprung up, and President Clinton cut the ribbon for the first new inner-city shopping center in Cleveland in years. Closer to downtown, sleek new glass and steel buildings replaced some of the vacant, weed-filled lots. To everyone's astonishment, even a few McMansions graced Chester Avenue.

In 1999, we attended a conference, in a drab, stuffy auditorium in downtown Cleveland, where Stella Adams, a rousing community activist from North Carolina, described, in stark detail, loan abuses she was seeing in her state. Riveted, we nodded in recognition. We, too, had been hearing about rapacious loans. Activists and government officials told us about lenders who refinanced zero-interest Habitat for Humanity loans into loans with high fees and interest rates of over 15 percent. Mortgage brokers were going door-to-door in neighborhoods with modest homes and persuading homeowners to take out loans that they could not afford. Foreclosure rates were starting to rise. It seemed that just when property values were going up in Cleveland, lenders and brokers were showing up to extract borrowers' wealth.

In that instant, we knew we would tackle the problem of subprime lending. We understood how unethical mortgage brokers could charge inflated commissions. But we could not fathom why lenders would make loans that borrowers could not afford to repay. Foreclosures yield about fifty cents on the dollar. So why would lenders do business when the endgame was foreclosure? We set out to answer this question.

Little did we know that our quest would consume us for the next ten years. We certainly had no idea that bad loans in Cleveland would ultimately play a role in freezing world credit markets and pushing the United States into a recession. Even more absurd was the notion that subprime loans would prevent a small town in Norway from paying its municipal workers or cause the cost of sawdust to rise 25 percent. But all this happened, and this book explains how.

When we started digging for explanations for why lenders were making loans that were doomed to fail, we tripped upon a whole new mortgage market—the subprime market—that offered loans that were strikingly different from traditional "prime" loans. What we saw resembled the wild West. Subprime interest rates were sometimes double the rates on prime loans. Closing costs on one loan alone could add up to tens of thousands of dollars. Borrowers could not lock in their interest rates, and lenders pulled bait-and-switch scams at closings.

During the 1990s, the subprime market had a subterranean existence that was barely apparent to middle-class whites. Lenders marketed these loans to people who had been turned down for credit in the past because of discrimination or bad credit or both. This meant people of limited means and people of color. Subprime lenders plied racially mixed neighborhoods with credit, posting ads on telephone poles and billboards. Mortgage brokers, the foot soldiers of the subprime industry, hawked shady loans door-to-door.

On the surface, what we observed reeked of old-fashioned loan sharking. But when we looked more closely, we found a highly institutionalized industry. Even in the 1990s, some subprime lenders were bank affiliates with names that obscured their ownership ties to banks. Other subprime lenders were independent, publicly traded companies. Wall Street was also heavily implicated as the major financier of subprime loans.

Initially, one of our challenges was to explain how subprime lending had gotten its start. Throughout the 1980s, the problem was lack of credit, not abusive loans. Banks were redlining inner-city neighborhoods, and blacks and Hispanics had difficulty getting loans. People with poor credit or low savings could forget about getting a mortgage.

So why did easy credit arrive on the scene in the 1990s? We discovered that the mortgage industry had undergone a radical transformation. Previously, one lender had done it all: solicited loan applications and underwritten, funded, and serviced loans. Then subprime securitization—a novel technique on Wall Street for financing loans—transformed the market. Rather than have one entity serve all the functions related to loans, securitization led to the evolution of a lending food chain that involved entities from mortgage brokers and lenders, to investment banks and rating agencies, each of which collected upfront fees and passed the risk of a bad loan down the line, ultimately stopping with investors.

Although we came to understand why lenders made subprime loans, there was still the question why borrowers would enter into these loans. This query led us into the field of behavioral economics. Borrowers bring psychological biases to their decision-making and sometimes act in ways that are not rational. Brokers and lenders, in turn, exploit borrowers' irrationality by offering bafflingly complex products and using clever marketing techniques.

Another puzzle was why competition did not drive down the price of subprime loans. There was compelling evidence that borrowers who would have qualified for cheap prime loans received high-cost loans, which suggested that subprime loans were overpriced. When we looked into this phenomenon more closely, we found that subprime lenders competed to lock borrowers into loans instead of trying to underprice each other. Their goal was to pinpoint likely borrowers before their competitors did and quickly induce them to agree to loans with onerous terms. The complexity of subprime loans helped brokers and lenders snare their prey, by making comparison shopping difficult. As long as this system worked and generated high fees, there was no reason for a subprime lender to break free from the pack and try to undercut the competition on price.

The pieces of the puzzle were still not complete, however. Investors were purchasing bonds backed by subprime loans, enthused by their high returns. As we tried to understand their investment decisions, we realized that, in many ways, subprime investors and borrowers were in parallel situations. Subprime mortgage-backed bonds are complex instruments that rarely trade publicly. It is difficult and costly to calculate the risk of the underlying loans and thus the value of the bonds.

Given these complexities, many investors relied on rating agencies' grades of the quality of mortgage-backed bonds, in the belief that investment grade bonds were good investments. Investors, big and small, also took advice from sophisticated bond dealers who recommended subprime bonds. Ultimately, investors' unrealistic expectations and greed, coupled with the impossibility of valuing the actual investments, caused them to take on risks they did not appreciate.

During the Clinton administration, we began crafting a proposal to remedy abuses in the subprime market. Our work built on the efforts of many who went before us, including Bill Brennan, Jim Carr, Kurt Eggert, Daniel Ehrenberg, Ira Goldstein, Dan Immergluck, Cathy Lesser Mansfield, and Patricia Sturdevant. The landmark treatise by Kathleen Keest and Elizabeth Renuart, *The Cost of Credit*, served as our guide as we parsed the maze of lending laws. Writings by housing economists such as George McCarthy, Roberto Quercia, Anthony Pennington-Cross, Susan Wachter, John Weicher, and Peter Zorn also influenced our work.

In spring 2001, at a Federal Reserve Board conference in Washington, D.C., we unveiled our proposal to tackle abusive loans, borrowing from legal principles in the securities world.[1] When people buy securities, the law requires brokers to recommend only securities that are suitable to their customers' circumstances and goals. There is no comparable protection for home mortgages, even though most Americans' single biggest investment is their home. It seemed unfair to protect investors more than homeowners, especially when people have so much of their wealth tied up in their homes. So we proposed that lenders and brokers who make subprime loans should only recommend loans that are suitable given borrowers' individual circumstances.

In the banking world, proposals like ours were greeted with derision. The man who eventually became the chief regulatory risk manager for National City Corporation expressed merriment at our proposal. A senior officer at one of the nation's largest banks called suitability our "little red wagon." When we presented our proposal at a national banking conference, some attendees audibly heckled.

Still, there was a sense during the Clinton administration that legal reforms were possible. Ellen Seidman proposed strong anti-predatory lending regulations for thrifts as director of the Office of Thrift Supervision. Donna Tanoue, the chairman of the Federal Deposit Insurance Corporation, publicly pointed out the dangers of the subprime securitization machine. The Federal Trade Commission under President Clinton brought a spate of high-level enforcement actions against alleged predatory lenders. The Department of Justice settled a series of landmark lending discrimination lawsuits. Ruth Clevenger and others in the Federal Reserve System actively championed research, including ours, on the problems with abusive subprime loans. In 2001, the Federal Reserve Board even amended its regulations to stamp out abusive practices in the costliest subprime loans.

The real action was happening, however, at the local level. Rumblings about abusive loans in cities and states sparked a movement for anti-predatory lending laws, with North Carolina taking the lead. Thanks to the efforts of Stella Adams, Martin Eakes, and others, North Carolina passed the first comprehensive state anti-predatory lending statute in 1999. Over pitched opposition from the lending industry, the credit-rating agencies, and worst of all the federal government, the majority of states would follow suit in years to come.

Once the George W. Bush administration settled in, the door slammed shut on any hope of federal reforms. At first, the policy shift took the form of federal inaction. Ellen Seidman's successor as the director of the Office of Thrift Supervision unceremoniously canned Seidman's proposal. At the behest of Bush administration appointees, the Federal Trade Commission, with one notable exception,[2] brought enforcement actions for abusive mortgage lending to a halt. A veil of silence descended over the lending discrimination unit at the Justice Department's Civil Rights Division. Over on Capitol Hill, Congressmen Paul Kanjorski and Bob Ney (who was later convicted in connection with the Jack Abramoff lobbying scandal and forced out of office) successfully waged a fight to block enactment of a meaningful federal anti-predatory lending law. Senator Phil Gramm, the man who brought us the Gramm-Leach-Bliley Act and deregulated credit default swaps, claimed that predatory lending could not be defined, so it could not be addressed.[3]

The Bush administration knew that it had to maintain some semblance of concern about predatory lending for the sake of political credibility. Consequently, the federal government pushed for financial literacy and consumer education. Financial literacy, according to Federal Reserve chairman Alan Greenspan and other federal officials, would empower consumers without limiting their freedom of choice. More window dressing than anything, the financial literacy campaign did not amount to much. Indeed, in 2004, the General Accountability Office concluded that federal consumer education initiatives were "of limited effectiveness in reducing predatory lending."[4] Suffice it to say, those initiatives did not stop the subprime crisis.

Further, the Bush administration's financial literacy campaign betrayed a punitive attitude toward ordinary Americans that fit comfortably with its laissez-faire ethos. Behind these programs lurked the insidious question: why should the government protect people from the consequences of their bad decisions if they refuse to comparison-shop for subprime loans? The debate was couched as a morality play: should the government halt financial exploitation or should individuals be solely responsible for harm that befell them?

During the George W. Bush administration, we personally experienced resistance to reform during our encounters with federal banking regulators and the Federal Trade Commission. Alan Greenspan at the Federal Reserve was refusing to regulate subprime lending, saying, "We are not skilled enough in these areas and we shouldn't be expected to [be]."[5] For part of that period, from 2002 through 2004, one of us—Pat—served on the Consumer Advisory Council (CAC) of the Federal Reserve. The council was so named even though representatives from the banking industry held the majority of seats on the CAC, which was handpicked by the Fed. Pat and other CAC members alerted the board to the dangers of subprime loans and subprime mortgage-backed securities, and tried to convince the board to exercise its authority to regulate mortgages. At the time, only one Fed governor, Ned Gramlich, advocated for greater regulation of abusive subprime loans. Under Greenspan's aegis, however, the board refused to take corrective action and failed to update its mortgage disclosures, which were so obsolete they were worthless to most consumers. Even worse, by 2004, Greenspan was encouraging homeowners to take out risky adjustable-rate mortgages instead of safer fixed-rate loans.[6]

The Fed was not alone. Greenspan had a soul mate in John Reich, the Federal Deposit Insurance Corporation's vice chairman (Reich would go on to become the director of the Office of Thrift Supervision and eventually resign from that position after exploding mortgages brought down the nation's largest thrift). At a 2004 FDIC meeting on regulatory reform that one of us attended, Reich made clear that his agenda was not to improve consumer welfare, but to water down consumer regulations to relieve the regulatory burden on banks. Later, Reich would become a cheerleader for the thrift industry's most noxious home mortgages.

Throughout this period, the federal government also promoted research that championed the subprime industry. One of the leading mortgage industry think tanks was the Credit Research Center (CRC) at Georgetown University. The CRC was known for producing subprime studies favorable to the American Financial Services Association, the self-described "national trade association for the consumer credit industry."

The CRC was quick to publish research that promoted industry positions, but never gave outside researchers access to the data the researchers used to generate their pro-industry reports. Staff members at the Federal Reserve Board were cozy with the CRC, liked to tout its research, and sometimes left to work there. In one instance, economists at the Federal Reserve even enlisted the CRC to analyze the sensitive question of racial disparities in subprime loan prices as part of a Fed study on fair lending enforcement. The Fed incorporated the CRC's findings, which downplayed racial disparities, even though the CRC had not allowed Fed researchers to examine the data for themselves.[7]

On one occasion, we even became the objects of a clumsy attempt to muffle research critical of the subprime industry. In the early fall of 2002, we both received a generic email from the Federal Trade Commission announcing that in a few weeks the agency would be holding a roundtable on consumer protection in mortgage lending, including subprime loans. The email arrived out of the blue with no message attached or invitation to speak. Later, we learned that the email was a response to complaints by consumer advocates that the agency's proposed roundtable was slanted toward the lending industry. Pointing to the email, FTC staff protested that they had "invited" us to speak. At the urging of consumer groups, Kathleen attended the roundtable, which ended up being a rehash of an industry-friendly conference that the Credit Research Center had recently sponsored.

Researchers and consumer advocates suffered from a serious handicap relative to places like the CRC. Almost all the information on mortgage loans was gathered and controlled by the financial services industry, which thwarted attempts by independent academic researchers to study the growing dangers from subprime loans. The lending industry maintains huge proprietary databases with vast amounts of information on borrowers and their loans. Researchers who wanted to study subprime lending but who had no affiliation with the industry had limited or no access to these databases. This was because licenses to use the data were either prohibitively expensive (upward of $200,000) or off-limits to outside researchers at any price.

Researchers without ties to the financial services industry were generally limited to using publicly available mortgage data collected under the Home Mortgage Disclosure Act, or HMDA. These data are deficient in many respects. Most importantly, the data does not contain information on borrowers' creditworthiness, the actual cost of loans, or the default history of loans. As a result, attempts by university researchers to study key public policy questions such as racial discrimination against subprime borrowers or the effect of subprime loan terms on default rates almost always hit a wall. Meanwhile, the Credit Research Center and other mortgage lending industry outlets pumped out one multivariate regression study after another criticizing regulation and extolling the benefits of subprime loans. All the while, they challenged reports by consumer advocates on the grounds that they were anecdotal and not based on comprehensive data on subprime lending.

We, too, encountered difficulties due to industry firewalls protecting proprietary data. In 2004, we published our first study analyzing the perverse incentive structure that caused subprime securitization to fuel the lax underwriting of subprime loans. We followed that up with a second, larger study of the moral hazard posed by subprime bonds in early 2007.[8] Researching private-label securitization was maddening during this period because the industry operated under a cloak. The credit-rating agencies offered some telling analyses of the problems in the subprime industry, but it was only by perfecting our web search skills and digging into prospectuses and transcripts of investor conference calls that we were able to stumble on illuminating industry analyses for free.

As the Bush administration became increasingly emboldened, what started out as federal inaction turned into active obstruction of state and local legislative attempts to rein in predatory lending. In 2004, the administration launched an offensive against the new state anti-predatory lending laws. That year, a little-known agency in the Treasury Department called the Office of the Comptroller of the Currency (or OCC for short) adopted a rule exempting national banks and their mortgage lending subsidiaries from most state lending laws protecting consumers. The OCC rule was patterned on a similar Office of Thrift Supervision (OTS) rule from the 1990s exempting federal thrifts from state lending laws.

The OCC rule might not have been so bad if the OCC had replaced state anti-predatory lending rules with stringent rules of its own. But it did not. Meanwhile, the OCC and OTS rules created the impetus for subprime lenders to duck state restrictions on subprime mortgages by becoming subsidiaries of national banks or federal thrifts. The OCC and OTS rules created such an unlevel playing field that the FDIC even considered adopting a copycat rule for the state-chartered community banks that were subject to FDIC supervision.[9]

The State of Michigan challenged the OCC rule in a case that eventually made it to the U.S. Supreme Court. Along with many consumer law professors, we hoped that Justice Scalia and other conservative justices on the Court, with their strong views on states' rights, would strike down the OCC rule. Our hopes were dashed in April 2007 when the Court affirmed the OCC rule, just in time for the unfolding subprime crisis. The dissent included an odd assortment of bedfellows, including Justice Scalia, Chief Justice Roberts, and Justice Stevens.

While Michigan's challenge to the OCC rule was working its way through the courts, home prices were rising steeply in many parts of the country and borrowers were finding it harder to qualify for standard fixed-rate mortgages. By 2005, subprime loans had captured 20 percent of the lending market, double their share four years earlier. These new subprime loans were even riskier than subprime loans from the late 1990s. Many of the 2005 vintage loans dispensed with documenting borrowers' incomes. Adjustable-rate mortgages (known as ARMs for short) with introductory rates that reset to much higher rates after set initial periods became the norm. Numerous borrowers with so-called hybrid ARMs found their monthly payments doubling overnight when their introductory periods expired. Finally, lenders were liberally waiving down-payment requirements, leaving borrowers with scant equity in their homes.

To us, these trends meant double trouble. On the consumer side, borrowers were so stretched financially that they could not afford down payments or safer fixed-rate mortgages. On the industry side, lenders and brokers were resorting to desperate risks to keep up loan volumes. We also worried that no-documentation loans were just a pretext for fraud.

By 2006, reports were surfacing in the press that lenders were qualifying borrowers based on low introductory interest rates, rather than on the higher eventual interest rates they would have to pay. Often borrowers who obtained these loans could not afford the new rates when they reset. Furthermore, many of them relied on assurances by their brokers that they could refinance if their monthly payments became unaffordable. That strategy only worked if home prices continued to rise, but they did not. In short, the breakdown in subprime underwriting standards was a train wreck waiting to happen.

The first signs of serious subprime distress appeared in late 2006 and finally stirred federal officials from their slumber. That fall, the Federal Trade Commission held a roundtable on the risks presented by hybrid ARMs and other exotic mortgages. The roundtable made a serious attempt to analyze the emerging dangers of these products.

Not long after the FTC roundtable, federal banking regulators finally rolled out a guidance warning about the dangers of exotic mortgages. While it was better than nothing, the guidance was only advisory in nature. Lenders did not have to follow it, and many of them did not. Even when the subprime house of cards collapsed in early 2007, federal regulators continued to drag their feet. It was not until July 2008 that the Federal Reserve Board finally issued a comprehensive, binding rule on subprime mortgages. By then, those mortgages were failing in droves and the pillars of the global financial system had begun to crumble.

The subprime story is the tale of how consumer abuses in an obscure corner of the home mortgage market spawned a virus that led to the near meltdown of the world's financial system. The virus had several strands. In the first, lenders cooked up hazardous subprime loans and peddled them to people who they knew could not afford to repay the loans. In the second, Wall Street sliced and diced subprime risk and spread it to the global financial system. In the third, traders bought trillions of dollars in credit default swaps with little or no margin on the bet that the whole enterprise would come crashing down. In the fourth and final strand, the federal government witnessed what was happening and made a deliberate decision to desist from any meaningful action. These strands combined to unleash untold economic harm.

It took the subprime crisis to prove that not protecting consumers could bring the world to the brink of financial collapse. When too many ordinary people have trouble paying their loans, financial systems can fail, both abroad and at home. For the sake of individual citizens and for the sake of financial stability worldwide, the country must take consumer protection seriously.

This book is born of frustration: frustration that Congress and federal regulators refused to heed warnings about the subprime market and let subprime loans spiral out of control. Some people like to call the subprime crisis a perfect storm. That's not what it was. It was a localized virus that slowly spread to infect the world financial system. Had anyone in Washington cared, the virus could have been checked.

# Part I

# The Subprime Market Takes Off

The astonishing thing about the subprime crisis is that something so small wreaked so much havoc. Subprime loans started out as just a pocket of the U.S. home loan market, then mutated like a virus into a crisis of global proportions. Along the way, brokers, lenders, investment banks, rating agencies, and—for a time—investors made a lot of money while borrowers struggled to keep their homes. The lure of money made the various actors in the subprime food chain ever more brazen and, with each passing year, subprime crowded out safe, prime loans, putting more homeowners at risk of losing their homes and ultimately pushing the entire world economy to the edge of a cliff.

# 2

▷

# The Emergence of the Subprime Market

A busive subprime lending burst into public consciousness in 2007, but its legacy dated back years. As early as the 1990s, consumer advocates were reporting predatory lending in lower-income neighborhoods. This early period was the first iteration of subprime lending. Only later did subprime loans morph into products that ultimately brought down the financial system.

## FROM CREDIT RATIONING TO CREDIT GLUT

To trace the emergence of subprime lending, we have to begin with the home mortgage market in the 1970s. Back then, mortgage lending was the sleepy province of community thrifts and banks. Banks took deposits and plowed them into fixed-rate loans requiring down payments of 20 percent. Consumers wanting mortgage loans went to their local bank, where loan officers helped them fill out paper applications. The applications then went to the bank's back office for underwriting. Using pencils and adding machines, underwriters calculated loan-to-value and debt-to-income ratios to determine whether the applicants could afford the loans. In addition, underwriters drew on their knowledge of the community to assess whether the customers were "good folk" who would repay their loans.

Banks kept their loans in their portfolios and absorbed the loss if borrowers defaulted. Knowing that they bore the risk if loans went bad, lenders made conservative lending decisions. They shied away from applicants with gaps in employment, late payments on bills, and anything less than solid reputations in the community. People of modest means could rarely obtain loans because their incomes were too low and they couldn't afford the high down payments. For people of color, obtaining credit was even harder. Many lenders refused to serve African-American and Hispanic borrowers at all, even when they had high incomes and flawless credit histories.

### Deregulation

Just as mortgage lending was conservative, so was regulation. Throughout most of the 1970s, federal and state governments imposed interest rate caps on home mortgages. Some states banned adjustable-rate mortgages (ARMs), loans with balloon payments, and prepayment penalties, which are charges for refinancing loans or paying them off early. These regulations had the effect of limiting or delaying opportunities for homeownership.[1]

The interest rate restrictions and bans on certain types of mortgages did not last forever. From 1972 to 1980, the average interest rate on thirty-year fixed-rate mortgages rose from 7.38 percent to 13.74 percent a year.[2] These high rates hurt lenders and borrowers alike. Mortgage lending and real estate sales declined. In states where market interest rates exceeded the state's interest rate cap, some lenders stopped financing home mortgages altogether. To add insult to injury, depositors were flocking to withdraw their money from banks to invest in money market funds, which offered higher returns because they were not subject to interest rate caps on bank accounts. The outflow of deposits meant banks had less money to lend, further curtailing the availability of mortgage loans.

Eventually, as the banking industry faltered and real estate sales dried up, Congress took action to dismantle the regulatory apparatus. First, it passed a law in 1980 eliminating interest rate caps on first-lien home mortgages. Then, in 1982, it permitted loan products other than fixed-rate, fully amortizing loans. Overnight new products sprung up, including ARMs, balloon payment loans, and reverse mortgages.[3] Congress, in a sweeping move, also overrode state and local provisions that were inconsistent with the 1980 and 1982 laws.[4]

Deregulation addressed the immediate pressures facing banks. The abolition of interest rate caps allowed banks and thrifts to charge market rates of interest. At the same time, the proliferation of new loan products broadened the array of loans available to borrowers. Borrowers who knew they would only be in their homes for a few years could opt for low-interest loans with a five-year balloon to be paid when they sold their homes. Other borrowers were attracted to ARMs offering initial interest rates below the rates on fixed-rate mortgages. Many of these borrowers planned to refinance later if fixed-rate loans dropped in price.

Deregulation was not all good news. Without the constraint of interest rate caps, lenders were free to charge exorbitant interest rates. They also had carte blanche to dream up an endless menu of exotic loan products that borrowers had no hope of understanding.

### Technological Advances

Starting in the 1980s, technological innovation also transformed the home mortgage market and paved the way for subprime lending. Lenders, in the past, had been extremely careful about borrowing decisions. They had erred on the side of caution because they did not know how to calculate the risk that borrowers would default. When underwriting loans, they had used rules of thumb to help ensure repayment, such as a total debt-to-income ratio of 36 percent, a 20 percent down payment, and three months of savings in the bank.

When the mainframe computer arrived on the scene, lenders could suddenly analyze vast stores of data on borrowers and their credit histories. Statisticians began using the power of computing to identify the factors that best predicted whether borrowers would make their mortgage payments. They used these factors to develop models for determining the risk that individual borrowers would default. The models were called automated underwriting and were dubbed *AU*. With AU, loan officers and brokers could take information from the loan applications of potential borrowers and run it through a computer program to determine the applicants' default risk and their eligibility for loans.

AU dashed a number of hoary maxims about traditional loan underwriting. Out went requirements that borrowers make down payments of 20 percent and have savings equal to three months of expenses. Out, too, went an insistence on pristine credit records, low debt-to-income ratios, and full documentation of income. The old-fashioned underwriting rules and underwriters' seat-of-the-pants judgment gave way to fancy statistical models, giving lenders the confidence to lend to borrowers with damaged credit or no credit history at all.

Equally important, AU made underwriting quick and cheap. In the "old days," it took weeks to get a loan approved. With AU, lenders could shorten the underwriting period to seconds. New Century Financial, now a bankrupt lender that approved loans through a call center, advertised: "We'll give you loan answers in just 12 seconds." AU not only saved time. It also saved money. AU software reduced underwriting costs by an average of $916 per loan.[5]

The mortgage finance giants Fannie Mae and Freddie Mac set the gold standard for AU systems with their Desktop Underwriter and Loan Prospector programs for prime loans. Later, Fannie Mae designed a program called Custom DU, which was supposed to automate the underwriting of subprime loans. Other companies designed their own AU models for subprime mortgages.[6]

Although automated underwriting was a valuable innovation, it had downsides, especially when it came to subprime loans. One problem was that many models assumed that housing prices in the United States would go up indefinitely, which was an unfounded and foolish assumption. AU systems also had a garbage in, garbage out problem. AU is only as good as the data that are entered. For example, if a broker entered false information, by inflating borrowers' income or the value of their property, the computerized assessment of the borrowers' risk would come out wrong.

When it came to subprime loans, there was even greater reason to question the reliability of automated underwriting. AU was originally developed for the prime market, using decades of data on the performance of prime loans. There was scant evidence, however, that these models yielded accurate results for subprime loans because there was little historical data on subprime loans. Despite these problems, AU gave the appearance of reliable underwriting, which was enough to embolden the market.

### Securitization

Perhaps the biggest factor contributing to the subprime boom was the securitization of home mortgages. Securitization quietly entered the scene in the 1970s. The idea behind securitization is ingenious: bundle a lender's loans, transfer them to a legally remote trust, repackage the monthly loan payments into bonds rated by rating agencies, back the bonds using the underlying mortgages as collateral, and sell the bonds to investors. It is a bit more complicated than this description suggests; we save the nitty-gritty of securitization for the next chapter.

The roots of securitization date back to the 1930s, when Congress established the Federal National Mortgage Association (Fannie Mae) as a federal agency to increase the money available for home mortgages. Initially, Fannie Mae purchased FHA-insured mortgages and in the process replenished the funds that lenders had on hand to make home mortgages.[7] Thirty years later, Congress spun Fannie Mae off into a government-sponsored entity (GSE) and created a new GSE, the Federal Home Mortgage Corporation (Freddie Mac). Both securitized mortgages and eventually became private sector companies owned by shareholders. The government exempted the GSEs from state and local taxes. In exchange, Fannie and Freddie agreed to meet affordable housing goals set by the U.S. Department of Housing and Urban Development (HUD). This public mission meant that Fannie and Freddie had two masters to serve: their shareholders and the government.

The way that GSE securitizations work is that lenders originate mortgage loans that they sell to the GSEs. Only loans that meet Fannie's and Freddie's underwriting standards and that fall below a certain dollar threshold are accepted for securitization by the GSEs. In the industry, these loans are called "conforming loans." Once they acquire the loans, the GSEs package them into pools. Those pools then issue bonds backed by the loans. As part of the bond covenants, Fannie and Freddie guarantee investors that they will receive their bond payments on time even if the borrowers default on their loans.[8]

Seeing the success of GSE securitization, investment banks and other financial institutions wanted in on the game. Fannie and Freddie had captured most of the prime mortgage market, but had not yet tapped subprime mortgages for securitization. This set the wheels in motion for "private label" securitization of subprime loans. *Private label* is the term used for any securitization other than those orchestrated by one of the GSEs. Some private-label securitizations were done by lenders. For example, Countrywide Financial Home Loans, one of the largest subprime lenders, packaged and securitized the loans it originated. More often, however, subprime loans were securitized by Wall Street investment banks. By 2006, up to 80 percent of subprime mortgages were being securitized.[9]

Securitization revolutionized home mortgage finance by wedding Wall Street with Main Street. It tapped huge new pools of capital across the nation and abroad to finance home mortgages in the United States. Lenders, in a continuous cycle, could make loans, sell those loans for securitization, and then plow the sales proceeds into a new batch of loans, which in turn could be securitized.

Securitization also solved an age-old problem for banks. In the past, banks had held home mortgages until they were paid off, which meant they were financing long-term mortgage loans with short-term demand deposits. This "lending long and borrowing short" destabilized banks. If interest rates rose, banks had to pay depositors rates that exceeded the interest rate borrowers were paying on older mortgages. And if interest rates dropped, borrowers would refinance to less expensive loans. This "term mismatch" problem was a direct cause of the 1980s savings and loan crisis. Securitization solved that problem by allowing banks to move mortgages off their books in exchange for upfront cash.

It was not only banks that benefited from the advent of securitization. All of a sudden, thinly capitalized entrepreneurs could become nonbank mortgage lenders. They financed their operations not with deposits, but by borrowing money to fund loans, which they paid back as they sold the loans for securitization. The new lenders operated free from costly and time-consuming banking regulation and flew under the radar by making loans through brokers. Many had no physical presence in the communities where they operated and were anonymous unless borrowers read the fine print.

By the time everyone was toasting the millennium, subprime lending was poised to take off. Soon what had been a credit drought would become a glut of credit.

## Macroeconomic and Public Policy Factors

Macroeconomic forces also helped spawn the subprime boom. Ironically, two financial busts helped clear the way for subprime lending's phenomenal growth in the 2000s. One of those grew out of the Asian flu. In July 1997, the Asian financial crisis ignited in Thailand, driving down the value of assets and currencies throughout Southeast Asia. In a domino effect, the crisis reduced the demand for oil, which contributed to a financial crisis in Russia the following year. After Russia defaulted on its debt, fearful investors began dumping both Asian and European bonds. The crisis spread to the United States when Long-Term Capital Management (LTCM), a highly leveraged hedge fund that made its money through arbitrage on bonds, lost money and experienced crippling redemptions. The Federal Reserve Board (the Fed) orchestrated a private bailout of LTCM of over $3.5 billion. With LTCM's collapse, the bond markets erupted in chaos, briefly paralyzing private-label securitization and resulting in a liquidity crunch. Several subprime lenders found themselves unable to raise working capital, and ultimately their businesses failed.[10]

During the same period, the dot-com bubble was swelling. In 2000, the bubble burst and stock values plunged. By August 2001, the S&P 500 Index was off 26 percent from its former high. Then on September 11, 2001, terrorists attacked the United States. As the country grieved, the faltering economy attempted to revive, only to sustain another body blow in December 2001 when Enron filed for bankruptcy. As one corporate scandal after another came to light, confidence in the stock market crumbled. The S&P 500 dropped another 15 percent and the country slid into a recession.

Throughout it all, the housing and credit markets were a beacon of hope for the economy. Alan Greenspan, the chairman of the Federal Reserve Board, seized on mortgage loans and other consumer credit as the way out of the slump. In mid-2000, the Fed exercised its "Greenspan put" and slashed interest rates, causing housing prices to grow at a steady clip of 10 percent a year nationally. After the 9/11 attacks, with the recession in full swing, the Fed ordered further rate cuts in order to jump-start the economy. Between August 2001 and January 2003, the Fed chopped the discount rate from 3 percent to 0.75 percent. This series of cuts drove down interest rates on prime loans. The cuts also made it possible for subprime lenders to borrow money at low rates, charge high rates to borrowers who couldn't qualify for prime loans, and make money on the spread when they sold the loans.[11]

Low interest rates answered President Bush's post-9/11 call for Americans to go shopping. Suddenly spending money became patriotic, and many consumers financed their purchases with credit cards that charged exorbitant interest and late fees. Too often, families converted their credit card debt into mortgage debt or refinanced their homes to pull out equity. As Greenspan noted, "Consumer spending carried the economy through the post-9/11 malaise, and what carried consumer spending was housing."[12] Programs advertising "Your Home Pays You Cash" urged people to borrow against their homes. Companies also promoted the idea that credit was the way to live the good life. Citibank spent $1 billion on a "live richly" campaign designed to lure people into home equity loans. PNC ads for second mortgages showed a wheelbarrow with the slogan, "The easiest way to haul money out of your house."[13]

The constant message was that people should feel good about using credit. Debt, which used to be considered embarrassing and a sign of poor discipline, had stopped being shameful. As a sign of this cultural shift, between 2001 and 2007, overall household debt grew from $7.2 trillion to $13.6 trillion, a 10 percent increase each year.[14]

The Fed under Greenspan not only kept interest rates low, but also refused to intervene to protect consumers despite growing evidence of abusive mortgages. Likewise, Congress and federal regulatory agencies were unmoved by stories of defrauded consumers. The dominant ideology was that if there were problems with mortgage lending, the market would solve them. In addition, if consumers were taking on credit they couldn't afford, that was their choice and their problem. The market's job was to offer consumers choices, and consumers' job was to take personal responsibility for the choices they made. On the corporate side, responsibility meant maximizing the bottom line for the benefit of shareholders, without regard for the consequences of abusive lending to consumers or society.

These dynamics coincided with a huge federal push for homeownership. This push began in the mid-1990s under President Bill Clinton, when HUD coordi-

**FIGURE 2.1.**
U.S. President George W. Bush makes remarks on home ownership at the Department of Housing and Urban Development. (Luke Frazza/ AFP/ Getty Images).

nated a public-private partnership designed to increase homeownership.[15] When President George W. Bush came into office in 2001, he went further, advocating that everyone should own a home as part of his vaunted "Ownership Society" initiative. In response, HUD increased its pressure on Fannie Mae and Freddie Mac to finance an ever greater number of mortgages to people with modest incomes and to borrowers of color. The Bush administration embraced subprime loans as the key to growth in homeownership. By 2004, even the chief counsel of the Office of the Comptroller of the Currency, Julie Williams, was lauding "the rise of the subprime segment . . . in advancing homeownership, especially for minority Americans."[16]

Ultimately, the forces of technology, financial engineering, and public policy converged to fuel the growth of the subprime market. Starting in 2000 the subprime market grew exponentially, capturing 36 percent of the mortgage market at its height in 2006, up from 12 percent in 2000, before crashing and infecting the world economy.[17]

## PREDATORY LENDING

The first iteration of subprime lending—coined *predatory lending*—began in the 1990s and was targeted at people who historically had been unable to get loans. Some had blemishes on their credit or limited credit histories that made them ineligible for prime credit with its stiff underwriting standards. Others were eligible for prime loans, but did not know how to go about applying for credit or, because of past discrimination, mistrusted banks. These people were ready prey for a new class of brokers and lenders, who targeted unsophisticated borrowers.

In these early days, mortgage brokers were small-time operators, soliciting borrowers over the phone or door-to-door like Fuller Brush salesmen of yore, armed with a menu of loan products from various lenders. Lenders back then were often small finance companies that generated money for loans through warehouse lines of credit. Some lenders worked solely with brokers, but many had storefronts where they took applications directly. One of the early entrants was Citigroup, which bought the Baltimore subprime lender Commercial Credit and later renamed it CitiFinancial, CitiFi for short.

Finding potential borrowers and getting them to commit to loans was the key to success. Existing homeowners were the most frequent targets because they had equity and were easy to identify through property records, unlike prospective homeowners. Brokers and lenders perfected marketing strategies to find naïve homeowners and dupe them into subprime loans. Some hired "cold callers" who would contact homeowners to see if they were interested in a new mortgage. The cold callers got paid a few hundred dollars for each successful call. Brokers and lenders also used municipal records to identify prospects. They scoured files at city offices to find homes with outstanding housing code violations, betting that the homeowners needed cash to make repairs. They read local obituaries to identify older women who had recently lost their husbands, surmising that widows were financially gullible. They also identified potential borrowers through consumer sales transactions. For example, in Virginia, Bennie Roberts, who could neither read nor write, bought a side of beef and over 100 pounds of other meat from a roadside stand on credit from the notorious subprime lender Associates First Capital. In talking with Mr. Roberts to arrange the consumer loan, the loan officer from Associates learned that Mr. Roberts had no mortgage on his home. He soon convinced his new client to take out a loan using the client's home equity. Associates refinanced that mortgage ten times in four years. The principal after the refinancings was $45,000 of which $19,000 was paid to Associates in fees.[18]

High fees were not the only thing that typified predatory loans. Interest rates, too, could be astronomical. In 2000, the *Baltimore City Paper* told the story of the Pulleys, who had overextended themselves with credit card debt. In 1997, the Pulleys "were barraged with letters and calls from mortgage lenders offering to consolidate [their] existing mortgage . . . and all their other debts into a new loan," which would supposedly save them $500 per month. "Needing the cash and not well-versed in such dealings," the Pulleys made a deal with Monument Mortgage for an adjustable rate mortgage loan with an annual interest rate that increased every six months up to 19.99 percent.[19]

Some brokers and lenders had understandings with real estate agents and home improvement contractors to refer homeowners to them for loans. This network also worked in reverse, when mortgage brokers received kickbacks for suggesting contractors to borrowers who were seeking loans for home repairs. These referrals generated good money for everyone except the borrowers, who ultimately paid for the referrals out of the loan proceeds or through up-front fees.

Shady contractors who helped homeowners finance repairs were rife. In Cleveland, Ruby Rogers had a mortgage-free home she had inherited from her uncle. Citywide Builders, a contractor, helped her obtain a loan through Ameriquest Mortgage to update the home. Over six months, the contractor arranged repeated refinancings of Ms. Rogers' loan until the principal hit $23,000. Of that amount, Ms. Rogers only saw $4,500. Meanwhile, Citywide Builders walked off the job after doing $3,200 of work on the house. Ms. Rogers was left with a leaking roof, peeling tiles, warped wall paneling, and a hole in the wall. After Citywide Builders went bankrupt, Ameriquest sued Ms. Rogers for foreclosure.[20]

Brokers and lenders also targeted black and Latino neighborhoods, where they knew credit had been scarce and demand for loans was high. As electronic databases of consumers became more sophisticated, lenders could "prescreen for vulnerability," picking out people they could most easily dupe.[21] Loan officers at one lender reportedly referred to neighborhoods with a high percentage of borrowers of color as "never-never land."[22]

For homeowners, the arrival of brokers and lenders offering them credit seemed like manna from heaven. Some lenders even invoked heaven in luring borrowers. Gospel radio station Heaven 600 AM aired advertisements for refinance loans through Promised Land Financial. To help brokers win customers' confidence, First Alliance Mortgage Company, nicknamed FAMCO, had brokers watch movies to help them understand borrowers' points of view. They were instructed to watch *Boyz N the Hood* to experience inner-city life and *Stand and Deliver* to get a feel for Hispanic borrowers.[23]

Loan officers and brokers were trained to make customers feel that they were acting in their best interests, even going so far as to provide attorneys to "represent" particularly leery borrowers.[24] They were told to "establish a common bond . . . to make the customer lower his guard." Suggested common bonds included family, jobs, and pets.[25] Clueless that they were being targeted, residents welcomed the salespeople who befriended them into their homes. There the pitchmen would ply them with offers of loans to fix a sagging porch, pay for a child's education, or buy a car. One borrower, whose loan was flipped multiple times, said, "Everyone was just so buttery and nice."[26]

Some brokers were people that borrowers knew through work or church. For many people, especially those who had been victims of redlining in the past, working with someone familiar or recommended felt safer than going to a bank. Often that was a mistake. The head deacon of the Message of Peace Church in South San Francisco allegedly used his position to exploit Brazilian immigrants who were parishioners at his church, by encouraging them to finance their home purchases through him. After they placed their trust in the deacon, he completed their loan applications, reportedly falsified documents, and agreed to terms on their behalf. One borrower said that when she uncovered what the deacon had done, he threatened to report her to the Immigration and Naturalization Service for overstaying her visa and then tried to bribe her with $5,000 to keep quiet.[27]

Much early predatory lending involved extracting equity from people's homes. Lenders or brokers would convince homeowners to take out high-cost loans that the salespeople knew would eventually become unaffordable. The loans might contain balloon payments coming due in a few years or adjustable rates that would only go up. Just when borrowers were on the brink of defaulting, the brokers or loan officers reappeared on their doorsteps, ready to refinance the borrowers into new loans. Some went so far as to adopt systems for tracking the amount of equity borrowers had in their homes. Each "loan flip" resulted in more fees for the brokers and lenders, which they tacked onto the principal. With each flip, the borrowers' equity shrank and their monthly payments went up, until their equity disappeared and they could no longer qualify for loans.[28]

By design, these subprime loans were unaffordable. The easiest loans to flip were those that borrowers couldn't afford in the first place. The higher the interest rate, the bigger the monthly payment and the more likely the borrower would default. Reports abounded of subprime mortgages with fixed rates of 18 percent and adjustable rates of close to 30 percent.[29]

One of the sadder instances of loan flipping involved Mary Podelco, a former waitress with a sixth-grade education who had lost her husband in 1994. She used his life insurance to pay off the mortgage on her family home. A year later, in need of new windows and a heating system, she took out a loan with Beneficial Finance for $11,921. Just one month later, Beneficial convinced her to refinance the loan for $16,256. Soon other lenders got into the game, each promising Ms. Podelco a loan that was superior to the one she had. Over the course of a year, lenders flipped her loan at least five times, increasing her outstanding debt to over $64,000. Unbeknownst to Ms. Podelco, she was paying exorbitant charges with every flip. On July 26, 2001, long before the subprime heyday, she told her story to the Senate Committee on Banking, Housing and Urban Affairs.[30]

Sometimes lenders urged borrowers to take out mortgages and use the funds to pay off outstanding medical debts, credit cards, or other bills. By consolidating their debts, lenders argued, borrowers would get lower interest rates and lower monthly payments. What the lenders didn't say was that by converting unsecured debt into debt secured by their homes, the borrowers put their homes at risk. Going into bankruptcy, more-over, would not wipe out their mortgages, unlike other debts.[31]

Another early predatory tactic was charging borrowers for credit insurance that would be used to pay off their loans if they became disabled or died. These policies charged a one-time premium in the many thousands of dollars that was paid at the closing and financed as part of the loan. Because borrowers had to pay interest on the premiums, the effective cost was as much as three or four times the original amount. This practice made the front page in 2002 when Citigroup ponied up $240 million to settle litigation against Associates First Capital, which Citigroup had purchased in 2000 for $31 billion amid allegations of similar abuses. These were not the only allegations against Citigroup. Reporter Michael Hudson, who wrote an early exposé on CitiFi, told of a borrower whom CitiFi convinced to take out not only credit life insurance but also disability and unemployment insurance.[32]

Lenders packed other exorbitant fees into loans. FAMCO, one of the largest and earliest predatory lenders, reportedly charged borrowers as much as 25 percent of their loan amount in discount points. This meant a borrower with a $100,000 loan would pay $25,000 in points. Typically, FAMCO's loans also included prepayment penalties and high interest rates. Eventually, FAMCO limited its points to 10 per-cent of the loan amount because of concern about the "sound-bite effect of high origination fees."[33]

Bait-and-switch schemes were also rife. At the time of application or shortly after-ward, lenders would describe the loan terms to borrowers, but not actually lock in the terms. Lenders would then change the terms after the borrowers were psychologically and financially invested in the loans. This was countenanced by federal disclosure laws, which only prohibited lenders from changing loan terms if they had made binding offers. In the subprime market, offers were almost never binding. Borrowers would show up at their loan closings expecting the promised loan terms, only to find that the terms had become worse in major ways. Fixed-rate loans became adjustable and interest rates soared. Surprise fees popped up in the loans. Second mortgages suddenly appeared in the documents.

Often the borrowers did not even recognize these changes in the hubbub of the closing. The closing agents would sit the borrowers down with a big stack of papers and flip the pages, directing borrowers to sign next to the sticky arrows. If the borrow-ers protested that things were moving too fast, that they wanted to review the docu-ments, or that the terms appeared different, the response would be, "Don't worry, I'll take care of that, just sign here."[34]

FAMCO reportedly pulled such a bait and switch on Bernae and Scott Gunder-son. After the loan closing, Ms. Gunderson looked through the loan documents and saw that the terms were worse than the ones she and her husband had agreed to. She talked with a manager at FAMCO, who assured her that the loan terms were as promised. Unbeknownst to the manager, Ms. Gunderson recorded the conversation. That recording proved invaluable after the Gundersons determined that FAMCO had added $13,000 in fees to the loan and put them in a loan with an interest rate that rose 1 percent every six months.[35]

Others were not so lucky. Roberta Green thought she was applying for a $6,000 home equity loan at a fixed rate. The broker filled out the loan application for Ms. Green and, as required by law, disclosed the interest rate and fees. Later, the loan closing was so rushed that Ms. Green did not realize she had agreed to refinance her current mortgage for $76,500 with a higher adjustable interest rate and $6,500 in additional fees, none of which the broker had previously mentioned.[36]

Lenders and brokers even resorted to duress to close loans. Back in 2001, *Crain's Chicago Business* published a report about a mentally disabled couple who had fallen behind on their real estate taxes. A broker approached them offering a loan to cover their taxes, using the equity in their home. On the day of the closing, a limousine brought the couple from Chicago's South Side, where they lived, to an office on the north side of Chicago near O'Hare International Airport. When the couple examined the loan documents, they discovered that the loan terms had been changed. They were far from home and did not know where they were or how to get home so they caved in and signed the papers.[37]

Intimidation was another tool of the subprime trade. A borrower with a CitiFinancial loan reported that when she missed some loan payments, a CitiFi manager threatened to have her arrested and to tell her boss that "she was a deadbeat."[38]

The most brazen lenders and brokers lied about loan terms. It was common to tell borrowers that their loans were for fixed rates when, in fact, they were not. Other misrepresentations took the form of false promises. Lenders would tell borrowers that they would quickly refinance their loans to lower the interest rate. Later, when the borrowers pressed the lenders to honor their promises, the lenders would concoct excuses why better rates were not possible.[39]

The exploitative practices of early predatory lenders were summed up in the 1998 testimony before the Senate Special Committee on Aging by a former finance company employee under the pseudonym of Jim Dough:

> My perfect customer would be an uneducated widow who is on a fixed income—hopefully from her deceased husband's pension and social security—who has her house paid off, is living off of credit cards, but having a difficult time keeping up [with] her payments, and who must make a car payment in addition to her credit card payments. . . .
>
> We were instructed and expected to flip as many loans as possible. . . . The practice is to charge the maximum number of points legally permissible for each loan and each flip, regardless of how recently the prior loan that was being refinanced had been made. The finance companies I worked for had no limits on how frequently a loan could be flipped, and we were not required to rebate any point income on loans that were flipped. . . .
>
> Our entire sale is built on confusion. Blue-collar workers tend to be less educated. I know I am being very stereotypical, but they are the more unsophisticated. They can be confused in the loan closings, and they look to us as professionals. . . . [T]hey are more trusting toward us.[40]

## SUBPRIME GOES MAINSTREAM

Over time, the subprime industry began moving from fringe to mainstream as commercial banks, investment banks, hedge funds, insurance companies, and other financial giants saw the profits that could be made. They soon started buying subprime lenders. Small mortgage banks mushroomed into large national behemoths, absorbing smaller entities along the way. All this buying of subprime lenders led to widespread consolidation in the industry. For example, one of Cleveland's leading bank holding companies, National City Corporation, bought the subprime lender First Franklin in 1999 for $266 million. In a few short years, First Franklin's subprime lending volume skyrocketed from $4 billion to $30 billion. With a subprime lender in its pocket, National City Bank could originate prime loans in its own name and, in the words of its chief executive, David Daberko, refer otherwise lost prospects "immediately to the nonprime company."[41] Later First Franklin became infamous for bringing down both National City Bank and Merrill Lynch.[42]

The global banking giant HSBC bought its own subprime lender, Household International, in 2003 for $14 billion. Investment banks Credit Suisse, Bear Stearns, Lehman Brothers, Merrill Lynch, Morgan Stanley, and Goldman Sachs all bought or founded nonbank subprime lenders to feed their securitization machines. As a *Wall Street Journal* reporter noted, "Without a production-line of mortgages, the inventory for all those fee-paying securities would dry up."[43] Private equity firms like New York's Capital Z Partners snapped up subprime lenders. Even blue-chip companies got swept up in the buying frenzy. General Electric bought WMC Mortgage Corporation in 2004. H & R Block bought Option One Mortgage Corporation in 1997.

The new owners of the subprime lenders piously avowed that they had cleaned up "shop" and would never sanction abusive lending. In testimony before the House Committee on Government Oversight and Reform, the former chief executive officer of Lehman Brothers, Richard Fuld, said: "When we bought [subprime lenders], we changed management, we changed underwriting standards to make them much more restrictive, to improve the quality of the loans that we did in fact originate so that those loans that we did then put into securitized form would be solid investments for investors."[44]

At the same time, independent mortgage banks that once had bit roles grew into mammoth institutions fed by securitization. Ameriquest and Countrywide were two of the most egregious mega-subprime lenders. Initially a small California thrift called Long Beach Savings and Loan, Ameriquest became a privately held mortgage lender in 1994 and quickly grew to secure a position as one of the largest mortgage companies in the United States. Ameriquest made loans through retail operations and independent mortgage brokers. The latter branch of the company went by the name Argent. Ronald Arnall, who founded Long Beach and stood at Ameriquest's helm, was the country's 106th wealthiest billionaire by 2004. By 2005, Ameriquest was reaping sufficient fees to sponsor the Super Bowl XXXIX half-time show in Jacksonville, Florida. The Ameriquest blimp hovered over the stadium touting the company's success.[45]

Arnall and his wife, Dawn, were big political contributors, raising over $12 million for President George W. Bush and various conservative advocacy organizations.[46] On August 1, 2005, President Bush nominated Arnall to be the next ambassador to the Netherlands, a position he held until 2008. On the same day that Bush nominated Arnall for the ambassadorship, Ameriquest agreed to fork over $325 million to settle pending lawsuits and investigations centered on Ameriquest's and Argent's questionable lending in dozens of states.[47] By 2007, Ameriquest had tanked. It shut down its retail mortgage shop and sold what was left of the company to Citigroup.

Countrywide, like Ameriquest, grew at an astounding rate and generated huge returns for its investors. Between 2000 and 2006, its securities trading volume went from $647 billion to $3.8 trillion. *Fortune* magazine reported that a $1,000 investment in the company in 1982 was worth $23,000 twenty years later. This 2,200 percent return more than outpaced returns at Wal-Mart and even Warren Buffett's Berkshire Hathaway. Members of Countrywide's board of directors were handsomely compensated, with some receiving over half a million dollars a year. Countrywide's chief executive officer, Angelo Mozilo, was paid up to $43 million a year.[48]

By 2005, Countrywide had become the nation's largest subprime lender. Two years later, the company went into a subprime skid and, in 2008, was acquired by Bank of America amid rumors that the lender was on the verge of bankruptcy. Shortly after Bank of America completed the sale, Countrywide committed over $8 billion to settle abusive lending claims with dozens of states.[49]

## Lending Channels

Borrowers could get subprime loans through three main channels: the retail channel, the wholesale channel, and the correspondent channel. The retail channel is the simplest to explain. Retail lenders took applications in person, over the Internet, and through call centers, using in-house loan officers instead of outside mortgage brokers. These lenders processed the applications, underwrote the loans, and funded them once approved. Many retail lenders were depository institutions. For example, Washington Mutual Bank (WaMu), the savings and loan giant, made subprime loans directly to borrowers through its retail branches.

More subprime loans, however, came through independent mortgage brokers, not loan officers at retail lenders. This was known as the wholesale channel because brokers generated loan applications for wholesale lenders who underwrote and funded the loans. Wholesale lenders could either be depository institutions or nonbank finance companies that raised money on the capital markets and used the money to fund their loans. Eventually, the loans were sold, at which time the wholesale lenders would profit from the difference between the sales price and the cost of funding the loans. At the peak of subprime lending, almost 80 percent of subprime loans were originated through some form of wholesale lender.[50]

The third channel was called correspondent lending. Correspondent lenders, which could be depository institutions or finance companies, had retail operations where they took applications and made loans pursuant to underwriting standards set by a wholesale lender, who committed in advance to buy the loans at a set price. In the correspondent setting, the wholesale lenders served as loan aggregators.

Mortgage channels had two more twists. The first was an arrangement known as table-funding, where on paper brokers appeared to make the loans, but in reality, the brokers only held the loans for a matter of seconds. The brokers would immediately endorse the loan notes over to wholesale lenders who were the true funders of the loans. Table-funding enabled brokers to make more fees.

The other twist was net branch banking, through which brokers became temporary employees of wholesale lenders, typically to avoid disclosing to borrowers the commissions that they received and to circumvent state licensing requirements. Many lenders used multiple channels. One lender could have retail and wholesale operations and also purchase loans from correspondent lenders.[51]

## Housing Bubble

The supply of subprime loans increased as the subprime industry went mainstream and investors flooded the market with capital. At the same time, there was increased demand for subprime loans. Demand was driven by a combination of stagnant real wages for most workers, rising interest rates, and rising home prices. The average U.S. home rose over 50 percent in value between 2001 and 2005. On the West Coast, the increases were even higher, with homes increasing 20 percent in just one year between 2004 and 2005. By 2006, only 17 percent of California households could afford a median-priced single-family home.[52]

The subprime industry contributed to rising home prices. Easy credit generated greater demand for housing, which, in turn, drove up housing prices. Higher-priced homes meant that homebuyers had to borrow ever larger amounts of money. Even borrowers with good credit histories found that they could not qualify for safe loans because they could not afford the monthly payments for fixed-rate, fully amortizing mortgages. In high-priced markets, some borrowers had to resort to jumbo nonprime loans because the loans they needed exceeded Fannie and Freddie limits on the size of the loans they would buy. Real estate investors also added to the demand. These purchasers bought homes with the intention of selling them in a few years and cashing in on the expected rise in home values.

Housing developments sprung up like weeds in western deserts, trash-strewn lots in cities, and farmland in the Midwest. Some developments were geared to high-end buyers who wanted McMansions with in-home movie theaters. Others marketed cheap, remote tracts to first-time homeowners. Developers partnered with lenders and brokers, providing buyers with one-stop shopping for a house and a loan. Countrywide established nearly 800 local offices that solicited loans through home builders and real estate agents. Developers and lenders sent a message that anyone could own a home and that people should dream big.[53]

## Feeding the Mortgage Machine

From lenders' perspective, the mortgage machine needed constant feeding in order to generate constant fees. Volume was what mattered. Lenders bought "leads" from firms that gathered consumer information from banks and credit bureaus and culled public records to create mega-databases on consumers. These databases, referred to as "farming kits," contained information on individual borrowers that lenders used to personalize their solicitations. Between 2004 and 2006, Countrywide mailed between six and eight million targeted solicitations each month and made many tens of thousands of phone calls. The solicitations made people believe that the new loan products were designed for them and were all pleasure and no pain.[54]

The president of one data firm explained that the people his company identified as prospects included consumers who were in financial trouble and likely needed to refinance to avoid default. Lenders could buy a list of 2,500 distressed subprime borrowers for about $500. Some lenders mined their own data to pinpoint borrowers in need of refinancing. Countrywide reportedly identified borrowers who were behind in their payments and offered to refinance their loans. In 2004, one out of every nine loans by Ameriquest refinanced a loan that Ameriquest had made within the previous two years.[55]

Credit bureaus offered other ways to identify people to target. Each time individuals submitted applications for mortgage loans, lenders contacted credit bureaus to check their credit. The credit bureaus compiled lists of borrowers on whom inquiries were made and sold the lists to other lenders, who would then solicit the borrowers. In addition to supplying data, these firms developed models, using information on borrowers' behavior, to create profiles of borrowers who showed a "statistical propensity to acquire new credit."[56]

## Dodgy Practices

Although subprime lending moved from sketchy to mainstream institutions, the industry did not clean up its practices. Bait-and-switch tactics persisted, with lenders surprising borrowers at loan closings with thousands of dollars in unexpected fees and higher interest rates. Often the new interest rates were adjustable and could double or triple over time. When borrowers protested, lenders assured them that they would soon be able to refinance. What lenders did not say was that when the borrowers refinanced, they would have to pay origination and closing fees all over again plus likely prepayment penalties for the early payoff of their loans.[57]

Lenders made out big from steering, which was the practice of conning borrowers who qualified for cheap prime loans into agreeing to costlier subprime loans. Behind the scenes, lenders set minimum prices (a combination of the interest rate, points, and fees) they would accept for each type of loan, taking into account borrowers' credit scores and factors like the amount of equity they had in their homes. This resulted in a sliding scale of prices, a practice known as risk-based pricing. Subprime lenders kept the real risk-based price a secret; borrowers only knew the price they were offered, which often exceeded the risk-based price. When borrowers paid more than the minimally acceptable price, lenders made more money. According to the *Wall Street Journal,* 55 percent of all subprime loans in 2005 went to people with sufficiently high credit scores to qualify for prime loans.[58]

Another gambit was to generate hundreds of dollars in "junk" fees for checking borrowers' credit, processing applications, and preparing loan documents. Firms charged borrowers up to $75 just to send emails. Lenders captured profits through other means, too. Investors paid more for certain loan attributes, with default interest rate clauses being a favorite. Under these clauses, the interest rate would skyrocket if a borrower missed a payment. Of course, if the interest rate went up, so did the likelihood of future defaults.[59]

Prepayment penalties were found in about 80 percent of subprime loans and typically required borrowers to pay six months' worth of interest if they refinanced within a stated period, commonly one to five years. On a $150,000 loan with a 12 percent interest rate, the prepayment penalty would be $7,500. A 2004 study estimated that prepayment penalties cost borrowers a total of $2.3 billion a year.[60] Prepayment penalties had pernicious effects, including locking borrowers into high-cost loans. As their credit profiles improved, borrowers could not refinance into cheaper loans unless they generated the cash to pay the penalties. Prepayment penalties also increased the odds of default by trapping borrowers in high-cost loans. One study found that loans with prepayment penalties longer than three years were 20 percent more likely to default than comparable loans without those penalties.[61]

### Lending According to Stereotype

The race-based targeting that was a signature of early predatory lending also continued unabated. Subprime mortgages were more heavily concentrated in predominantly black and Latino neighborhoods relative to white communities, even when controlling for income and credit scores. Researchers estimated that half of home mortgage loans made to African-Americans before the housing market collapsed were expensive subprime loans.[62]

Damning evidence to this effect appeared in an affidavit by former Wells Fargo loan officer Tony Paschal. Paschal asserted that Wells Fargo employees referred to borrowers of color as "mud people" and their loans as "ghetto loans." Loan officers, he reported, lowered interest rates for whites when interest rates fell before closing, but told black borrowers that their rates were "locked" and they could not take advantage of interest rate declines. Paschal also accused Wells Fargo of deliberate marketing practices directed at African-Americans, including a software program that would send flyers to consumers based on their "language." One such "language" was "African-American."[63] Another former Wells Fargo loan officer, Elizabeth Jacobson, attested that the company approached black churches in hopes that each minister would "convince the congregation to take out subprime loans with Wells Fargo."[64]

Lenders and brokers saved the worst deals for borrowers they considered easy marks. In a study of loans insured by the Federal Housing Administration, researchers looked at differences in the amounts borrowers paid in fees based on race and education. The study controlled for factors such as credit scores and home values that could have influenced default risks and therefore the cost of credit. On average, African-American borrowers paid $414 more in fees and Latinos $365 more than equivalent whites.[65]

These findings were not unique. Studies by governmental agencies and consumer groups have consistently found that people of color pay more for credit even after controlling for creditworthiness. Setting the cost of mortgages based on borrowers' race is blatantly unfair and discriminatory. It also increases the likelihood that borrowers will lose their homes because their mortgages are less affordable than those offered to equivalent white borrowers.[66]

Education mattered, too. In one study, borrowers with college degrees paid, on average, $1,100 less than those without a college education even though the latter borrowers purchased essentially the same products, presented the same level of default risk, and lived in similar communities and types of housing.[67] Not surprisingly, given these results, subprime loans are concentrated in areas where people have lower educational levels, even when those areas have the same default risk as neighborhoods with better educated residents.[68]

## Outright Fraud

The quest for ever higher revenues went hand in hand with fraud. Too often, brokers and lenders did whatever it took to close a loan. That might involve padding a borrower's income or assets (with or without the borrower's knowledge), commissioning inflated appraisals, manufacturing fake pay stubs and W-2s, altering credit reports, and creating fictitious checks and investment statements. These practices, according to a study by Fitch Ratings, were more pronounced among loans made through independent brokers than through loan officers. This was probably because brokers didn't make any money if borrowers could not satisfy lenders' underwriting criteria.[69] In Cleveland, for example, eighty-three people were charged with mortgage fraud in a scheme to defraud lenders by fabricating employment and income records and then hiring people called "backstoppers" who would verify the information when lenders called as part of the underwriting process.[70]

Lenders and brokers did not work alone. There are stories of professionals who helped them commit fraud, like the CPA who allegedly was in the "back pocket" of a New Century account executive, providing letters verifying borrowers' self-employment income that did not exist.[71] A bank teller reportedly doctored bank statements for loan originators to help borrowers qualify.[72] According to the *New York Times,* some brokers even offered bribes to underwriters to accept loan applications that other lenders had rejected.[73] In 2002, following an intense FBI investigation, "two accountants, four title companies, five appraisers, eight underwriters and forty mortgage brokers" were indicted for their involvement in a mortgage fraud scheme allegedly orchestrated by American Home Loans.[74]

Brokers and lenders were skillful at finding appraisers who would come in with property valuations that would satisfy underwriters. In a practice called "hitting the bid," they would handpick appraisers and tell them what the property needed to be worth for the loan to go through.[75] Appraisers reported feeling "bulldozed" into inflating the value of homes and misrepresenting the condition of properties.[76] When the State of New York got wind of allegations of such practices at Washington Mutual, it brought a lawsuit against an appraisal outfit that reportedly succumbed to pressure from WaMu. According to the complaint, WaMu generated a list of preferred appraisers from eAppraiseIT who could be counted on to bring in high valuations.[77]

Some loan originators engaged in even more blatant forms of fraud. One mortgage bank made a name for itself by having borrowers sign duplicate copies of their loan and mortgage agreements. The lender would then sell the notes to two different entities, each of which thought it held the "real" note. This practice, called "double-booking," enabled the mortgage bank to retain all the funds from the sale of both notes. The borrowers would only pay on one of the notes, not realizing they owed on two. The investor that was not receiving any payments would then go after the borrowers, only to discover the fraud.[78] In other situations, borrowers would attempt to refinance their loans, only to learn that there were multiple fictitious mortgages on their property.[79]

In a damning affidavit, a former account executive for a subprime lender described his firm's practices:

- Ameriquest taught . . . Account Executives to inflate the stated value of the customer's property for the purpose of qualifying them for a refinance loan. I recall an Ameriquest area manager indicating that appraisal values should regularly be pushed by at least 10–15 percent.
- It was a common and open practice at Ameriquest for Account Executives to forge or alter borrower information or loan documents. For example, I saw Account Executives openly engage in conduct such as altering borrowers' W-2

forms or pay stubs, photocopying borrower signatures and copying them onto other, unsigned documents, and similar conduct . . .

- Account Executives regularly concealed or obfuscated that a loan was an adjustable rate mortgage, rather than a fixed. In fact, it was common practice for Account Executives to refer to adjustable rate loans as "fixed adjustable" loans.[80]

## FOLLOW THE MONEY

People wonder why brokers and loan officers wanted to rip-off their customers with high-cost products. The answer is commissions. Think used car salespeople. In fact, the disreputable subprime lender FAMCO "recruited highly paid automobile sales representatives, who were at ease with the 'hard sell' but tired of the long evening hours and weekend work that auto sales involved."[81]

Every day lenders sent brokers and loan officers—if they had retail operations— rate sheets reflecting the minimum price they would accept for each type of subprime product they offered. Products varied by interest rate, points, and prepayment penalties. The prices took into account product features and borrower information like credit scores.[82] Most importantly for brokers, the rate sheets spelled out the commissions, called yield spread premiums (or YSPs), that brokers could earn if they steered borrowers to higher interest loans with prepayment penalties. Banks often had parallel compensation systems for their loan officers, called "overages," if they induced borrowers to take out loans on costlier terms. Both types of compensation were essentially legalized kickbacks.

Brokers and lenders virtually never gave borrowers copies of the rate sheets or told them the lenders' bottom line prices. And, most lenders expressly prohibited disclosure of their rate sheets to borrowers. Every incentive was for brokers and loan officers to use the rate sheets to steer borrowers into high-priced loan products to maximize their commissions.[83]

Some firms were particularly generous with their YSPs. New Century, which is now among the ranks of bankrupt lenders, rewarded brokers with handsome YSPs. Amber Barbosa, who got into the loan origination business as an employee at New Century, eventually became an independent mortgage broker. At twenty-eight years old, with no college degree, Ms. Barbosa made $500,000 a year in YSPs. She drove a Mercedes CLS 500 and a Cadillac Escalade and owned three pieces of property, including one with an ocean view. She described YSPs of $15,000 to $20,000 "as kickbacks."[84]

YSPs and the complex loan terms that usually accompanied them had significant effects on the price of credit. One study found that borrowers paid between $800 and $3,000 extra per loan if the lender paid a YSP to the broker, with an average added cost to borrowers of $1,046.[85] Another study revealed that subprime borrowers who did not use brokers paid almost $36,000 less over the life of a loan than their counterparts who went through brokers.[86]

There were other pecuniary incentives for loan officers to steer borrowers who applied for prime loans to subprime products. According to Elizabeth Jacobson, formerly at Wells Fargo, loan officers in the prime division made more money if they referred prime-eligible borrowers to loan officers handling subprime products. They would persuade borrowers to make the switch from prime to subprime saying that the processing time was shorter and required less documentation and no down payment. Others advised borrowers not to make down payments, which then made them ineligible for prime loans.[87]

Commissions were often based on a percentage of the loan principal, which meant that the larger the borrower's loan, the larger the commission. This led loan originators to encourage borrowers to take on more debt than they had originally requested. Brokers and loan officers could also generate fees by packing in products like credit life insurance.

All these opportunities for compensation were pernicious, not just because borrowers paid more than they should have. By inflating the interest rates, the size of the loans, and the various fees borrowers had to pay, the commissions substantially increased the likelihood that subprime loans would default and go into foreclosure. This increased risk was not insubstantial. Economists have calculated that for every 1 percent increase in the initial interest rate of a home mortgage, the chance that a loan will go into default rises by 16 percent a year.[88]

## THE RACE TO THE BOTTOM

Starting in 2003, the competition for loans to securitize got fierce. Everyone who wanted to refinance had done so, and there were more and bigger lenders flocking to the market. As one insider put it, "We ran out of borrowers. . . . Everybody that could qualify, anybody that could fog a mirror . . . had basically been refinanced once, twice, three, sometimes four times."[89] At the same time, the spread between the interest rate lenders paid to borrow money and the interest rate they could charge borrowers was narrowing because of increased competition.

The year 2003 was when interest rates started to rise. Borrowers were increasingly shut out of the mortgage market because of higher home prices and higher interest rates. The once-booming mortgage business stalled, leading one reporter to write, "Fear is rampant that the housing boom is over. . . . [W]ill the financial companies that rode the rocket fizzle along with their best product, mortgages?"[90]

Lenders were desperate for new sources of mortgages. The "solution" was the expansion of the market through two techniques: risky new products called "nontraditional mortgages" and relaxed underwriting standards and loan terms, both of which were designed to qualify more borrowers. Most of the new, nontraditional mortgages combined artificially low initial payments with eye-popping monthly payments after a few years. This allowed lenders to qualify borrowers for loans based solely on the lower initial payments, without regard to whether the borrowers could make higher monthly payments later on. The assumption was that the borrowers could always refinance out of these loans if and when their payments became unaffordable because housing prices would keep going up. In describing a nontraditional loan known as a hybrid ARM, New Century personnel laid out the risks: "Inevitably, the borrower lacks enough equity to continue this cycle (absent rapidly rising property values) and ends up having to sell the house or face foreclosure."[91]

### Nontraditional Mortgages

Lenders peddled a cornucopia of risky nontraditional mortgage products to borrowers during the housing bubble: hybrid ARMs, interest-only loans, pay-option ARMs, and loans with negative amortization. The emergence of these products marked a new phase in the subprime market. Historically, subprime had referred to features of borrowers. Typically, subprime borrowers had been people with blemished credit histories, often with significant amounts of equity in their homes. In the second iteration of subprime lending, the word *subprime* shifted to describe the type of loan, not the features of borrowers. These new products were also referred to as Alt-A or nonprime loans; prime loans were called A loans.

Nontraditional mortgages experienced a meteoric rise. Of these, hybrid ARMs, interest-only mortgages, and pay-option ARMs accounted for a growing share. Pay-option ARMs and interest-only mortgages went from 3 percent of all nonprime originations in 2002 to well over 50 percent by 2005.[92]

The most common nontraditional mortgages were hybrid ARMs. By 2004 and continuing through 2006, hybrid ARMs represented about three-fourths of the loans in subprime securitizations. Hybrid ARMs had fixed initial rates that reset into adjustable rate mortgages in a set number of years. Often they were called 2/28s or 3/27s; the two numbers referred to the respective lengths of the fixed-rate and adjustable-rate periods. For example, a 2/28 had a fixed rate for two years and then converted to an adjustable rate for the next 28 years, with the rate usually adjusting every six months. The adjustable rate was calculated by adding a "margin" to an abstruse index such as the London Interbank Offered Rate (LIBOR), which is the rate at which London banks lend to each other. For example, say that a hybrid ARM had a margin of 4 percent and LIBOR was currently 5 percent; the adjustable rate would be 9 percent.[93]

Hybrid ARMs contained a hidden risk of payment shock—the risk that monthly payments would rise dramatically upon rate reset. The potential payment shock was worse than with traditional ARMs, which had lower reset rates and manageable lifetime caps. Indeed, with hybrid ARMs, the only way interest rates could go was up. During the housing bubble, many subprime hybrid ARMs had initial rate resets of three percentage points, resulting in increased monthly payments of as much as 50 percent.[94]

Even more dangerous were interest-only ARMs. With these loans, borrowers only paid interest for an initial period of anywhere from six months to five years. Once the introductory period expired, the borrowers' payments went up, often substantially, for the same reason as hybrid ARMs, plus two more. First, after the initial period, the loan began to amortize and borrowers had to pay principal as well as interest. In addition, the principal payments were higher than they would be under a fully amortizing loan because there were fewer years left to pay off the principal. As a result, the payment shock on interest-only ARMs was often worse than on hybrid ARMs.[95]

The most toxic nontraditional mortgages, however, were "pay-option" or "pick-a-pay" ARMs. These loans allowed borrowers to select among three options each month: (1) paying the full principal and interest; (2) paying only the interest; or (3) paying some set amount that was less than the interest payment. When borrowers chose the third option, the principal balance of their loans actually grew over time until the principal reached a set limit, usually around 120 percent of the original loan balance.

Seventy percent of borrowers with pay-option ARMs picked the minimum payment option until they hit their limit, at which point their loans were "recast." Then they faced much higher monthly payments that amortized the principal, including the interest that had been deferred, plus interest. The monthly payments went up even more because the loan was amortized over the remaining loan period, not the full loan term. In the process, borrowers' payments easily doubled or tripled overnight.[96]

The loan disclosures for pay-option ARMs typically only showed what the payments would be if borrowers made the minimum payments before recasting. With respect to possible, later higher payments, the disclosures often only provided a hypothetical involving a $10,000 loan and let the borrowers do the math.[97] Not surprisingly, with their woefully deficient disclosures and their high-risk profile, pay-option ARMs were "the most likely" of all nontraditional mortgages "to default."[98]

Lenders deliberately marketed pay-option ARMs to borrowers to obfuscate the back-end risk. For instance, Countrywide reportedly required the loan officers in its Full Spectrum Lending Division to memorize the following script: "Which would you rather have, a long-term fixed payment or a short-term one that may allow you to realize several hundred dollars a month in savings? I am able to help many of my clients lower their monthly payments and it only takes a few minutes over the phone to get started."[99] Edward Marini, a disabled veteran who had a pay-option ARM with Countrywide, was left believing that his mortgage had low payments for five years. To his surprise, three years after the closing, he learned that his monthly payment was about to triple from $1,300 to $3,800. The new payment amount exceeded his monthly income of $3,250.[100]

Lenders knew they were potentially putting pay-option ARM borrowers in untenable positions with these products that were untested in the mass market. Countrywide's chief executive officer, Angelo Mozilo, was quoted as saying that lenders were "flying blind on how [they would] perform in a stressed environment of higher unemployment, reduced values and slowing home sales."[101] That did not deter his company from making almost $750 billion worth of pay-option ARMs between 2004 and 2007.[102]

## Easy Terms and Loose Underwriting Standards

During the housing bubble, the other way lenders kept up volume was to loosen underwriting standards to qualify more borrowers for loans. If a down-payment requirement or low equity was a concern, no problem: the lender just reduced the minimum required equity in the home. If the borrower's income was an issue, no problem: the lender would just do a stated-income loan.

Loans with high loan-to-value (LTV) ratios reduced the need for borrowers to come up with large down payments when buying homes. Similarly, high LTV loans made it possible for borrowers to refinance with little or no equity. As a result, between 2001 and 2006, the average LTV among subprime loans increased from 79.4 percent to 85.9 percent. Some loans even had LTVs of over 100 percent, meaning they exceeded the value of the homes that served as the collateral. Not surprisingly, loans with high loan-to-value ratios were more likely to default.[103]

Piggyback loans were another technique to reduce down-payment or minimum equity requirements. These loans had the added attraction of obviating the need for borrowers to pay private mortgage insurance (PMI). In the past, if borrowers did not make down payments of at least 20 percent, they had to buy PMI, which would pay off the lenders if the borrowers defaulted. During the lending boom, lenders skirted these requirements by using piggyback loans.

Piggyback loans worked like this: The lender gave the borrower a first mortgage for 80 percent of the value of the home. Then it granted a second loan covering all or part of the difference between the first 80 percent and the remaining value of the home. Piggyback loans and other loans with combined LTVs of 100 percent grew at exponential rates, reaching almost 40 percent of all subprime loan originations by 2006.[104]

Piggyback loans layered another level of risk on top of subprime mortgages. When piggyback loans left borrowers with no equity, any depreciation in their homes put their loans "under water." And if the first mortgage was sold through securitization, the loan's new owner often did not know that there was a "silent second" loan or that the home was 100 percent leveraged. Countrywide's Angelo Mozilo wrote in an internal email that he had "never seen a more toxic product."[105]

Lenders further dropped their underwriting standards in response to the fact that housing prices were rapidly outstripping workers' stagnant wages. They did this by lowering or eliminating their documentation requirements for income, assets, and jobs. In a "stated-income" or low-documentation loan, applicants reported their income, but did not provide proof. In a no-documentation loan, the loan was underwritten with no information at all on the loan applicant's income, stated or otherwise. With a NINA (no income, no assets) loan, the income and asset fields were left blank on loan applications. The only thing worse were NINJA (no income, no job, no assets) loans, which lenders made without any information on loan applicants' income, assets, or jobs.

At the outset, stated-income loans were limited to prime, fixed-rate loans requiring higher credit scores to qualify. This changed over time as lenders abandoned their underwriting requirements. Estimates are that at the top of the bubble, 80 percent of Alt-A loans and almost 40 percent of subprime loans were low-doc or no-doc loans. Low-doc and no-doc loans were most prevalent in rapidly appreciating markets like California, Nevada, Florida, and Arizona, where high prices made it hard for borrowers to qualify for loans. And like high LTV loans, stated-income and no-doc loans were more likely to default than full-documentation loans.[106]

Low-doc and no-doc loans were particularly noxious because they invited deception. They soon became known as "liar's loans." Borrowers could put whatever figure they wanted down for their income and not back it up with tax returns or pay stubs. Likewise, examples a bound of brokers or loan officers who entered false income, asset, and job information on loan applications without borrowers' knowledge. World Savings Bank, which Wachovia Corporation later purchased, allegedly qualified a widow for a loan based on her deceased husband's income with the knowledge that he was no longer alive.[107] According to one study, close to 60 percent of applications for stated-income loans inflated borrowers' incomes by at least 50 percent above the amounts reported to the IRS.[108] Another study of loans that went into default shortly after they were originated found that up to 70 percent of the loan applications in question contained false information.[109]

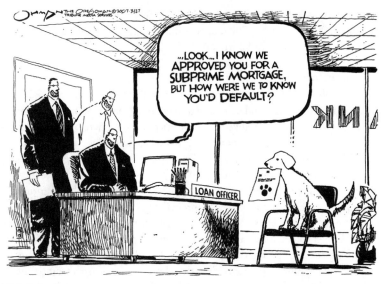

**FIGURE 2.2.**

Lenders could have verified borrowers' income, but few bothered to do so. Not verifying borrowers' income and assets made underwriting faster and cheaper. Washington Mutual allegedly promoted low-doc and no-doc loans with a flier stating that "a thin file is a good file."[110] Countrywide called its low-doc product "Fast and Easy" because Countrywide could issue loan approvals without having to wait for pay stubs or income tax returns from applicants.[111]

Brokers and loan officers often earned higher commissions on low-doc and no-doc loans. Fees on a $300,000 stated-income loan went as high as $15,000. A comparable fixed-rate, full-documentation loan would generate less than $5,000 in fees. No wonder brokers and loan officers often tried to steer borrowers to reduced documentation products. Borrowers often fell for the ruse, either because brokers or loan officers convinced them that they had to close the deal quickly before rates went up or because they liked the convenience of low-doc and no-doc loans.[112]

Another way to cut corners was to qualify borrowers based on their monthly payments for principal and interest without escrowing for homeowner's insurance and property taxes. Historically, lenders had required borrowers to escrow insurance and property taxes as part of their monthly mortgage payments. Lenders would disperse the escrow funds when the tax and insurance bills came due. By not escrowing these expenses, lenders could make unaffordable loans appear affordable. The danger, however, was that when the bills for taxes and insurance came in the mail, borrowers would not have the money to pay them.[113]

As if the risk of any one of these practices or products was not enough, lenders began layering multiple risks. For example, a lender might combine an interest-only ARM with a piggyback loan and dispense with verifying the borrower's income. Each of these features increased the risk of the loan. A 2008 study found that stated-income loans with 100 percent loan-to-value ratios were particularly treacherous and had the highest rates of default.[114]

All told, the new loan products spurred a sixfold increase in nonprime lending from 2000 through 2005. By January 2009, outstanding subprime mortgage debt, including Alt-A mortgages, was close to $2 trillion.[115]

## Crowd-Out Effect

ARMs offered lower initial monthly payments than fixed-rate, fully amortizing loans, which allowed irresponsible lenders to outcompete safe lenders. Soon, banks and other conservative lenders came to realize that it didn't pay to compete on fixed-rate prime loans, so they expanded into the nonprime market as well. That is why hybrid sub-prime ARMs, interest-only mortgages, and pay option ARMs captured a growing part of the market during the housing bubble.[116]

Lenders were under constant pressure to increase production "by hunting down more borrowers, selling more loans, and processing loans as quickly as possible."[117] This pressure led to problems at every stage of loan production. Lenders competed fiercely for brokers' allegiance. To entice brokers to throw loans their way, lenders scrapped their documentation requirements and slashed their approval times. One company, NovaStar Financial, reportedly sent a brochure to brokers trumpeting, "Did You Know NovaStar Offers to Completely Ignore Consumer Credit!"[118]

Lenders also turned a blind eye to wrongdoing by brokers. One WaMu senior underwriter reported noticing that a broker was targeting seniors and minorities and flipping loans. He informed WaMu's senior management and said he was going to decline the next loan submitted by the broker. To his dismay, management report-edly rejected his decision on grounds that "the broker gave WaMu a lot of loans."[119] Another executive complained that the subprime lender People's Choice knew about broker fraud, but "calculated that it would have been too complicated and expensive to go after [it]."[120]

Lenders set up incentive systems for loan officers, rewarding those who met min-imum production goals with lavish vacations and bonuses. One former Ameriquest employee described "the drive to close deals and grab six-figure salaries" as lead-ing "many Ameriquest employees astray. They forged documents, hyped customers' creditworthiness and 'juiced' mortgages with hidden rates and fees." A loan officer from Ameriquest reported coming across "co-workers using a brightly lighted Coke machine as a tracing board, copying borrowers' signatures on an unsigned piece of paper."[121] A former employee at WaMu said "she coached brokers to leave parts of applications blank to avoid prompting verification if the borrower's job or income was sketchy."[122] In Los Angeles, the FBI uncovered a document forger who created false W-2s, pay stubs, and other documents verifying borrowers' credit, employment, and identification for use by over 100 mortgage professionals.[123]

In the frenzy, lenders "lost sight of the basic tenets of underwriting and risk." A quality assurance manager at one lender described his company as "going through the motions" of risk management during the "free for all to approve loans by the thou-sands." The most graphic description of the breakdown in risk management came from a former WaMu underwriter, who said, "If you had a pulse, WaMu would give you a loan."[124]

It was loan underwriters' job to review loan files for creditworthiness and rule out fraud, but they rarely had enough time to thoroughly review files, given the constant pressure to approve loans. In addition, lenders increasingly overrode underwriters' loan decisions by making "exceptions" to the underwriting criteria. Underwriters claimed that when they nixed loans as too risky, senior management would reverse their decisions and approve the loans as exceptions. Sometimes refusal to approve a loan would be grounds for disciplinary action or retaliation against an underwriter.[125] At New Century, one underwriter told of a salesman who hit her desk with a baseball bat when she "cut" his deal. The same underwriter reported that she was "constantly told 'If you look the other way and let an additional three to four loans in a day that would mean millions more in revenue for New Century over the course of the week.'"[126] Lenders used carrots as well as sticks. At some companies, underwriters who met or exceeded their targets for loan approvals earned bonuses as high as $5,000 per month.[127]

Some subprime lenders outsourced loan underwriting to contract underwriters for as little as $10 per loan application. With such low fees, it was not cost-effective to verify incomes and evaluate credit risk carefully. As a result, contract underwriters had economic incentives to dispense with careful verification of borrowers' eligibility for credit and deceive participants down the line about the risks of subprime loans.

In a 2006 review of a sample of loans with early defaults, Fitch Ratings uncovered compelling evidence of a "race to the bottom" in underwriting. Fitch concluded that "in many instances, misrepresentations and altered documentation [were] evident in the physical files." It found that "loan files of borrowers with very high [credit] scores showed little evidence of a sound credit history but rather the borrowers appeared as 'authorized' users of someone else's credit." In other files, they found errors in the calculation of borrowers' debt-to-income ratios, incomes reported in low-doc and no-doc loans that were "unreasonable," and "substantial numbers of first-time homebuyers with questionable credit/income." One file included an admission by the borrower that he was a "'straw buyer' in a property flipping scheme." Fitch concluded that "poor underwriting processes did not identify and prevent and, therefore, in effect, allowed willful misrepresentations by parties to the transactions, which . . . exacerbated the effects of declining home prices and lax program guidelines."[128]

A 2009 study by the General Accountability Office confirmed the deterioration in loan quality. With every vintage, the percentage of subprime loans defaulting within three years got worse. For loans originated in 2004, the three-year default rate for loans was 5 percent. For loans originated in 2005 that rate was 8 percent, and for 2006 loans, the rate rose to 16 percent.[129]

The crowd-out effect also drove out affordable loans designed for borrowers with weak credit. Throughout the subprime boom, the Federal Housing Administration (FHA) and Veterans Affairs (VA) offered safer and cheaper alternatives to subprime loans. However, as subprime loan products proliferated, FHA and VA loans lost favor. From 1999 through 2006, for example, FHA's market share by dollar volume fell from 7.96 percent to 1.75 percent. VA loans experienced a similar drop. In 2005 alone, the volume of FHA loans fell 39 percent, and VA loans fell 30 percent.[130]

There were many reasons for this decline. Government loan programs required detailed documentation and down payments and capped the size of eligible loans. FHA and VA loans were slower to process because of paperwork requirements and mandatory inspections. For some borrowers, the loans may have seemed like a hassle. Brokers also had lots to gain from putting borrowers in subprime loans with their high fees and reduced documentation, and lots to lose if they offered FHA and VA loans. The suppression of safe substitutes for subprime loans during the housing bubble was one more indication that subprime loans had crowded out prime loans.[131]

The crowd-out effect also tilted Fannie Mae and Freddie Mac toward buying increasingly dangerous loans. In 2003, the GSEs dominated the issuance of mortgage-backed securities, with 78.4 percent of the market. Just two years later, in 2005, their combined market share had plummeted to 44.7 percent, a drop of 42 percent, as lenders sold more and more loosely underwritten loans to the private-label market. In response to this shift and under pressure from Congress to make more loans to low- and moderate-income borrowers, the GSEs made a conscious decision to push deeper into the subprime market, buying ever riskier loans for securitization, including stated-income loans, balloon loans, and loans with high LTVs.[132] Fannie Mae also purchased Countrywide's Fast and Easy low-doc loans. Initially, Countrywide had required Fast and Easy borrowers to have high FICO scores and down payments of at least 10 percent. Over time, however, Countrywide relaxed its requirements for low-doc loans and, despite these changes, Fannie Mae continued to buy them.[133] In the words of the former loan-servicing director for Fannie Mae, the company "didn't know what [it was] buying . . . The system was designed for plain vanilla loans, and we were trying to push chocolate sundaes through the gears."[134]

## PASS THE TRASH

In theory, lenders and brokers should have shied away from making abusive loans because their reputations and their solvency were at stake. Yet none of these concerns proved to be roadblocks. Brokers exploited borrowers and left town when homeowners or enforcement agencies were on their trail. States lacked any strong requirement that brokers be capitalized or bonded, which effectively made brokers judgment-proof.

Lenders should have worried even more that bad lending would hurt their business. After all, lenders had substantial assets that borrowers could go after and reputations to preserve. The risk of lawsuits and damage to reputation didn't seem to sway subprime lenders, however. Until the mortgage crash, even lenders who were embroiled in massive, nationwide lawsuits were able to stay in business. CitiFinancial, Ameriquest, and other major subprime lenders survived well-publicized consumer litigation and managed to keep their lending shops open. And, despite the bad press, borrowers still flocked to them for loans, and capital markets continued to finance their lending.

The reason subprime lenders did not worry about their solvency was securitization. Securitization allowed lenders to shift most of the default risk on to investors, who bore the financial brunt if the loans went belly-up. In other words, lenders could "pass the trash." In the past, when most mortgage lenders were regulated banks and thrifts that held their loans in portfolio, lenders took care when underwriting loans. Back then, default was a serious financial event. With securitization, lenders—both regulated and unregulated—could roll the loans off their balance sheets. As New Century's bankruptcy examiner explained: "So long as investors continued to be willing to purchase New Century loans, New Century apparently did not believe it needed significantly to improve loan quality."[135]

Securitization also altered the compensation structure of subprime lending. Lenders made their money on upfront fees collected from borrowers and the cash proceeds from securitization offerings, not on the interest payments on loans. This gave lenders the security of being paid in advance, instead of having to wait for uncertain monthly payments over the life of loans. As a result, lenders had even less reason to care about how well their loans performed. Instead, all that mattered was generating fees and quickly getting the loans off their books.

Some lenders even had two sets of underwriting standards: high standards for loans they kept on their books and lax standards for ones that they securitized. Researchers have confirmed the moral hazard problems created by securitization. When lenders sold loans to outside buyers, the loans were more likely to default. This suggests that lenders were more careful about the default risks if they had formal relationships with the purchasers of their loans, for example, if the lenders and purchasers were owned by the same holding company. One of the most compelling studies compared functionally equivalent subprime loans, some of which fell just below the threshold for securitization (a FICO credit score of 620)[136] and those with scores just above the threshold. These loans should have had similar default rates. Instead, the authors found that the loans right above the 620 threshold—the ones more likely to be securitized—had higher rates of default. These results were strongest for stated-income loans, where the borrowers' true incomes were unknown.[137] Another study compared loans that were sold through securitization with those held in banks' portfolios. Overall, the loans that lenders sold on the secondary market did not perform as well.[138] An obvious conclusion from these studies is that lenders were less concerned with carefully underwriting loans that they knew were going to be securitized.[139]

## WHAT ABOUT THE BORROWERS?

Without a doubt, most borrowers with subprime loans would have been better off with loans on better terms or with no loans at all. It is natural, then, to ask why borrowers ever agreed to ridiculously expensive subprime loans.

For one thing, many borrowers lacked full information when choosing subprime loans. Subprime loans were known for their complexity. The loans had multiple moving parts, from interest rates that depended on the interest rate that London banks charged each other to dozens of different fees.

Complexity made it difficult for borrowers to determine the true cost of loans, which made it hard to comparison-shop. Plus, lenders and brokers were unwilling to give firm price quotes when borrowers were shopping for subprime loans. Federal mortgage disclosures were too outmoded, complicated, and late to help consumers shop or to alert them to the back-end risks of toxic ARMs.[140]

People fell for abusive subprime loans for another reason: information overload. When people have to evaluate deals with multiple features, they tend to focus on one or two features. There is simply too much information to consider all the variables. In the case of subprime loans, people often concentrated on the initial interest rate or the initial monthly payment. Behavioral economists call these rules of thumb "choice heuristics." Choice heuristics can lead consumers to make decisions that are not in their best interests. Subprime lenders and brokers exploited these behavioral tendencies by

"As an alternative to the traditional 30-year mortgage,
we also offer an interest-only mortgage, balloon
mortgage, reverse mortgage, upside down mortgage,
inside out mortgage, loop-de-loop mortgage, and the
spinning double axel mortgage with a triple lutz."

**FIGURE 2.3.**

offering complex products to borrowers and then directing them to consider only the initial monthly payment: was it more or less than what they were paying and could afford? Many borrowers, suffering information overload, would latch on to the initial monthly payments for exotic ARMs in the mistaken belief that lenders and brokers were acting in their best interests.[141] What they did not know, though, was that their monthly payments could ultimately soar.

Overoptimism was another reason that borrowers took out subprime loans. People tend to look on the bright side. This can lead them to misjudge their ability to afford future increases in their mortgage payments. People also place excessive importance on immediate gains while discounting potential future losses. In the mortgage context, empirical studies have found that when consumers look at a loan amount and payment schedule, they tend to underestimate the cost of the interest rate they will pay.[142] This explains why people might have preferred loans that put cash in their pockets over no-cash-out loans with lower interest rates and fees that would have reduced the odds they would lose their homes.[143]

Whether you call it predatory, nontraditional, Alt-A, nonprime or subprime lending, making loans with terms that borrowers could not understand or afford was a recipe for disaster. It was with these loans that the subprime virus took off.

3

▷

# A Rolling Loan Gathers No Loss

If lenders had kept their subprime loans on their books, they probably would have made fewer loans and taken greater care with the ones they made. With securitization, however, they could write risky loans and shed them quickly for cash. The buyers, mostly Wall Street banks, converted the loans into securities and passed the risk onto investors. That risk then "went viral" with the creation of trillions of dollars in complex credit derivatives built on subprime loans. Commercial banks, investment banks, insurance companies, hedge funds, pension plans, and governments around the world bought subprime derivatives, which depended on one thing: the timely payment of U.S. subprime mortgages. When that edifice cracked, the structure of private-label securitization came tumbling down.

*Securitization* did not even appear in Webster's dictionary until 1981.[1] Although the word is still in its infancy, most people in the United States sense that securitization had something to do with the subprime crisis. This chapter introduces readers to the process of securitization and to the actors who helped convert mortgage loans into complex financial instruments. It then explains how that process went haywire despite warnings to the market and the government years in advance.

## A THUMBNAIL SKETCH OF SECURITIZATION

At its core, securitization is rather simple. Investors provide lenders with capital to make mortgages or other loans. In return, the investors receive bonds backed by the loans.

During the credit boom, there were two main branches of residential mortgage securitization: agency securitization and private-label securitization. Agency securitization refers to the securitization of loans by Fannie Mae and Freddie Mac. Historically, loans meeting Fannie's and Freddie's requirements for purchase were called conforming loans. Private-label securitization financed non-conforming loans, such as subprime loans and jumbo prime loans, and was orchestrated by Wall Street firms. In this chapter, we will primarily be concerned with private-label securitization.

When a lender made a subprime loan with an eye to securitization, typically it sold the loan to an investment bank, whose function was described as the arranger, sponsor, or underwriter. We use the term *arranger* in this book. The job of the arranger was to convert loans into securities.

In a typical securitization, the arranger bundled a group of loans into a pool and created bonds out of the loan pool. These bonds were called *residential mortgage-backed securities* (RMBS) because they were backed by collateral consisting of the loans in the loan pool. Rating agencies then rated the bonds based on the expected likelihood of default. Once the arranger had the ratings in hand, it priced the securities and readied them for sale. Ultimately, the loans were transferred to a special purpose vehicle (SPV), which usually took the form of a trust. The SPV insulated the loans from seizure by the lender's creditors in case the lender became insolvent. Then the trust issued the securities and sold them to investors through broker-dealers, who often were affiliates of the arranger. Other entities, the servicers, did the heavy lifting of collecting the payments from borrowers, paying taxes and insurance, forwarding funds for disbursement to investors, and managing the loans. A final entity, the trustee for the trust, was typically some other Wall Street investment bank that sent the payments on the bonds to the investors.

### Arrangers

Arrangers of private-label securitizations were usually investment banks. In 2007, Lehman Brothers, Bear Stearns, Morgan Stanley, and JPMorgan Chase were the top

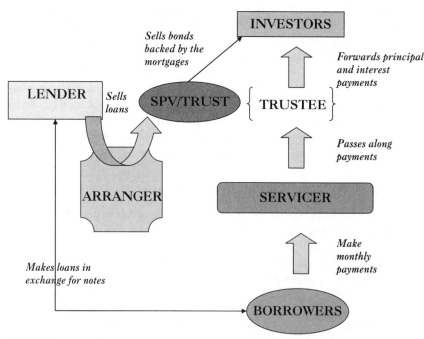

**FIGURE 3.1.**
Flowchart of securitization.

four arrangers of private-label securitizations. In a few cases, such as Countrywide, lenders directly issued their own securitization offerings.

Arrangers needed a constant flow of loans to generate securitization fees. One way they achieved this was by buying subprime lenders outright. Another way was by providing lenders with warehouse lines of credit to fund the loans they made. In return, the lenders granted the arrangers the right to purchase the loans. These warehouse lines were significant. At its peak, New Century had over $14 billion in warehouse lines from banks and other sources.

Arrangers also struck "selling forward" deals in which they agreed to buy loans from lenders, subject to stipulations, before the loans were made. For example, a lender might agree on October 1 that on December 1 it would deliver 2,000 adjustable-rate mortgage loans with an average interest rate of 6 percent, of which half would be subject to a prepayment penalty. The sales price was usually the face value of the loans plus a few percentage points. Based on stipulations regarding the characteristics of the loans, an arranger might agree to pay 102.25 percent of the original loan principal. In other words, the purchaser would agree in advance to pay the amount of the principal plus 2.25 percent. If the loans actually delivered had a slightly higher or lower average interest rate, the stipulations would specify an adjustment to the premium that was added to the principal.

## Lender Representations and Warranties

When arrangers purchased loans, they required lenders to provide them with representations (reps) and warranties about the quality of the loans. These reps and warranties included assurances that the loans complied with state and federal laws and satisfied stated underwriting criteria. To further sweeten the deals, lenders agreed to recourse clauses, in which they promised to buy back loans that violated the reps and warranties or that went into early default. Recourse clauses lulled some investors into believing that they did not have to carefully review the actual loans. After all, the thinking went, if a loan violated the reps and warranties the lender would have to repurchase it.

Reps and warranties were only as good as the promises they made. For example, failing to confirm a borrower's income did not violate the reps and warranties unless the lender specifically stated that it verified borrowers' incomes.

## Due Diligence

Arrangers did not rely on reps and warranties alone when buying loans. To assuage investors and ensure that the securities would receive the highest, investment grade ratings, arrangers commissioned due diligence reviews of loan pools. Generally, they hired outside due diligence firms that would review a sample of loans in a pool to confirm that the loans met the lenders' underwriting standards and procedures. Ideally, due diligence firms also verified information on borrowers' applications and made sure that all the loan documents were in order. These firms would then report their findings to arrangers for use in securities disclosures. This due diligence review was the only time that individual loan files normally received outside scrutiny during the securitization process.

With the growth of subprime lending and exotic new loan products, arrangers should have intensified their due diligence reviews. Instead, due diligence became perfunctory. During the subprime bubble, the quality of due diligence reviews declined, and so did the number of loans that underwent review. In 1995, due diligence reviewers sampled up to 30 percent of the loans in a loan pool. In 2005, arrangers were instructing due diligence firms to review only 5 percent.[2]

Other developments around the same time contributed to the decline in the quality of due diligence reviews. With the emergence of no-doc and low-doc loans, borrowers' loan files often did not contain paystubs or tax returns proving their income. In those cases, due diligence firms could not verify borrowers' stated incomes based on the loan files.

Due diligence also took on a new meaning. In the past, due diligence had focused on the quality of loans, including borrowers' ability to repay their loans. As subprime lending accelerated, the inquiry narrowed to the single question: did the loan adhere to the lender's guidelines? If the guidelines did not require a hard-nosed assessment of a borrower's ability to repay, then the due diligence review did not look at that issue.[3]

Like others in the securitization food chain, the people who conducted due diligence reviews were under constant pressure to sign off on dubious loans. For example, one employee of the due diligence firm Watterson-Prime, whose chief client was the now-defunct Bear Stearns, claimed that she rejected loans only to be overruled by her supervisors. According to the employee, 75 percent of the loans she rejected ultimately made it into subprime loan pools. When she showed her supervisors loan files that lacked proof that the borrowers made the incomes reported on their applications, her supervisors responded, "Oh, it's fine. Don't worry about it."[4]

A key feature of any due diligence report was information on the number of loans that flunked the underwriting criteria specified in the lender's reps and warranties. These loans were called "exceptions" and were more likely to default for obvious reasons. By 2006 and 2007, in some securities offerings, the number of exceptions exceeded the number of loans that met the lender's underwriting standards. In some deals, up to 80 percent of loans were exceptions.

Lenders came up with various justifications for deviating from their underwriting standards. For example, New Century allowed exceptions for people who demonstrated pride of ownership by keeping their homes in better shape than their neighbors.[5] When due diligence firms brought high exception rates to arrangers' attention, their concerns were often dismissed. One executive at a major due diligence firm complained that people at his company felt like "potted plants" as they watched investment banks scoop up mortgages that flunked due diligence reviews.[6]

Lenders had strong incentives to stuff in exception loans with "good" loans that were destined for securitization, and so did arrangers. First, passing the trash made it easier for all concerned to satisfy investors' demand for subprime RMBS. Otherwise, they had to find a replacement for every loan they rejected from a pool. Another reason arrangers threw rotten apples in with the good had to do with their contracts with lenders. It was "a generally accepted practice" for arrangers and lenders to negotiate a cap on the percentage of loans that an arranger could return to a lender.[7] New Century, for example, extracted promises from investment banks to reject no more than 2.5 percent of the loans they purchased.[8] These agreements provided lenders like New Century with incentives to slip bad loans into pools.

Arrangers counted on investors and rating agencies not to notice suspect loans. It helped that arrangers kept the due diligence reports mum. As we write this book, the New York attorney general, with the cooperation of a leading due diligence firm, is investigating reports that investment banks withheld damaging information in due diligence reports from rating agencies and investors. Allegedly, "Some Wall Street firms concealed information about exceptions . . . in a bid to bolster ratings of mortgage securities and make them more attractive to buyers."[9]

## Structuring the Bonds

Purchasing and reviewing loans were just two of the tasks of arrangers. Their main job was carving the principal and interest payments from borrowers into tranches (which is French for slices). Each tranche had its own bond, with its own yield, maturity date, and level of risk. A single deal could have over twenty tranches. The top tranche was the safest, with the lowest interest rate, and was paid off first. The tranche right below the senior tranche was paid off next and had a slightly higher risk with a slightly higher interest rate. And so it went down the line to the last tranche, the junior tranche or equity tranche. The equity tranche was the last to be paid, offered the highest interest, and was the first to absorb losses if borrowers defaulted.

The rating agencies assigned ratings to each of the tranches, using a unique combination of upper- and lower-case letters. For example, Standard & Poor's usually gave the top tranche a AAA rating; Moody's used Aaa. The next highest tranche received an AA, while the medium risk (mezzanine) tranches were ranked A to BBB. Any tranche rated BB or lower was below investment grade. The equity tranche was not rated at all. Often lenders owned the equity tranche. The theory was that if lenders held the riskiest tranches, they would exercise more caution when underwriting loans. However, as we discuss later on, lenders figured out how to hedge the equity tranches or sell them for resecuritization and unload that risk.[10]

Arrangers had other responsibilities, too. They had to create the trusts that would hold the assets and issue the securities. They drafted prospectuses and offering memoranda that informed investors about lenders' underwriting criteria and the risks associated with the securities. They also made other needed filings with the Securities and Exchange Commission (SEC) and ensured that all of the necessary regulatory approvals were obtained.

Arrangers made millions of dollars on every deal they put together. Underwriting fees were usually at least 1 percent of the value of the collateral and deals were in the billions of dollars. To get a sense of the total magnitude of this compensation, arrangers underwrote $2.1 trillion in subprime mortgage-backed securities between 2000 and 2007. One percent of $2.1 trillion is a very large number.[11]

## Rating Agencies

Arrangers worked closely with the three big rating agencies, Standard & Poor's ("S&P"), Moody's, and Fitch, whose task it was to grade each tranche based on the credit risk associated with that security. In rating mortgage-backed securities, the agencies relied on data from arrangers about the loans and the borrowers. These data included borrowers' credit scores, loan-to-value ratios, whether the borrowers documented their incomes, whether the properties were owner-occupied, and whether the loans were used to refinance an existing loan or to buy a home. The rating agencies also reviewed the lenders' reps and warranties and their reputations. Using this information, the agencies calculated the default risk for each of the tranches.

In rating RMBS, the rating agencies lacked one key source of information: the due diligence reports. The agencies maintained that "due diligence duties belonged to the other parties in the process."[12] On some occasions, rating agencies did request due diligence reports from arrangers, but were turned down.[13]

The SEC designated all three rating agencies Nationally Recognized Statistical Rating Organizations (NRSROs). For arrangers, garnering top ratings on mortgage-backed securities from one or more of these NRSROs was critically important. They prized a rating agency's NRSRO status because state and federal laws prohibited banks, insurance companies, and pension plans from investing in securities that did not have investment grade ratings from an NRSRO.[14]

The law conferred another important benefit on rating agencies that other market participants like securities analysts and accounting firms did not enjoy. They had immunity from broad swaths of legal exposure under the First Amendment and federal securities law. Practically, this meant that rating agencies could evaluate risks, give opinions on those risks through ratings, and not have to answer for their errors in judgment.[15]

No bond issue could earn a AAA rating without protections known as credit enhancements. Credit enhancements were supposed to minimize risk to investors by creating a cushion to absorb losses in the event of widespread defaults. These enhancements together with strong ratings were designed to give investors confidence to invest in the securities. Credit enhancements included overcollateralization, where the total balance of the principal of the loans exceeded the outstanding principal balance on the securities, and excess spread, where the interest payments from borrowers exceeded the interest owed to bondholders.

Bond insurance was another common form of credit enhancement. Issued by monoline insurers, such as Ambac and MBIA, bond insurance kicked in if the mortgage payments on a pool of loans fell too low to pay the trust's obligations to investors. The top bond insurers had vaunted AAA ratings and were considered "good for the money." At least one major bond insurer reportedly never expected to have to pay out on its policies and did not review the quality of the mortgages backing the securities it insured, something that only came to light in 2009.[16]

For many years, rating agencies functioned in the shadow of subprime securitization. Their role in the crisis did not become apparent until journalists and regulators began to dig deeper. Startling evidence of poor judgment eventually came to light. For example, from 2000 through 2006, Standard & Poor's took the position that piggyback loans—those with simultaneous second mortgages—were just as safe as loans in which borrowers had equity in their homes. This defied common sense. When S&P later discovered that piggyback loans were 43 percent more likely to default than other loans, it still did not downgrade securities backed by piggyback loans, saying it "had to further monitor the performance of loans."[17]

Speed was the name of the game at the peak of subprime. This encouraged less-than-careful work by rating agency analysts. Inundated with requests to assess new issues from arrangers, the agencies could not keep up. Sometimes the deadlines were so tight that analysts only had one day to evaluate submissions from arrangers.[18] According to the SEC, an analytical manager at one firm warned in an internal email: "We ran our staffing model assuming the analysts are working 60 hours a week and we are short on resources. . . . The analysts on average are working longer than this and we are burning them out."[19]

The problems at the rating agencies were not limited to flawed assumptions and overwork. An even bigger issue was their compensation system. In the past, rating agencies made money by selling their ratings to investors for use in their investment decisions. Having investors, not arrangers, pay for ratings was key to rating agencies' objectivity because, as a former Moody's vice president said in 1957, "We obviously cannot ask payment for rating a bond. To do so would attach a price to the process, and we could not escape the charge . . . that our ratings are for sale."[20]

Despite this admonition, in the 1970s the SEC began allowing arrangers to pay the rating agencies for rating the securities they were underwriting. Suddenly, the agencies were beholden to Wall Street for revenue.[21] An employee from Standard & Poor's structured finance division captured this mentality in an email saying that a deal "could be structured by cows, and we would rate it."[22]

The rating of a mortgage-backed security garnered fees that were four or five times the fees from rating a municipal bond offering. These fees propelled Moody's average profit margin to 53 percent.[23] From 2000 to 2006, Moody's had a 375 percent increase in profits, and its stock value increased fivefold.[24] The compensation

Stu's Views        © Stu  All Rights Reserved  www.STUS.com

How many sleazy rating agencies does it take to change a light bulb, and wreck the global economy?

Three?

**FIGURE 3.2.**

structure, along with arrangers' ability to shop for ratings, led to ratings inflation. Eighty percent of securities backed by subprime mortgages were rated AAA, and 95 percent were rated A, AA or AAA.[25] As one Moody's employee reportedly wrote in an email, the ratings suggested incompetence or that the firm had "sold [its] soul to the devil for revenue."[26]

Rating agencies snared business by satisfying their customers. In doing so, they *did* put their ratings up for sale. According to *New York Times* reporters, rating agencies were collaborators who worked "behind the scenes, with the underwriters that were putting . . . securities together." The reporters explained that underwriters didn't "assemble a security out of home loans and ship it off to the credit raters to see what grade" it would get. Rather, underwriters "work[ed] with rating companies while designing a mortgage bond or other security."[27] The rating analysts would advise the arrangers "how to structure the bonds to achieve maximum triple-A ratings."[28] The agencies also provided software that originators, investment banks, investors, mortgage insurers, and other entities could use to get a sense of what it would take for a deal to receive an investment grade rating.[29] Arrangers could plug various numbers into the software until they came up with a structure that would generate a AAA rating for the top tranche. This practice enabled investment banks to "game" the system.[30]

Arrangers wielded a great deal of power. The rating agencies needed their business, and most of that business came from a handful of arrangers. In the RMBS market, a dozen arrangers were involved in 90 percent of the deals.[31] According to industry insiders, arrangers would shop among the rating agencies to see who would give them the best rating on their securities. This practice was known as "maximizing value" or "best execution."[32] In the drive to secure business, firewalls designed to insulate rating agency analysts from influence broke down. An SEC report revealed internal emails from one rating agency suggesting that analysts should consider the impact of changes to their ratings methodology on the firm's market share. The same report told of analysts being involved in discussing the agency's fees with arrangers and sometimes even participating in fee negotiations. [33]

Arrangers actively lobbied analysts, hoping to influence their ratings. Raymond McDaniel, the chief executive officer of Moody's, reportedly described this phenomenon to his board of directors in a memo discussing "ratings erosion by persuasion." McDaniel explained that analysts and managing directors were "continually 'pitched' by bankers, issuers, investors . . . whose views can color credit judgment, sometimes improving it, other times degrading it (we 'drink the kool-aid')."[34] Drinking the Kool-Aid often meant "adjusting the criteria . . . because of the ongoing threat of losing deals."[35]

To their credit, some rating analysts refused to succumb to pressure from arrangers. Such refusals could generate calls from irate arrangers who would ask the agencies to assign a new analyst to rate the deal. The *Wall Street Journal* reported that clients of Moody's who complained about the conclusions Moody's analysts reached on deals, at times, had their reviews transferred to other analysts. Countrywide had a reputation of complaining to Moody's that its assessments of Countrywide's issues were "too tough." Moody's response was to "soften[] its stance on Countrywide securities . . . even though no new and significant information had come to light."[36]

In 2008, the SEC investigated rating agencies' processes and found numerous problems. The agencies used ratings criteria that they had never published. They failed to document their policies and procedures for rating subprime bonds, and had no method for detecting errors in their models. One of the more alarming findings was that the agencies sometimes deviated from their own models in a practice known as "'out of model' adjustments" when issuing ratings. These adjustments tamped down the losses that the agencies' models otherwise would have predicted. When the SEC asked about these deviations, the staff at the agencies was not always able to offer an explanation. The fate of billions of dollars turned on these inexplicable ratings.[37]

As authors of a *New York Times* op-ed put it, "In pursuit of their own short-term earnings," the rating agencies "did exactly the opposite of what they were meant to do: rather than expose financial risk they systematically disguised it."[38]

## Selling the Securities

Once the arranger worked out the details of a securitization, it parked the loans in an SPV that was the actual issuer of the securities. Broker-dealers then stepped in and marketed the securities to investors. Selling mortgage-backed securities was a lucrative business, with revenues consisting of a cut of the sales proceeds in the form of discounts, concessions, or commissions.[39]

It was not unusual for broker-dealers to hold some of the securities, either as investments or because there was no market for a particular tranche. Sometimes investors rejected the top tranche because the yield was too low. At other times, arrangers like Merrill Lynch held on to senior tranches in the mistaken belief that the tranches were "shielded from falls in the prices of mortgage securities."[40] Citigroup made the same mistake. In 2008, Citigroup ended up with $20 billion in senior mortgage-related securities on its books even after taking write-downs on some of those securities of up to 80 percent.[41] Both companies suffered grievous losses as a result.

## Servicers

Servicers were key players in securitizations. They collected and processed borrowers' mortgage payments and passed the monthly loan proceeds on to the trust after taking out their servicing fees and any escrow payments for real estate taxes and insurance. The trustee then distributed the principal and interest payments to the investors.

Loan servicers got a nice piece of the subprime pie. Some of their revenue consisted of a cut of the interest that borrowers paid on loans. For prime, fixed-rate loans, this was usually 0.25 percent of the loan amount. For subprime loans, it was usually 0.50 percent. ARMs garnered even higher fees because servicers had to process the various rate adjustments over time. For FHA loans, VA loans, and subprime loans, the servicers' cut was also substantial because these loans were more likely to go into default and required more servicing.

Servicers had other sources of revenue as well. They were allowed to retain late fees and received additional compensation if they met performance goals for loss mitigation. These fees were not benign. They created an incentive for servicers to delay posting payments and employ aggressive tactics to get borrowers to come up with money for their loan payments.[42]

## CDOs and Their Cousins

Residential mortgage-backed securities were simple compared to what came next. Wall Street began concocting collateralized debt obligations (CDOs), which involved pooling tranches of bonds and converting them into new securities. Drexel Burnham Lambert invented CDOs in the late 1980s as a way to unload corporate bonds. Only later did the model expand to mortgage-backed securities. In a process that paralleled the securitization of mortgages, arrangers constructed CDOs by taking lower-rated tranches of mortgage-backed securities (including junk RMBS), pooling those tranches, and dividing the pool into a new set of tranches for sale to investors. Alternatively, arrangers built "synthetic" CDOs out of sellers' obligations to pay on credit default swaps on subprime bonds.

Rating agencies reviewed the CDOs and gave the senior tranches AAA ratings. Just as with mortgage-backed securities, the top tranche carried the least risk and offered a lower yield than the junior tranches. For CDOs, the rating process was somewhat different than for RMBS. A CDO's assets were actively managed and were constantly changing. As a result, rating firms could not base their ratings on the assets that were actually backing a CDO. Instead, they reviewed the restrictions on the collateral the CDO was permitted to hold and used this information to make judgments about the risks associated with each tranche of the CDO.[43]

The complexity ran riot with the resecuritization of CDO tranches. CDOs were pooled and tranched into CDOs[2] and CDOs[2] were resecuritized into CDOs[3]. The astonishing thing about CDOs (whether they were plain, squared, or cubed) was that the underlying bonds could be junk, yet the top tranche of any CDO could carry a AAA rating. Essentially, CDOs purported to make steak out of chicken. Arrangers pooled tranches of mortgage-backed securities with low or no ratings (the chicken) and sliced those pools into tranches, with the top tranche earning a AAA rating (the steak).

**FIGURE 3.3.**
Drawing by Kagan McLeod.

It was too good to be true. Just because a CDO had a AAA rating didn't mean the assets backing it were top flight. Up to 80 percent of CDOs had AAA ratings, even though as many as 70 percent of the underlying RMBS had ratings below AAA.[44] All a AAA rating meant was that the AAA tranche would get paid first. Being first in line is irrelevant, however, if there is nothing to get. That is exactly what happened. When droves of subprime mortgages went into default, the most junior mortgage-backed securities received no payments and neither did the CDOs containing these tranches, regardless whether those CDO tranches were rated AAA or D. CDOs had other problems. Some CDOs were formed and sold before arrangers had assembled all the collateral that would go into the pool. This meant that investors had to trust arrangers' assurances about what would go into the pools, with no ability to verify the collateral before deciding to invest.[45]

Lack of diversification was another issue. Some pools contained as few as twenty assets. And even CDOs with hundreds of different assets could lack diversity if most or all of the assets came from the same sector, such as residential mortgage-backed securities. This was not a hypothetical concern. According to one report, RMBS grew from making up 43.3 percent of CDO portfolios in 2003 to 71.3 percent in 2006. In some cases, RMBS represented 90 percent of CDOs' portfolios. So much for CDOs as risk-diversifying instruments.[46]

Mortgage-related CDOs and their squared and cubed cousins were scarce until the mid-1990s, when JPMorgan Chase dove into the market. At the top of the market in 2006 and 2007, banks issued over $200 billion worth of CDOs backed by risky mortgage-backed securities.[47] The underwriting fees were astronomical, with some arrangers garnering 2.5 percent of the value of a CDO offering. Citigroup alone issued $20 billion worth of CDOs in 2005. Merrill Lynch bested Citi in 2007, creating more than $30 billion in mortgage-backed CDOs in just seven months.[48]

Investors flocked to CDOs. During the housing bubble, hedge funds bought over 45 percent of CDOs; insurance companies, banks, and asset managers held most of the rest. As would be expected, banks held the top-rated tranches, while hedge funds preferred the equity tranches.[49]

## SIVs

Banks were not keen on keeping RMBS and CDOs on their balance sheets, so they found a way to off-load these risky holdings through entities called structured investment vehicles (SIVs). With an SIV, a bank could sell its mortgage-backed securities to its SIV, which became the actual owner of the securities. To pay for the securities, the SIV issued commercial paper—a fancy way of saying it borrowed money, often from money market funds—at low rates and for short terms. The SIV's RMBS and CDOs served as the collateral for the loans. If the return on the SIV's assets exceeded the interest rate on its loans, the SIV made a profit.[50]

SIVs were a bright spot for a time. Citigroup first introduced SIVs in the late 1980s, and by 2007, banks had created over twenty SIVs with total assets ranging from $350 to $400 billion. The business model of SIVs was inherently unstable. The SIVs' securities had lengthy maturities, but their commercial paper came due in less than nine months and sometimes in only a few days. To keep SIVs going, managers had to constantly issue new commercial paper to refinance the old. Consequently, SIVs' success depended on their liquidity, and their liquidity depended on the strength of their assets. If they could not roll over their commercial paper because of faulty collateral, the SIVs would inevitably fail.[51]

Because SIVs were new on the block, there was no history to consult in predicting their future performance. This concerned investors who bought SIVs' commercial paper. They worried that if an SIV's RMBS and CDOs started defaulting, the SIV would not be able to pay back its loans. This was a risk that investors were unwilling to take. The solution was to extract informal promises from banks to make good on their SIVs' obligations if the SIVs' collateral failed to perform. The SIVs implemented these promises with guarantees, called "liquidity puts," issued to their investors. Despite these promises, in a seemingly masterful but ultimately disastrous sleight of hand, the banks did not book the SIVs' debts on their balance sheets when they made their promises.[52]

### Credit Default Swaps

The proliferation of credit derivatives did not stop with CDOs and SIVs. The risk that RMBS and CDOs might default spawned another product called credit default swaps (CDS). CDS were a tool for hedging default risk. A swap purchaser—usually a bank or other investor—would buy swap protection from a swap seller that would cover any losses if a bond covered by the swap defaulted. Investors liked swaps because swaps limited their exposure to default risk (so long as their swap seller was solvent if and when they needed to collect). Swap sellers were willing to provide swaps because the swap premiums were lucrative and sellers thought it was unlikely they would ever have to pay out on the swaps.[53]

In addition to their hedging function, swaps were used for speculation. Investors bought and sold swaps as bets on the performance of bonds. In cases of pure speculation, neither the buyer nor the seller actually owned the bond in question. Instead, they were betting on the performance of a bond held by someone else. Nothing limited the number of credit default swaps referencing a single security. For example, bonds valued at $1 million could be the basis for a hundred bets totaling $100 million on the performance of those bonds. The dominant seller of credit default swaps on mortgage bonds was American International Group (AIG).

We could go on to describe further complexities in financial products. The point, however, is not to inundate readers with descriptions of financial products, but to show how securitization, in the words of law professor Kurt Eggert, was "able to spin endless amounts of Wall Street gold . . . out of even the most suspect and speculative straw."[54]

### The Quants

Mathematical wizards, known as "quants," made subprime mortgage-backed securities possible by developing complex algorithms that calculated the risk of RMBS, CDOs, $CDOs^2$, and $CDOs^3$ as well as swaps. Over time, modeling complex financial instruments became a religion on Wall Street. As a "recovered" Wall Street model builder wrote, "Throw some epsilons and thetas on a paper, hoist a few Ph.D.'s behind your name, and now you're an expert in divining the future."[55] These models helped arrangers figure out how to structure deals, assisted rating agencies in deciding what grade to assign each tranche and aided swap dealers in pricing swaps.[56]

Not everyone believed in the quants' models. Long before the crash, Warren Buffett famously warned: "Beware of geeks bearing formulas." Even earlier, after the collapse of Long-Term Capital Management, a 1998 Merrill Lynch memo reportedly cautioned that financial models "may provide a greater sense of security than warranted; therefore reliance on these models should be limited." Merrill Lynch later failed to heed its own advice. The skeptics were right: the geeks' formulas were deeply flawed.[57]

Quants often made mistakes in their assumptions when designing models. Some assumed that historically low mortgage default rates would continue. Many did not even consider the possibility that subprime loans might have higher default rates than prime loans. And, few models incorporated the possibility that a financial cataclysm would increase default risk. The thinking was that because there had been no recent crises, the coming years would be free from crises too.[58]

Even when quants factored past market crashes into their risk models, the models were not fail-safe. They did not always include extreme, "tail" events. As one risk consultant put it, "Historic[al] data only has rainstorms and then a tornado hits."[59] The tail event that many, including modelers at Citigroup, did not consider was the risk that houses could lose value nationwide. Economists know that even tiny mistakes in assumptions can dramatically skew the predictive power of models. The risks from mistaken assumptions were particularly potent in the mortgage sector, where the effect of each mistake was compounded whenever a security was resecuritized.[60]

Another problem for the quants was the newness of subprime lending. Quants had plenty of information on the performance of prime loans but little information on the performance of subprime mortgages. As lenders devised new types of loans, the quants had to estimate new risks with no historical experience. No one who was honest could be confident about the quants' predictions during the infancy of subprime. This did not prevent the rating agencies from awarding AAA ratings to securities backed by subprime mortgages.

As the subprime market matured, quants did have opportunities to revise their models to account for new information on subprime loan performance. That did not always happen. For example, rating agency quants reportedly used data from 2001 through 2003 (when losses were 6 percent) to predict the risk on subprime loans made in 2006. The rating agencies' sloppiness could not have come at a worse time— just when new subprime products were entering the market and borrower quality was declining.[61]

Rating agencies also could have used default and other performance metrics to adjust their ratings on the securities that were already on the market. These adjustments—rating upgrades or downgrades—were infrequent and usually too late. In fact, agencies often neglected to monitor the performance of subprime securities unless they had some reason to know the securities were in trouble. As a consequence, investors did not have access to timely information about the quality of previously issued bonds.

Frank Raiter, the former managing director and head of the residential mortgage-backed ratings group at Standard & Poor's, explained the situation in testimony before the House Committee on Oversight and Government Reform:

The stress for profits and the desire to keep expenses low prevented us from in fact developing and implementing the appropriate methodology to keep track of the new products.

As a result, we didn't have the data going forward in 2004 and 2005 to really track what was happening with the subprime products and some of the new alternative-payment type products. And we did not, therefore, have the ability to forecast when they started to go awry. As a result, we did not, by that time, have the support of management in order to implement the analytics that, in my opinion, might have forestalled some of the problems we're experiencing today.[62]

Lastly, the quants' models could be gamed. As we mentioned earlier, the arrangers ran potential deals through rating agency models to see what structures would generate the best rating at the least cost. Law professor Frank Partnoy wrote about this in the context of CDOs, saying, "The process of rating CDOs [became] a mathematical game that smart bankers [knew] that they [could] win. A person who under[stood] the details of the model [could] tweak the inputs, assumptions, and underlying assets to produce a CDO that appear[ed] to add value, though in reality it [did] not."[63]

### Arrangers as Market Makers

It is easy to view investment banks and other arrangers as mechanics who simply operated the machinery that linked lenders to capital markets. In reality, arrangers orchestrated subprime lending behind the scenes. Drawing on his experience as a former derivatives trader, Frank Partnoy wrote, "The driving force behind the explosion of subprime mortgage lending in the U.S. was neither lenders nor borrowers. It was the arrangers of CDOs. They were the ones supplying the cocaine. The lenders and borrowers were just mice pushing the button."[64]

Behind the scenes, arrangers were the real ones pulling the strings of subprime lending, but their role received scant attention. One explanation for this omission is that the relationships between arrangers and lenders were opaque and difficult to dissect. Furthermore, many of the lenders who could have "talked" went out of business. On the investment banking side, the threat of personal liability may well have discouraged people from coming forward with information.

The evidence that does exist comes from public documents and the few people who chose to spill the beans. One of these is William Dallas, the founder and former chief executive officer of a lender, Ownit. According to the *New York Times*, Dallas said that investment banks pressured his firm to make questionable loans for packaging into securities. Merrill Lynch explicitly told Dallas to increase the number of stated-income loans Ownit was producing. The message, Dallas said, was obvious: "You are leaving money on the table—do more [low-doc loans]."[65]

Publicly available documents echo this depiction. An annual report from Fremont General portrayed how Fremont changed its mix of loan products to satisfy demand from Wall Street:

The company [sought] to maximize the premiums on whole loan sales and securitizations by closely monitoring the requirements of the various institutional purchasers, investors and rating agencies, and focusing on originating the types of loans that met their criteria and for which higher premiums were more likely to be realized.[66]

In a 2008 lawsuit against Countrywide, the State of California made similar allegations:

> In order to maximize the profits earned by the sale of its loans to the secondary market, Countrywide's business model increasingly focused on finding ways to generate an ever larger volume of the types of loans most demanded by investors. For example, Countrywide developed and modified loan products by discussing with investors the prices they would be willing to pay for loans with particular characteristics (or for securities backed by loans with particular characteristics), and also would receive requests from investors for pools of certain types of loans, or loans with particular characteristics. This enabled Countrywide to determine which loans were most likely to be sold on the secondary market for the highest premiums. . . .
>
> The information regarding the premiums that particular loan products and terms could earn on the secondary market was forwarded to Countrywide's production department, which was responsible for setting the prices at which loans were marketed to consumers.[67]

To ensure a constant supply of loans to feed their securitization machines, arrangers bought subprime lenders and made them captive. Ultimately, many investment banks had vertically-integrated production factories with lenders, servicers, and insurers. The only piece of the action that arrangers wanted no part of was the retail side of mortgage originations. They believed that by having a layer—mortgage brokers—between borrowers and their firms, they could eliminate their exposure to fair lending and consumer protection claims.[68]

Working in tandem, investment banks extended credit to their affiliates to make loans, purchased those loans for securitization, put securitization deals together, bought and sold the securities through their broker-dealer arms, and serviced the loans.[69] Bear Stearns, for example, had a Web-based platform that allowed mortgage brokers to search loan types and prices, submit loan applications, and obtain automated approvals. A Bear Stearns affiliate then took the loans and put them into securitization deals. The company's broker-dealers sold the securities and Bear Stearns's servicing arm, EMC Mortgage, collected the borrowers' monthly payments.[70]

Bear Stearns was not alone. Lehman Brothers owned numerous wholesale mortgage companies, including BNC Mortgage and Finance America, as well as a servicer, Aurora Loan Serving. In 2006, Morgan Stanley acquired Saxon Capital, a servicer and lender. Commercial banks also pursued vertical integration strategies, buying up and merging with loan servicers, originators, and broker-dealers. Even hedge funds, in a departure from their usual mode of operation, adopted vertical integration. For example, Cerberus Capital Management and Fortress Investment Group owned lenders and servicers.[71]

The following excerpt from a Morgan Stanley prospectus gives a sense of firms' tentacle-like components:

The sponsor is Morgan Stanley Mortgage Capital Holdings LLC, a New York limited liability company ("MSMCH"), successor-in-interest by merger to Morgan Stanley Mortgage Capital Inc. MSMCH is an affiliate, through common parent ownership, of Morgan Stanley Capital Services Inc., the interest rate swap provider and interest rate cap provider, and Morgan Stanley & Co. Incorporated, the underwriter. MSMCH is also an affiliate of the depositor and a direct, wholly-owned subsidiary of Morgan Stanley (NYSE:MS). As a result of a merger, completed on December 4, 2006, between a subsidiary of MSMCH and Saxon Capital, Inc., MSMCH is an affiliate, through common parent ownership, of Saxon Mortgage Services, Inc., one of the servicers.[72]

At the end of the day, financial institutions had their fingers in every piece of the pie and generated fees from origination through foreclosure.[73] This prompted Senator Schumer to charge: "The bottom feeders of society, these predatory lenders, reach up to the highest economic titans in society, and the two work together."[74]

In just a few years, mortgage-backed securitization and related services had become huge profit centers, stepping into the breach after 9/11 and Enron, when the initial public offering market dried up. Countrywide reportedly issued $647 billion in mortgage bonds in 2000 and $3.8 trillion in 2006.[75] In 2006, the financial services industry contributed over 8 percent of the country's gross domestic product and employed over six million people.[76] At the big investment banks, chief executive officers pulled down indecent amounts of pay. In 2006, the chief executive officer of Morgan Stanley received over $40 million in bonuses and his counterpart at Goldman Sachs scored even more—a $53.4 million bonus.[77]

## INVESTORS

So far we have been discussing the financial institutions that issued subprime bonds, not the investors who snapped up those bonds. Buyers of mortgage-backed securities hailed from all over the world—from small shires in Australia to major Chinese banks. University endowments, pension funds, insurance companies, banks, mutual funds, and municipalities all clamored for investment grade subprime RMBS and CDOs. More aggressive investors, like hedge funds, went for the riskier tranches with their higher yields.

Investors took to subprime mortgage-backed securities like fish to water. At their peak, subprime bonds were considered excellent investments. There were lots of reasons for investors to like them. One was the fact their yields exceeded those on conventional government and corporate bonds; some returns were even triple the yield on U.S. Treasuries. RMBS and CDOs also appeared to offer sufficient diversification to make the risk worth taking. The thinking was that, even if a few loans went bad, the pools were large enough and diverse enough to absorb an occasional default. Furthermore, rating agencies touted the top-rated subprime bonds—ranging from AAA down to A—as hardly ever defaulting. Other high-yield options, like bonds issued by countries with emerging economies, were considered substantially riskier.[78]

Mortgage-backed securities were appealing for another reason. Investors who were looking for highly rated securities had very few options. For example, "Only five non-financial companies and a few sovereigns had AAA ratings as of 2007."[79] In contrast, most tranches of mortgage-backed securities had investment grade ratings. For the same reason, investors eagerly bought the asset-backed commercial paper issued by SIVs. With banks essentially guaranteeing the SIVs' loans, investors felt protected from any defaults on the underlying RMBS and CDOs.

State and federal laws also spurred demand for investment grade mortgage-backed securities. Insurance companies, pension plans, and banks were all subject to laws restricting their bond holdings to investment grade debt. Institutional investors who wanted to expand beyond cash and corporate bonds turned to highly rated RMBS.

Even Fannie Mae and Freddie Mac bought securities backed by subprime loans. Rules governing the GSEs restricted Fannie and Freddie from purchasing loans that did not comply with their anti-predatory lending rules. But no similar restriction applied to their purchases of subprime bonds. Indeed, the Department of Housing and Urban Development (HUD) permitted Fannie and Freddie to fulfill their affordable lending obligations by purchasing securities backed by subprime loans. And so they did. Between 2004 and 2006, Fannie Mae and Freddie Mac purchased a total of $434 billion in subprime mortgage-backed securities, the bulk from Countrywide, New Century, and Ameriquest.[80]

## Challenges Facing Investors in Subprime Bonds

Investing in mortgage-backed securities was not a simple task. It was nearly impossible for investors to grasp their potential exposure and nearly impossible to know if they were getting fair deals. Take just one security—a $CDO^2$, which is a collection of tranches of CDOs. The CDOs in the pool underlying the $CDO^2$ would themselves include tranches from RMBS, which in turn incorporated pools of subprime mortgages. The word *opaque* does not begin to describe these products. Credit default swaps were even harder to value. As one investment bank manager reportedly said, "We can't accurately price [credit default swaps], although we're confident that we're getting a good price for them."[81]

Both Alan Greenspan and Ben Bernanke recognized that complexity made valuing securities challenging. In 2005, when discussing CDOs, Greenspan drew attention to a study that found that "understanding the credit risk profiles of CDO tranches poses challenges to even the most-sophisticated of market participants." Greenspan went on to advise investors "not to rely on rating-agency assessments of credit risk."[82] Later, a reporter overheard Chairman Bernanke say in reference to mortgage-backed securities, "I would like to know what those damn things are worth."[83]

Given that neither the former nor the current chairman of the Fed could harness the formidable resources at their fingertips to determine the value of mortgage-related securities, it is not surprising that investors couldn't either. In active markets, like publicly traded stocks, prices have a semblance of reliability because markets are liquid and prices are publicly posted. That was not true for subprime bonds. RMBS and CDOs were not traded on an exchange; rather, they were traded on the over-the-counter (OTC) market. Dealers executed OTC trades with customers on an individual basis, without publicly posting the sales volume or the sales price. Because these bonds were so opaque, the volume of RMBS and CDOs that were resold was small. With little

This derivative investment is so complicated that no investor will truly understand it. Thanks!

**FIGURE 3.4.**

active trading and no public resale market, there was no reliable mechanism for the market to set the price and investors could not determine whether the subprime bonds were accurately valued.

There was one vehicle that indirectly tracked the value of subprime mortgage-backed securities: the ABX index. Some credit default swaps traded with frequency and the ABX index tracked those deals. But the ABX index wasn't perfect. Critics complained that it only captured 3 percent of the mortgage market and overstated potential losses.[84]

Arguably, investors could have used their own mathematical tools and had their own quants appraise the value of subprime bonds that were offered for sale. This, however, was an expensive enterprise for most investors. Some commentators maintained that investors chose not to investigate the bonds because they "didn't want to spend the time and money required to be prudent investors at a time when low interest rates had everyone reaching for higher returns without contemplating the higher risks."[85]

Whatever the reason, most investors did not conduct their own due diligence. Instead, they relied on issuers' offering documents, ratings from the rating agencies, the structure of the deals, and assurances from broker-dealers. The offering documents often omitted critical information and sometimes were just wrong. According to the SEC, Countrywide misled investors by characterizing borrowers with FICO scores as low as 500 as having prime loans, even though the industry considered any borrower with a FICO score below 620 as subprime.[86]

Whether through necessity or choice, it was easiest for investors to rely on the rating agencies. If a bond had the Good Housekeeping seal of approval from Standard & Poor's, Moody's, or Fitch, investors considered the security a good investment without ever assessing the agencies' methods or the information the agencies relied on to issue the ratings. This myopia was particularly alarming because the rating agencies claimed they had no duty to confirm the truth of the information they received from arrangers. Too late in the game, investors learned that elevating rating agencies to "god-like status" had been a mistake.[87]

In the CDO market, the situation was even more worrisome. Investors would commit to purchasing CDOs before the arrangers could even tell them what collateral would back the bonds, "making a mockery of anyone who tried to do a fundamental analysis . . . before agreeing to buy."[88] To make matters worse, competition to purchase the securities meant investors had to make decisions on the fly. Credit committees for investors often only had a couple of days or sometimes just hours to review an offering. In the rush, they often just asked for the price.[89]

Investors also rashly relied on the advice of broker-dealers, mistakenly believing that the middlemen were speaking the truth. This reliance blinded them to the need to carefully review prospectuses and independently evaluate the risks involved in transactions.[90] Investment advisors had the strongest influence over pint-sized institutional investors like school districts and small municipalities. Whitefish Bay, Wisconsin, for example, listened to its investment banker and together with four other school districts bought $200 million worth of synthetic CDOs. An analyst in Chicago explained that "Selling these products to municipalities was pretty widespread. They tend to be less sophisticated. So bankers sell them products stuffed with junk."[91]

## THEY SAW IT COMING

Some people maintain that the subprime collapse was a surprise. The truth is, many saw it coming and others could have had they not been blinded by euphoria or greed. Starting in 2000, lenders were making increasingly risky loans, and by the end of 2005, "Degradation of the subprime market was apparent."[92] Even in 2004, lenders were experiencing a rise in early payment defaults, which are loans that default within a few months of origination. New Century's rate of early payment defaults, for instance, was already 7.24 percent in 2004.[93]

Other evidence abounded. Starting in the 1990s, there was a constant drumbeat of congressional hearings about abuses in the subprime market. In 1997, for example, Margot Saunders of the National Consumer Law Center alerted members of the Senate Banking Committee that home foreclosures had tripled in the past fifteen years, cautioning: "It does not help Americans to tantalize them with the dream of homeownership without providing the support to allow them to maintain that homeownership." Drake University law professor Cathy Lesser Mansfield advised the House Banking Committee in 2000 that high-cost subprime loans accounted for 22 percent of all foreclosures in 1998. In 2001, the Senate Banking Committee held a hearing where Allen Fishbein of the Center for Community Change testified that the "'dirty, rotten secret' of predatory lending is that many of the worst abuses are not necessarily illegal under existing consumer protections." In 2004, Norma Garcia from the Consumers Union told the House Banking Committee that "too many subprime loans" were "simply unaffordable and destined to fail."[94]

Over that same period, there were consumer protection lawsuits and enforcement actions against lenders across the country, many settling for huge amounts of money. For example, in 1999 Lehman Brothers faced predatory lending allegations when making a bid to acquire a Delaware bank. Lehman resolved the problem by agreeing that the bank would not "engage in predatory pricing" and would adopt procedures to "identify predatory pricing practices."[95] In 2002, Citigroup settled a Federal Trade Commission predatory lending claim for $215 million.[96] In 2003, the Federal Reserve Board fined CitiFinancial, Citibank's subprime arm, $70 million for making abusive loans. Around the same time, Household Finance, owned by HSBC, paid $484 million to settle consumer claims by state attorneys general. Ameriquest followed suit in 2006, paying $325 million to resolve similar claims by 48 states.[97]

For a time, government agencies were actively tracking the problems with subprime loans. In 1998, HUD and the Federal Reserve Board issued a report on deficiencies in subprime mortgage disclosures.[98] The Department of Treasury and HUD followed two years later with a major report on subprime abuses.[99] The Office of Thrift Supervision closed Superior Bank, FSB, in Chicago in 2001 after the bank made billions of dollars worth of loans to unqualified subprime borrowers.[100] Even President George W. Bush knew about the dangers of subprime loans. In 2006, top White House advisors warned him of a housing bubble and that the country would soon face a foreclosure crisis.[101]

The experience in individual states also provided evidence of the building storm. Beginning with North Carolina in 1999, states passed a succession of anti-predatory lending laws. These laws were a clear signal that states were contending with mounting problem loans.

Behind the scenes, investment banks knew that lenders were up to no good. That knowledge did not stop them from opening the money spigot to lenders. Nor did it stop them from buying loans for securitization. Take American Business Financial Services (ABFS), a subprime lender in Philadelphia. ABFS raised money by selling notes with high interest rates directly to individuals—mostly senior citizens—through newspaper ads. ABFS then used the proceeds to make high-cost mortgage loans. Wall Street firms greased ABFS' operations by lending it money and by buying its loans for securitization. Eventually, when ABFS collapsed and went into bankruptcy in 2005, investors lost over $600 million. According to the *Wall Street Journal*, during the bankruptcy proceedings, emails surfaced showing that investment banks had known as early as 2001 that ABFS was exploiting investors and engaging in dicey lending practices.[102]

Investment banks were also aware that lenders were relaxing their underwriting standards in ways that increased the risk of default. They had forty years of evidence that highly leveraged borrowing went hand in hand with heightened defaults, yet they continued to finance and buy loans even when the borrowers had no equity in their homes.[103] Wall Street firms also knew that mortgage-backed securities and related derivatives were spawning manic risks. As a former risk manager at Morgan Stanley told a *New York Times* reporter:

You absolutely could see it coming. You could see the risks rising. However, in the two years before the crisis hit, instead of preparing for it, the opposite took place to an extreme degree. The real trouble we got into today is because of things that took place in the two years before, when the risk measures were saying things were getting bad.[104]

In 2005, Fannie Mae's chief risk officer wrote a memo about the subprime-backed bonds in Fannie's portfolio, warning that the loans backing the securities would lose value if housing prices dropped. He also expressed concern that the rating agencies had not adequately assessed the risk in subprime and Alt-A loans.[105] The previous year, Freddie Mac's chief risk officer had advised his higher-ups that subprime loans "would likely pose an enormous financial and reputational risk to the company and the country." The response from the head of Freddie Mac was that the company "couldn't afford to say no to anyone."[106] The same sentiment reigned at Citigroup, where Charles Prince, the former CEO, said, "As long as the music is playing, you've got to get up and dance."[107]

Rating agencies were alert to the looming crisis, too. As early as 2003, a director at Fitch Ratings reported that his firm was "watching closely for a loosening in underwriting guidelines. . . . [I]f we start to see changes for the worse, moving down the credit scale, that would raise red flags."[108] By 2005, the rating agencies were fielding complaints that their ratings on mortgage-backed securities were too high and did not accurately reflect default risk.[109] In December 2006, a Standard & Poor's employee described his firm's ratings of CDOs as creating "an even bigger monster—the CDO market. Let's hope we are all wealthy and retired by the time this house of cards falters."[110]

AIG is another case in point. AIG stopped writing credit default swaps on subprime bonds in 2005 after consulting with Wall Street firms. This move was in response to concerns about deterioration in the quality of subprime loans.[111] In a 2007 investor conference call, AIG explained its decision to exit the market:

> We were seeing . . . through the many meetings that we held with everyone related to the market, from the managers, the originators, the servicers, the repackagers, we met all of them. And we came back from our trips thinking things are changing and they are clearly not changing for the better. So as a result, we stopped accepting the collateral and pulled out of the business.[112]

Perhaps the strongest evidence that players knew of the risks associated with subprime lending comes from history. The subprime mortgage crisis that began in 2006 was not the first. During the 1990s, companies like Green Tree Financial were financing the purchase of manufactured homes—trailers and double-wides. Like subprime mortgages, these manufactured home loans had terms that borrowers often could not afford.[113] At the end of each month, Green Tree's underwriting was at its weakest as salespeople tried to meet quotas and bonus targets.[114] A 2001 article reported: "The go-go years in manufactured homes were driven by loose accounting practices, inflated reports to investors and high-pressure sales tactics, at the local level. . . . Many consumers who bought mobile homes looked only at the monthly payment."[115] Green Tree, which later became part of Conseco, sold the loans for securitization on Wall

Street. Eventually, Green Tree brought down Conseco in 2002 and forced it into bankruptcy.[116]

During the heyday of manufactured home lending, there were also several good-sized subprime mortgage lenders plying high-risk loans that were ultimately securitized. In 1998 and 1999, several of these firms failed. At the time, investors complained that the investment banks had done a poor job structuring the deals and that the rating companies were incompetent.[117]

The subprime auto finance market tells a similar story. In the late 1990s risky subprime car loans prompted a spate of bankruptcies among auto finance companies. Cutthroat competition was one cause of this distress:

> The environment of readily available credit resulted in many new entrants in the subprime industry. . . . As the number of subprime automobile finance companies increased exponentially, competition for market share intensified. More competition caused credit quality to deteriorate, while increasing the pricing of loans.[118]

It's a sadly familiar tale.

## POLICING THE MARKET

What is hard to understand is why no one but consumers, their advocates, outside researchers, and a handful of politicians yelled "fire" even though the flames were at the windows. After all, one would think that if lenders were making loans to borrowers who could not afford their monthly loan payments, the market would have shut them down. Why didn't that happen? The answer is that all the various actors, from mortgage brokers to securities brokers and every institution in between, believed they could make money on subprime and pass the risk down the subprime food chain. In the words of George W. Bush, "Wall Street got drunk."[119]

The dominant ideology under the Bush administration was that the market would sniff out mortgage abuses and excess risk and police them. But market discipline of that sort did not happen. Instead, market participants blithely believed that if the market started to tank, they could protect themselves by selling any risky holdings. With no one caring about the harm to borrowers, to society, or even to themselves, subprime lending and subprime securitization descended into a Hobbesian nightmare.

Mortgage brokers originated high-risk subprime loans because they did not bear any credit risk and collected their fees at closing. Lenders made risky loans because they earned up-front fees while dumping the loans on investors by way of arrangers. Investment banks glossed over the risks of subprime loans because their earnings came from securitization. For all these entities, any check on abusive lending would have been bad for business. As Donna Tanoue, the former chairman of the Federal Deposit Insurance Corporation, warned: "The underwriter's motivation appears to be to receive the highest price . . . on behalf of the issuer—not to help curb predatory loans."[120]

At least investors should have cared about shoddy loans, even if the middlemen did not. After all, next to borrowers, investors had the most to lose from bad subprime lending. In reality, investors threw caution to the wind. They believed that they were insulated from credit risk. The ratings were strong and investors received their interest payments consistently for years so they did not question the performance of the underlying loans. They also hedged that risk by buying swap protection on the underlying securities.

There were some potential sources of market discipline. For example, lenders were often required to retain the riskiest equity tranches of RMBS when they securitized their loans, which should have given them reason to care about the quality of the loans they made. That isn't what happened. Instead, lenders often disposed of the risk by bundling and repackaging their equity tranches and resecuritizing them into CDOs. Wall Street liked to tout recourse clauses as another form of market discipline. As long as the vast majority of loans kept performing, however, investors had no reason to insist on recourse. In 2006, when borrowers began defaulting on their mortgages at high rates, so many subprime lenders wound up in bankruptcy court or disappeared altogether that recourse clauses became unenforceable. In short, recourse provisions were only as good as a lender's solvency and clearly were not effective at curtailing high-risk lending.

Even legal judgments did not slow down the frenzied pace of subprime securitizations. A test case arose involving Lehman Brothers and First Alliance Mortgage Company (FAMCO). Lehman Brothers bought hundreds of millions of dollars of loans from FAMCO at the same time that states were publicly investigating FAMCO's lending practices and consumers were suing FAMCO for predatory lending.[121] In one consumer class action lawsuit, consumers named Lehman Brothers as a defendant, claiming that the firm had aided and abetted FAMCO's abusive lending. The evidence in support of the claim included a 1995 memo from a Lehman executive describing FAMCO as a "sweat shop" that used "high pressure sales for people who are in a weak state."[122] Ultimately, after protracted litigation that ended up in bankruptcy court, Lehman Brothers was found liable and had to pay five million dollars in damages. That wasn't much for a financial giant and was certainly not enough to motivate Lehman Brothers or any other Wall Street firm to screen out abusive loans. If anything, it gave investment banks confidence that their relationships with predatory lenders would not bring them down. All told, the saga of subprime securitization rendered true the industry mantra that "a rolling loan gathers no loss."

# Part II

▷

# Contagion

Like a troupe of acrobats, Wall Street attempted to pull off a delicate balancing act, with RMBS depending on the performance of the underlying subprime mortgages, CDOs depending on the underlying RMBS, and credit default swaps depending on the entire edifice. If anyone wobbled, the pyramid would come crashing down. That is exactly what happened beginning in 2006.

Defaults soared on subprime mortgages, erupting into contagion in early 2007. Subprime lenders dropped like flies and private-label mortgage securitization collapsed. By the end of 2007, the United States was in a full-blown recession; by September 2008, the world's financial system was in meltdown.

Subprime mortgages were to blame and private-label securitization rested on their rotting foundation. Once subprime delinquencies took off, the pillars of securitization gave way. Often the same subprime loan backed multiple bonds, including RMBS, CDOs, and CDOs². If the loan went into default, it jeopardized payment on all three bonds.

Many of the same banks that shed their subprime loans through securitization reinfected themselves by buying private-label RMBS and CDOs and taking those risks back onto their books. As borrowers defaulted, those holdings lost value and banks responded by reining in lending, which only served to deepen the recession.

Meanwhile, investors that had used their subprime bonds as collateral for loans inadvertently contaminated other markets. Banks had pledged subprime bonds for short-term loans from other banks. Corporations had borrowed money from other corporations, issuing commercial paper backed by subprime bonds. When those subprime securities collapsed in value, lenders called in their loans and credit markets slowed to a crawl.

Soon investor panic was in full bloom. Banks did not want to lend to other banks for fear that subprime losses might be lurking on their counterparts' books. Investors shied away from all types of bonds backed by mortgages because they had lost faith in the ratings. Stocks in commercial banks, insurance companies, and Wall Street firms took a beating because investors did not know where the subprime assets were hidden. In fact, investors stopped trusting practically everyone because they did not know who was tainted by subprime lending. Through these vectors of contagion, the subprime virus spread far and wide.

# 4

▷

# Prelude to the Storm

## SEISMIC TREMORS

In early December 2006, two large subprime lenders capsized, sending shockwaves through the mortgage market. One was Ownit Mortgage Solutions in California, the eleventh biggest wholesale subprime lender. The other was Sebring Capital Partners LP, located outside Dallas, a smaller lender operating in forty-one states. At the start of the New Year, another big subprime lender, Mortgage Lenders Network USA in Middletown, Connecticut, shut its wholesale lending operation. By February 2007, all three were bankrupt.[1]

These failures were harbingers of bigger problems to come. All three companies were wholesale lenders that relied heavily on outside mortgage brokers for originations, and all three were independent, nonbank lenders with no deposit base. As such, they depended on short-term, "warehouse" lines of credit from Wall Street firms to fund their loans. Once the loans were securitized, the lenders used the proceeds to pay down their lines of credit.

In 2006, a liquidity crisis hit wholesale lending. Default rates were climbing on subprime loans, and Moody's revealed that unexpected numbers of borrowers had defaulted without ever making loan payments.[2] All this led Wall Street to lose confidence in the lenders they financed. In Ownit's case, Merrill Lynch, JPMorgan Chase, and other Wall Street firms cut the company's credit lines and, pursuant to recourse clauses, demanded that the lender buy back millions of dollars in bad loans. Mortgage Lenders Network went into death throes after Merrill Lynch, GMAC-RFC, and other large investors refused to buy its loans and also pelted the company with demands to buy back loans. Similar problems brought down Sebring. In the meantime, a spike in early payment defaults on loans made by the three failed firms raised larger questions about the exposure of Merrill Lynch (which owned 20 percent of Ownit) and other large investment banks such as Lehman Brothers and Bear Stearns that were heavily ensconced in subprime securitization. According to a mortgage banker, Merrill Lynch termed its invest-ment in Ownit "one of the worst mortgage trades the investment banker had ever made."[3]

These problems were not isolated. Jitters set in after UBS told investors in a conference call in November 2006 that subprime delinquencies of sixty days or more had reached 8 percent, almost double the level the year before.[4] For the fourth quarter of 2006, the Alt-A lender IndyMac Bancorp reported higher loan losses and delinquencies. Wells Fargo also announced higher than expected losses from wholesale lending.

The subprime market softened, driving down stock prices for two leading independent subprime lenders, New Century Financial and Novastar Financial. Owners of large subprime lenders such as Champion, First Franklin Financial Corporation, Ameriquest Mortgage, GMAC-RFC, and Option One Mortgage Corporation, put their companies up for sale. Meanwhile, Goldman Sachs and Balestra Capital placed lucrative bets that subprime investments would fall in value.

By spring 2007, it was official: the United States was in a housing bust. In the first quarter of 2007, housing prices declined nationwide, sharply in some markets, for the first time since the Great Depression. For borrowers facing difficulty making monthly payments, falling home prices severely limited their options. One way out was to refi-nance into a cheaper mortgage, but that became harder as home values dropped, often below the balance on borrowers' mortgages, leaving many distressed borrowers with no or even negative equity in their homes. Another solution was to pay off the loan by selling the home, but falling home prices eliminated that option for many people as well.[5]

HAUNTED HOUSES

**FIGURE 4.1.**

As distressed borrowers got boxed in, defaults soared and so did foreclosures. While all types of mortgages started to experience problems, the biggest problem initially was with subprime and Alt-A adjustable-rate mortgages. In July 2005, 5.63 percent of subprime ARMs and 0.43 percent of Alt-A ARMs were ninety days or more past due or in foreclosure. A year later, in July 2006, this rate had climbed to 8.16 percent for subprime ARMs and 0.74 percent for Alt-A ARMs. From that point on, things deteriorated quickly. By July 2007, this delinquency rate hit 14.63 percent and 3.06 percent respectively for subprime and Alt-A ARMs. A new high came in November 2007, when a shocking one-fifth of subprime ARMs were at least ninety days delinquent or in foreclosure, often because of defaults within months of the loan's closing.[6]

Meanwhile, during the first six months of 2007, close to eighty mortgage lenders failed. Others underwent fire sales or curtailed major lending operations because of rising defaults or liquidity crunches. A website suddenly appeared called the Mortgage Lender Implode-O-Meter, which tracked the serial implosions of mortgage lenders. The biggest that spring was the second-ranked subprime lender in 2006, New Century Financial Corporation, which filed for bankruptcy on April 2.[7] Some of the afflicted players were banks such as HSBC, but the lenders most affected during this period were independent, nonbank companies with heavy reliance on Wall Street funding.

Although Wall Street was reluctant to finance subprime lenders, investment banks continued to pump out bonds during the first half of 2007, using loans that they had previously acquired for securitization. In February, Wall Street issued $108.2 billion in private-label residential mortgage-backed securities, actually topping the monthly average for 2006. In retrospect, it was the securitization industry's last gasp; lenders and Wall Street had been frantically unloading their worst mortgages like hot potatoes onto investors before the securitization door slammed close.[8]

There were other signs of trouble. Consumer spending was losing steam and so was new home construction. Standard & Poor's and Moody's cut ratings on scores of classes of subprime bonds in response to unexpectedly high defaults on the underlying mortgages, giving investors a rude shock.[9]

In June 2007, losses from mortgage defaults engulfed two Bear Stearns subprime hedge funds, setting off a run by investors. Unable to satisfy the barrage of redemption requests, both hedge funds sank in July, to the market's consternation. Bear Stearns fired its co-president, Warren Spector, and replaced him with Alan Schwartz. Although few appreciated it at the time, the hedge funds' troubles were a premonition that Bear Stearns was headed for disaster.

The Bush administration and the Federal Reserve were not perturbed. By most appearances, the rest of the economy looked stable during the first half of 2007. The nation's gross domestic product was growing at a 2.25 percent annual clip, the stock market was booming, and unemployment was holding steady at 4.5 percent.[10] The Federal Reserve's main concern was the possibility of a resurgence in inflation, not a recession.

Indeed, Fed chairman Ben Bernanke felt bullish enough to opine on June 5: "The troubles in the subprime sector seem unlikely to seriously spill over to the broader economy or the financial sector."[11] Treasury secretary Henry Paulson echoed Bernanke's sentiment, saying that "the housing market is at or near the bottom" and that the problems in the housing market were "largely contained."[12] Taking heart, the stock market surged, with the Dow Jones Industrial Average surpassing 14,000 for the first time on July 19.

## FAMOUS LAST WORDS

Within weeks, events proved Bernanke wrong. The beginning of the end came during the summer of 2007, when the foundation of the private-label mortgage-backed securities market collapsed. On July 10, Moody's and Standard & Poor's announced they were slashing ratings or considering downgrades on 1,043 tranches of subprime mortgage-backed securities and CDOs. The implications went far beyond the affected bonds, throwing the entire rating methodology of the two giant rating agencies into doubt.[13]

The rating agency downgrades drove up the number of subprime bonds "for sale" and drove down their prices. The increase in bonds for sale was, in part, because investors lost confidence in the subprime bonds, and also because the law required banks, insurance companies, and pension funds to sell any bond holdings downgraded below investment grade. Bond purchasers disappeared overnight because they had no easy way to evaluate the creditworthiness of private-label RMBS and CDOs. By August 2007, the private-label market had dried up. Figure 4.2 illustrates the decline in agency (Fannie Mae, Freddie Mac, and other government-related) securitizations and nonagency (private label) securitizations. As liquidity evaporated, financing dis-

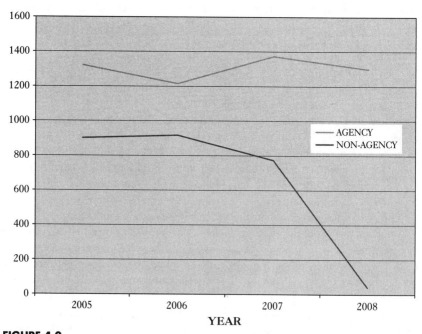

**FIGURE 4.2.**
Total volume of U.S. agency and nonagency securitizations, in billions of dollars: 2005–2008. *Source*: Securities Industry and Financial Markets Association.

appeared not only for subprime mortgages, but also for jumbo mortgages, Alt-A mortgages, commercial mortgages, credit cards, and auto loans.

More mortgage lenders toppled once the private-label securitization spigot closed for good. Lehman Brothers shuttered its subprime lender, BNC Mortgage, and First Magnus, another subprime lender, filed for bankruptcy.[14] The liquidity crunch even jeopardized Countrywide Financial Corporation, the nation's leading mortgage lender. In early August, Countrywide warned investors that "market demand" for its mortgage-backed securities "was negatively affected by investor concern about credit quality" and that "the impact on the Company is unknown." With 75 percent of its short-term funding sources no longer "reliable," Countrywide announced plans to fund more loans using deposits from Countrywide Bank and to hold loans in portfolio. Later that month, Bank of America threw Countrywide a lifeline, agreeing to buy $2 billion in Countrywide stock.

Investors became increasingly skittish, and not just about investments linked to subprime mortgages. Anxiety mounted when on July 31, a third Bear Stearns hedge fund with no major subprime ties announced it was halting redemptions to stop a run.[15] Michael Metz, the chief investment strategist at Oppenheimer & Company, explained: "We really don't know who's caught with the garbage in their portfolios."[16] In a flight to safety, investors yanked their uninsured funds out of financial institutions and invested them in Treasury bonds.

## PROBLEMS AT AIG

Meanwhile, the sprawling global insurance company American International Group (AIG) was reeling from problem swaps sold by its subsidiary AIG Financial Products. Financial Products had sold massive quantities of credit default swaps on the safest tranches of subprime mortgage CDOs through 2005. Even though the firm had exited the market early, it was still liable on almost a half trillion dollars in older swap deals.[17]

Financial Products was in trouble on many fronts. First, the company's risk models grossly miscalculated the possibility that the CDOs would default. Expecting only a 0.15 percent risk of loss, Tom Savage, the president of Financial Products, told the *Washington Post* that AIG had believed that its "risk was so remote that the fees were almost free money."[18] This view pervaded the company. The firm's chief operating officer, Joseph Cassano, had reported that "It is hard for us, without being flippant, to even see a scenario within any realm of reason that would see us losing one dollar in any of these transactions."[19] These beliefs had given AIG the confidence to tie up its investments in highly illiquid assets that were tough to sell when the company had to raise cash collateral for the swaps.

AIG had gravely underestimated two other risks. One was market risk, which was the risk that AIG's swaps might drop in value, forcing AIG to take major write-downs and losses to capital. The second risk was that AIG's counterparties would demand additional collateral from AIG to back its guarantees. When AIG had initially sold its swaps, the firm had a AAA credit rating, which enabled it to sell CDS with no reserves or collateral so long as AIG retained its stellar rating and the value of the bonds that it insured did not decline. AIG was convinced that there would be no substantial collateral calls.[20] Even after the two Bear Stearns hedge funds blew up in the summer of 2007, Cassano remained bullish about AIG's ability to withstand collateral calls. He estimated its collateral call exposure on June 30 at only $847 million, just a drop in the bucket compared to AIG's total swap exposure. In August, one of Cassano's colleagues emailed him a *Wall Street Journal* story questioning AIG's assessment of the risks it was insuring. Cassano's response reportedly was, "Hopefully people just ignore it. It is not a real story."[21]

Cassano's words failed to soothe AIG's counterparties, especially Goldman Sachs. By September 2007, Goldman and other counterparties were pressing AIG for billions of dollars in added collateral. AIG had "significant" differences with its counterparties about the value of its CDS and the collateral AIG needed to post.

Company executives, including Cassano, scrambled in September 2007 to develop a new valuation model—the "Binomial Expansion Technique," or BET model—to reflect the deterioration in the credit markets and assuage counterparties. In the end, the BET model, like AIG's other models, was based more on mark-to-myth than mark-to-market. In November 2007, AIG issued a quarterly report saying that the value of AIG Financial Product's credit default swaps had dropped at least half a billion dollars. In a shocking admission, AIG said that it had no idea what its swaps were really worth, because of disruptions in the securitization market and recent ratings downgrades.

Things came to a head in an investor conference call on December 5, 2007, when Cassano admitted that any attempt to assign a dollar value to AIG's CDS portfolio was "not grounded in reality." He had "no idea" if AIG's CDS would rise or fall in value. In addition, he allowed that capital adequacy had not been his priority at AIG Financial Products, saying: "It's clearly on my list of things to work through." At that point, AIG Financial Products only had about $2.1 billion in capital, and most of that was not high quality. In the December 5 conference call, AIG higher-ups also admitted underpricing some of AIG's swaps. According to Cassano, AIG had faced pricing pressure "because there are other folks that are desperate to do business." AIG executive Andrew Forster added: "We may have…compromised our pricing objectives to win a transaction."[22]

AIG further conceded fatal flaws with the models it had used to estimate possible default rates on the CDOs it insured. AIG's models had been developed by a quant named Dr. Gary Gorton, back then a finance professor at the Wharton School. Under questioning during the conference call, Gorton admitted that his model had not taken into account the fact that underwriting standards in home mortgage loans had deteriorated or that there had been a "huge run up in home prices." Cassano added: "We also realized the model was incapable of dealing with [the] fundamental shift" in the mortgage market, including "teasers and all these option ARMs." Three months later, Cassano retired from AIG.

**THE VIRUS SPREADS**

Meanwhile, redemption requests were surging at European investment funds. In early August 2007, the biggest public bank in France, BNP Paribas, temporarily halted redemptions in three subprime funds because it could not value their holdings. At the same time, concerns about bank runs were roiling the market for interbank loans (where banks lend money to one another). In anticipation of the worst, banks sought to boost their reserves by stepping up their borrowing from other banks. As the demand for interbank credit spiked, so did the federal funds rate and LIBOR (the key interbank interest rate), jacking up the cost of interbank loans. The Federal Reserve and the European Central Bank were forced to flood the banking system with funds in early August to bring those rates back down.

The subprime virus was in full swing and soon it spread to SIVs—the bank-created entities that borrowed short-term funds using mortgage-related securities as collateral. The market in asset-backed commercial paper had grown to $1.2 trillion by 2007 and made up over half of the commercial paper issued in the United States.[23] Once the price of subprime bonds plunged, the asset-backed commercial paper market choked. In August 2007, BNP Paribas announced that it could not even value asset-backed commercial paper. More alarm bells went off after Countrywide failed in an attempt to sell its commercial paper, forcing the bank to turn to forty banks for an $11.5 billion loan to shore up its cash. Meanwhile, money market funds and other lenders that had bought commercial paper to juice their returns wanted out. SIVs were in a jam. For their business model to work, they had to constantly roll over their short-term commercial paper, but no one wanted to buy it. As a result, they were unable to pay back their loans on time. When lenders did not get paid as expected, the market descended into further panic. By late August, the fabled chief investment officer at PIMCO, Bill Gross, pronounced the asset-backed commercial paper market "history."[24]

It wasn't just SIVs that had problems with their collateral. Large institutions, including hedge funds, state and local governments, insurance companies, pension funds, and major corporations, owned subprime bonds that they had pledged as security for loans. When the value of their subprime collateral dropped through the floor, lenders hit the borrowers with margin calls and demanded that they post additional security. In the ensuing scramble to raise cash, institutional borrowers flooded the market with "for sale" subprime bonds. The prices for subprime bonds fell further, and buyers became so scarce that institutional borrowers started selling off their corporate bonds and stocks to raise cash for collateral calls. In the words of onetime fund manager Richard Bookstaber, "If you can't sell what you want to sell, you sell what you can sell."[25] Fleeing to safety, investors continued to cash out their stocks and bonds and invest in Treasury bonds and gold. As the selling pressure mounted, the price of corporate bonds and stocks dropped en masse, exacerbating the difficulties institutions were having raising cash and meeting redemptions and margin calls.

Even in transactions involving no subprime collateral, concerns about the subprime crisis had a ripple effect, making it hard for companies and government entities across the board to secure financing. Banks did not want to lend to other banks for fear that undisclosed subprime losses were lurking on their sister banks' books. Investors did not want to buy bonds backed by student loans, car loans, or leveraged syndicated loans financing takeovers, because they had lost faith in credit ratings and could not assess the quality of the underlying collateral. Hedge funds lost the confidence of investors, who could not peer into the makeup of their portfolios. Stocks in commercial banks, insurance companies, and Wall Street firms took a beating because investors feared subprime write-downs. Junk bond issuances dropped and spreads on junk bonds widened. Cities had trouble floating municipal bond offerings because the credit ratings of municipal bond insurers slipped as their subprime liabilities mounted. Investor panic crippled the market for auction-rate securities, and initial public offerings dried up. Because they did not know exactly who was tainted by subprime, investors stopped trusting anyone except Uncle Sam.

"I THOUGHT WE WERE JUST BUYING A HOUSE!"

**FIGURE 4.3.**

### DITHERING BY THE FEDERAL RESERVE

Throughout August 2007, the stock market experienced wild price swings almost every day. Despite the growing turmoil, the Federal Reserve was slow to react. On August 7, the Federal Open Market Committee issued a press release declining to cut the target federal funds rate, saying that fears about inflation outweighed the risk of a contraction in the economy. The markets reacted negatively to the Fed's indecision. Fed minutes show that after the August 7 meeting, the interbank loan market showed immediate "signs of stress," and the availability of interbank loans became "significantly impaired." Conditions became so precarious that just three days later, on August 10, the Federal Open Market Committee convened an emergency teleconference call. According to the minutes, this was the first time the committee came to grips with the worsening strains in the credit markets. Immediately afterward, the Fed issued a short press release attempting to offer reassurance. In it, the Fed stated that it was "providing liquidity to facilitate the orderly functioning of financial markets" and emphasized that the discount window was always available for backup liquidity needs.

The Fed's efforts to calm the markets had no effect. Credit market conditions continued to unravel, prompting the committee to convene another emergency teleconference call on August 16. On August 17, the Federal Reserve finally issued a statement acknowledging that "disruptions in financial markets" were having "adverse effects on the economy" and stating that it was prepared to "mitigate" those effects.

As an initial step, the Fed liberalized its discount window loans to banks in four ways. First, the central bank cut the interest rate on discount window loans—known as the discount rate—by half a percent. Next, it announced that banks could roll over their discount window loans every thirty days, instead of having to repay them overnight. In addition, the Fed said it was willing to accept home mortgages as pledges for discount window loans, sending a signal that the Fed was prepared to finance the home mortgage market if Wall Street was not. Finally, the Fed actively urged banks to borrow from the discount window in order to tamp down concerns about stigma. (Banks normally regard discount window loans as a sign that the borrowing bank is in financial trouble.) To further remove the whiff of stigma, the Fed orchestrated discount window loans of $500 million each to the nation's four biggest banks. The Fed's eagerness to tout discount window lending—and to allow banks to roll over their loans every thirty days instead of overnight—betrayed the governors' worry about the liquidity of banks, the health of the interbank loan market, and the reluctance of banks to make ordinary loans. Some wondered if a big bank had a problem.[26]

## A DECEPTIVE CALM

In September 2007, private-label mortgage-backed securitization was in shambles, other securitization markets were on the ropes, and mortgage defaults were climbing with no end in sight. Lenders had tightened underwriting standards and consumers were finding it hard to get loans. Nevertheless, spurred by a Federal Reserve half a percent reduction in the target federal funds rate in September, credit markets displayed some modest improvement, although generally with higher spreads. The commercial paper market started to breathe again and so did the market for interbank loans. Activity picked up in leveraged buyouts, junk bond issuances, and offerings of investment-grade corporate bonds. The stock market recovered and barreled on, with the Dow Jones Industrial Average hitting a high of 14,164.53 on October 9.

Federal officials continued to insist that banks and the larger economy had escaped the subprime fallout. In speeches throughout the fall, federal banking regulators took pains to assure the public that subprime problems had not infected the larger economy. On October 15, for example, Chairman Bernanke said that "direct evidence of" housing "spillovers onto the broader economy has been limited."[27] Bernanke reiterated that view on November 8, when he told Congress that there was "scant evidence of spillovers from housing to other components of final demand."[28]

Bernanke and other federal banking regulators also had reassuring words about the banking system's ability to weather the storm. On September 5, the comptroller of the currency, John Dugan, advised the House Financial Services Committee that national banks had "strong levels of capital" and that the nation's banking system was "safe and sound."[29] Bernanke echoed that sentiment on October 15, observing that the financial system entered the crisis "with strong capital positions" and the "banking system [was] healthy."[30] On October 24, John Walsh, the OCC's chief of staff, claimed that while the largest U.S. banks "were engaged in sophisticated lending and market operations, they managed their exposures to these risks effectively." He smugly compared the United States to Britain, saying that unlike Northern Rock—a British bank that needed a government infusion in September 2007—"there was never a liquidity problem at any of our banks."[31]

The calm had a short life and the Fed was worried. On December 11, the Federal Reserve again cut the discount rate by another quarter percent. According to the minutes of that meeting, those present "agreed that the housing correction was likely to be both deeper and more prolonged than the Board had anticipated in October." The next day, the Fed took action of a more momentous nature, unveiling the first of a set of extraordinary steps to address the liquidity problems facing banks. In conjunction with the central banks of Canada, England, Europe, and Switzerland, the Fed announced it was creating a "Term Auction Facility" (TAF) to alleviate the pressure in the interbank market.[32] Under TAF, the Fed started holding biweekly auctions to allow banks to bid for loans of twenty-eight or thirty-five days and post a wide assortment of collateral. The collateral provision was key because it allowed banks to post as security troubled mortgage-backed securities and other assets that private market participants considered taboo.

The Fed created TAF in part because ordinary discount window lending remained low, likely because of the associated stigma. The hope was that TAF would inject liquidity into the banking system without raising reputational concerns for banks. The creation of TAF seemed to initially help the troubled credit markets; immediately afterward, the LIBOR spread dropped to its previous level.[33]

Still, the U.S. banking system was showing serious cracks. The year 2007 witnessed the failure of three small banks, the first since 2004. Of greater concern, though, was the fact that large commercial banks were reeling from multiple problems. Some major banks had originated large quantities of subprime and Alt-A mortgages with the intent of securitizing those loans. When the securitization market shut down, the banks were left holding the bag, with billions of dollars in questionable mortgages stuck in the securitization pipeline and portfolios full of subprime bonds that were shrinking in value. Banks had few options. They could sell the assets at a loss, with a corresponding hit to earnings, or retain the assets on their books, with exposure to possible future losses, higher capital charges, and potentially deep write-downs.[34]

Big banks had another problem: the SIVs. As we discussed in the previous chapter, banks had informally promised the buyers of their SIVs' commercial paper that if the SIVs' assets failed to perform, the banks would make good on the SIVs' obligations. When it became impossible for the SIVs to roll over their commercial paper, the banks were faced with the unpalatable choice of lending money to the SIVs, taking the SIVs' assets and debts onto their balance sheets, or trying to sell the securities the SIVs owned in an already depressed market. The choice was made for the banks on December 3, when Moody's revealed that it planned to make downgrades on SIV obligations of as much as $116 billion.[35] Moody's actions cut off other options, and the banks, determined to honor their promises, took the SIVs' assets back on their books. Citigroup alone took back $49 billion in assets from failed SIVs.[36] Big banks' balance sheets, which were already swollen with toxic assets, groaned under the strain of even more noxious bonds and loans.

All of these problems took a toll on the capital cushions and reserves of banks. Institutions now stuck with risky mortgages, subprime bonds, and assets of SIVs had to hold more capital against those assets. Bank reserves had hit a low in 2006 and by 2007 were badly depleted. Meanwhile, losses were eating through capital like acid. Large customers were drawing down their lines of credit just when banks needed to replenish their capital.

Federal regulation subjects banks to minimum capital rules. When banks can't raise needed capital, they can't extend more loans. Fearful of runs and desperate to conserve funds, banks started hoarding cash and became wary of new credit extensions. Businesses that needed credit to expand or simply to meet fluctuating needs for cash had difficulty getting loans. The result was an economic chokehold.[37]

The big banks stumbled through the fourth quarter. Bank of America and Wachovia Bank ended 2007 in positive territory, but net incomes for both had slid over 70 percent in the prior six months. Wells Fargo Bank saw a 26 percent drop in net income in the last half of 2007. Citibank was in even worse shape. On November 5, Citigroup forced out Chuck Prince as CEO after announcing $11 billion in unexpected write-downs due to subprime losses.[38] Citibank closed out 2007 with a fourth quarter loss of $4.5 billion. Only JPMorgan Chase ended the year on a bright note, with higher quarterly earnings. Otherwise, the overall earnings reports were so bad that the interbank markets froze again, pushing the LIBOR spread to a new high of 108 basis points on December 6.[39]

FDIC chairman Sheila Bair foresaw more problems on the horizon. She warned that small banks were starting to feel the pinch as borrowers began defaulting on construction and development loans, mainstays of small, regional banks.[40] For the banking industry as a whole, net income plummeted 98 percent in the last half of 2007 and almost hit zero by year end.

The Big Five investment banks had their own woes and almost all of them were hemorrhaging red ink. At Bear Stearns, the summer's hedge fund fiasco was just an inkling of things to come. For the fourth quarter of 2007, Bear reported an $854 million loss due to write-downs on bad subprime investments. It was the first loss in Bear's eighty-four-year history. The same quarter, Morgan Stanley reported a $3.5 billion loss, also due to mortgage-related write-downs. Lehman Brothers' earnings were dropping steadily, but remained positive. Merrill Lynch's financial woes, meanwhile, became the stuff of public spectacle. On October 25, the company announced a third-quarter loss of $2.2 billion, mostly from subprime mortgages and CDOs. On Halloween, just six days later, Merrill Lynch spooked Wall Street with the news that it was taking another $3.4 billion in subprime write-downs. Upon the announcement, Stan O'Neal immediately resigned as Merrill's CEO. In the last quarter of 2007, Merrill reported red ink of $9.8 billion, dwarfing its $2.2 billion loss from the previous quarter.

Sovereign wealth funds from abroad, betting that U.S. bank securities were undervalued, sent their dollars across the ocean. In late November, the Abu Dhabi government

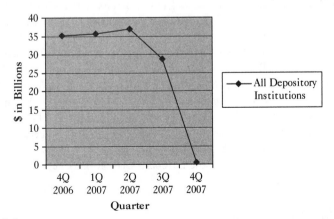

**FIGURE 4.4.**
Net income of U.S. depository institutions, 4th quarter 2006–4th quarter 2007.
*Source*: FDIC.

bought a $7.5 billion stake in Citigroup, followed by a $6.88 billion infusion by Singapore and a $3 billion investment by Kuwait in January 2008. In December, China's state-run investment fund came to Morgan Stanley's rescue with a $5 billion capital infusion. The same month, UBS sold a stake of more than 10 percent to a sovereign wealth fund in Singapore and an unnamed Middle Eastern investor. The new year brought another Kuwaiti investment, this time for $2 billion in Merrill Lynch.[41]

## GLOBAL CONTAGION

Some of the earliest banks to fail from subprime losses were located overseas. In fact, the swift emergence of subprime contagion abroad was one of the shocking things about the early stage of the subprime crisis. In addition to the three BNP Paribas hedge funds that suffered runs in August 2007, losses on subprime investments a month earlier had pushed a regional German bank, IKB Deutsche Industriebank, into insolvency. Subprime woes sank another German bank, Sachsen Landesbank, that August. In short order, Australian banks and hedge funds announced subprime losses, as did the Dutch lender NIBC Holding. In August, the public learned that the Bank of China held over $9 billion in dubious subprime mortgage-backed securities and CDOs. On August 9, the European Central Bank flooded the Eurozone banking system with over $130 billion to ease the nervous interbank market. It injected another $200 billion-plus on August 10.[42]

In September 2007, write-downs on U.S. subprime bonds triggered a severe bank run at Britain's fifth largest mortgage lender, Northern Rock. The run unhinged British depositors to such a degree that the Bank of England felt compelled to issue an unprecedented blanket guarantee for all deposits at British banks. Northern Rock was too ill to be saved, and ultimately the Bank of England was forced to nationalize the bank. Meanwhile, the U.K. housing market was starting to cool off and prices dropped sharply in November. In early December, the British banking regulator, the Financial Services Authority (FSA), warned that mortgage defaults were rising and that lenders should plan for the "worst."[43]

Northern Rock, Sachsen Landesbank, and IKB Industriebank were not the only overseas victims of the subprime fallout. The Swiss bank UBS, which had aspired in 2006 and 2007 to dominate subprime securitization, wrote down $3.7 billion in U.S. subprime assets on October 1 and another $10 billion in December. Across the English Channel, Barclays announced $1.6 billion in subprime write-downs on November 15. The Royal Bank of Scotland followed suit, disclosing over $2.5 billion in subprime write-downs of its own on December 6. On December 10, the French bank Société Générale bailed out a sinking investment fund for $4.3 billion. Even the little Arctic town of Narvik, Norway (pop. 18,000) succumbed and became insolvent in December 2007 because of bad bets on subprime bonds.[44] Desperate to stem the crisis in Europe, on December 18, the European Central Bank poured another $500 billion into the market.

## SUBPRIME SPILLOVER

As the financial sector experienced serial convulsions, the subprime virus extended its reach. Wall Street firms, struggling to gain control of their balance sheets, began massive layoffs. Lehman Brothers dismissed 2,450 workers in 2007 and another 1,300 at the start of 2008. Bank of America announced the elimination of 3,000 jobs in the fall of 2007. By early 2008, Citigroup had let 75,000 of its 375,000 employees go. Moody's cut its workforce by 7 percent. Wall Street bosses were predicting that 20 percent of the workers on "the Street" would be laid off in 2008. By far the biggest losses were at subprime lenders themselves. In California alone, 12,000 people who worked for subprime lenders had lost their jobs by year's end.[45]

All the market turmoil was bad for consumers too. Banks suddenly needed to increase their capital and reduce losses. In what seemed like a flash, the flow of easy credit stopped and tough new underwriting standards took its place. Option ARMs disappeared altogether and low-doc and no-doc loans became rarities. The same was true for 100 percent loan-to-value and piggyback loans. The evaporation of liquidity crippled financing not only for subprime mortgages, but also for prime jumbo mortgages and Alt-A mortgages.

Ever more cautious banks required creditworthy prime borrowers to make larger down payments, have higher credit scores, and pass tougher underwriting standards. To get the best rates, some lenders required borrowers to prove that they had savings worth three years of mortgage payments. Lenders routinely closed the door to self-employed borrowers and those with irregular earnings. No longer did lenders calculate the affordability of loans based on the initial rates; instead, they used the highest interest rates borrowers could possibly have to pay. Eventually, the drought of mortgage credit became so severe that any mortgage not backed by Fannie Mae, Freddie Mac, or the federal government became extremely expensive or just plain unavailable.[46]

Even Fannie Mae and Freddie Mac were running scared. They imposed new charges on loans they purchased and guaranteed. All borrowers had to pay a surcharge of 0.25 percent of their loan amount. Those with credit scores below 680 and loans with loan-to-value ratios more than 70 percent paid an additional surcharge based on their credit score. In a further effort to reduce its risk, Fannie Mae imposed larger down-payment requirements in areas that were experiencing the most dramatic falloffs in home values. This last requirement was rescinded six months later in response to intense political pressure.[47]

The housing market became ever thinner as fewer borrowers could qualify for loans. Between 2006 and 2007, the number of sales of new homes dropped over 25 percent. Sales of existing homes dropped 13 percent. Qualified borrowers who wanted to take advantage of declining home prices and upgrade to nicer homes were stuck with homes they couldn't sell.[48]

Other forms of consumer credit became scarce. Almost all credit is securitized, which means any crimp in the securitization markets trickles down to restrict credit to consumers. Credit card companies began canceling credit cards, cutting credit lines, and raising minimum payments and interest rates, often without explanation, even if customers had had no change in their credit scores. Borrowers who in the past had tapped home equity lines to pay credit card and auto loans had their lines reduced. Auto finance companies and student loan programs stiffened their underwriting standards. Small businesses were also in a bind. In October 2007, 85 percent of banks reported that they had tightened the requirements for business loans.[49]

## Movement to Loan Modifications

The more serious problem involved borrowers who did not have the money to pay their debts, especially their mortgages. Defaults and foreclosures were escalating across the country. Serious delinquencies for subprime ARMs were almost 16 percent in August 2007. To analysts' consternation, even prime mortgages—long deemed a bastion of safety—were experiencing higher defaults.[50]

Banks and consumer groups urged policymakers to develop government programs to refinance borrowers out of unaffordable loans and buy troubled loans to help unclog the credit markets. Bank of America proposed that the government buy loans at a discount, forgive the difference between the original loan amounts and the market value of the homes, and then refinance the loans through the FHA. Other proposals called for lenders to write down the loan principal to the market value of the property. The difference between the market value and the indebtedness would turn into a second lien on the property that borrowers would pay off if they sold the property for a price above the new mortgage amount. For a time, there was even some momentum behind a proposal to temporarily freeze the interest rate on ARMs.[51]

Many of these proposals met with resistance, in large part because they were seen as subsidies to greedy borrowers and the financial institutions that brought down the economy. There was also concern that any program that benefited delinquent borrowers would encourage other borrowers to default so they could qualify for the program. (Of course, this kind of ruthless default would be costly to borrowers because it could hurt their credit scores and hinder their ability to obtain credit in the future.)[52]

Some political leaders did try to address loan defaults. Senator Chris Dodd of Connecticut was one of the first on the scene. Lacking sufficient support to get legislation passed to force loan modifications, in 2007 he summoned banks to a Homeownership Preservation Summit where he pushed lenders to modify loans with high reset rates. The banks were unmoved.[53] For its part, the Bush administration was resistant to foreclosure prevention relief or anything else that smacked of a bailout of homeowners. It rejected proposals for mandatory foreclosure mitigation and higher conforming loan limits for Fannie and Freddie designed to allow more homeowners to refinance their loans into fixed-rate loans. The White House also fought changing the bankruptcy laws to allow judges to reduce the amount distressed borrowers owed on their homes, known as principal cram-downs, and refused to consider appropriations for homeowner counseling.[54]

The only government program that Bush put forward was FHA Secure, which enabled borrowers to refinance into FHA-insured mortgages. In announcing the program, Bush said, "It's not the government's job to bail out speculators or those who made the decision to buy a home they knew they could never afford."[55] As a result, the government only made the program available to borrowers with good credit histories.[56] FHA Secure was intended to help 80,000 borrowers, but over the course of more than a year, only 4,100 borrowers qualified and HUD eventually shut down the program.[57]

Over time, the idea that gained the most traction was loan modifications, which typically involve changes to the interest rate, principal, or repayment period of loans. The goal of modifications is to restructure loans to bring them current, that is, no longer in default. Examples of modifications include:

- Tacking overdue payments onto the end of the loan term and extending the repayment period
- Wrapping overdue payments into the principal amount owed, increasing borrowers' monthly payments
- Extending the loan term, for example, from thirty to forty years
- Suspending payments for several months (forbearance)
- Extending the period in which the initial interest rate is fixed, thus postponing payment shock when an ARM resets
- Forgiving overdue loan payments
- Lowering the interest rate
- Reducing the principal

Consumer advocates supported loan modifications on grounds that most consumers were duped into high-cost loans and deserved better loan terms. Plus, if government funds were being used to bail out financial institutions, why shouldn't the government bail out borrowers, too? Pragmatists argued that the social costs of foreclosures far outweighed any arguments against modifications. On the other side of the debate were those who wanted the government to stay out of the fray and let the housing market sort itself out.

In the end, and after a lot of public pressure, Treasury secretary Paulson announced the creation of a government loan modification program, the Hope Now Alliance, in October 2007. Hope Now was a voluntary program that included Fannie Mae and Freddie Mac, credit counselors, eleven servicers who serviced about 80 percent of subprime loans, and other entities involved in the mortgage market. Hope Now created a hotline that was designed to match borrowers with counselors who would work with servicers to modify borrowers' loans. Eligibility was limited to people who took out loans between January 2005 and July 2006 and who had a record of timely mortgage payments. They also had to be facing rate resets that increased their monthly payments by at least 10 percent and have loans with loan-to-value ratios of over 97 percent. Eligible borrowers would have their principal reduced to 90 percent of the market value of their homes and would be refinanced into fixed-rate FHA loans.[58]

Hope Now did not stand the test of time. Six months after its inception, the program claimed to have prevented 1,035,000 foreclosures. No one ever took those figures seriously, especially after an OCC study reported a modification rate under the program that was one-sixth what Hope Now had reported.[59] To the extent Hope Now did aid homeowners, it was just window dressing that did not slow the tide of foreclosures. Studies found that 63 percent of the Hope Now modifications simply tacked overdue payments on to borrowers' loans, and less than 20 percent of borrowers had their monthly payments reduced.[60]

Although the Bush administration wasn't willing to take meaningful steps to help homeowners, Sheila Bair, the chairman of the FDIC, took a proactive stance, arguing that adjustable rate mortgages should be frozen at their initial rates to avoid widespread foreclosures. In her view, servicers did not have the staffing or the time to craft individualized loan modifications. Bair called on the financial industry to adopt her proposal and "show policy makers that the industry is . . . working to find a solution." She went on to say that if the industry did not adopt voluntary modification programs, Congress would "do it for them."[61]

### Servicing and Foreclosure Abuses

Servicers and lenders not only resisted meaningful loan modifications, they resorted to aggressive tactics to collect money and push homes into foreclosure before the market slid further. Reports streamed into courtrooms of servicers inflating the amounts borrowers owed, failing to post payments, losing borrowers' checks, and charging bogus fees. A fax might cost $50 and overnight delivery fees $137.[62] Distressed borrowers often did not have the resources or information to detect frivolous charges or errors in lenders' and servicers' accounting.

Servicers played hardball in loan modification negotiations, too. Stories surfaced of servicers who made borrowers waive their right to sue lenders as a condition of obtaining loan modifications. This meant that borrowers who had been defrauded by their lenders had to give up the right to sue the fraudsters before servicers would modify their loans.[63]

Some borrowers were savvy enough to take on lenders and servicers that had misstated their debt, including Michael Jones, who proved that Wells Fargo overcharged him $24,451. This amount included $6,742 that was erroneously reported as owed to the sheriff's office and the costs for sixteen property inspections over twenty-nine months.[64] Eventually, the Federal Trade Commission became involved in pursuing abusive servicers. In one of its most noteworthy cases, the FTC extracted $28 million from Bear Stearns and its servicing arm, EMC Mortgage, to settle claims that the companies had misrepresented borrowers' indebtedness, charged excessive and wrongful fees, and employed illegal debt-collection practices.[65]

The courts began catching on to another problem with foreclosures. When borrowers are served with foreclosure papers and know they have defaulted on their mortgages, they often don't appear in court. That can be because they have no defense to the creditors' claims, cannot afford a lawyer, or can't take the time off from work. Typically if a defendant (the borrower) does not appear, the court issues a default judgment, which is a ruling that the plaintiff (the lender or the trust) automatically wins because the defendant was a "no show."[66] In foreclosure actions, courts were entering default judgments without looking at the underlying documents to ensure that the lender had the lawful right to foreclose. The same was true in states that allowed foreclosure without any judicial review. Foreclosure papers passed through the system without anyone assessing whether the company seeking foreclosure was entitled to the borrower's property.

Each time a loan changes hands it must be endorsed, like a check. The only entity with the right to foreclose on a note is the one that holds the note, and the note must have the proper endorsements. It turns out that in the flurry of securitizing loans, obtaining endorsements fell to the wayside and notes were often misplaced. Trusts were going into court and securing orders to foreclose even though they had not proven that they had the right to foreclose.

A few diligent judges began noticing these types of irregularities in foreclosure complaints. In 2007, a Bush appointee to the federal district court in Cleveland, Christopher Boyko, on his own initiative, looked into the documents supporting a set of Deutsche Bank complaints to foreclosure. Judge Boyko discovered that the bank had not demonstrated that it owned the notes and, therefore, did not have the right to pursue the collection action. In legal parlance, this is called "lack of standing." Judge Boyko entered an order dismissing all the cases and in a colorful footnote addressed an assertion by Deutsche Bank's lawyer that the judge "just [didn't] understand how things work[ed]":

> There is no doubt every decision made by a financial institution in the foreclo-
> sure process is driven by money.... [U]nchallenged by underfinanced opponents,
> the institutions worry less about jurisdictional requirements and more about
> maximizing returns.... [T]he arguments made by the Counsel for the institu-
> tions...utterly fail to satisfy their standing and jurisdictional burdens. The insti-
> tutions seem to adopt the attitude that since they have been doing this for so
> long, unchallenged, this practice equates with legal compliance. Finally put to
> the test, their weak legal arguments compel the Court to stop them at the gate.
>
> The Court will illustrate in simple terms its decision: "Fluidity of the
> market"—"X" dollars, "contractual arrangements between institutions and
> counsel"—"X" dollars, "purchasing mortgages in bulk and securitizing"—"X"
> dollars, "rush to file, slow to record after judgment"—"X" dollars, "the jurisdic-
> tional integrity of United States District Court"—"Priceless."[67]

Judge Boyko was not alone. Many Ohio federal judges followed his lead and began scouring foreclosure complaints to determine whether the lenders had standing, dis-missing the cases of those that did not. In New York, Brooklyn judge Arthur Schack also began demanding proof of ownership in foreclosure actions and, by his own account, denied more complaints to foreclose than he granted.[68]

## Hopes for Good News Dashed

In December 2007, the United States officially entered a recession.[69] The next year opened with major political news and more cracks in the financial system. The head-lines were abuzz with Barack Obama's victory in the Iowa caucuses, giving his presi-dential bid new life.

Rumors also began to circulate that Countrywide was headed for bankruptcy. Gigantic losses from questionable mortgages, coupled with dwindling cash, had pushed Countrywide to the brink. Without the subprime securitization machine, Countrywide had limped through the end of 2007 with an uncertain patchwork of bank deposits, credit lines, discount window loans, and advances from the Federal Home Loan Bank system, plus the equity infusion from Bank of America. Its assets were a mess. Dicey subprime loans that had been slated for sale on the secondary mar-ket littered the firm's books. As of December 31, 2007, Countrywide's nonperforming loans had jumped 359 percent from 2006 levels, and almost one-third of the company's subprime loans were delinquent or in foreclosure. Its prime loans were experiencing unprecedented losses, too. To make matters worse, Countrywide was weighed down by two SIVs that it had subsidized and was finally forced to terminate in December 2007. After a $1.2 billion loss in the third quarter of 2007 and a $421 million fourth-quarter loss, Countrywide closed out the year with a net loss of $703 million.

On January 8, Countrywide's stock price took a 28 percent nosedive, to $5.47, off 89 percent from its high. Three days later, on January 11, Bank of America announced that it would buy Countrywide Financial for $4.1 billion, saving the company from looming failure. But Countrywide's stock price continued to fall and by the time the sale was consummated in July 2008, Bank of America only paid $2.5 billion for the once-proud lender.

Meanwhile, in a musty corner of the bond market, trouble was brewing for the bond insurance industry. In the old days, monoline bond insurers had mainly guaranteed boring municipal bonds. During the housing boom, however, they expanded into something much more glamorous--providing guarantees on subprime mortgage-backed securities and CDOs, as part of the credit enhancements on securitization deals. By 2008, with mortgage delinquencies triggering defaults on bonds, the insurers suddenly faced liabilities that could jeopardize their AAA ratings. This was no small matter. If the large bond insurers lost their sterling ratings, $2.4 trillion worth of municipal and structured bonds could be subject to ratings downgrades.[70] In addition, any loss of confidence in bond insurers' ability to make good on their promises could have systemic effects, according to an official at Fitch Ratings.[71] Most importantly, if bond insurers lost their AAA ratings, banks would face added pressure to take further write-downs on their subprime bond holdings.

The carnage among bond insurers began in earnest on January 18, when Fitch cut Ambac Financial Group's AAA rating. Moody's did the same to the Financial Guaranty Insurance Company on February 14. MBIA later lost its AAA rating in June 2008.

As each piece of bad news rolled in, the stock market took more hits. The Dow fell 1.9 percent on January 8. On January 17, Citigroup and Merrill Lynch dropped bombshells, announcing enormous write-downs totaling $18.1 billion and $14.1 billion respectively. The Dow plunged another 2.5 percent on the news. With that drop, the index was down 14 percent from its October 9, 2007, high. The following Monday, on January 21, stock markets in London and Europe plunged, suffering their single biggest daily loss since the terrorist attacks on September 11, 2001. Fear was in the air, with the *Wall Street Journal* describing global markets as "in free fall amid recession fears."[72]

The Federal Reserve responded to the downward spiral in the stock markets with a surprise rate cut, slashing the discount rate and the target federal funds rate by a whopping three-quarters of 1 percent. It was the Fed's biggest rate cut in twenty-five years. The Federal Open Market Committee had its regularly scheduled meetings on January 29 and 30. By then, the Federal Reserve governors were seriously concerned that the widening economic fallout would affect households' buying power. According to the committee's minutes, many of the participants feared that shrinking stock portfolios, along with falling home prices, "would likely damp consumer spending." Adding to that concern, the unemployment rate had edged up from 4.4 percent to 4.9 percent between March and December. To further stimulate the economy, the Federal Reserve ordered another half a percent rate cut on January 30. In five short months, the Fed had cut interest rates by 2.25 percent.

## FISCAL STIMULUS

Up to this point, the federal government had mostly addressed the crisis through monetary policy and exhortations. But in January 2008, pressure grew on the Bush administration to take bolder action as the presidential primaries heated up and economic conditions unraveled. Within weeks, the federal government approved its first fiscal stimulus of the crisis.

On January 24, during the fallout from the stock market panic, the Bush administration and Congress hammered out an agreement for a $168 billion economic stimu-
lus plan that President Bush signed into law on February 13. The centerpiece of the
stimulus plan, known as the Economic Stimulus Act of 2008,[73] was tax rebate checks
to households, ranging from $300 to $1,200, and bonus depreciation allowances to
spur capital investment by businesses. The law also raised the conforming loan limits
for Fannie Mae and Freddie Mac loans as high as $730,000; this allowed the GSEs
to buy larger loans. By leaning on Fannie and Freddie to revive the faltering home
mortgage market, Congress encouraged the two GSEs to take on additional risk when
they were least equipped to absorb it.

Neither the Fed's late January rate cut nor the fiscal stimulus plan was enough to
calm the shell-shocked markets. On January 30, Standard & Poor's came out with
more bad news, saying that it had downgraded or threatened to downgrade 8,342
classes of subprime mortgage-backed securities and CDOs. With this announcement, S&P cast doubt on almost half of the U.S. subprime MBS rated in the eighteen
months beginning on January 1, 2006, plus 35 percent of CDOs sold during that
period.[74] On February 1, President Bush described the country's economic situation
as "a rough patch."[75]

By February 2008, there were unmistakable signs that the credit meltdown had
spread to the economy as a whole. At its meetings that month, the Group of Seven
finance ministers projected that worldwide write-offs on U.S. subprime mortgages
could reach $400 billion. Mario Draghi of the Bank of Italy, the chairman of the
Financial Stability Forum, called the next ten days to two weeks "crucial" as companies
issued their annual reports.[76]

As Draghi intimated, more bad news surfaced. Within a month, AIG announced a
$5.2 billion, fourth-quarter loss. Credit Agricole in France lost $1.3 billion that quarter, UBS in Switzerland lost $4 billion for all of 2007, and HSBC, Britain's biggest
bank, reported a loss of $17.2 billion in 2007, all due to write-downs on subprime and
Alt-A assets and credit default swaps.

By late February, companies were rushing to dump even more assets to raise cash,
causing asset prices to slide further. By the week of March 3, Thornburg Mortgage
plus hedge funds run by Carlyle Capital Corporation and Peloton Partners had run
out of cash after trying (unsuccessfully) to meet their margin calls. Bear Stearns and
Lehman Brothers, sitting on $6 billion and $15 billion of Alt-A mortgages respectively, were in danger of a similar fate.[77]

## THE FED AS MATCHMAKER

March opened with the short-term credit markets again approaching collapse. On
March 3, the Bank for International Settlements reported that "Parts of the credit market remained largely dysfunctional," with widening loan spreads, "adding to perceptions
of systemic risk."[78] In order to stockpile cash, banks and other lenders were cutting their
credit lines or canceling them outright. Overnight loans became costly or scarce at any
price, threatening big investment banks that relied on overnight loans for their survival.

On March 11, the Federal Reserve attempted to shore up Wall Street firms with
a new, $200 billion rescue program called the Term Securities Lending Facility, or

TSLF. For the first time since the Great Depression, the Fed expanded the New York Fed's long-standing program in which it lent Treasury bonds overnight to "primary dealers." Primary dealers consisted of twenty-odd investment banks and other firms that traded with the Fed. With the TSLF, the Fed liberalized its securities lending program in two ways. First, the New York Fed agreed to make loans for up to twenty-eight days, instead of overnight. Second, it agreed to take risky, top-rated subprime mortgage-backed securities as collateral. This allowed investment banks to swap their untouchable subprime bonds for highly liquid Treasury securities, which they could then post as collateral for short-term, private loans. The first TSLF auction was scheduled for March 27.[79]

That was too late to save Bear Stearns, which was hurtling toward insolvency.[80] Bear was up to its ears in debt, depending on short-term—often overnight—loans for over 96 percent of its working capital. Of the Big Five investment banks, Bear Stearns was the most exposed to subprime bonds and loans. After the big subprime write-downs by major banks in February 2008, the cost of credit default swap protection on Bear's obligations had skyrocketed. On Monday, March 10, Moody's downgraded fifteen Bear Stearns mortgage issues, and confidence in Bear took a nosedive. Investors placed bets that Bear would fail, and some lenders canceled the firm's credit lines. Other lenders, increasingly gun-shy of Bear's subprime collateral, demanded more collateral and higher rates for Bear's overnight loans. On Tuesday, March 11, Securities and Exchange Commission (SEC) chairman Christopher Cox told the press that he had "a great deal of comfort" in Bear's capital cushion.[81] But behind the scenes that day, Bear protested some collateral valuations and missed a number of margin calls. Nevertheless, during a CNBC interview that Tuesday, Bear's chief financial officer said, "There is no liquidity crisis. No margin calls."[82]

Meanwhile, Bear was suffering the twenty-first-century equivalent of a bank run, only the run was on free-cash accounts, not on bank deposits. As rumors circulated that Bear was running out of cash, traders yanked their business from the firm. Hedge funds and mutual funds withdrew their prime brokerage accounts and moved their funds elsewhere. Redemption requests quickly drained Bear's liquid assets, which dropped from $18.1 billion on March 10 to only $2 billion on March 13. By Friday morning, March 14, Bear could not repay its overnight loans.[83]

At the New York Fed, President Timothy Geithner agonized that if Bear Stearns defaulted on its overnight obligations, its creditors would instantly seize and liquidate their collateral. The resulting sell-off would further depress asset prices, which could jeopardize the solvency of a string of other financial firms. After marathon meetings and phone calls throughout Thursday night, the Federal Reserve agreed at dawn on Friday, March 14, to funnel a discount window loan to Bear through JPMorgan Chase for as long as four weeks. The Fed issued a cryptic press release confirming the loan and saying that it was "monitoring market developments closely" and continuing "to provide liquidity as necessary to promote the orderly functioning of the financial system." Bear, apparently, was "too big to fail."

By midafternoon Friday, however, it was clear that the Fed's loan had not staunched the bleeding at Bear Stearns. The rating agencies had slashed Bear's credit ratings Friday morning, lenders were refusing to extend overnight loans at any price, and hedge funds were in a panic to withdraw their funds. Convinced that Bear could not survive until Monday morning, Henry Paulson and Geithner called Bear's chief executive officer, Alan Schwartz, Friday night and demanded that Bear find a buyer by Sunday night or file for bankruptcy.

On Sunday, March 16, after protracted negotiations, the Federal Reserve engineered an emergency takeover of Bear Stearns by JPMorgan Chase. To avoid rewarding Bear's shareholders, Paulson insisted that JPMorgan pay them no more than $2 a share. As a sweetener, the Federal Reserve agreed to take Bear's most questionable assets onto the Fed's balance sheet in exchange for a loan to Bear Stearns, through JPMorgan Chase, of up to $30 billion.[84]

Faced with a crisis of systemic proportions, the Fed was forced to improvise. The financial health of Bear's creditors—which included such titans as Morgan Stanley and Goldman Sachs—was inextricably tied to Bear's ability to honor its financial obligations. Another problem involved the sellers of credit default swaps on Bear's debt, who would have to pay out if Bear couldn't meet its commitments. As Ben Bernanke later told Congress, the "sudden failure of Bear Stearns likely would have led to a chaotic unwinding of positions" and "cast doubt on the financial positions of some of Bear Stearns' thousands of counterparties."[85]

The Federal Reserve's loan to Bear Stearns was precedent-shattering. The Fed had opened its discount window to a nonbank company for the first time since the Great Depression. To do so, the Fed invoked its extraordinary powers under Section 13(3) of the Federal Reserve Act, which allowed the Fed to make discount window loans to "any individual, partnership, or corporation" under "unusual and exigent circumstances."[86] With this move, the Fed sent an unmistakable signal that Wall Street firms could act irresponsibly and still escape bankruptcy if they were too interconnected to fail. In so doing, it crossed a point of no return.

The Fed did not stop there. That night, it also opened its discount window to twenty other investment banks on the same terms as commercial banks, with no limits on loan size. Until then, the Fed had limited its lending of last resort to commercial banks, in return for stiff federal regulation of their balance sheets and activities. In addition to giving investment banks unprecedented access to the discount window, the Fed accepted a broader range of collateral, including highly rated subprime bonds. Again, the Fed cited "unusual and exigent circumstances" and invoked Section 13(3). By that point, the Federal Reserve had committed over half of its balance sheet to quelling the credit crisis.

Former Fed chairman Paul Volcker later criticized both moves, saying: "Sweeping powers have been exercised in a manner that is neither natural nor comfortable for a central bank."[87] Volker was concerned that by throwing investment banks a lifeline, the Fed had exposed the nation's financial system to more systemic risk in the future. Within weeks, Lehman Brothers would securitize $2.26 billion of its illiquid loans, get the rating agencies to give those bonds an A rating, and then exchange the bonds for cash from the Federal Reserve. Lehman dubbed its securitization vehicle "Freedom" because "it was designed to give Lehman freedom to tap as much cash as possible" from the Fed. Wall Street observers termed the move "brilliant."[88]

In expanding the reach of the discount window to investment banks, the Fed imposed a quid pro quo: any banks that used the discount window had to open their books to Fed scrutiny. This condition, however, did not apply to Bear Stearns because the Fed's new oversight rules did not go into effect until the day the Fed gave Bear access to the discount window.[89] As a result, the Fed was flying blind when it assisted Bear.

Worse yet, the Fed was forced to pump tens of billions of dollars into Bear Stearns with no legal tools to wipe out Bear's shareholders. Under the American free market system, shareholders are supposed to reap the profits if their company succeeds and lose their investment if their company fails. This market discipline is harsh, but it does a good job of rewarding efficient businesses and punishing the inefficient ones. When the federal government bails out a company, it is even more imperative to wipe out the shareholders so they are not rewarded for reckless behavior. Consider, for example, when the Federal Deposit Insurance Corporation (FDIC) seizes a failing bank or thrift. Under bank receivership law, the insured depositors are protected, but the shareholders usually receive nothing. The shareholders have no choice in the matter; they are not allowed to vote the receivership up or down. By denying the shareholders the right to vote on closure, Congress made sure that bank shareholders are not rewarded for playing dice with depositors' funds.

Bear Stearns was not a depository institution and, therefore, was not subject to FDIC receivership rules. This meant that the Fed had no legal authority to wipe out Bear's shareholders when it saved the firm. In fact, unlike shareholders of depository institutions in similar straits, Bear's shareholders had tremendous leverage in the deal. Under Delaware law, no merger could go through without the shareholders' approval. This law gave the shareholders a powerful card to play and the shareholders played it well. They refused to sanction the merger unless JPMorgan sweetened the share price from $2 to $10.[90] Due to rushed legal work by JPMorgan's lawyers, JPMorgan had agreed to guarantee Bear Stearns' liabilities for a year even if Bear's shareholders repeatedly voted down the merger.[91] As a result of the one-year guarantee, JPMorgan could not just walk away from the merger, which forced it to accede to the shareholders' price demands.

With the Ides of March, the federal government had opened a brand new chapter in its response to the financial crisis. Before, Washington had relied on traditional monetary policy, some mild fiscal relief, and strictly voluntary foreclosure prevention to patch up the faltering economy. Bear Stearns marked a new approach, in which the federal government was prepared to bail out financial firms deemed systemically important, one by one. Although Bernanke and Paulson would warn major banks in coming months that they could not rely on a similar bailout, that warning was not taken seriously on Wall Street. Instead, in the eyes of key financial firms, the federal government assumed a new role in the spring of 2008: that of matchmaker and financier.

## GOING THROUGH THE MOTIONS

The political climate changed with the Bear Stearns rescue. Henry Paulson knew that the public would demand fundamental reform to avoid further bailouts. In an effort to assuage voters, on March 31, 2008, he rushed out a Treasury Department blueprint for modernizing U.S. financial regulation.[92] Paulson knew that the blueprint, without more, would not allay public outrage over the Fed's rescue of Wall Street while leaving homeowners struggling. Thus, his next step was to shore up the secondary market in an effort to stimulate lending for home mortgages.

On Sunday, March 16, 2008, Paulson made an urgent phone call to the two chief executive officers of Fannie Mae and Freddie Mac, entreating both companies to raise capital so they could buy more mortgage loans. Paulson prevailed, and on March 19, Fannie Mae and Freddie Mac agreed to buy more jumbo mortgages and refinance distressed borrowers out of unmanageable subprime loans. Eight days later, the administration took a further step by cutting Fannie Mae's and Freddie Mac's capital surcharge, thus allowing the GSEs to buy $200 billion more in questionable subprime bonds. This was an abrupt about-face for the Bush administration, which, in prior years, had tried to dismantle Fannie and Freddie and had criticized both companies for taking on too much risk.

While the new plans for the GSEs were touted as tools for bringing down mortgage rates, they had another equally important objective: to get the subprime mortgage-backed securities off the books of ailing banks and onto the balance sheets of the GSEs. It was no secret that the subprime bonds that the GSEs took onto their books would likely require write-downs, something the GSEs could ill afford. Fannie's and Freddie's capital levels were already half that of ordinary banks. Further capital reductions opened them up to even more risk. Plus, the two companies had lost around $9 billion in the last half of 2007 and more losses were expected.

The administration's attempts to prop up housing finance did not stop there. On March 24, it convinced the Federal Housing Finance Board to allow the twelve regional Federal Home Loan Banks to buy up to $160 billion in Fannie and Freddie mortgage-backed securities, doubling their holdings. The Federal Home Loan Banks are owned by over 8,000 depository institutions, credit unions, and insurance companies and exist to provide advances to their owners. Countrywide and other ailing mortgage lenders had liberally tapped those advances in 2007 after other financing had evaporated. Like the GSEs, the Federal Home Loan Banks were already thinly capitalized. Despite the danger of loading them up with even more risk, the administration hoped that if the Fed, the GSEs, and the Federal Home Loan Banks bought more home mortgages, interest rates would fall on residential loans.

## A THOUSAND CUTS

Piecemeal rescues and infusions of money did not still the waters. The LIBOR spread ballooned again and investors fled for cover, sending gold to a record $1,000 a troy ounce in March.[93] Federal Reserve officials became concerned that the financial markets were "unusually fragile" and that lenders were unwilling to lend. There was "little indication" that home prices had hit bottom. Fed officials worried about "an adverse feedback loop," in which tight credit "prompts a deterioration in the economic outlook that, in turn, spurs additional tightening in credit conditions." In their view, "A prolonged and severe economic downturn could not be ruled out."

There was evidence everywhere that this vicious cycle had kicked in. Between February and May 2008, unemployment climbed from 4.8 percent to 5.5 percent. Consumer confidence tumbled to lows seen only during past recessions. Lenders became stingy about extending car loans, and GM, Toyota, Ford, and Chrysler reported double-digit drops in car sales by U.S. customers in March 2008 alone. The student loan market was under severe strain. The federal deficit ballooned, and corporate income tax receipts were down. Home values continued to slide. Hedge funds totaling nearly $4 billion in assets closed in the first three months of the year. Once again the Fed took action. Between March 15 and March 18, the Federal Open Market Committee lowered the discount rate a full percentage point, from 3.5 percent to 2.5 percent, and cut the target federal funds rate three-quarters of a point, to 2.25 percent.

Spring's first-quarter earnings reports brought more bad news. Subprime CDOs dropped sharply in value in March, requiring huge write-downs and hammering earnings reports. Goldman Sachs, Bank of America, and Lehman Brothers squeaked by with modest quarterly profits. Lehman pulled that off only by reporting a one-time noncash gain. Elsewhere, big losses came rolling in: $393 million at Wachovia, $1.96 billion at Merrill Lynch, $5.11 billion at Citigroup, $2.2 billion at Fannie Mae, and $200 million at the smaller Freddie Mac. The world's biggest bond insurer, MBIA, clocked in with a $2.4 billion loss. Countrywide Financial lost $893 million amid reports that federal investigators had proof that Countrywide officials had deliberately made loans despite knowing that borrowers' incomes were inflated.[94] Washington Mutual lost $1.1 billion and AIG a staggering $7.81 billion due to write-downs on its credit default swap portfolio.

These losses paled compared to losses at UBS. On April 1, the Swiss investment bank giant announced a first quarter loss of $18.12 billion, mostly on subprime and Alt-A investments. The news precipitated the ouster of its chairman, Marcel Ospel. By that point, UBS's total write-downs from its subprime activities topped $37 billion. Next door, in Germany, Deutsche Bank announced a $3.9 billion write-down for the quarter. Britain's second largest bank, Royal Bank of Scotland, announced it was increasing its 2008 charge-offs to $11.7 billion—again, due to write-downs on mortgage-backed securities. Fitch Ratings put Icelandic banks on watch due to liquidity concerns.

Back in the U.S., officials at the Federal Reserve and the SEC were prodding big banks to raise more long-term capital. Many of them succeeded, to the total tune of $28 billion. JPMorgan Chase and Citigroup each sold $6 billion in preferred stock. Merrill Lynch sold $9.5 billion in preferred shares and senior debt. Goldman Sachs sold $1.5 billion in ten-year notes, and Lehman Brothers raised $4 billion in preferred shares. Investors led by the private equity group TPG invested $7 billion in Washington Mutual; another private equity confab led by Corsair Capital pumped $7 billion into National City Corporation. And Fannie Mae raised $7.4 billion that May. According to the *Financial Times*, "Many investors believe[d] the worst write-downs on mortgage-related assets and leveraged loan commitments [were] over."[95]

Still, skeptics abounded. The spotlight was on Lehman Brothers, whose condition looked increasingly like Bear Stearns. Nearly one-third of Lehman's assets were troubled subprime and Alt-A mortgage investments. Lehman was highly leveraged; on February 29, 2008, its leverage ratio stood at 31.7 percent, meaning that the company's capital barely exceeded 5 percent of total assets. Lehman's stock had fallen 40 percent in 2007, and short sales of the company's stock took off in March and April. (Short sales are essentially bets that a company's stock price will drop.) It did not help that Lehman had to liquidate three of its funds and take a total of $1.8 billion in troubled assets back on its books.

At the end of April 2008, the Federal Open Market Committee met again and found continued strain in the banking sector. The Fed decided to expand monetary relief on several fronts, including a quarter percent cut to the target federal funds rate and discount rate, bigger swap lines with central banks in Europe, and expansion of the Term Auction Facility. All this was on top of the March rate cuts.

## INVESTOR OF LAST RESORT

The Fed and the Bush administration continued to expand the federal role as financier of last resort by creating new government markets for illiquid assets. In late April 2008, the Fed quietly started to allow investment banks to post AAA-rated CDOs as collateral for loans from the Term Securities Lending Facility. This move was designed to offer temporary liquidity for hard-to-sell subprime CDOs that were lurking on banks' books.

Three weeks later, Education secretary Margaret Spellings and Treasury secretary Henry Paulson unveiled plans to revive the student loan market, which by then was on life support. Sallie Mae, which had been the primary originator of federally-insured student loans, was considering exiting the guaranteed student loan business, and dozens of lenders had dropped out of the student loan market altogether. There were two reasons for this transformation. The first was that the market for bonds backed by student loans had dried up and the second was that, in 2007, the federal government had dramatically reduced the size of the subsidy it gave private lenders for making student loans.

The few lenders left in the field had all raised interest rates and imposed stiffer underwriting requirements, making it harder for students to qualify for loans. State-sponsored student loan programs also started to disappear, often because the crisis in the bond markets made it impossible to raise funds to finance those programs. As a stopgap, Spellings and Paulson announced that the federal government would finance federal student loans itself for the coming school year. As part of that plan, the federal government would forge its own securitization market for student loans. If necessary, Spellings added, the federal government would make student loans directly. The *Wall Street Journal* remarked: "The injection of federal funds into the student-loan arena [was] the latest move by Congress and the administration to head off an election-year collapse of that market."[96]

In a further attempt to boost the housing and credit markets, the federal government cut Fannie Mae's capital surcharge again in mid-May, this time from 20 to 15 percent. It was prepared to do the same for Freddie Mac if Freddie raised additional capital, but Freddie never succeeded. With more resources, Fannie Mae was able to buy even more loans and securitize more mortgages, partially filling the hole left by the demise of the private-label mortgage securitization market. By July 2008, Treasury secretary Paulson would call the GSEs "the only functioning secondary mortgage market" in the United States.[97]

## SINKHOLE

During the summer of 2008, as the presidential campaign was heating up, the U.S. economy continued its descent. Unemployment shot up 24 percent, reaching 6.2 percent. Manufacturing contracted, home construction shrank, and auto sales tumbled further. The Dow Jones Industrial Average declined 8.66 percent from the beginning of June to the end of August. Crude oil hit record prices, and U.S. gasoline passed $4 a gallon for the first time.[98]

Second-quarter earnings reports brought a fresh round of misery. GM announced a $15.5 billion quarterly loss, while Ford's was $8.7 billion. Wachovia bled $8.9 billion, its largest quarterly loss ever, and ousted its chief executive officer, Ken Thompson. Analysts reeled at news that Fannie Mae had lost $2.3 billion. AIG lost $5.4 billion, spurring the departure of Martin Sullivan, its CEO. Losses totaled $2.5 billion at Citigroup, $821 million at Freddie Mac, and $1.76 billion at National City Corporation. Merrill Lynch's loss weighed in at $4.65 billion and Washington Mutual's at $3.33 billion. Overseas, UBS took a $329.3 million hit, and Royal Bank of Scotland was out $1.56 billion. Lehman Brothers was still in center stage with a $2.8 billion quarterly loss, sparking a crisis of confidence and leading to the ouster of its president and the demotion of its chief financial officer. On July 11, Lehman's stock hit a new low, down 83 percent from its 2007 high.

Short sales spiked, driving down the price of financial stocks. There was concern that naked short sales—short sales accomplished without borrowing the stock being shorted—were fueling ruinous speculation. On July 15, the SEC entered an emergency order placing a brief ban on naked short sales of nineteen financial stocks, including Fannie Mae, Freddie Mac, and the nation's largest banks.

By midsummer, it was clear that the financial crisis had become a banking crisis of major proportions. Before July 2008, the credit crisis had claimed seven small banks and thrifts, but no big ones had capsized. That all changed on Friday, July 11, when the crisis toppled the first large bank. IndyMac Bank, FSB, with $32.3 billion in assets, became the second largest United States depository institution in the country's history to fail, succumbing to rash mortgage loans. IndyMac was in such rough shape that no buyer wanted to touch it when the FDIC seized the bank. The following Monday, when the FDIC reopened the thrift, depositors, almost all of whom were FDIC-insured, formed lines outside the bank, desperate to withdraw their cash.

Fannie Mae and Freddie Mac were on the skids, too. On Monday, July 7, a Lehman Brothers report questioned the capital adequacy of both GSEs.[99] With that report, GSE stockholders dumped their shares, on fears that investors might refuse to roll

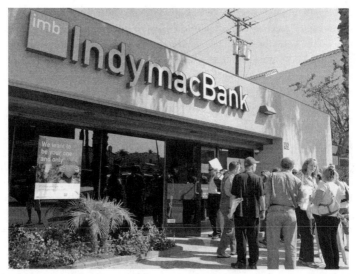

**FIGURE 2.5.**
Customers line up in front of IndyMac. (Gabriel Bouys/Getty Images News/ Getty Images).

over the GSEs' debt, creating a replay of Bear Stearns that could reduce shareholders' equity in the process. At midweek things got worse after William Poole, president of the St. Louis Fed, told Bloomberg News that Fannie and Freddie were insolvent and might require a government rescue.[100]

On the morning of July 11, the *New York Times* reported that senior Bush administration officials were preparing plans to seize Fannie Mae and Freddie Mac if their conditions worsened.[101] That day, their stock prices plunged about 50 percent before stabilizing after Paulson doused the *Times* report in a carefully worded press release. In it, Paulson said that "our primary focus is supporting Fannie Mae and Freddie Mac in their current form." Pundits read Paulson's words to mean that the Treasury secretary had ruled out government nationalization of the mortgage giants.

Paulson's next move, however, suggested that the GSEs' only likely source of fresh capital was Uncle Sam himself. By now, the Bush administration was depending on Fannie and Freddie to keep housing finance alive and needed to keep the GSEs afloat. On Sunday, July 13, Paulson came up with a plan to shore up the GSEs; his plan ultimately became part of the Housing and Economic Recovery Act of 2008 (HERA),[102] which the president signed into law on July 30. HERA gave the Treasury Department authority to invest in the GSEs' stock and bonds. It also created a new regulator for the GSEs, the Federal Housing Finance Agency (FHFA), and gave it the authority to place the GSEs in conservatorship or receivership, if need be.

HERA also expanded FHA lending, by authorizing FHA to guarantee up to $300 billion worth of refinanced mortgages. The guarantees only applied if lenders agreed to refinance borrowers into fixed-rate FHA mortgages after reducing the principal to 90 percent of the homes' appraised values. Lenders had to absorb the losses from the principal reduction, but, in exchange, FHA guaranteed the loans. The hitch for borrowers was that they had to pay high fees and share any future appreciation with the FHA. The new program, called Hope for Homeowners, or H4H for short, anticipated helping 400,000 distressed borrowers refinance. In order to qualify for H4H, borrowers had to have unaffordable loans and be unable to refinance because their homes were worth less than the amount due on their loans. HERA also created the Neighborhood Stabilization Program to provide grants to states and local governments to address foreclosures and abandoned property. The other noteworthy piece of HERA was the requirement that all states establish a registry for mortgage brokers and a system for educating and licensing those brokers.[103]

While HERA had some consumer-friendly provisions, the bill's main focus was the GSEs. Many people rightfully believed that the government was preparing to seize the GSEs. In testimony before Congress, Paulson suggested otherwise, saying: "If you've got a bazooka, and people know you've got it, you may not have to take it out."[104] Of course, the administration did not want to use the bazooka because it would mean another bailout on its watch. The White House hoped to funnel cash to the GSEs without having to make a politically controversial fiscal outlay. So it turned to the Fed for further help in stabilizing the GSEs. On Sunday, July 13, the Federal Reserve issued a terse press release stating that it was opening the discount window to Fannie Mae and Freddie Mac. The Fed defended this extraordinary expansion of its discount window facility as necessary "to promote the availability of home mortgage credit during a period of stress in financial markets." Unimpressed, the *Wall Street*

**FIGURE 4.6.**
U.S. Treasury Secretary Henry Paulson (*left*) and Federal Reserve Board Chairman
Ben Bernanke testify before the Senate Banking, Housing and Urban Affairs
Committee on Capitol Hill. (Chip Somodevilla/AFP/Getty Images)

*Journal* criticized Paulson for passing the buck to the Fed and called on him to make
an immediate federal injection into both companies to boost their sagging capital.[105]
That didn't happen.

In the meantime, Washington Mutual was battling liquidity problems of its own.
On July 24, a research analyst at Gimme Credit reported that uninsured depositors
and providers of commercial paper were quietly pulling their funds out of WaMu.
That day, U.S. financial stocks experienced their worst one-day drop since 2000.
Washington Mutual hastily tapped the Fed's discount window, Federal Home Loan
Bank loans, and open market operations to assemble $10 billion in fresh cash.[106]

Behind the scenes, some Federal Reserve officials worried that the credit markets
were coming unglued again. On July 30, the board announced that it was extending its
emergency liquidity programs through January 30 and started offering Term Auction
Facility loans of up to eighty-four days.[107]

### THE DEAD OF SUMMER

In Washington, as elsewhere, August was sleepy, apart from the thrill of the 2008
Olympics in Beijing and the Democratic and Republican political conventions at

home. There were few financial developments, and they largely went unnoticed. The Danish central bank seized Roskilde Bank after falling real estate values drove the lender into insolvency.[108] Big banks agreed to legal settlements in July and August to take huge sums of worthless auction rate securities back onto their books.[109] Near the end of the month, Bloomberg News issued a shocking figure: total write-downs and credit losses at the world's biggest banks to date had topped half a trillion dollars.[110]

The public's attention, however, was elsewhere. Michael Phelps won a record eight gold medals for swimming at the Beijing Olympics. Later, on August 27, the Democratic Party nominated Barack Obama to be the nation's first African-American president. John McCain accepted the Republican nomination for president after choosing Alaska governor Sarah Palin for his vice presidential running mate.

August was also a quiet time at the Federal Reserve Board. The Federal Open Market Committee met and decided not to lower interest rates. Some present were sanguine and ventured "that risks to the financial system had receded." According to the minutes, the committee members "generally anticipated that the next policy move would likely be a tightening" of interest rates. They did not meet again until September 16.

# 5

▷

# Meltdown

In an address in Singapore in mid-August 2008, Kenneth Rogoff, the former chief economist of the International Monetary Fund, warned his audience, "The worst is to come."[1] He was right.

## BAZOOKA

During the summer of 2008, Henry Paulson assured Congress that by creating a mechanism for placing Fannie Mae and Freddie Mac into conservatorship, Congress would calm investors. Paulson had expressed confidence that he would never actually have to use his "bazooka" to rein in the GSEs. Less than two months later, however, the Treasury secretary pulled the trigger.

On the weekend of September 6, 2008, Paulson summoned the CEOs of Fannie Mae and Freddie Mac and told them they had to step down.[2] The government was seizing both companies and putting them into conservatorship. Fannie and Freddie would continue to operate but under federal control, with U.S. taxpayers absorbing their losses. The federal conservator would have full voting control over the companies. According to Paulson, the conservatorship would give policymakers a "time-out" to decide how to restructure the GSEs going forward.[3]

What accounted for the GSEs' demise? In the 1990s—as best we know—Fannie and Freddie confined their loan purchases to prime mortgages and the best Alt-A loans. During the housing bubble, however, both firms lost market share as private-label subprime securitization boomed and consumers were shunted into nontraditional loans. At the same time, Congress expected the GSEs to increase their purchase of mortgages to lower-income neighborhoods and borrowers.

As private companies with a public mandate and implicit government backing, the GSEs served two masters, neither well. As private concerns, they were under pressure from shareholders to meet their quarterly earnings targets. Under their public mandate, Congress expected the firms to meet affordable housing goals to expand access to credit. To satisfy both sets of demands, in 2005 the companies began ramping up their purchases of poor quality subprime loans. They also made the misguided decision to invest in large quantities of private-label subprime bonds, partly because it allowed them to meet their affordable housing goals.

Both business strategies backfired, with disastrous results. By mid-2007, Fannie and Freddie were bleeding ink and more huge losses were on the horizon. Worse yet, the companies had almost no financial cushion because the federal government only required them to hold minimum capital of a measly 2.5 percent of total assets (plus 0.45 percent of off-balance sheet items). The boards of the GSEs resisted raising more capital because they wanted to avoid diluting shareholders' holdings. Shareholders, in turn, became increasingly nervous about the companies' meager capital and accounting integrity. Voting with their feet in the summer of 2008, they forced Fannie's and Freddie's share prices down sharply.

Foreign investors became anxious that the GSEs might renege on their debt. They curtailed their purchases and demanded higher risk premiums on Fannie and Freddie bonds. Analysts became concerned that investors would flee GSE bond offerings altogether, which would have been tantamount to a run. The administration could not afford this exodus because the U.S. housing market was relying on Fannie and Freddie for 70 percent of home mortgages. In August, the screws tightened further after Freddie Mac tried to float a belated stock offering to raise new capital. Investors rejected the offering out of hand, spooked that a possible federal takeover could wipe out their investment. Both companies' stocks were in a nosedive, having fallen almost 90 percent in the first eight months of 2008.

Alarmed, Treasury started drawing up contingency plans and sent in Morgan Stanley analysts to examine Fannie's and Freddie's books. What they saw was ugly. Freddie Mac had used clever accounting tricks to make it appear adequately capitalized. It was still holding delinquent mortgages and subprime bonds at full value on its books. In addition, the company had inflated its net worth with deferred tax credits for which it had no use because it was not making any profits. Fannie Mae had used similar strategies to a lesser extent.[4] By August 26, the capital position of both companies was so dire that Paulson placed a video conference call from a bunker under the West Wing of the White House to Crawford, Texas, to brief President Bush at his ranch. By Labor Day weekend, plans to put the GSEs into federal conservatorship were under way.[5]

In the most striking feature of the conservatorship, the federal government made the implicit federal guarantee of Fannie and Freddie explicit by guaranteeing principal and interest payments on both companies' debt and mortgage-backed bonds. This propped up private financing for both firms by ensuring that holders of the bonds would be timely repaid in full. The rescue did not extend to Fannie's and Freddie's shareholders, whose dividend payments were canceled and who stood last in line for recovery.[6]

Under the terms of the conservatorship, the federal government pledged to pump enough money into the companies to restore them to positive net worth. Originally that pledge was capped at $100 billion apiece. In return, Uncle Sam received senior preferred shares in both companies paying 10 percent a year, plus unspecified quarterly payments. Effectively that made the government the controlling shareholder of Fannie Mae and Freddie Mac. In addition, the government received stock warrants—that is, purchase rights—entitling it to buy up to 79.9 percent of each company's common stock for less than $1 a share.[7]

In another major feature of the takeover, the federal government made sure that Fannie and Freddie could borrow to finance their operations, under the Housing and Economic Recovery Act. Treasury arranged this support by giving both GSEs direct borrowing privileges under the new Secured Lending Credit Facility if the private debt markets dried up.[8] In addition, Treasury and the Fed began buying large quantities of Fannie and Freddie mortgage-backed securities and debt on the open market to bring down interest rates on home mortgages.

The rescue of Fannie and Freddie demonstrated that the financial system had become too dependent on the implicit federal guarantee of the GSEs to let the companies fail. Too many banks had invested in Fannie and Freddie bonds and many would have toppled if those bonds had gone into default. Likewise, central banks and other investors around the world, including China, had purchased Fannie and Freddie MBS in the belief that the bonds were virtually risk-free. A default would have shattered the faith of global investors in anything remotely smacking of a U.S. obligation. "Because the U.S. Government created these ambiguities," Paulson asserted when taking control of the companies, "we have a responsibility to both avert and ultimately address the systemic risk now posed by the scale and breadth of the holdings of GSE debt and MBS."[9]

There was another rationale for bailing out Fannie and Freddie. If the government had let them default on their bond obligations, most of what remained of the U.S. system of residential finance would have collapsed, wiping out home values and deepening what was already the worst recession since the 1930s. The administration viewed Fannie Mae and Freddie Mac as "critical to turning the corner on housing" and was determined not to let them fail.[10]

The price tag was enormous. After the GSEs were put into conservatorship, their losses continued to mount, further depleting their capital. By October 2009, the federal government had injected $96 billion into the GSEs in the form of senior preferred stock to keep them afloat. Treasury and the Fed had also bought $1 trillion or so in GSE mortgage-backed securities and well over $100 billion in debt issued by the two firms.[11]

As with Bear Stearns, when the government seized the GSEs, it was still attacking the financial crisis one institution at a time. But the model that the government used for Fannie and Freddie was distinct from the one it used to rescue Bear Stearns. For one thing, under the rules of the GSEs' conservatorship, shareholders moved to the back of the line for recovery. In that way, conservatorship meant that shareholders did not profit from their recklessness at the expense of taxpayers. That was a big improvement over the deal with Bear Stearns. Another major difference was that the federal government bought outright equity stakes in both companies. The purpose of outright ownership was to allow U.S. taxpayers to reap any profits from the bailouts, but the structure also put Uncle Sam in the uncomfortable position of partially nationalizing two large financial concerns. Nevertheless, the preferred stock ownership model used for the GSEs would become the template for numerous federal bailouts to come.

## THE SITUATION ON MAIN STREET

While tumult reined on Wall Street, individuals who bore no blame for the subprime crisis were feeling their own pain. Businesses that relied on home sales, like title insurance companies, laid off thousands of workers. The construction trades were hit hard because there was no market for new homes. Workers lost their jobs and developers were stuck with large inventories of unsold homes; many ultimately went under, often losing their personal savings along the way. Appliance manufacturers, carpet installers, and paint companies felt the sting, too. Children's furniture sales dropped and home supply stores like Linens 'n Things closed up shop.[12]

In a sharp example of the spillover effects from subprime lending, breeders of mice felt the pinch when the decline in home construction reduced the amount of available sawdust, driving up the price of the sawdust they needed for their kennels. It wasn't just the mice breeders. Farmers, ranchers, wineries, oil companies, and particle-board and auto-parts manufacturers all use sawdust. For some companies, the lack of sawdust meant they had to reduce their production, which then led to lay-offs, and so the cycle continued.[13]

Working people who had money in mutual funds holding subprime securities and stocks experienced deep dives in the value of their assets. Pension funds were big investors in mortgage-backed securities and even funds with no direct exposure to subprime mortgages were losing value. When the value of pension assets tumbles, companies have to drum up cash to meet the shortfall. If a private plan fails, the federal Pension Benefit Guaranty Corporation has to step in to cover the plan's obligations. By the end of 2008, the pension funds at the country's 1,500 biggest companies were underfunded to the tune of $409 billion. The public sector similarly suffered. At the end of 2008, public pension funds' liabilities exceeded their assets by an average of 35 percent. In the hardest hit states, the differential was as high as 50 percent. In response, states faced the uncomfortable choice of increasing taxes to cover the shortfall, postponing workers' eligibility for retirement, or deferring funding of public plans.[14]

## LEHMAN BROTHERS TOPPLES

Back on Wall Street, the venerable Lehman Brothers, founded in 1850, was in dire straits. Lehman Brothers' balance sheet looked disconcertingly like Bear Stearns' six months earlier. Lehman had aggressively expanded into subprime and Alt-A securitizations and was up to its ears in troubled mortgage assets. In addition, the firm's commercial real estate investments had been hammered by falling real estate prices. And like Bear, Lehman had barely any capital. At one point in March 2008, its leverage ratio hit 44 percent. Lehman had also numbered among the ten biggest sellers of credit default swaps on subprime debt.

To make matters worse, Lehman took its time shedding bad assets and raising capital when the subprime crisis began because it did not want to record write-downs or dilute shareholders. Once Bear was gone, investors had Lehman in their crosshairs and shorting Lehman stock became a sport. Every drop in Lehman's stock price made it harder for the company to raise capital, triggering a vicious cycle.

Given Lehman's heavy subprime bets, losses were inevitable, and eventually they materialized in June 2008. Although Lehman could tap the Fed's discount window, investors were anxious because the firm had not found a solution to its financial woes. Plans to sell off Lehman's investment management unit had gone nowhere; so had plans to segregate its troubled assets into a separate "bad bank." One management shakeup followed another.

Lehman had been urgently searching for a buyer. It had reached out to Warren Buffett in March, to no avail; Morgan Stanley had already shrugged Lehman off. By late summer, Lehman was pinning its hopes on the Korea Development Bank or Bank of America. Secretary Paulson and the New York Fed's Timothy Geithner had even hosted a secret rendezvous at a New York Fed dinner on July 21 to allow Richard Fuld, the CEO of Lehman, to make a proposition to Ken Lewis, the CEO of Bank of America, but Lewis did not bite.[15]

Earlier that year, Lehman had balked at selling its bad assets at a loss and now it was paying the price. By early September 2008, Lehman's toxic assets outstripped its capital by more than two to one. On Tuesday, September 9, the press announced that Korea Development Bank had cut off talks with Lehman. That day, Standard & Poor's and Fitch sounded the death knell, putting Lehman on review for a credit downgrade. On the news, Lehman's stock plummeted 45 percent, while the cost of insuring its debt skyrocketed.

Wednesday morning, the *Wall Street Journal* opined: "The market is close to giving up on Lehman."[16] Richard Fuld reported that day that the company had suffered a $3.9 billion loss in third quarter 2008 and was now thinking about selling major assets. His assurances failed to placate investors, sending the firm's stock down 77 percent for the week. In a terrifying replay of Bear, Lehman's lenders demanded more collateral and quietly cut their credit lines. Hedge funds pulled their prime brokerage accounts from Lehman, while CDS buyers scrambled to sell their protection contracts back to the firm.

Friday night, September 12, Henry Paulson, Ben Bernanke, Timothy Geithner, and SEC chairman Christopher Cox convened a meeting of Wall Street titans and gave them an ultimatum: there would be no federal bailout for Lehman Brothers; any solution had to come from "the Street." According to reports, Paulson and Bernanke drew a line in the sand because unlike Bear, Lehman had had time to raise capital. Even more importantly, the economic leaders knew that a second bailout would embolden investors into thinking that the government would always be at the ready to bail out large banks.

That week, Bank of America had been reconsidering a merger with Lehman, but it walked away once Paulson made it clear there would be no federal support. Sunday afternoon, September 14, Barclays jilted Lehman after the Federal Reserve refused to guarantee the ailing firm's assets. Despite marathon weekend meetings at the New York Fed, no other firm was willing to step up to the plate, either singly or together, to buy Lehman Brothers. Swap traders rushed to their desks that Sunday to line up swap sellers who were prepared to replace the enormous sums of CDS contracts sold by Lehman.

Over that weekend, other financial giants became engulfed in crises as well. One was Merrill Lynch, of the "thundering herd" fame. The Wall Street firm, with over $900 billion in toxic assets, was vulnerable to the same type of run as Lehman Brothers and Bear Stearns, and its share price had plunged 38 percent in just four days. After Paulson and Bernanke decided to nix federal aid to Lehman, Merrill Lynch realized it would be the next domino to fall unless it found an immediate suitor. In record time, on Sunday night, September 14, Bank of America hastily struck a deal to buy Merrill Lynch, ending the firm's proud ninety-four years of independence. Bank of America's shareholders voted to approve the acquisition on December 5, 2008, after which two disturbing facts emerged. First was the bombshell that Merrill had paid $3.6 billion to its traders in bonuses right before the merger became final, leading the judge who later reviewed the case to exclaim: "Do Wall Street people expect to be paid large bonuses in years when their company lost $27 billion?"[17] Second, Bank of America discovered $12.5 billion in after-tax losses at Merrill Lynch, almost four times more than anticipated, a discovery the firm supposedly made after the vote.[18]

There were rumblings at Washington Mutual as well. Losses were soaring on its $50 billion portfolio of pay-option ARMs, particularly on West Coast homes, where property values had collapsed. The thrift's stock price had dropped 92 percent over the course of one year. On September 4, WaMu's board forced out Kerry Killinger, the company's CEO, after a string of multi-billion dollar losses. On September 9, the public learned that WaMu's board had signed a secret supervisory agreement—a bellwether of serious trouble—with the thrift's regulator, the Office of Thrift Supervision. Moody's and Fitch thereupon downgraded the company and observers began forecasting the thrift's demise.

AIG was deep in trouble, too. Moody's and Standard & Poor's had already changed their outlook for AIG to negative in February 2008 and had downgraded its credit rating that May. Write-downs on credit default swaps and mortgage-backed securities had forced AIG to record net losses of $13.2 billion for the first half of 2008, eroding its capital. Together, the downgrades and the write-downs exposed AIG to substantially higher collateral calls that the company did not have the cash to meet. Analysts started hounding AIG for additional write-downs on its swaps portfolio, especially after Merrill Lynch decided to slash the value of its own swaps to thirteen cents on the dollar in July 2008. Between September 2007 and September 2008, AIG's stock price fell over 80 percent.

On September 12, 2008, Standard & Poor's issued a warning that AIG faced another possible downgrade, pushing AIG's stock price down 30 percent. Every time its stock price slid, AIG found it harder to attract new capital. The company scrambled unsuccessfully to raise $40 billion in cash. On Sunday, September 14, AIG executives approached Geithner at the New York Fed for a bridge loan. They walked away empty-handed.

That night, the Federal Reserve Board girded itself for chaos. The Fed knew that investment banks and hedge funds relied on short-term loans through the "repo" market as their lifeblood. In the repo market, a dealer or other investor sells securities for cash to a buyer with an agreement to repurchase the securities in the near future, rarely longer than thirty days, at a set price. These repo agreements, in effect, are loans backed by securities. If the dealer fails to make good on the promise to repurchase the securities, the buyer can sell the collateral. Buyers' willingness to enter into repo agreements is based, in large part, on their expectations about the value of the collateral.

With multiple cracks appearing on Wall Street, the Fed became worried that the repo market would freeze up. So on Monday, September 15, the Fed announced that it was replicating the repo market at the discount window. Investment banks could obtain loans at the discount window, posting the same type of collateral (including stock) permitted for repo loans. To shore up Wall Street, the Fed also expanded the collateral that investment banks could exchange for Treasury bonds. In addition, the

Fed temporarily relaxed its conflict-of-interest rules to allow insured banks to pump money into their affiliates in exchange for investment-grade subprime bonds.

## ALL HELL BREAKS LOOSE

Monday morning, September 15, 2008, Lehman Brothers became the biggest U.S. bankruptcy filing in history, sending worldwide markets into a panic. Investors dumped stocks, especially financial stocks, for the safety of Treasury bonds. By the time trading closed at 4:00 P.M., the Dow Jones Industrial Average had plunged 504.48 points or 4.4 percent, its biggest drop percentage-wise in over six years. The Tokyo stock market dropped 5.1 percent; the Hang Seng index in Hong Kong slid 6.1 percent. Fear was rampant. Traders were terrified that companies that had sold credit default swap protection on Lehman's debt would be forced to make large cash payouts when they could least spare the cash. Companies that had bought swap protection from Lehman faced write-downs on those swaps, inflicting a further hit to their capital.

The stock markets were not the only trading posts affected. The market for interbank credit choked, pushing LIBOR up to 3.106 percent, a 44 percent increase in just one day. To relieve the funding pressure on banks, central banks from Europe to China flooded the global banking system with cash.

### Zig-Zag

Meanwhile, on the evening of Monday, September 15, AIG was holding on for dear life. Late that afternoon, Standard & Poor's and Moody's had downgraded the company's long-term rating three notches, causing AIG's stock to plummet 60 percent. The downgrades forced AIG to raise considerably more cash—as much as $75 billion—to cover its credit default swap obligations. On Monday, the New York insurance department had given AIG permission to pull $20 billion in cash out of its insurance subsidiaries in exchange for illiquid assets worth the same amount. Still, that was just a drop in the bucket and time was running out. AIG did not have the time it needed to sell huge sums of assets at distress sale prices to raise more funds. The company's last best hope evaporated when JPMorgan Chase and Goldman Sachs, unable to pin down the size of AIG's financial hole, refused to make it a bridge loan.

The thought of an AIG bankruptcy struck terror in federal officials. Countless banks and mutual funds owned AIG debt, which would instantly go into default if AIG filed for bankruptcy. In addition, AIG was one of the biggest worldwide sellers of credit default swap protection on corporate bonds, mortgage-backed securities, and CDOs. With $441 billion in swap obligations, AIG's reckless swap activity dwarfed Lehman Brothers'. Goldman Sachs alone had $20 billion in exposure to AIG swaps. If AIG failed and reneged on its swaps, institutions that had bought default protection on the bonds they held would be forced to take write-downs, eroding their capital and forcing them to raise more equity just when the stock markets were in disarray. Some of them would not survive. The panic that had erupted after Lehman Brothers filed for bankruptcy only compounded fears about a chain reaction of horrific proportions.

On Tuesday, September 16, Paulson and Bernanke blinked and agreed to a federal rescue of AIG to avoid financial conflagration. That evening, after an afternoon briefing to President Bush, the two men went to Capitol Hill and informed stunned congressional leaders that the Federal Reserve was planning to throw AIG an $85 billion lifeline. Bernanke warned legislators that an AIG collapse could trigger a massive run on mutual funds because AIG was one of the ten most common stock holdings in 401(k) plans.[19] Congressman Barney Frank asked Bernanke if he had $85 billion on hand, to which Bernanke reportedly replied, "I have $800 billion." Frank later complained to the press: "No one in a democracy unelected should have $800 billion to dispense as he sees fit."[20] The public learned of the rescue later that night.

To finance the bailout, the Federal Reserve took the extraordinary step of opening the discount window, this time not to a commercial bank or even an investment bank, but to an insurance company. As legal authority for this unprecedented step, the Fed invoked the "unusual and exigent circumstances" clause in Section 13(3) of the Federal Reserve Act, just as it had in the Bear Stearns rescue.

The Fed did not let AIG off lightly. The U.S. government received a 79.9 percent equity stake in AIG as recompense for the bailout. In addition, the Fed charged a punitive interest rate of LIBOR plus 8.5 percent on its $85 billion loan. In return, AIG pledged all of its assets as collateral, including its stock in its insurance companies. It had twenty-four months to repay the loan, and the Fed expected it to sell off its noncore businesses to retire the debt. Heads rolled, too, and one was AIG's CEO, Robert Willumstad, whom Paulson personally asked to step down.[21]

When the United States bought AIG, it chewed off more than it realized. Once the federal government became AIG's controlling shareholder, it felt compelled to pour more money into AIG to salvage its investment. On October 8, just three weeks after the bailout, the press reported that AIG had already drawn down over $61 billion of its $85 billion loan. The Fed made AIG another loan of $37.8 billion that day to tide over the company. As a former chief accountant for the SEC, Lynn Turner, told Congress: "This is hardly a situation . . . that instills confidence or trust."[22]

Three weeks later, on October 30, the Fed allowed AIG to borrow an additional $20.9 billion under its commercial paper program. The following month, continued distress at AIG compelled the Treasury Department to restructure AIG's bailout package and increase the total aid to the company to $150 billion. In early March 2009, Washington upped AIG's aid package by another $30 billion and relaxed the terms of AIG's loan.[23] It did so right before AIG announced its biggest quarterly loss ever, of $61.7 billion. On April 17, the Treasury Department injected another $29.8 billion and by year-end 2009, the government had pumped $182 billion into AIG. A General Accountability Office report in September 2009 glumly concluded that AIG's ability to fully repay its federal aid "remain[ed] uncertain."[24]

The AIG fiasco was compounded by the federal government's ill-fated decision nearly ten years earlier to exempt credit default swaps from regulation. This meant the Fed did not know what AIG's books looked like when the company was effectively nationalized. Once again, the Fed was flying blind when making critical decisions, just as it had with Bear Stearns.

Other problems arose because the Fed lacked regulatory authority. When depository institutions fail, regulators have clearly delineated steps for resolution. This was not the case with AIG. The only two options for resolving the company were bankruptcy or a government bailout. Understandably skittish about forcing AIG into bankruptcy, the Fed chose the safer route and overnight came to control the world's largest insurance company. By permitting AIG to live and condemning Lehman to die, it opened itself up to criticism that it was picking winners and losers.

## The Ship Cracks

On Tuesday, September 16, AIG was not the sole preoccupation of the Fed. The Federal Open Market Committee met and voted to leave the federal funds target rate untouched at 2 percent. Although the target rate was 2 percent, the actual rate that banks were charging each other for overnight loans was 4 percent, so the Fed poured $50 billion into the market to bring the rate down to the 2 percent target.

Other markets were experiencing severe distress. Overnight LIBOR had more than doubled, from 3.10625 percent to 6.4375 percent, putting intense strain on banks that needed to borrow. Interest rates on asset-backed commercial paper jumped as well. On Tuesday, the Tokyo and Shanghai stock markets lost 5 percent; the major Russian stock exchange Micex fell 17.45 percent, bringing trading to a halt.

Even more frightening, a $65 billion money market fund—the Reserve Primary Fund—had "broken the buck." The news came as a shock because investors viewed money market funds as the ultimate in safety and depended on getting $1 back for every dollar they invested. The Primary Fund had purchased commercial paper from Lehman Brothers, which had been wiped out in bankruptcy. Those losses, plus heavy redemption requests, limited the fund to paying out ninety-seven cents for every dollar invested. In addition, the fund announced it would delay further redemptions for up to seven days, as permitted by law. The Primary Fund was not alone. Two other money market funds "broke the buck" that day.

Investors, from the biggest Wall Street houses to the average Joe on Main Street, were spooked. The $3.4 trillion money market industry had been considered a safe haven, one many investors had flocked to when the economic crisis began. Eighty percent of U.S. companies and 20 percent of households held cash in money market funds.[25] Now, to everyone's shock, their principal might not be safe.

Unable to tell which funds were viable, investors pulled their cash out of money market funds, setting off what would become a $200 billion net outflow. Shortly after the Reserve Fund news, Putnam liquidated its Prime Money Market Fund because of a run, further rattling investors. To stave off heavy redemptions, some fund sponsors hastily proclaimed that they would subsidize their funds if necessary to maintain the $1 share value. Behind the scenes, other money market funds quietly placed limits on large redemption requests, unable to liquidate their commercial paper holdings fast enough to meet redemption demands. The commercial paper market quickly jammed.

The havoc escalated on September 17. The New York Times reported that "many credit markets [had] stopped working normally."[26] Short-term debt markets froze as money market funds, the lifeblood of those markets, stopped buying commercial paper. Central banks around the world, including the Fed, pumped wads of money into the global financial system in a desperate attempt to thaw the credit markets. Investors rushed to safety, at one point sending the yield on one-month Treasury bills below zero; they were essentially taking a loss to gain security. Fear gripped the market for corporate bonds, pushing their spread over U.S. Treasury bonds to the widest level in years.

Shareholders headed for the doors. The Dow Jones Industrial Average plunged 449 points. Goldman Sachs and Morgan Stanley suffered mass sell-offs of their stock, while the cost of protecting their debt hit new highs as investors bit their nails about both firms' dependence on leverage. Morgan Stanley wooed Citigroup as a suitor, then Wachovia. Short sales hammered Washington Mutual's stock, prompting reports that WaMu, too, was contemplating a sale. In Washington, the SEC strengthened its curbs on naked short sales, while federal banking regulators rushed out a proposal to encourage bank mergers by allowing purchasers to count goodwill toward their capital requirements. Meanwhile, President Bush was nowhere in sight.

By then, it was painfully clear that the subprime crisis had engulfed the global financial system and was in danger of decimating the life savings of average men and women. The markets that Americans relied on for their retirement savings—the stock market, the corporate bond market, and even money market funds—were imploding all at once. An unknown number of banks were hovering on the brink of failure. No one wanted to lend because they could not tell where the financial time-bombs were hidden. Even Goldman Sachs's viability was in doubt. Washington's style of crisis management by improv was provoking hysteria. Commentators accused Bernanke and Paulson of playing "whack-a-mole," hitting one mole just as another mole popped up elsewhere.[27]

## No More Whack-a-Mole

With the financial system in cardiac arrest, Bernanke and Paulson jumped into action. On Thursday, September 18, the Federal Reserve funneled $300 billion into the credit markets, to no avail. Next, Paulson announced that the U.S. Treasury Department would tap the Exchange Stabilization Fund to issue a one-year, $50 billion blanket guarantee of all balances in participating money market funds as of September 19. Simultaneously, the Fed announced it was again invoking its extraordinary authority under Section 13(3) to funnel loans immediately to money market funds through banks to allow the funds to honor their redemption requests and buy commercial paper.[28] Paradoxically, these moves made money market funds even safer than bank deposit accounts.

The night of Thursday, September 18, Bernanke and Paulson went back to the White House, where they informed the president and his economic team that the credit markets were still frozen and drastic action was needed. The president was stunned and after a moment asked, "How did we get here?"[29] We don't know how Bernanke and Paulson responded. What we do know is that they returned to Capitol Hill, where they told ashen legislators that the financial system was on the verge of collapse, putting their constituents' investments at risk. The time had come, they argued, for a comprehensive taxpayer bailout of banks.

Their proposal was to have the Treasury Department buy up toxic subprime assets from distressed financial firms and hold those assets for sale until asset prices improved. In a public statement on Friday, Paulson argued that removing the bad assets parked on banks' books would free them to lend to consumers and businesses again. With luck, the government would even make money that would eventually benefit taxpayers.

The markets reveled in the news, sending the Dow up 368 points on Friday. But serious doubts surrounded the plan from the start. Were banks really willing to sell their assets at fair market value? After all, many banks had not yet written down the assets to realistic values. If they sold their toxic holdings at fair market value, they would have to record gigantic losses, eating into their capital and requiring them to raise more equity at the worst imaginable time. Alternatively, if Washington offered to pay a higher price, U.S. taxpayers would be staring at a big loss, and banks would be rewarded for irresponsible past practices. Anyway, how could anyone determine fair market value when the assets were not trading? If Paulson was wrong, the potential cost to taxpayers could be enormous.

Paulson delivered his proposal to Congress on Saturday, September 20. The bill, only three pages long, was breathtaking in its audacity. The draft was silent about limits on executive compensation, aid to homeowners, or capital infusions to banks. The Bush administration was casting aside free-market ideology to ask Congress for the biggest appropriation in history—$700 billion—to buy mortgage-related assets from U.S. financial institutions with no judicial review. President Bush took to the airwaves to push for the bill.

From legislators' perspective, the timing was disastrous. There were seven weeks to go before the hotly contested presidential election. A third of the Senate and every member of the House of Representatives was up for reelection that fall. Congress was scheduled to recess on September 26 and hit the campaign trail, where legislators would be asking taxpayers to pony up $700 billion to bail out big banks. Democrats insisted on relief for homeowners in return. Republicans gagged at the prospect of a government bailout of such massive proportions.

## The Demise of the Independent Investment Bank

While Congress commenced negotiations over the bailout bill, the era of the independent investment bank was nearing its end. Of the Big Five independent investment banks that were standing on March 1, 2008, only Morgan Stanley and Goldman Sachs remained. Bear Stearns and Lehman Brothers had bitten the dust, while Merrill Lynch had rushed into Bank of America's arms.

Goldman and Morgan Stanley had lower leverage ratios than Lehman or Bear, but with no secure base of bank deposits to tap, both firms depended on the short-term debt markets to finance their operations. Now that those markets were paralyzed and the cost of credit default swap protection on their debt was soaring to new highs, their independence looked precarious. Investors were asking whether the investment bank business model worked any more, and short-sellers were hammering both companies' stock, prompting the SEC to slap a temporary ban on short sales of 799 financial stocks on Friday, September 19.

Goldman and Morgan Stanley did have a lifeline through the Fed's discount window. However, their discount window privileges were temporary and eventually the Fed would rescind them. To avoid Lehman's fate, Goldman Sachs and Morgan Stanley each filed rush applications with the Federal Reserve to become bank holding companies under the Fed's supervision. To accomplish this, both firms proposed taking industrial loan companies that they already owned and turning them into banks. On Sunday, September 21, the Fed approved both applications on an emergency basis.

By relinquishing their independence and submitting to Federal Reserve oversight, Goldman and Morgan Stanley gained distinct advantages. Importantly, they could wean themselves from the short-term debt markets by using more secure bank deposits to fund their trading operations. In addition, their newfound status gave them permanent access to the Fed's discount window and allowed them to post a wider range of collateral for discount window loans. In exchange, Goldman and Morgan Stanley gave up their cherished independence for daily supervision by federal banking examiners, higher capital requirements, and heavy restrictions on their ability to engage in nonfinancial activities. With the shift, the era of the big independent Wall Street firm was over.

## TARP

With all eyes on Washington, Congress postponed its September 26 recess and took up work on the bailout bill. On Tuesday, September 23, and Wednesday, September 24, Paulson and Bernanke testified in Congress in defense of the bill, where they were raked over the coals. The bailout bill quickly became embroiled in electoral politics when presidential hopeful John McCain, who just nine days earlier had reassured voters that "the fundamentals of our economy are strong,"[30] announced that he was suspending his campaign and Friday's presidential debate to work on the bill. McCain and Barack Obama joined congressional leaders at the White House on Thursday, September 25, with the goal of hammering out the final details. The talks deteriorated into acrimony and no deal was struck.

Markets were holding their breath, waiting for action on the bill. The financial system continued its slow-motion crash. On Wednesday, September 24, the Bank of East Asia in Hong Kong suffered a run. On Thursday, September 25, Washington Mutual collapsed following a devastating silent electronic run on its deposits. The FDIC seized the bank and arranged an immediate sale of most of WaMu's assets to

**FIGURE 5.1.**
Bush, McCain, Obama, and congressional leaders meet on financial crisis. (Mark Wilson/Getty Images News/Getty Images).

JPMorgan Chase at no cost to the Deposit Insurance Fund. WaMu's shareholders and bondholders were wiped out.

On Friday, September 26, congressional leaders resumed negotiations and on Sunday night, the leadership announced agreement on a final bailout bill, giving Treasury the power to buy "troubled assets." The legislation came up for a vote in the House of Representatives the next day. In a shocking upset, the House voted down the bill 228 to 205, mostly along partisan lines with some defections by conservative Democrats. The general election was five weeks away.

On the news of the bill's failure, the markets exploded in chaos. Monday afternoon, the Dow Jones Industrial Average fell 777.68 points, a 7 percent drop. The price of oil plunged over $10 a barrel. In a coordinated move, central banks flooded the world financial system with more liquidity. On the heels of WaMu, Wachovia Bank was undergoing its own silent run. Monday night, to staunch the run, the FDIC announced that Citigroup was buying Wachovia for $1 a share. The transaction had been brokered and financed by the FDIC following consultation with President Bush himself. A few days later, Wells Fargo made a better bid and Wachovia ditched Citibank for the bank of Pony Express fame.

Across the Atlantic, things were unraveling as well. Monday, September 29, the Benelux countries nationalized the failing bank Fortis, with $1.533 trillion in assets, while Britain seized the mortgage lender Bradford & Bingley. Iceland bailed out Glitnir, its third largest bank, as Fitch cut Iceland's sovereign debt rating. To avert panic, Ireland announced a blanket deposit guarantee for six Irish banks. Tuesday, France and Belgium rescued Dexia, a lender with $913 billion in assets, which was on the ropes following disastrous losses in its American operations.

It took panic on Wall Street to kick Congress into action. On Wednesday, October 1, just two days after Monday's stock market dive, the Senate approved the bailout bill 74 to 25, after loading it up with favors to induce members to vote yes. On Friday, October 3, a chastened House of Representatives approved the bailout bill by a margin of 263 to 171 after the Bureau of Labor Statistics reported that the economy had shed 159,000 jobs in September. Within hours, President Bush signed the Emergency Economic Stabilization Act of 2008 (EESA) into law. The final legislation, larded with $150 billion in pork barrel projects, was 451 pages long.[31]

EESA's centerpiece was the $700 billion Troubled Asset Relief Program (TARP), which allowed Treasury to buy toxic assets from banks. The funds were divided into two installments of $350 billion each. Treasury could not receive the second installment without approval from Congress. At the insistence of Congressman Barney Frank and fellow Democrats, Congress had added measures to the law for foreclosure prevention relief, executive compensation limits for TARP recipients, and closer scrutiny of Treasury's TARP decisions. EESA also temporarily increased federal deposit insurance from $100,000 to $250,000 per depositor.

Most of the EESA's provisions were designed to place restrictions on TARP expenditures. There was one aspect of EESA, however, that was broader than policymakers had originally contemplated. In defining "troubled assets," Congress included not just mortgage-related assets, but "any other financial instrument" that the Treasury secretary, after consultation with the chairman of the Fed, "determines the purchase of which is necessary to promote financial market stability."[32] Conceivably, that could

**FIGURE 5.2.**
Congress races to hammer out deal for bailout legislation. (Alex Wong/Getty Images News/Getty Images).

include stock in financial institutions themselves. Paulson had made sure he had that authority because, as he later said: "It was clear to me by the time [EESA] was passed on October 3rd that . . . purchasing troubled assets—our initial focus—would take time to implement and would not be sufficient given the severity of the problem."[33]

There was one policy initiative that did not make its way into the final EESA: giving bankruptcy judges the power to reduce the principal borrowers owed on their mortgages, known as cram-downs. Under bankruptcy laws, judges can reduce the principal borrowers owe on credit cards, boats, and even second homes, but not on primary residences. Mortgage cram-downs were included in versions of the proposed bailout legislation, but they encountered strong opposition from lenders, who claimed that cram-downs would increase their losses and the cost of credit to borrowers. They also contended that bankruptcy cram-downs would create perverse incentives for homeowners who were underwater—whose homes were worth less than their mortgages. The argument was that these borrowers would use the bankruptcy courts to secure loan modifications.[34] There were also concerns that if the cram-down legislation passed, the rating agencies would downgrade mortgage-backed securities because the legislation could reduce investors' expected returns. Investors who were restricted to holding investment grade securities would then have to sell their holdings in an already illiquid market. Banks arguably would have to further write down the value of their holdings and raise additional capital.

Congress capitulated and omitted the cram-down provisions from the law. It is worth noting that for about fourteen years, the federal courts were split on whether bankruptcy judges had the authority to reduce the principal of residential loans. Researchers looked at mortgage markets in the different jurisdictions during that period and concluded that "mortgage markets are largely indifferent to bankruptcy modification outcomes."[35]

**FIGURE 5.3.**
National Credit Union Administration poster announcing increase in federal
deposit insurance. (National Credit Union Administration).

In the meantime, the Hope for Homeowners (H4H) FHA refinancing program
hit the ground in October with high expectations.[36] Those hopes were ratcheted down
when in the first two months of the program, only 200 borrowers applied for H4H
and not a single loan was refinanced.[37]

### A No-Confidence Vote

When Monday, October 6, arrived, the headlines were overflowing with grim economic news. Iceland was on the verge of bankruptcy. The solvency of the Italian
bank Unicredit was in doubt. At home, Republican governor Arnold Schwarzenegger
announced that California could not sell its short-term debt on the bond markets and
might need a federal loan. Other states, including Massachusetts, discovered to their
dismay that bond investors would no longer buy their debt. The Dow Jones Industrial
Average dropped below 10,000 for the first time in four years; European stocks suffered their biggest daily drop since 1988. Clearly, the passage of the EESA had not
restored anyone's confidence.

Back in the United States, the commercial paper market remained under severe
strain. Determined to administer a shock to revive the market, the Federal Reserve
pulled out its extraordinary Section 13(3) powers again on October 7 and announced

that it would start issuing three-month commercial paper directly to U.S. companies. With a stroke of the pen, the Fed became the main prop of the U.S. commercial paper market. It was the first time since the Great Depression that the Fed had lent directly to the general business sector instead of using banks as conduits.[38]

Wednesday, October 8, brought more disconcerting news. In a sign of how dire things had become, the Federal Reserve and other major central banks announced their first joint rate cut since the aftermath of September 11, 2001. The Federal Open Market Committee dropped the target federal funds rate to 1.5 percent. The S&P 500 stock index closed at 909.92 the same day. In just seven trading days, the S&P had fallen 22 percent, a drop unmatched except in 1987 and the Great Depression.

On Thursday, October 9, Iceland's financial system collapsed. The Icelandic krona stopped trading, the government seized the country's three biggest banks, and the stock exchange abruptly closed. It was left to the International Monetary Fund to bail Iceland out.

The next morning, the Dow fell 697 points (8 percent) in the first 8 minutes of trading and panic was everywhere. At 10:25 A.M., President Bush tried to reassure the nation in an address from the Rose Garden, to no effect. The Dow continued to experience convulsions, swinging a full 1018.77 points from high to low. It was the Dow's biggest one-day swing ever and its worst week in its 112-year history. The VIX Index—a key indicator of stock market volatility that is normally in the teens— shot up to 69.95. The LIBOR-OIS spread[39]—a measure of stress in the interbank market—rose to unheard of heights, hitting 365 basis points (see figure 5.4). Typically, the LIBOR-OIS spread is between 5 and 10 basis points. Around the world, stock markets had fallen more than 50 percent from their highs.

While people in Washington were trying to figure out how to value troubled assets for purchase through TARP, European nations were taking a different tack. In Britain, Her Majesty's Treasury announced plans on October 8 to inject £50 billion in equity into British banks, including Royal Bank of Scotland, HSBC Bank, Lloyds TSB, HBOS, Barclays, and other giants. On October 9, the White House floated a trial balloon, announcing that it might use TARP funds to buy equity stakes in U.S. banks as well.

A few blocks west of the White House, world finance ministers were attending the annual meeting of the International Monetary Fund. During the tumultuous day of Friday, October 10, Paulson took time to confer with the G-7 ministers. Afterward, he emerged with earthshaking news: the U.S. government had decided to buy stock in "a broad array of financial institutions." For Paulson, one of the original architects of the troubled assets plan, it was an abrupt about-face and a bitter pill to swallow, given his strong aversion to government ownership of firms in a free market economy. Paulson, in reality, had no choice. European countries had already unveiled plans to recapitalize their banks. If Paulson did not follow their path, he would inadvertently give investors the impression that Europe was a safer place to invest.

Paulson summoned the chief executive officers of the nation's nine largest banks to a 3:00 P.M. meeting on Monday, October 13, at the Treasury Department. Ben Bernanke, Sheila Bair, Timothy Geithner, John Dugan, the comptroller of the currency, and Federal Reserve governor Kevin Warsh also attended. There, to their shock, Paulson presented each CEO with one-page contracts, obligating their companies

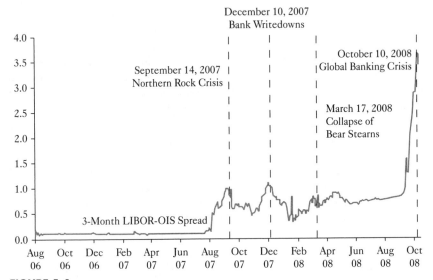

**FIGURE 5.4.**
3-month LIBOR-OIS spread: August 2006–October 2008. *Source*: Sengupta and Tam (2008).

to sell the federal government senior preferred stock. As the quid pro quo, the government would inject up to $25 billion in capital into each bank using TARP funds. Determined not to take no for an answer, Paulson told the men that they had to sign the agreements before leaving "for the good of the American financial system."[40]

Some of the bankers balked at the provisions subjecting the top five executives at each bank to strict executive compensation limits until the bank repaid its TARP funds. Those limits would expire, however, for any bank that conducted a successful private stock offering and repaid the government. The bailout was not all bad news for the banks. The preferred shares paid a 5 percent dividend for the first five years, which was cheap compared to private sources of capital. In fact, Jamie Dimon at JPMorgan Chase thought the proposition seemed "pretty good once he ran the numbers through his head."[41] It was also reassuring that the government could not exercise ordinary voting rights.

The FDIC also held out two irresistible carrots to the bankers. FDIC chairman Sheila Bair described plans to grant a temporary, blanket guarantee of the senior debt (including senior commercial paper, interbank loans, and promissory notes) of all FDIC-insured banks and thrifts. Further, to halt future runs on uninsured deposits, the FDIC would grant a breathtaking temporary expansion of deposit insurance to include all non-interest-bearing checking accounts in any amount. These inducements carried the day. By 6:30 Monday evening, all nine CEOs had agreed to sign.

The day after the fabled bankers' meeting, Paulson brought his plan to recapitalize "healthy" banks to the public. Under the Capital Purchase Program, Treasury would use $250 billion in TARP funds to inject capital into U.S. financial institutions by purchasing preferred stock and warrants. The goal, Paulson stressed, was to enable banks to "make more loans to businesses and consumers across the nation."

At the same time, the FDIC announced the two new guarantees that it had touted the day before to the bank CEOs, under the rubric of a new Temporary Liquidity Guarantee Program. The FDIC guarantee of new senior unsecured debt issued by depository institutions and their holding companies would last through June 30, 2012, and included commercial paper, interbank loans, and promissory notes. The unlimited deposit insurance guarantee for interest-free transaction accounts, targeted mainly at business checking accounts, would expire earlier, at the end of 2009 (later extended by the FDIC to December 31, 2010). After the first thirty days, participating banks and thrifts would pay fees to participate in these programs.

Together these measures expanded FDIC guarantees to unprecedented levels. The actions were so extraordinary, in fact, that the FDIC's board and the Treasury secretary were both required by statute to first determine that the steps were necessary to prevent systemic risk, following consultation with President Bush and the Federal Reserve Board.

Infusing banks with capital did not preclude Treasury from implementing the original troubled assets purchase plan. But Paulson ultimately had a change of heart and moved the plan to the back burner, declaring that "purchasing illiquid mortgage-related assets . . . is not the most effective use of TARP funds" and saying that it would no longer receive priority.[42]

By October 28, 2008, the George W. Bush administration had started the process of partial nationalization of U.S. banks. In the first round of payments, Wells Fargo, Citigroup, and JPMorgan Chase each received $25 billion in TARP funds, followed by $15 billion to Bank of America[43] and $10 billion apiece to Morgan Stanley and Goldman Sachs. As President Bush later admitted to CNN: "I . . . abandoned free-market principles to save the free-market system."[44]

## DODGING THE BULLET

While Paulson was banging heads in the Treasury Department's gilded conference room on Monday, October 13, world leaders took sweeping action to gird the world economy. Britain stated that the Exchequer would buy controlling stakes in the Royal Bank of Scotland and Lloyds TSB in return for capital infusions. Germany, France, Austria, Spain, and the Netherlands announced over €1.3 trillion in capital injections and inter-bank loan guarantees. In a tandem effort, the central banks of Britain, Europe, Switzerland, the United States, and Japan announced they were further liberalizing access to liquidity. Momentarily, world stock markets broke out in joy. On October 13, European stock markets saw gains of up to 11 percent and the Dow's performance was even better.

The elation was short-lived as more depressing economic news sent the markets down again. For third quarter 2008, the U.S. economy had suffered its most severe contraction since the 2001 recession. Consumer spending had fallen 3.1 percent, the first decline in seventeen years. Manufacturing was down and so were real estate sales. The governors of New York and New Jersey told Congress that their states were facing disastrous budget cuts. Unemployment continued to climb. Both Fannie Mae and Freddie Mac reported third-quarter losses of over $25 billion. In a symbol of the times, the VIX Index hit a shocking high of 80.06. (See figure 5.5.) There was even talk of deflation, which struck fear in economists because consumers and companies would defer spending if they anticipated more price drops.

On October 29, the Federal Open Market Committee met. After deciding that "a forceful policy response" was needed, it cut the target federal funds rate by a half percent, to 1 percent. The Fed matched that with a half percent cut to the discount rate, lowering it to 1.25 percent. At the end of the meeting, the committee resolved that "it would take whatever steps were necessary to support the recovery of the economy." As far as interest rates were concerned, however, the Fed had little room left to maneuver.

As the presidential campaign sprinted to the finish, the public's mood was sour. Economic insecurity was palpable, foreclosures were mounting, and 401(k) balances had plunged. Millions of workers were out of work, being placed on furloughs, or suffering wage cuts. There was red-hot outrage that the big banks that had caused the crisis had been bailed out with taxpayer funds. The United States was waging hostilities on two fronts, in Iraq and Afghanistan, and voters were weary of incessant war. Revolt was in the air.

## ELECTION DAY

Election Day, November 4, arrived with anxious anticipation. The results came in: Barack Obama would be the next president of the United States, winning 53.4 percent of the popular vote. The Democrats gained seven seats in the Senate, for a 58-member majority, and twenty-one seats in the House, for a 257-member majority. The voter turnout rate hit 61.6 percent, the largest in more than forty years.

Still, the inauguration seemed far away, while the lousy economic news just kept rolling in. With the Bush administration a lame-duck presidency and the Obama administration not yet in power, Washington was in a state of suspended animation. Starting three days after the election, on November 7, President-elect Obama gave an unprecedented series of televised press conferences designed to buoy the public. Holding press conferences was not the same, though, as holding the reins of power.

The federal government's actions that fall had stopped the economy from collapse but not from a slow deterioration. Days after the election, the Labor Department

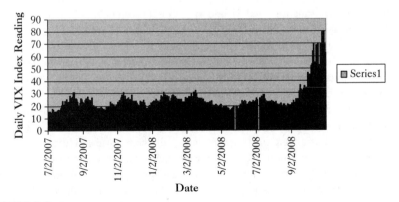

**FIGURE 5.5.**
VIX index levels: July 2, 2007–October 27, 2008. *Source*: Chicago Board Options Exchange.

announced that unemployment had hit 6.6 percent in October, the highest rate in four-teen years. In early December, the Mortgage Bankers Association reported shocking news: almost 10 percent of U.S. residential mortgages were past due or in foreclosure in third quarter 2008.[45] Christmas sales were dismal. Major companies were seeking bank-ruptcy protection: Circuit City Stores, the Tribune newspaper chain, and the chicken-processing firm Pilgrim's Pride. Europe was officially in recession; so was Japan. Even Toyota and Goldman Sachs reported quarterly losses shortly before Christmas.

By November, the Big Three U.S. automakers were all on the ropes. The recession and tight credit had choked off auto sales. In 2008, Chrysler's sales had dropped 30 percent compared to 2007, GM 23 percent, and Ford 21 percent. All three were clos-ing plants and ordering layoffs. GM and Chrysler were in particularly bad shape, hav-ing gone through $14.6 billion in cash in the third quarter alone. (Ford had stockpiled cash to help weather potential losses.)

On Tuesday, November 18, the chief executive officers of the Big Three companies appeared before the Senate Banking Committee to beg for a rescue. The venture was a failure. The CEOs had no detailed turnaround plans to provide the committee. Then the press reported that all three men had flown to Washington on their private jets to testify. Two weeks later, they returned to Capitol Hill, having driven from Detroit by car, with more detailed proposals in hand for the Senators. Unmoved, Congress refused to lend them any aid.

Nevertheless, the Bush administration was under growing pressure to forestall the mammoth job loss that the automakers' bankruptcy would entail. On December 19, President Bush broke down and announced a package of short-term loans and stock warrants to tide over General Motors and Chrysler until March 31, 2009. Under the plan, the administration committed $13.4 billion in TARP funds to shore up the two auto manufacturers. In turn, both companies promised to provide the White House with restructuring plans on February 17, 2009. They also agreed to relinquish their golden parachute packages, rein in executive pay, and sell their corporate jets.

Ten days later, on December 29, Treasury announced that it was taking a $5 bil-lion equity stake in GMAC LLC, General Motors' ailing finance arm, using TARP funds. The apparent purpose was to support consumer financing for car purchases. In addition, the government loaned $1 billion to GM to help GMAC qualify as a bank holding company. Later, on January 16, the administration made a $1.5 billion loan to a Chrysler Financial entity to finance auto loans.

While the automakers were making their pleas, federal banking regulators were plugging various financial holes. On November 10, the Treasury Department and the Fed increased their aid to AIG and substantially cut the interest rate on AIG's loan. On November 23, Citigroup got its second federal bailout, this time $20 billion in TARP funds plus a federal guarantee on $306 billion in real estate loans and securi-ties that the Fed said were in danger of "unusually large losses." These moves gave the federal government more than a 7 percent equity stake in Citigroup. The FDIC, which issued part of the guarantee, extracted heavy concessions in exchange, including tighter controls over executive pay and company acquisitions and a three-year ban on dividends. In a deft move, the FDIC also conditioned FDIC aid to Citigroup on an agreement that the bank adopt a FDIC-designed loan modification plan. It was the first time that TARP funds had been conditioned on increased foreclosure relief.

On the last working day of the Bush administration, the public learned that Bank of America's chief executive officer, Ken Lewis, had told Paulson and Bernanke on December 17 that because of staggering, unexpected losses at Merrill Lynch, the bank was seriously considering backing out of its deal to acquire the firm. Bernanke replied that reneging on the Merrill Lynch deal "would entail significant risks, not only for the financial system as a whole but also for Bank of America itself." He urged Lewis to go forward with the transaction, signaling that it might be possible for Bank of America to receive further federal assistance.[46] Internally, Fed officials were incredulous that Bank of America's management had not discovered the losses sooner; some believed that "management should be downgraded."[47]

After intense, secretive negotiations with the bank, the federal government salvaged the deal by making another $20 billion in TARP funds available to Bank of America. The terms of this infusion were onerous. Uncle Sam increased its stake in Bank of America Corporation to about 6 percent and the bank agreed to tighter executive pay restrictions and more modifications of mortgages to help homeowners stay in their homes. As part of the deal, the federal government guaranteed approximately $118 billion of bad loans and mortgage-backed securities that Bank of America had assumed in the Merrill Lynch takeover.[48] The announcement was timed to precede Bank of America's news of a $1.79 billion fourth-quarter loss and a disastrous $15.3 billion fourth-quarter loss for Merrill Lynch.[49] In a briefing memorandum to Bernanke on the upcoming rescue, Fed governor Kevin Warsh added an aside: "happy inauguration day, mr. president."[50]

The liquidity crunch continued to have a devastating effect on small businesses and consumers. Banks were paring back credit lines even further, and credit became noticeably tighter for small businesses and consumers. The TARP funds to the banks weren't leaving the vaults as planned.[51] Credit card companies unilaterally slashed cardholders' credit lines and jacked up interest rates. The public, already financially besieged, was enraged.

The Federal Reserve stepped in to provide some relief by proposing the creation of the Term Asset Backed Securities Loan Facility, slating $20 billion in TARP funds to help finance credit cards, student loans, car loans, and federally guaranteed small business loans. The Fed's new brainchild, dubbed TALF, was created under Section 13(3). That same day—November 25—the Fed announced plans to directly buy debt and mortgage-backed securities issued by Fannie Mae, Freddie Mac, and the Federal Home Loan Banks in an effort to bring down mortgage rates and boost the housing market.

Fannie and Freddie also expanded their loan modification efforts for delinquent borrowers whose loans were backed by GSE guarantees. The GSEs' programs capped borrowers' monthly payments at a percentage of their income and restructured borrowers' loans by reducing the interest rate, extending the payment period, and delaying principal payments. The Fannie and Freddie programs, while laudable, failed to reach the bulk of subprime and Alt-A borrowers whose loans were part of private securitizations.[52]

Investor blues continued and the Dow Jones Industrial Average sank further. December 11 brought new tremors to Wall Street: Bernard Madoff, the former chairman of the NASDAQ stock exchange, had pulled off the biggest Ponzi scheme in history, racking up $50 billion in losses. Again, investors turned to Treasury bills and again there were bids for negative returns. On December 16, the Federal Open Market

Committee dropped the target federal funds rate, this time to a range between zero and 0.25 percent.

## THE TIRELESS SHEILA BAIR

Although most of the federal banking regulators were singularly focused on financial institutions and credit markets, Sheila Bair of the FDIC considered a broader landscape and was thinking hard about how to curb foreclosures. As part of that effort, the FDIC crafted a model for streamlined loan modifications, called "mod in a box." Bair's proposal was to reduce the monthly payments for delinquent borrowers to as low as 31 percent of their monthly, pretax income. The reduction would come through interest rate cuts, extensions in the length of the loans, forbearance, and principal reductions. After a set period of time, borrowers' interest rates would adjust 1 percent annually until they reached the market rate. As an inducement to servicers, Bair proposed that the federal government pick up half the losses if borrowers whose loans were modified under this program redefaulted.[53]

The FDIC had already implemented a "mod in the box" program when it took over failed IndyMac Bank. The IndyMac program allowed borrowers who were behind on their payments to participate in a streamlined modification program that reduced their monthly payments. Not every borrower was eligible for the IndyMac program. In cases where foreclosure would reap a larger return than a loan modification, IndyMac could go forward with foreclosure. The initial estimates were that the IndyMac program would reach almost two-thirds of the bank's delinquent borrowers. Ultimately, the number of borrowers eligible for the IndyMac program was smaller than expected, but there were still many thousands of borrowers who had their IndyMac loans modified. The average reduction in monthly payments was $380. The projected redefault rate among loans modified through the IndyMac program was 40 percent.[54]

**FIGURE 5.6.**
Sheila Bair, Chairman of the Federal Deposit Insurance Corporation. (Bloomberg/ Getty Images).

## YEAR'S END

When 2008 came to an end, the year's statistics revealed a portrait of economic wreckage. Twenty-six banks had failed that year. The U.S. government owned stock in 208 banks—plus AIG—through capital infusions under TARP. The markets for commercial paper, bank debt, mortgage-backed securities, and asset-backed securities were on life support from the federal government. The S&P 500 Index was down 38.5 percent for the year, its worst performance since 1931. On the last day of 2008, the Dow closed lower than it had opened ten years earlier, meaning that the Dow had lost money over the past decade.

This carnage paled compared to the suffering on Main Street. Distressed mortgages were at a record high since the Great Depression. At the end of 2008, 11.93 percent of all home mortgages—and 48 percent of subprime ARMs—were past due or in foreclosure. Close to three million people were sixty days late or more on their loans. The foreclosure rate had risen 63 percent. As the recession dug in its heels and the unemployment rolls kept rising, even borrowers with prime loans began defaulting. At year's end, the number of prime borrowers who had missed two or more loan payments surpassed the number of subprime borrowers in that situation.[55]

The housing market was at a standstill even though interest rates on mortgages were at record lows. The low interest rates were of no use because so many borrowers owed more on their mortgages than their homes were worth, discouraging them from selling their homes. The percentage of underwater loans was staggering. In Nevada, half the homeowners with mortgages had no equity in their homes. In some communities, the fraction of underwater homeowners was close to 90 percent.[56] Some borrowers just gave up and handed their homes back to banks, leading to the term "jingle mail"—letters from borrowers to lenders that contained their house keys.

Subprime lending, which had been lauded as the tool to increase homeownership, was now responsible for a decline in homeownership. In 2004, homeownership had peaked at 69 percent; by 2008, the homeownership rate was down to 67.9 percent. Among African-Americans, the decline in homeownership was even more dramatic, with a drop from 49.1 percent to 47.4 percent.[57]

At the start of the George W. Bush administration, there were 17.1 million manufacturing jobs; by the end, there were 13 million. When the administration first took office, unemployment was 3.9 percent; at the end, the jobless rate was 7.2 percent. Over the course of the Bush presidency, the national debt per person jumped from $24,500 to $34,750. At the start of the administration, 13.7 percent of Americans lacked health insurance; at its end, the percentage of uninsured stood at 15.3. On Inauguration Day, 2001, the Dow closed at 10,587.59; eight years later, it closed at 8,281.22. Over 2.5 million people were out of work, the most since 1945.

When President Bush was asked to survey the scene near the end of his presidency, here is how he responded: "I'm not real happy about the fact that there have been excesses in the financial markets which are affecting hard-working people and affecting their retirement accounts."[58] Eventually, the sorry year of 2008 drew to a close, and not a minute too soon.

# 6

▷

# Aftermath

Inauguration Day arrived on January 20, 2009, ushering in a national day of festivity. Briefly, the problems facing the nation were put aside as Barack Obama took the oath as the first African-American president of the United States.

Immense challenges confronted the new president. The FDIC was closing banks practically every Friday night and the balance sheets at most banks were tenuous, at best. The stock market was sinking, consumer demand was sickly, and unemployment was in full ascent. A frightening negative feedback loop had emerged, with each new round of job losses generating fresh loan defaults and reductions in consumer spending. The United States was waging war on two fronts, in Iraq and in Afghanistan, and Islamic extremists were resurgent. The president's economic team was still being formed and fundamental financial regulatory reforms were just an idea.

On Monday, January 26, the Senate ratified Timothy Geithner as Treasury secretary despite embarrassing questions about Geithner's past tax returns.[1] The Senate's haste was an indication of the urgent need to get a Treasury secretary in place. Former Treasury secretary Lawrence Summers, former Fed chairman Paul Volcker, Ben Bernanke, Sheila Bair, budget director Peter Orszag, and Christina Romer, the new chair of the Council of Economic Advisers, rounded out the president's economic team. Meanwhile, the Senate released the second, $350 billion shot of TARP funds on January 16 to give the new administration added economic firepower.

The United States lost 741,000 jobs in January 2009, the biggest monthly decline in sixty years.[2] The unemployment rate hit 7.7 percent that month and was expected to go higher. By that point, American households had lost $10 trillion in wealth during the economic crisis.[3] There was a profound sense that no sector of the financial markets was truly secure. Money market funds could lose money; banks could fail and uninsured deposits could go up in smoke; insurance companies could become insolvent and default on annuities; employers could go bankrupt and renege on pensions; the Dow could drop by half and wipe out 401(k)s; states could override hard-won union contracts.

The collapse of the housing sector added to the distress. By early 2009, home values had fallen an average of 23 percent from their high, with the biggest declines in California and Florida.[4]

Almost 70 percent of borrowers were not eligible for refinancing, many because they did not have enough equity in their homes.[5] Stocks of unsold homes were soaring because there were too many sellers and not enough buyers. The situation was made worse by the expiration of foreclosure moratoria that many states and the GSEs had adopted in 2007 and 2008. As the moratoria ran their course, servicers began dumping increasing numbers of foreclosed homes on the market.[6]

With the nation's economic fabric in shreds, Washington could no longer afford to ignore ordinary citizens' plight. The Obama administration aggressively attacked these problems on multiple fronts. First, it instituted massive federal spending intended to boost consumer spending and create jobs. Second, it rolled out a series of programs designed to alleviate foreclosures. Third, it expanded initiatives originally undertaken by the Bush administration to stabilize the banking system. Finally, the administration proposed an ambitious array of bills to enact long-term, fundamental reforms to the nation's system of financial regulation.

## THE ECONOMIC STIMULUS PLAN

Despite the vast sums of money that the Bush White House spent to combat the financial crisis, most of that federal aid had been channeled to banks, not households. In the first days of the new Obama administration, Congress and the White House took steps to fight unemployment and jump-start the economy. The hope was that through stimulus checks, jobs, foreclosure relief, and increased consumer credit, individual households would experience some relief.

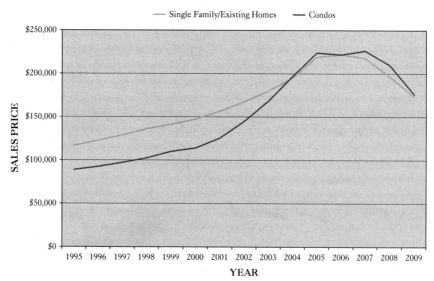

**FIGURE 6.1.**
Median U.S. home sales prices, 1995–2009. *Source*: U.S. Census Bureau.

Harkening back to the New Deal days of Keynesian economics, the administration drew on a broad array of tools to preserve jobs and stimulate consumer spending. One of the administration's earliest and most notable accomplishments was passage of a massive economic stimulus plan. On February 17, 2009, President Obama signed the American Recovery and Reinvestment Act,[7] a $787 billion economic stimulus package.

The stimulus act attacked unemployment on multiple fronts. First, Congress undertook an ambitious program of job creation through $120 billion in public works projects including mass transit, bridges, and roads. Because few public works projects were ready to hire immediately, Congress earmarked another $100 billion in stimulus funds to save existing jobs at public schools and universities. The Recovery Act also boosted funding for the Neighborhood Stabilization Program that was started under the Housing and Economic Recovery Act (HERA) back in 2008. To assist the long-term unemployed, the act increased weekly unemployment benefits and extended them by twenty more weeks. Finally, a new, $2,500 higher education tax credit encouraged people who were out of work to return to school to learn new skills.

Another key objective of the stimulus plan was to resuscitate the economy by reviving consumer spending. In pursuit of that goal, Congress handed out cash to consumers via a one-time middle-class tax cut of up to $400 for individuals and $800 for couples. To prod consumers to spend the money instead of using it to pay down debt, the Internal Revenue Service implemented the tax cut by reducing tax withholdings from workers' paychecks. Congress also doled out $250 in cash to every Social Security and disability recipient and increased food stamp, Medicaid, and unemployment benefits.

Some of the stimulus measures were aimed at sparking consumer spending while achieving ancillary goals. A temporary $8,000 tax credit for first-time homebuyers had the added purpose of stabilizing home prices.[8] An alternative energy tax credit had the dual goal of increasing energy efficiency. The most successful example was the wildly popular "Cash for Clunkers" program, which bestowed up to $4,500 in credits on automobile owners for trading in their gas guzzlers for fuel-efficient cars.

## The Automotive Sector

Despite its popularity, Cash for Clunkers was not enough to solve the ongoing crisis at the big Detroit automakers. In February 2009, Chrysler and GM submitted their second round of restructuring plans, which landed in Washington with a thud. President Obama nixed both companies' plans, instructing Chrysler to reach agreement with its creditors by April 30 or lose federal funds. Meanwhile at GM, Obama forced out the company's chief executive officer, Rick Wagoner, and delivered a like ultimatum: GM had ninety days to downsize and win major concessions from its unions, parts suppliers, and bondholders or else.

GM's and Chrysler's bondholders, however, refused to agree to the drastic debt forgiveness concessions that the federal government demanded to avert bankruptcy. On April 30, 2009, Chrysler was forced into Chapter 11 bankruptcy, followed by GM on June 1. So that both companies could quickly restructure and exit bankruptcy without emerging with a crushing load of debt, the White House agreed to provide debtor-in-possession financing—$3.3 billion to Chrysler and $30 billion to GM, on top of the

$20 billion it had already received—in exchange for an ownership stake, not debt. To speed the bankruptcy proceedings, the companies had hammered out understandings with the United Auto Workers to protect members' pensions and retiree health benefits in return for more plant closings and deep pay cuts.

Just forty-two days later, on June 10, Chrysler emerged from bankruptcy, after closing a fourth of its dealerships and forging a partnership with Fiat with financing from the federal government. A new, slimmed-down GM emerged from bankruptcy on July 10, after closing 40 percent of its dealerships and shedding its Saturn, Hummer, and Pontiac brands. Postbankruptcy, the UAW and the federal government became lead shareholders at both companies. The bailout came at a big price. According to a Government Accountability Office report in November 2009, "Treasury [was] unlikely to recover the entirety of its investment in Chrysler or GM," given how much both companies' value would have to grow to recoup that investment.[9]

Washington's efforts to salvage the U.S. car industry were not limited to direct support to GM and Chrysler. Prior to the bankruptcy filings, Treasury threw auto suppliers a lifebuoy in the form of $5 billion in TARP funds. All told, by November 2009 the U.S. government had shelled out $81.1 billion in TARP funds to save the domestic auto industry.[10]

## Consumer Lending

The Obama administration and Congress put high priority on cash subsidies, tax credits, and jobs as means to stimulate consumer demand. But increased employment and stimulus checks were not the only ways that Washington tried to increase consumer spending.

In the dark days of the crisis in October 2008, the securitization markets for credit cards, student loans, auto loans, and small business loans had dried up, contributing to the drought in consumer spending. To tackle the problem, in November 2008, the Federal Reserve Board had floated a proposal to revive those markets, called the Term Asset-Backed Securities Loan Facility or TALF. After Obama came to office, and after some tweaking by Treasury and the Fed, TALF was launched in early March 2009.

Like some of the Fed's other innovative facilities during the credit crisis, TALF opened the discount window to investors who would normally not qualify for discount window loans. The idea behind TALF was to extend up to $200 billion in nonrecourse loans to investors to buy AAA-rated securities backed by consumer credit or small business loans. Later in the spring of 2009, the Fed expanded TALF to a vastly broader array of asset-backed securities, backed by commercial mortgages, mortgage servicing advances, business equipment leases, vehicle fleet leases, and inventory loans to car dealers and home appliance stores.

## CREDIT CARD REFORMS

While the Fed was working to spur the consumer credit market, Congress was wrestling with complaints from constituents that credit card companies were gouging them and putting them at higher risk of default and bankruptcy. Politicians fast realized that financial losses to their constituents during the downturn, coupled with public anger over the fact that most card issuers had received billions of dollars in taxpayer-financed TARP funds, was a powder keg waiting to explode. With haste, Congress passed and the president signed the Credit Card Accountability, Responsibility, and Disclosure Act of 2009[11] in May to rein in the worst practices and clean up disclosures. The law banned retroactive rate increases, universal default clauses, and unfair late fee practices. In addition, Congress required credit card issuers to apply payments to balances carrying the highest interest rates first. Although the new act was well intentioned, it sparked even more rate increases by card issuers in the months before the law became effective.

## STEPPED-UP LOAN MODIFICATIONS

Foreclosure relief was at the top of the Obama administration's agenda from the start. Everyone agreed that voluntary loan modifications were not working. An OCC report found that over half of borrowers whose loans had been modified in the first half of 2008 had redefaulted.[12] The question was why. A study by the Federal Reserve Bank of Boston found that of 600,000 seriously delinquent loans examined, only 3 percent had received modifications that reduced borrowers' monthly payments.[13] A later study by Professor Alan White found that two-thirds of modifications actually increased borrowers' principal by adding overdue interest and fees to the original principal. The average increase in principal was $10,800.[14]

It was clear that servicers and lenders were not making modifications that made loans affordable. A director at Neighborhood Housing Services of Chicago reported that *after* loan modifications, one-third of borrowers had loan payments that were more than 60 percent of their income and another third had payments between 40 and 60 percent of their income.[15] Servicers' unwillingness to make modifications based on what borrowers could afford flew in the face of evidence by financial institutions, like Credit Suisse, that borrowers whose modifications involved principal reductions were less likely to redefault than borrowers who had other forms of modifications.[16] Similarly, a later analysis by the OCC and OTS found that "modifications that decreased monthly payments had consistently lower redefault rates, with greater percentage decreases resulting in lower subsequent redefault rates. While lower payments reduce monthly cash flows to mortgage investors, they tend to result in longer term sustainability of the payments."[17]

The low rate of loan modifications was puzzling because there were good economic reasons for doing workouts. When a home goes into foreclosure, the rule of thumb is that the holder of the loan will suffer a net loss of around 50 percent.[18] One explanation for the low modification rates was that lenders, servicers, and investors were excessively optimistic about the recovery of the housing market and, as a result, put all their eggs in that basket. A former manager at Bank of America said that his bank had been reluctant to modify loans because it was hoping that the economy and housing markets would bounce back and that delinquent borrowers would begin paying on their loans.[19] If this was the source of banks' resistance to modifying loans, it was a bad call. Even financial industry lobbyists contended that big banks "would have been better off had they agreed [in 2007] to address foreclosures systematically rather than pin their hopes on an unlikely housing rebound."[20]

Another factor impeding modifications was that servicers could not tell which delinquent borrowers would self-cure and resume payments without a modification and which needed a modification to avoid foreclosure. It only made sense to modify the latter. One study found that as many as one-third of borrowers resume timely payments even after being seriously delinquent.[21] By postponing modifications, servicers increased the odds that they would know each borrower's trajectory and whether a modification made sense. There was also the problem of redefaults. Modifications were of no value if they simply postponed the inevitable. Plus, with housing values dropping, delays in foreclosure could mean that homes would garner smaller proceeds when the inevitable foreclosure sales took place.[22]

Banks were also influenced by the effect that modifications would have on their balance sheets. Every time a loan was permanently modified, banks had to write down the value of the loan. In contrast, foreclosures can take months, giving banks more time to account for their losses, a practice some called "extend and pretend."[23] People in the industry also contended that if banks wrote down the value of a mortgage because of a modification, "there would be a strong argument that it would have to reduce the value on its balance sheet of all mortgages in the same geographic area to reflect that the region had hit an economic slump."[24] The more write-downs, the more capital banks had to raise.

With loan modification programs not fulfilling their promise, the bankruptcy cram-down idea gained renewed momentum with a new proposal entitled the Helping Families Save their Homes in Bankruptcy Act.[25] Citigroup publicly supported the bill. Supporters contended that if the law were passed, servicers and lenders would be under greater pressure to hasten loan modifications and to make them more effective. The House passed the proposed legislation in March 2009, but the Senate, in response to powerful lobbying by the banks, defeated the measure.[26]

In the meantime, in February 2009, the Obama administration had forged ahead with an expanded federal loan modification program, Making Home Affordable, with the intention of salvaging millions of loans. The program had multiple parts. Under one part of the program, borrowers with Fannie- and Freddie-owned or guaranteed loans could refinance into low-interest, fixed-rate loans so long as they had strong payment histories and met specific loan-to-value limits. Treasury allocated $200 billion to the GSEs to finance the program, called the Home Affordable Refinance Program (HARP).[27]

The other part of the program was nicknamed HAMP, for the Home Affordable Modification Program. HAMP created incentives for servicers to modify loans that were at least sixty days delinquent or at imminent risk of default. Eligibility was limited to borrowers with a debt-to-income ratio of over 31 percent who were occupying their homes. Loans had to be first liens and could not exceed $729,750. All servicers who received two or more rounds of TARP funds and who serviced loans guaranteed by Freddie Mac or Fannie Mae had to participate in HAMP. Otherwise, participation was voluntary. In total, servicers representing over 85 percent of the market signed on to HAMP.[28]

In HAMP, the government's goal was to reduce distressed borrowers' monthly mortgage payments to 31 percent of their gross monthly income. It sought to accomplish this objective through incentive payments to participating servicers and borrowers. Servicers under HAMP were instructed to achieve the 31 percent target first by reducing the interest rate, then by extending the loan term to up to forty years, and then, if necessary, by forbearing part of the principal. If the servicer had to resort to forbearance to hit the target, the borrower had to pay the forborne principal at the end of the loan term, but owed no interest on that amount. Under HAMP, borrowers needed to stay current on their initial trial modifications for three months and, if they did, their modifications became permanent. Other provisions of HAMP allowed interest rates to increase over time with caps, provided insurance to lenders and servicers against declines in home values, and created some mild incentives for extinguishing second liens on property.[29]

With HAMP, servicers only had to modify loans where the modified loan would have a higher net present value—that is, would be worth more—than an unmodified loan with a higher risk of foreclosure. Servicers received $1,000 for each modification and an additional $1,000 per year for the first three years after a modification if the borrower did not redefault. Borrowers also received $1,000 per year for five years if they did not redefault. These incentives also applied to modifications of GSE loans and loans made through H4H. Later, as part of the Helping Families Save their Homes Act in May 2009, Congress expanded HAMP to FHA loans.[30]

Making Home Affordable also addressed borrowers who could not afford their homes even with modifications that reduced their monthly payments. For these borrowers, the program created incentives for servicers to use alternatives to foreclosure. The two main alternatives were short sales, where borrowers sell their property for less than the loan amount due and the lenders absorb the difference, and deeds in lieu of foreclosure, where borrowers essentially turn the keys over to their lenders and the lenders waive the right to foreclose. Borrowers who participated in these alternatives to foreclosure were eligible for $1,500 in relocation expenses.[31]

There were other modification programs in narrow sectors. In February 2009, JPMorgan Chase announced that it would not only modify loans it owned outright, but also those that were part of securitized loan pools.[32] The preceding fall, Countrywide had agreed to implement a loan modification program as part of an $8.68 billion multistate settlement of claims that the company had violated consumer protection laws.[33] Around the same time, the Federal Reserve began a modification program that focused on principal reductions on loans it held through its takeover of Bear Stearns.[34]

The federal government also began experimenting with various programs to help keep homes occupied. Freddie Mac, for example, launched its REO Rental Option program in January 2009, which made it possible for owners who lost their homes to foreclosure to continue to reside in their homes as renters, paying market rental rates. The goal of the program was to keep properties occupied and in good condition to help "support local property values and promote a faster recovery in the housing market." Fannie Mae followed suit in November with the "Deed for Lease" program that enabled borrowers to remain in their homes for at least a year.[35]

### Increasing the Heat on Servicers

By mid-2009, despite the administration's efforts, one thing was clear: foreclosure rates remained alarming. In the first six months of 2009, 1.9 million foreclosure actions were filed and 4.3 percent of homes were in foreclosure. That same period, 3 percent of prime loans and over 15 percent of subprime loans were in foreclosure. 36 percent of home sales involved foreclosures or short sales, which pushed down home values. In Nevada, one out of every sixteen homes that carried a mortgage was in foreclosure during the first six months of 2009. Judges in one Florida county were hearing as many as 800 foreclosure cases each day in what was called the "rocket docket."[36]

There was no relief in sight. As figure 6.2 demonstrates, delinquency rates were climbing and many of those loans would work their way into foreclosure. These were not necessarily loans that had been priced out of borrowers' reach. To the contrary, the great bulk of defaults in 2009 were the result of unemployment, not costly loan terms.[37]

One theory for the spike in foreclosures was that complications from securitization were hindering workouts. With loans pooled and diced into tranches and with so many parties entitled to a cut of the revenue from a loan, borrowers in financial trouble had no easy way to renegotiate their loans. The entities that owned their notes were often passive trusts parked with unknown banks. It was nearly impossible for borrowers to even find the name of the trust and the trustees refused to negotiate with borrowers. The only other avenue for relief was the servicer, the entity that collected the borrowers' monthly payments and otherwise administered the loans.

Getting relief through servicers was not easy. Servicers were overwhelmed with calls from distressed borrowers. Chase Home Finance reported getting 40,000 calls a week in 2009. When borrowers or their credit counselors did get through to agents at call centers, the people at the other end of the phone typically didn't have the experience or authority to help. For their part, servicers complained that when they tried to reach out to borrowers in default, they often could not make contact because the borrowers were avoiding them or were suspicious of the servicers' motives. There was also a mismatch between servicers' skills and the foreclosure crisis. Servicing staff were trained to collect and distribute loan payments and help the periodic borrower who

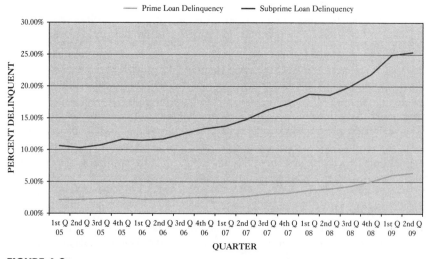

**FIGURE 6.2.**

Delinquent U.S. mortgages, 2005–2009. Note: Includes residential properties (1–4 units) with at least one payment past due, but not loans in the foreclosure process. *Source*: Mortgage Bankers Association.

encountered an unexpected financial crisis; they did not have the special skills needed to renegotiate thousands of loans.[38]

Servicers were inundated with paperwork. Loan files got lost or were incomplete. Borrowers would repeatedly submit the needed information only to have servicers repeatedly lose the documents in the frenzy. People who were eligible for modifications or refinancing were sometimes denied these options because the servicers could not keep up with their own record-keeping. For example, in an Arizona bankruptcy case a Wells Fargo officer claimed that the borrower had failed to submit a required financial worksheet and was, thus, ineligible for a modification. It turned out that Wells Fargo had never asked the borrower to complete the worksheet, which explained why the borrower never submitted it.[39]

Financial incentives also affected servicers' willingness to modify loans. When a loan went into default, servicers were obliged to advance to investors their share of the anticipated—not actual—principal and interest payments from borrowers, even though the borrowers had not made their payments to the servicer. When the property was sold at foreclosure, servicers recovered those payments plus any late fees charged to borrowers and the costs of foreclosing. This system of compensation created an incentive for servicers to move properties into foreclosure. In contrast, when a servicer modified a loan, it still had to advance to investors their share of any payments the borrowers missed; however, it could not recover those advances until the borrower made the overdue payments. If the overdue payments were tacked onto the end of the loan, the servicer would have to wait years to be reimbursed for the advances it made.[40]

A former Countrywide and Bank of America employee, describing the benefits to servicers of foreclosing over modifying, said if servicers "do a loan modification, they get a few shekels from the government." The shekels under HAMP were less than the fees servicers could generate by proceeding to foreclosure.[41]

To complicate matters, most of the loans that servicers handled were part of securitization deals, not whole loans owned by a single entity like a bank. Ostensibly, this created impediments to servicers' willingness to modify loans. Servicers for securitized loans operated subject to pooling and servicing agreements, which contained explicit and implicit limits on loan modifications.[42] Sometimes the explicit limits included terms that restricted the percentage of the loans—in absolute numbers or dollar amounts—in loan pools that servicers could modify without permission from investors or insurers.[43] The extent to which these terms existed and the extent to which they limited servicers' ability to modify loans was vigorously debated at the start of the foreclosure crisis, but by 2009, an executive with the American Securitization Forum stated that in the great majority of servicing contracts, "There [were] no meaningful restrictions on a servicer's ability to modify."[44]

Another problem arose because pooling and servicing agreements routinely required servicers to act in the best interests of investors. When housing values were appreciating, investors usually benefited more from foreclosures than modifications when borrowers defaulted. However, after home values plummeted and foreclosures on homes with subprime loans were bringing in only 50 cents on the dollar at best,[45] loan modifications may have been the better course. There was a potential glitch, however. Not all investors in mortgage-backed securities have the same interests. For reasons having to do with cash flows, holders of the top, AAA-rated tranches are better off if servicers foreclose; for holders of the equity tranches, foreclosures typically wipe them out, so they prefer modifications which at least preserve the possibility of future returns. With this conflict among the different tranche holders, servicers claimed it was impossible to determine what was "in the best interest of the investors." Supposedly to avoid lawsuits by investors claiming that servicers had not acted in their best interests, servicers stuck to the foreclosure track.

Choosing which tranche to "favor" was even more complicated for servicers that had an affiliation with entities that had invested in one or more of the tranches. Those servicers had reason to tread lightly when it came to modifications for fear of charges that they were picking favorites. It was a safer bet, some argued, to just pursue foreclosures as spelled out in the servicers' agreements.[46]

It is hard to know how much this "tranche warfare" actually influenced servicers' behavior. Research by the Federal Reserve Bank of Boston in 2009 suggested that potential conflicts among bondholders were not a real impediment. The researchers found no difference in modification rates on loans held in portfolio versus those that were part of securitized loan pools, which suggests that concern about taking actions that would benefit one tranche over another did not affect modifications.[47]

Congress helped address the threat of tranche warfare with the passage of two laws. The first was in July 2008 when, as part of HERA, Congress established that servicers are "deemed to act in the best interests of all . . . investors" when modifying a loan so long as (1) the loan was in default or default was "reasonably foreseeable"; (2) the borrower occupied the property; and (3) the net present value of the modification exceeded the likely recovery if the property went into foreclosure.[48] In May 2009, Congress created a safe harbor for servicers who complied with HERA's guidelines. The safe harbor insulated servicers from investor lawsuits based on servicers' modification activities.[49]

The new laws failed to clear the modification logjam. By May 2009, only one borrower had refinanced into a more affordable loan through H4H, which allowed borrowers to refinance into FHA loans. These results were surprising because H4H, unlike HAMP, made it possible for lenders to unload the risk onto the public sector. In contrast, lenders bore the risk of loans modified under HAMP. One explanation for H4H's failure was that lenders were unwilling to reduce the principal amount of loans, which was one of the requirements for the program. In addition, H4H required that any junior liens on property be eliminated as part of the refinancing—a requirement that investors and servicers both resisted.[50]

In May 2009, Congress amended H4H to relax the program's principal writedown requirement, from 90 percent of the value of homes to 93 percent. In addition, new provisions provided the owners of the original loans and second-lien holders with a share of any future appreciation of homes that were refinanced through H4H.[51] These amendments had no immediate effect. As of September 2009, only ninety-five borrowers had refinanced through H4H.[52] In October 2009, HUD tinkered with H4H again, this time replacing the shared appreciation provision with a cash payment to second-lien holders.[53]

HAMP modifications weren't faring much better. One problem, again, was the presence of second (often piggyback) mortgages. Almost half of borrowers who were seriously delinquent on their loans had second mortgages. Lenders and others holding these seconds knew they would never recover any money if underwater borrowers went into foreclosure. Even where there was some home equity, the equity usually did not generate sufficient proceeds to cover the first mortgage, let alone the second.[54]

Holders of second mortgages did, however, have some power. They could hold up modifications of first mortgages by refusing to release their liens on borrowers' homes. And so they did. By blocking the modifications of first lien mortgages, owners of seconds could extract a handout from the government.

There may have been another explanation why second mortgage holders clung to their stakes. The major banks in the country held $442 billion in second liens, including home equity lines of credit. If modifications brought the value of these liens to zero, the banks would have had to, once again, book the losses and take major write-downs—a step that was counter to their interests.[55] While this game of chicken played out, it was homeowners, neighborhoods, and states that suffered.

**TABLE 6.1.**

Estimates of nonprime borrowers with negative equity in selected metropolitan areas using the S&P/Case-Shiller Index, as of June 30, 2009.

| METROPOLITAN AREA | NUMBER OF NONPRIME BORROWERS WITH ACTIVE LOANS | ESTIMATED NUMBER WITH NEGATIVE EQUITY | ESTIMATED PERCENTAGE WITH NEGATIVE EQUITY |
|---|---|---|---|
| Las Vegas, NV | 92,949 | 87,685 | 94.3 |
| Phoenix, AZ | 131,069 | 117,185 | 89.4 |
| Miami, FL | 225,355 | 193,360 | 85.8 |
| Minneapolis, MN | 49,435 | 39,841 | 80.6 |
| Tampa, FL | 85,641 | 67,343 | 78.6 |
| San Diego, CA | 86,499 | 62,160 | 71.9 |
| Chicago, IL | 128,929 | 86,523 | 67.1 |
| Washington, DC | 130,760 | 83,682 | 64.0 |
| Los Angeles, CA | 315,289 | 201,009 | 63.8 |
| Atlanta, GA | 122,302 | 73,001 | 59.7 |
| San Francisco, CA | 103,369 | 61,652 | 59.6 |
| New York, NY | 295,932 | 76,204 | 25.8 |
| Seattle, MA | 69,353 | 17,327 | 25.0 |
| Boston, MA | 54,844 | 12,670 | 23.1 |
| Portland, OR | 42,014 | 5,323 | 12.7 |
| Denver, CO | 60,280 | 5,583 | 9.3 |
| Total | 1,994,020 | 1,190,548 | 59.7 |

*Source*: GAO analysis of LP data and S&P/Case-Shiller index.

At the end of April 2009, Treasury announced a new HAMP second-lien program. Servicers who participated in the program agreed to modify second mortgages if first mortgages were modified. The carrot consisted of more cash payments to servicers and borrowers. In addition, the government agreed to share the cost of any interest rate reductions on second liens or to pay the second-lien holders for releases of their liens.[56]

Slowly, trial modifications under HAMP began to pick up, but not enough to outstrip the rate of foreclosures. Banks like Wells Fargo and Citigroup hired thousands of employees to work on loan modifications, but the workout volumes were still low. Figures for early July showed 131,030 trial modifications, which was small potatoes relative to the estimates that over three million homes would go into foreclosure in 2009.

Timothy Geithner and the secretary of Housing and Urban Development, Shaun Donovan, were displeased with these numbers. In July, they summoned the top twenty-five servicers to Washington to press them to stem defaults. At the meeting, the secretaries urged the servicers to expand their operations to process more modifications and reach out to borrowers who could benefit from the Making Home Affordable programs.[57]

Trial modifications finally passed the 500,000 mark in the fall of 2009. A short time later, Credit Suisse estimated that eight million homes, representing 16 percent of all home mortgages, would go into foreclosure by the end of 2012. Some servicers and lenders took more active roles in modifications than others. Morgan Stanley's Saxon Mortgage Servicers led the pack with 41 percent of its eligible borrowers in trial modifications by the fall of 2009. Among the large banks, Citigroup hit 33 percent. Bank of America trailed far behind with only 11 percent of eligible borrowers in trial modifications.[58]

There were some signs of progress along the way. In October 2009, 10 percent of loan modifications involved principal reductions, a threefold increase from the first quarter of that year. Well over 75 percent of modifications involved reductions in monthly payments, which was a big change since the days of the Hope Now Alliance. Redefault rates, which dropped from 30 percent at the start of 2009 to 18.7 percent by the end of the year, reflected more aggressive loan modifications. The feeling on "the Street" was that at least some banks were finally recognizing that the economy wasn't going to bounce back any time soon and that they should consider modifying borrowers' loans instead of waiting for a miracle in the housing market.[59]

Still, modifications were not meeting targets and the administration resorted to rebuke. In November 2009, Treasury's assistant secretary for financial institutions reportedly said that the government would "use shame as a corrective, publicly naming those institutions that move too slowly to permanently lower mortgage payments."[60] Later that month, the administration announced it would soon unveil new metrics to "hold servicers accountable for their performance."[61]

Undaunted, the administration kept fine-tuning its various modification and refinancing programs. On November 31, 2009, the Treasury Department said it was going to send SWAT teams to servicing companies and check in with the largest servicers twice daily to get reports on their modification activities. The administration summoned servicers once more to Washington and even threatened them with monetary sanctions if they were not more successful. On December 1, 2009, HUD announced a plan to pay servicers who negotiated short sales and second-lien holders who released liens to permit short sales. With each programmatic change, servicers and credit counselors had to train their staffs, change their Web sites, and sometimes refine their models. The more time spent trying to keep up with the changes and the more staff time spent in training sessions, the less resources there were to actually orchestrate modifications.[62]

## FORECLOSURE RESCUE AND OTHER SCAMS

As more and more people fell behind on their mortgage payments, "foreclosure rescue" companies appeared on the scene, ready to exploit them. These for-profit companies offered to negotiate modifications of borrowers' loans to make them more affordable. These "services," mostly scams, cost several thousand dollars in upfront fees and rarely led to meaningful change in borrowers' loan terms. Some companies took people's money and did nothing. The worst created fake documents showing that the lenders had dismissed their foreclosure actions altogether. Others filed bankruptcy actions to stay foreclosures without borrowers' consent or knowledge. The operators of rescue scams could easily identify potential victims by reviewing public foreclosure notices— clear signs of borrowers in need of rescue.[63]

Some foreclosure rescue companies were former subprime lenders that resurfaced to "rescue" borrowers from the same bad loans they had made. When the California Department of Real Estate shut down over 200 businesses that were offering foreclosure relief without a license, half the people in these companies had prior connections to the mortgage or real estate industries.[64] As a partner at FedMod, a loan modification company, said, "We just changed the script and changed the product we were selling." Desperate borrowers would call FedMod's office, often in tears. To receive FedMod's services, they had to pay $3,495. The salespeople received a 30 percent commission on each "sale." A salesman described the hard sell: "A big grabber was that [the borrower's] loan will be reduced to 2.5 to 5 percent on a 30-year fixed rate loan. They'd print out all these mythical success stories for us to read over the phone." To seal the deals, FedMod had the sales force say, "You can pay me or you can lose your house." The borrowers would give FedMod "every dime they had, opening credit cards," but, the salesman reported, "I never saw one client come out of it with a successful loan modification."[65]

The FTC sued FedMod in April 2009 for deceptive and unfair practices.[66] The suit was part of an interagency effort in 2009 to shut down foreclosure relief scams. State attorneys general began prosecuting similar companies for fraud and theft. But with Web-based marketing and the ability to disappear and reappear under a new guise, the mortgage rescue companies were always several steps ahead of the enforcers.[67] Companies that used *Federal* in their names were of particular concern because borrowers could easily believe that the companies were government sponsored or sanctioned. FedMod's full name was the Federal Loan Modification Program, and some salespeople even told borrowers, "We're the federal government."[68]

Incentive programs under HAMP also inadvertently funneled money to some of the bad actors in the subprime lending arena. Countrywide's servicing arm, for example, was eligible to earn over $5 billion in incentives through HAMP. Other recipients included a subsidiary of AIG and two subsidiaries of Merrill Lynch. A report by the Center for Public Integrity found that twenty-one of the top twenty-five firms receiving HAMP money had strong connections to the subprime industry.[69]

## THE RESURGENCE OF FHA

When subprime lending tanked, FHA-insured loans experienced a remarkable resurgence. In 2006, FHA loans represented only 2.6 percent of the home mortgage market. By 2009, they had captured a market share of 23 percent. FHA loans appealed both to borrowers, who only had to put together down payments of 3.5 percent, and to investors, who bought Ginnie Mae securities that were backed by FHA-insured loans. More investors translated into more FHA lending at lower prices. There was also an increase in refinancing into FHA loans in part because investment firms were purchasing subprime loans at deeply discounted prices and then refinancing the borrowers into FHA-insured loans.[70]

Not everyone believed that FHA's meteoric rise was a good thing. Critics claimed that the premium borrowers paid for FHA insurance would be insufficient to cover potential claims by lenders when borrowers defaulted. Evidence that 24 percent of 2007 vintage FHA loans and 20 percent from 2008 were in default by 2009 bolstered these arguments. To compound matters, the free fall in housing prices pushed borrowers with new, low-down-payment FHA loans into the ranks of underwater homeowners. By September 2009, the FHA's cash reserves had fallen below the minimum required by Congress, sparking concern that FHA, like Fannie and Freddie, would need a bailout.[71]

The risk to FHA was not simply the state of the market. For decades, researchers who studied FHA had raised concerns over moral hazard. FHA insurance steps in to cover mortgage payments and foreclosure costs when borrowers default. This insurance arguably reduces the incentives that originators have to carefully underwrite loans.

FHA lenders in 2009 were not a squeaky clean lot. Some were former subprime lenders who switched to FHA lending because that was where the money was. To write FHA loans, lenders had to obtain licenses from HUD. Not surprisingly, as lenders moved into FHA lending, HUD was inundated with requests for FHA licenses and simply did not have the resources to screen lenders or to adequately police the lenders they had licensed.[72] A September 2009 audit report by the HUD inspector general stated:

> FHA's lender approval process did not have sufficient controls and procedures to ensure that lenders met all applicable requirements for approval to participate in the FHA single-family program. In addition, FHA did not obtain or consider negative information on lenders from other HUD offices. . . . In fiscal year 2008, the number of [applications from lenders] approved by FHA totaled 3,297, more than triple the number approved in 2007. FHA officials told us that staffing levels had been near constant since 2005 and that the large increase in applications strained FHA's ability to review the applications.[73]

## STABILIZING THE BANKING SYSTEM

While jobs, foreclosure relief, and increased consumer spending were top priorities of the Obama administration, the White House could not afford to ignore the storm clouds over the banking industry as the nation's biggest banks reported more huge losses. When President Obama took office, he encountered a furious debate over whether to nationalize the biggest "zombie" banks, meaning banks whose liabilities exceeded their assets and who had no more room to lend. Citigroup was the most obvious candidate, with a stock price skirting $1 per share in March 2009, a loss of $8.29 billion in the fourth quarter of 2008, and two TARP bailouts to its name. Another was Bank of America, with two TARP infusions and a $1.79 billion fourth-quarter loss. Wells Fargo had avoided a second bailout but announced a $2.55 billion quarterly loss on January 28, 2009. A $2 billion loss at Morgan Stanley and a $2.1 billion loss at Goldman Sachs rounded out the disastrous fourth-quarter 2008 earnings news.

Nationalizing a zombie bank would have meant putting it into government receivership, wiping out the shareholders, replacing management, rehabilitating the bank, and returning it to private control as soon as possible. This was not a path the administration wanted to take. On Tuesday, February 10, Treasury secretary Timothy Geithner gave a long-winded press conference in which he announced a $2.5 trillion financial stability plan with three basic parts. First, Geithner proposed submitting all banks with over $100 billion in assets to a stress test to determine whether they had enough capital to weather different disaster scenarios. Second, the administration planned to spend up to $1 trillion to finance private purchases of toxic assets from banks. Finally, Geithner proposed expanding the Federal Reserve's TALF program to $1 trillion.

Geithner's plan was maddeningly short on details, and the markets responded glumly. That day, the Dow dropped 4.6 percent on the news. While Treasury mulled over how to implement the programs, the stock market continued its downward march, hitting bottom at 6,547.05 on March 9, off 54 percent from its October 9, 2007 high.

### Treadmill Test

The goal of Geithner's bank stress test was to determine whether the nineteen largest banking companies could survive an even worse recession than expected. The nineteen giants accounted for two-thirds of the assets and half of the outstanding loans in the U.S. banking system. There were several purposes for the stress test—or the Supervisory Capital Assessment Program, as it was officially called—the foremost being to remove the doubts hanging over the nation's largest banks. While all nineteen firms technically met their capital requirements, federal banking regulators wanted them to hold even more capital to absorb unexpected losses and to generate more lending, in view of their systemic importance. In quick order, the markets drew the conclusion that the stress-test banks were all too-big-to-fail.

The stress test did not just look at overall capital; it focused on having sufficient common shareholders' equity to withstand an economic shock during the next two years. Common stock is the highest quality capital, standing first in line to absorb losses. Based on a number of debatable assumptions about unemployment, GDP, housing prices, bank earnings, and mortgage defaults, the stress test estimated that the nineteen firms would suffer another $600 billion in combined losses. Those predicted losses were on top of the $350 billion in losses the banks had already experienced because of the crisis. The stress test's goal was for each bank to have sufficient added capital to survive even this higher level of loss.

Federal banking regulators made the astute decision to make the stress-test results public for every company tested, a sharp departure from the normal secrecy shrouding bank examinations. When the results were revealed on May 7, 2009, the Federal Reserve Board announced that nine of the nineteen firms had passed the stress test with flying colors.[74] Of the remaining ten, eight had mixed results.[75] Those eight had sufficient capital to withstand the disaster scenario with what is called Tier 1 capital of at least 6 percent, but their Tier 1 capital consisted of less than two-thirds common equity, below the level desired by regulators.[76] The remaining two banks, GMAC and Regions Financial, failed their stress tests altogether. Reportedly, the total capital shortfall at the ten banks that marginally passed or failed the stress test was $185 billion.[77] Regulators gave the ten until November 9, 2009 to boost their capital by selling off assets, raising stock, or taking a new injection of TARP funds. By November 9, all of the banks were able to raise the needed capital except for GMAC, which earned the dubious distinction of having to ask for a third injection of TARP funds.[78]

Pundits condemned the stress test's assumptions as too rosy,[79] and the press reported that Citigroup and other banks had bargained successfully with the Fed to reduce the size of their reported capital holes.[80] Nevertheless, once the stress-test results were announced, the Dow Jones Industrial Average took off, topping 10,000 on October 14, 2009. Apparently, the results provided needed assurance to the markets, which had been laboring under fears that the big banks remained undercapitalized, notwithstanding their TARP bailouts.

What that assurance consisted of was not clear. Had the markets concluded that the nineteen biggest banks were adequately capitalized after all? Or had the markets simply assumed that the government would bail the big banks out? Similarly, the stress test said nothing about the financial health of smaller banks, many of which continued to deteriorate throughout 2009. The rising spate of smaller bank failures, growing loan losses, and the slow pace of marking down toxic assets on banks' books maintained pressure on the Obama administration to continue to address capital adequacy at the nation's banks.

## Capital Infusions: The Sequel

Back in the fall of 2008, Henry Paulson had ditched his toxic assets plan to make capital injections into banks using TARP funds. The Obama administration continued this approach in a somewhat modified form in its new Capital Assistance Program, or CAP. Under CAP, any of the ten big institutions that failed to pass its stress test with flying colors could qualify for another TARP infusion if it could not raise sufficient private capital. In addition, the administration continued to make capital injections available to small banks and thrifts under Paulson's original Capital Purchase Program. The administration's new, improved version of these programs required recipients to report publicly on how they were using their TARP funds to increase lending.

Eventually, the Treasury Department folded CAP without disbursing a dime. The department had dragged out activating CAP to give the stress-test banks time to raise capital privately on their own. In November 2009, Treasury announced that nine of CAP's ten potential recipients had succeeded in raising common equity and that GMAC, the tenth, would likely receive a bailout from TARP's Automotive Industry Financing Program instead. With little fanfare, CAP was taken off the shelf unused.

The story of CAP's birth and death illustrates the dramatic change since fall 2008, when the banking industry was undercapitalized as a whole and banks needing capital found the equity markets closed to them. A year later, virtually all large banks were able once again to sell stock. This achievement attests to the fact that the combined actions of the Bush and Obama administrations, both in engineering the initial round of TARP bailouts and in ordering the stress test, spared the U.S. economy from going over the brink. Still, banks would continue to face threats to their capital levels in months to come.

### Toxic Assets

Despite the brief and uneventful life of CAP, the toxic asset problem had not gone away. Distressed home mortgages and private-label mortgage-backed securities and CDOs were continuing to weigh down financial institutions' books and eat into their capital. As capital shrank, banks had less money to lend.

For these reasons, Geithner's February 2009 plan included a new troubled assets purchase plan, called the Public-Private Investment Program, or PPIP. The main difference between Paulson's troubled assets plan and PPIP involved the identity of the buyer. Under Paulson's plan, the federal government would have bought troubled assets directly. Under Geithner's plan, long-term private investors—private equity, hedge funds, and vulture funds, as well as pension plans, sovereign wealth funds, endowments, and insurance companies—could bid for pools of toxic assets with generous financing from TARP, the Federal Reserve, and the FDIC.

Geithner envisioned a two-part PPIP scheme. In the "legacy loan" program, the FDIC would manage the sale of distressed mortgages by lenders under its systemic risk exception. Under a Treasury Department "legacy securities" program, the department would select asset managers and task them with organizing funds to purchase troubled mortgage-backed securities and CDOs. For the funds' working capital, part came from private investment and part came from the federal government.[81] Treasury hoped that using private investors instead of Uncle Sam as buyers would result in more accurate pricing and allow the government to shift some of the risk to investors.

PPIP's success hinged on the dubious ability of banks and investors to agree on prices. Banks were reluctant to sell low because their holdings were starting to gain value.[82] The stress-test results also removed pressure from the largest banks to get troubled assets off their books. Then, in April 2009, the Financial Accounting Standards Board (FASB) made banks even more unwilling to sell at deep discounts by narrowing the circumstances in which they had to mark troubled assets to market.[83]

Investors had their own reasons to shy away from participating in PPIP. Some worried about the appearance of profiting from misfortune. Others were unwilling to take the risk that the administration would subject them to TARP's executive pay restrictions. When investors did venture what they were willing to pay, their estimates came in low because many of the assets were too complex and opaque for them to value with any confidence.

Ironically, PPIP's very creation may have obviated its use. When Geithner unveiled PPIP's specifics on March 23, 2009, the Dow soared nearly 7 percent. From May to mid-June 2009, ten of the largest banks succeeded in raising $65 billion through stock offerings, which dampened their appetite for selling troubled bonds through PPIP.

Originally, Geithner had envisioned total PPIP investments of $500 billion to $1 trillion. But by early July 2009, the Treasury Department had scaled back its total estimates to just $40 billion for the legacy securities program. Under that program, only eight investment funds were off the ground as of March 31, 2010, with $25 billion in purchasing power.

The FDIC's legacy loan program fizzled almost from the start. Most banks considered the bids on distressed mortgages unacceptably low. In response, the FDIC delayed ramping up the program, apart from one test bid. The test bid, in September 2009, resulted in only one successful auction. The proceeds from that auction were less than a billion dollars and the auction was limited to loans acquired as part of an FDIC receivership, rather than loans sold by a bank that was still open.[84]

Ultimately, the failure to solve the troubled assets problem raised the risk of prolonging the economic crisis. It made banks vulnerable to even deeper losses on their assets if unemployment continued to rise and real estate values continued to fall. Similarly, it fueled the credit crunch by tying up capital that otherwise could be used to lend. In the meantime, investors looked askance at the financial statements of banks with large amounts of troubled assets because they could not tell what those assets were really worth. FASB's refusal to require banks to write down the toxic assets on their books turned bank financial statements into creative writing exercises that masked capital inadequacies at banks.

### The Deposit Insurance Fund Goes Broke

The FDIC had bigger problems on its plate. Although the federal government had resisted closing the biggest zombie banks, it was not reluctant to seize smaller banks and thrifts that were insolvent. By September 30, 2009, 124 insured banks and thrifts had failed during the crisis. Most of the bank failures arose from elevated defaults among commercial real estate and construction loans that were a consequence of the recession. This contrasted with 2008, when residential mortgages and bonds backed by subprime and Alt-A loans were the major drivers of bank insolvencies.[85]

Mounting bank failures took their toll, and the Deposit Insurance Fund became insolvent as of September 30, 2009, with an $8.2 billion hole.[86] Over a fourth of banks and thrifts were unprofitable, and noncurrent loans were growing faster than banks' loan loss reserves in the third quarter of 2009. At that point, 552 banks—one out of every sixteen institutions—were on the FDIC's problem bank list.

The Deposit Insurance Fund was also feeling strain from the decision to increase the ordinary deposit insurance coverage cap to $250,000 in the fall of 2008. Of even greater concern, the FDIC's average cost from banks that had failed since 2007 was 25 percent of assets. That was almost one-third higher than the average cost during the last big wave of bank failures from 1989 through 1995.[87] In other words, this time around, the losses were significantly worse than during the savings and loan crisis.

There was never any threat to insured deposits because the FDIC had strong safety nets in case the Deposit Insurance Fund became insolvent. Still, to recapitalize the fund, the FDIC faced three unappetizing choices. It could raise assessments on the banking industry. That option would force the industry to clean up the mess it created, but would come when banks could least spare the cash. Alternatively, the FDIC could tap its $100 billion line of credit with the Treasury Department. Doing so, however, would let banks off the hook while making the FDIC beholden to Treasury. Finally, the FDIC could ask Congress for taxpayer funds to replenish the fund. Ultimately, the FDIC chose the first route, imposing an initial special assessment in May 2009, raising premiums that September, and later ordering banks to prepay three years of premium payments by the end of 2009. Questions remained, however, whether those measures would be enough to preserve public confidence in the deposit insurance system and absorb the losses from bank failures yet to come.

## PAY RAGE

Throughout 2009, the Obama administration was under constant pressure to put fires out in every corner. Each problem and proposed solution generated extensive debate, but nothing triggered public ire more than bonus payments to the executives at companies that had received bailout money. In March 2009, the issue boiled over when the public learned that AIG had paid $165 million in executive bonuses at AIG Financial Products—the same unit responsible for AIG's credit default swap fiasco—after federal taxpayers had bailed out the company. Some AIG bonus recipients received death threats. New York attorney general Andrew Cuomo added further fuel to the flames with a report finding that six banks receiving TARP funds in 2008 had paid more money out in bonuses than they had made in profits that year.[88]

In response to the public furor, the Obama administration adopted new, stiffer executive pay standards for TARP recipients across the board.[89] In addition, the White House anointed a pay czar, Kenneth R. Feinberg, for every company that had received two or more TARP bailouts, namely, AIG, Bank of America, Citigroup, and the auto company recipients. At each of the companies, Feinberg became the final arbiter of executive pay packages. In short order, he altered each company's executive pay structure to stress long-term profitability over short-term profits. Under Feinberg, restricted, long-term stock was in; cash bonuses and salaries over $500,000 were out.[90] All told, Feinberg cut cash compensation at companies like AIG on average by more than 90 percent; he cut average total compensation, including restricted stock, by more than 50 percent.

Not to be outdone, the Federal Reserve Board launched a sweeping proposal in October 2009 to perform special reviews of executive compensation at the twenty-eight largest banking companies. In addition, the Fed proposed expanding safety and soundness examinations of all banking companies within its jurisdiction to scrutinize executive pay. Earlier that summer, the administration had proposed an even broader measure to make compensation committees more independent and institute "say on pay" at major companies, regardless of industry. These measures and those imposed by Feinberg represented a sea change in the "hands-off" approach to executive compensation formerly taken by the United States.

## LONG-TERM FINANCIAL REFORMS

In addition to stabilizing the banking system and making huge fiscal outlays to shore up jobs and spark consumer purchases, the Obama administration launched an ambitious program of proposals designed to achieve fundamental financial regulatory reforms. Treasury secretary Geithner unveiled the first of those proposals on March 26, 2009, with his plan to regulate systemic risk. In the plan, Geithner called for six key reforms: a systemic risk regulator, stricter regulation of too-big-to-fail firms, registration of hedge fund advisers, credit default swap regulation, stronger supervision of money market funds, and resolution authority for complex institutions. In June 2009, the administration followed the initiative with a bold proposal for a new Consumer Financial Protection Agency. Over the summer, the administration delivered more proposals to Congress on the topics of investor protection, executive pay, credit-rating agency reform, and regulation of over-the-counter derivatives.

Fall 2009 brought a frenzy of rival proposals, hearings, and lobbying in the House and in the Senate. In December, the House passed a financial reform bill. But with health insurance reform the Obama administration's top priority that fall, by year end 2009, no financial reform bill had emerged from the Senate. With financial markets improving and the midterm elections approaching in fall 2010, the pressure was on to make lasting financial reforms.

## COMMUNITY IMPACT

Much of the focus since the start of the crisis was on financial institutions and the federal government, but a walk through once-vibrant neighborhoods revealed that the rot of subprime lending was local.[91] Broken windows, missing shingles, and peeling paint scarred vacant homes. By 2008, 3 percent of homes were vacant and almost 10 percent of homes built between 2000 and 2009 were empty.[92] Vandals were breaking into houses and stripping everything of value, from copper pipes to bathtubs, in the end leaving buildings fit only for vermin.

When owners left their homes, the houses did not remain idle. Con artists changed the locks and then rented out the homes as if they were the owners. In one case, the supposed landlord rented the same property to two families, both of which tried to move in on the same day.[93] Abandoned homes also hosted prostitution rings and other criminal activities. Gang members used the homes to stash weapons. For drug dealers, empty homes were good cover—a place to store drugs or manufacture methamphetamine.[94]

The problem of abandoned homes was not confined to lower-income areas. High-flying Southern California, once home to four of the largest lenders in the country, fell particularly hard because the "economies [had been] self-feeding off the housing boom."[95] Lawns turned brown, algae formed in backyard pools, and trash piles multiplied at abandoned properties.[96] In places like Florida, where there was a high rate of foreclosures in condominiums, condo owners literally paid the price of abandonment. With fewer people paying fees into condo associations, the remaining owners had to cough up more in condo fees or perform property maintenance themselves. Some condo associations simply did not have enough money coming in through dues to keep the properties in habitable condition.[97]

Banks and other investors found themselves owning thousands of vacant homes. At foreclosure sales, when nobody shows up to buy the property, the mortgage holder becomes the owner. Before the wave of foreclosures, banks owned about 160,000 foreclosed homes (known in the industry as "real estate owned" or REO) at any given time. In November 2008, banks owned 900,000 REO properties, with expectations that this number would climb to 1.5 million.[98]

When far-off entities end up owning homes after foreclosure, they often lack incentives to adequately maintain the property. For cities, enforcing housing ordinances against absent owners was a challenge, especially because securitization made it nearly impossible for city officials to find the true owners. Even when cities could identify the usually remote trusts, servicers, or lenders responsible for a piece of property, they rarely received responses to their notices of violations or their summons to come to court.[99]

Irate over lenders not maintaining the properties they owned, towns began upping the ante. One California city passed an ordinance enabling the city to charge banks with criminal misdemeanors if they neglected their properties. Town officials used this ordinance to go after Citigroup for failing to clean up algae in the pool at a home. The police chief was quoted saying, "If I need to do it, I'll say 'Mr. Bank President, if you don't come and take care of your property, we're going to come arrest you and take you to court in California.'"[100] In the end, cities usually ended up stepping into the void to cut lawns, paint houses, board up broken windows, and remove trash, and then sought compensation through liens on the properties.[101]

The difficulties of maintaining property and the risk of liability for housing code and public nuisance actions led some lenders to sell homes in bulk. Investors bought up the empty houses at bargain prices and then peddled them to unsuspecting buyers. In 2009, we searched for homes on eBay and found some good deals. A three-bedroom home in Cleveland was listed with a starting bid of $7,000. The ad stated:

> Great Opportunity! Must Sell. You can live now, rent it out as your income property or even resale [sic] it to make some profit!! Seller want to sell it ASAP. You won't lose money for this investment! I spent money fo [sic] rehab, so you don't need to do anything. Great condition.[102]

Sometimes owners of loans decided that it was not in their interest to foreclose. If no one bid for the property at foreclosure, they would become the property owners and would be responsible for taxes, housing code violations, and upkeep, costs that could exceed a home's value. To avoid taking ownership, they would abandon foreclosure actions midstream. In the meantime, the borrowers would have moved out, believing they were about to lose their homes and be evicted. This phenomenon came to be known as "walkaways." Enforcing housing codes with walkaway properties was impossible. The owners would vacate the property when they received the foreclosure notice and would never know that the foreclosure was not completed and that they still owned their former homes. Lenders had no legal obligation to keep up the properties because they never completed the foreclosure process. In some cases, cities did catch up with the homeowners years later and handed them bills for thousands of dollars for back taxes, fines for housing code violations, and even demolition costs. Walkaways caused another problem: toxic titles. With no one claiming ownership of a walkaway property, the property was in limbo. If an entity or individual wanted to buy the house, there was no one who could sell it to them.[103]

Tenants in foreclosed rental properties were innocent victims of the crisis. As many as 40 percent of foreclosures were on rental properties and these foreclosures were concentrated in low-income neighborhoods.[104] Defaulting landlords often pocketed tenants' monthly rent, security deposits, and last month's rent and then disappeared without making mortgage or utility payments. Tenants found themselves without power and with an eviction notice posted on their door. Once a foreclosure sale went

**FIGURE 6.3.**
Struggling Cleveland. When Detective Cole finds a home that is already abandoned or vacant, he enters with his weapon drawn, to guard against squatters. (Anthony Suau).

**FIGURE 6.4.**
Condemnation notice, Cleveland. (Kathleen C. Engel).

through, new owners could evict tenants with as little as three days' notice. The tenants then lost not only their housing, but also any security deposit or advanced rent they had paid, which made it difficult for them to secure new housing. As a legal services lawyer commented, "Nationwide, tenants who did nothing wrong, except to rent from a defaulting owner are suffering harsh collateral damage from the mortgage fallout."[105]

In November 2008, Fannie Mae and Freddie Mac suspended all evictions on their REO properties until January 9, 2009. Both companies extended these suspensions while they developed new policies to permit renters in foreclosed properties to continue their tenancies.[106] The federal government also took notice of the impact that foreclosures were having on tenants and in May 2009 enacted a law requiring purchasers of homes at foreclosure sales to allow tenants to remain for ninety days or the remainder of their leases.[107]

As economic strain spread its tentacles to every part of the economy, cities and states experienced dramatic declines in tax revenues. Between the middle of 2007 and the end of 2009, communities and states lost $917 million in property taxes. Across the country, borrowers sought to have their homes reassessed to more accurately reflect the market value of their property and, thus, reduce their tax bills. Less consumer spending meant less sales tax revenue and job loss meant less in income tax for states. Friday furloughs became common by the summer of 2009, with many states closing all but the most essential offices several Fridays a month to reduce payroll costs.[108]

The decline in tax revenues coincided with increased demand for services. Cities had to commit scarce dollars to quelling fires in empty homes, fighting crime in abandoned neighborhoods, and boarding up and demolishing houses. The estimated costs to cities ran as high as $30,000 per foreclosed home.[109] Requests to cities for heating subsidies, rental assistance, and other social services were steadily rising.

The federal government was not blind to the despair pervading communities. Congress had authorized money to assist the hardest hit areas, dating back to the first Neighborhood Stabilization Program in 2008. In October 2009, housing finance agencies (HFAs) got a boost from the Obama administration, which announced a new initiative to finance the construction and rehabilitation of affordable properties for rent and purchase by buying bonds issued by state and local HFAs.[110]

Without a doubt, subprime lending hit fragile neighborhoods the hardest. Dan Immergluck and Geoff Smith have quantified the effect of foreclosures in low- and moderate-income areas, finding that for each foreclosure within one-eighth of a mile of any given home, the value of the home dropped by over 1.4 percent.[111] As blight infected modest neighborhoods, residents whose wealth was tied up in their houses were powerless to escape. Their homes, with manicured lawns and bright, geranium-filled window boxes, sat alongside boarded-up homes marred by graffiti.

For people of color, subprime lending was an unmitigated disaster. A Federal Reserve Bank of Boston study found that almost half of the African-Americans in Massachusetts who vacated their homes in 2007 moved following foreclosure.[112] In Chicago, half the properties that become bank-owned REO in the first quarter of 2009 were in neighborhoods where more than 80 percent of the residents were African-American.[113] These communities then got hit with a second blow: job loss. African-Americans, who never gained back the ground they lost in the 2001 recession, were looking at 15 percent unemployment as of August 2009. Hispanics were close behind at 13 percent.[114]

For almost two million children, subprime foreclosures meant having to move, sometimes to homeless shelters. Cleveland alone had 2,100 homeless children enrolled in its schools in April 2008, a 30 percent increase over the prior year. In some districts, school buses had stops at homeless shelters, motels, and RV parks. These children suffered gaps in their learning when they moved, and their friendships and sense of community were fractured. Studies on educational disruption uniformly find that children who move frequently perform less well on standardized tests and are more likely to be held back in school and to drop out.[115]

The one thing that is impossible to assess, but everyone knows is true, is that subprime lending extracted a tremendous emotional toll, especially on those who lost their homes. Homes are not simply assets. They are the places where people live, raise children, care for the people they love, and play, where life events are celebrated, rituals performed, and much more. When people lose their homes, they lose a deep emotional connection. For some people this loss was too much to bear. A woman in Massachusetts killed herself after faxing a letter to her mortgage company that she would be dead by the time people showed up for the foreclosure auction that afternoon. In Ohio, sheriff's deputies were standing with eviction papers outside the home of a ninety-year-old woman whose property had been foreclosed upon, when the woman shot herself multiple times.[116]

## A PERILOUS BALANCE

At the end of 2009, the country found itself at a delicate pass. Financial markets were slowly recovering, due in no small part to the bold and creative measures taken by Bernanke, Paulson, and Geithner. Corporate bond issuance had revived, the stock market had risen 23.5 percent, and municipal bond market conditions had improved.[117] By October 2009, the three-month LIBOR-OIS spread had returned to its precrisis

**FIGURE 6.5.**
All boarded up, Cleveland. (Kathleen C. Engel).

level of ten to fifteen basis points.[118] Financial markets had stabilized enough to end three of the federal government's extraordinary bailout programs: the Money Market Investor Funding Facility at the Fed, the Money Market Fund Program at the Treasury Department, and the Debt Guarantee Program at the FDIC.[119] In addition, the Fed and the Treasury had started scaling back other relief programs as private financing sources improved.[120]

In other respects, the nation's economy remained precarious. In 2008 and 2009, the United States lost 7.6 million jobs. Unemployment stood at 10 percent in December 2009 and the jobless ranks contained an unusually high percentage of the long-term unemployed, compelling Congress to extend unemployment benefits in November 2009 for up to ninety-nine weeks—almost two years. Even with federal aid, over half the people who became unemployed had to borrow money from family and friends. An equal number were forced to reduce their medical care. In 2009, bankruptcy filings jumped to 1.4 million, up 32 percent from 2008's rate.[121] As despair increased, so, too, did mental health issues, family conflicts, and feelings of shame.[122]

Poverty was also on the rise. Some experts predicted that by the end of 2009, one out of every seven people would be living below the poverty line of $22,000 per year for a family of four. The poverty rate among African-American and Hispanic people was almost 25 percent. Hunger was rampant, with forty-nine million Americans reporting a lack of food and one out of eight citizens on food stamps. Homeless shelters found more people at their doors. The housing market was not recovering and more borrowers were falling behind on their mortgages. By the fall of 2009, 7.5 million borrowers were thirty days or more behind on their loan payments or in foreclosure and 42 percent of all subprime loans were a month or more past due. Default rates on pay-option ARMs were expected to rise as borrowers experienced, on average, a 60 percent increase in their monthly mortgage payments when their rates adjusted.[123]

Pay-option ARMs were not the only time bomb. Almost three million people held interest-only mortgages worth over $900 billion. By September 2009, in California, Florida, and Nevada, more than 20 percent of borrowers with interest-only *prime* loans were at least sixty days late.[124] Goldman Sachs estimated that over 50 percent of all pay-option loans would eventually default.[125]

Housing prices appeared to stabilize briefly in the early fall of 2009, but there was concern about another downturn by year-end. With more foreclosed homes being put up for sale, housing prices continued to drop. Experts projected that the number of foreclosed homes on the market would exceed well over one million by the middle of 2010, an increase of 300,000 over July 2009's figure.[126]

Together, these problems in the labor and housing markets put added pressure on the financial health of banks. With each new wave of joblessness and each new drop in home values, loan losses grew. Toxic assets continued to drag down big banks and growing defaults in the commercial real estate market posed a fresh source of woes. Although bank runs had mercifully receded, banks were failing at an increasing rate in late 2009.[127]

Broad swaths of the financial system remained on federal life support. In the fall of 2009, nine out of ten new mortgages were financed by the U.S. government.[128] Public confidence in banks depended on higher basic deposit insurance plus a blanket guarantee of business checking accounts. Consumer lending was sickly and functioning

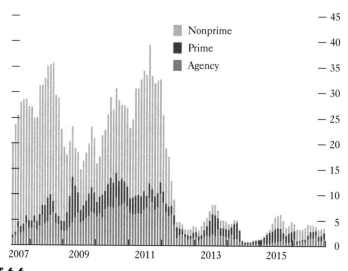

**FIGURE 6.6.**
Monthly mortgage rate resets (first reset in billions of U.S. dollars). *Source*: Credit Suisse.

only because of federal backing of the consumer asset-backed securities market. The commercial paper market, while improved, remained significantly below its mid-2007 high, making the Fed reluctant to close down its Commercial Paper Funding Facility.[129] In view of these concerns, in September 2009, the Treasury Department said that it was "unclear whether the improvements achieved to date will persist without a period of continued government support."[130]

The roots of the subprime crisis date back more than 20 years. Over that time, the federal government had the knowledge, the resources and the power to stem the tide of abusive lending. Instead, by failing to act, the government inflicted disastrous harm on the American people and backed itself into risky and tragic choices that would haunt the nation for years to come. For in saving the world's economy from the abyss, the U.S. government had sent banks an unmistakable sign that they could reap the profits from going for broke while saddling U.S. taxpayers with any losses.

# Part III

▷

# Regulatory Failure

Federal regulators acted in time to stop a complete collapse of the world economy, but where were they when consumers and their advocates, researchers, cities, and states were warning about the growing abuses in the subprime market? Even when the chorus reached a deafening crescendo in 2006, regulators continued to shrug their shoulders at the problems in subprime. Their indifference was part and parcel of the same deregulatory agenda that prompted Congress to abolish substantive controls on home mortgages in the early 1980s. From then on, the federal government embraced the credo that the market, not the government, was the one to fix problems in the mortgage market.

Federal regulators gave subprime lending their blessing by leaving subprime loans untouched, even though many of the loans violated the most basic tenet of lending: that no loan should be made unless the borrower can repay. Worse yet, federal regulators actively resisted using their substantial powers of rule-making, examination, and sanctions to crack down on the proliferation of virulent loans. At the same time, they gave banks the green light to invest in subprime mortgage-backed securities and CDOs, leaving the nation's largest financial institutions awash in toxic assets.

The subprime crisis didn't have to happen. It could have been stopped. We proceed with our cautionary tale of how federal regulators abdicated their responsibility.

▷

# The Clinton Years

Subprime lending took off in the early 1990s, while Bill Clinton was president. During the Clinton presidency, many of the same problems that resulted in the credit crisis in 2007 and 2008 came to light. These problems included high default rates, consumer abuses, bank failures from subprime loans, and the wholesale failure of subprime lenders in 1998 and 1999 due to illiquidity after investors briefly fled the subprime securitization market.

During the 1990s, the federal government's response to the hazards of subprime lending was uneven. Congress passed legislation governing subprime loans in 1994, but that law had little effect. At the other end of Pennsylvania Avenue, the Clinton administration took the subprime problem more seriously. However, Clinton left office before the administration's reforms could be completed.

## THE BANKING REGULATORS

Before we embark on our discussion of the Clinton era policy on subprime loans, it is important to describe the complex landscape of mortgage regulation, which encompasses Congress, a hodgepodge of federal agencies, and, to a limited extent, the states.

Mortgage lenders come in different varieties. Lenders that take deposits are called *depository institutions*. Depository institutions are either banks or thrifts (which are also called savings associations or savings and loan institutions).

In the United States, most ordinary corporations receive their charter—that is, their operating license—from a state. One of the oddities of U.S. banking is that banks and thrifts have the option of going to a state or the federal government to obtain their charters. A federally chartered bank is known as a *national bank*. You can usually recognize a national bank because the word *National* appears in its name or the term *National Association* (N.A.) is at the end. Thus, the First National Bank of Lawrence and Citibank, N.A., are both examples of national banks. Likewise, a federally chartered thrift institution is called a *federal savings association*. All federal savings associations have the word *Federal* in their name. Finally, depository institutions that obtain a state charter are known as state banks or state thrifts.

Starting in the 1970s, a new breed of mortgage lender emerged that did not take deposits and thus was neither a bank nor a thrift. Mortgage bankers and finance companies were examples of nonbank lenders. Some nonbank mortgage lenders were independent, freestanding corporations. Others were owned by banks or thrifts or otherwise affiliated with them.

To figure out who regulated a particular mortgage lender during the 1990s and 2000s, you needed to know whether the lender was a bank or a thrift or affiliated with one. Independent nonbank lenders were the easiest case. They were regulated primarily by the states. If an independent nonbank lender engaged in an unfair or deceptive act or practice in violation of the Federal Trade Commission Act, however, it also was subject to enforcement by the Federal Trade Commission. (See figure 7.1.)

The story for banks and thrifts was more complicated. As a matter of historical accident and definitely not planning, the United States ended up with four federal banking regulators. Together, they formed an alphabet soup of agencies, with each having jurisdiction over a different type of lender. To start with, all banks and thrifts had a primary federal regulator. For national banks, the regulator was the Office of the Comptroller of the Currency, or the OCC, an agency within the Treasury Department. The Federal Reserve Board regulated state banks that were members of the Federal Reserve System, while the Federal Deposit Insurance Corporation (FDIC) regulated state nonmember banks. Finally, the Office of Thrift Supervision (OTS), another agency within the Treasury Department, supervised all thrift institutions, whether they were federally or state-chartered. State banks and state thrifts were also regulated by state regulators. State regulators, however, did not supervise national banks or federal thrifts. How about nonbank lenders that were subsidiaries or affiliates of banks or thrifts? To make things even more complicated, they had different regulators. Nonbank lenders owned by national banks were supervised by the OCC. Nonbank lenders that were sister affiliates of a bank (whether state or national) were regulated by the Federal Reserve Board. Finally, nonbank lenders that were owned by a thrift institution or a savings and loan holding company were regulated by OTS.

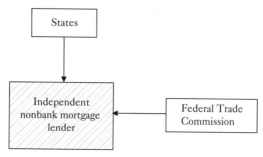

**FIGURE 7.1.**
Regulation of independent nonbank mortgage lenders.

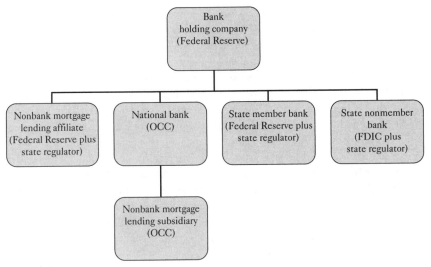

**FIGURE 7.2.**
Regulation of mortgage lenders owned by bank holding companies.

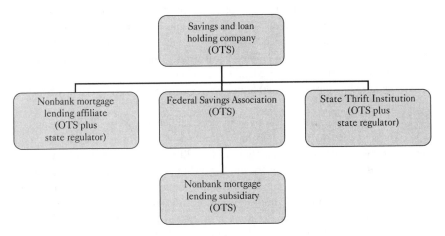

**FIGURE 7.3.**
Regulation of mortgage lenders owned by savings and loan holding companies.

## THE CLINTON ERA

President Clinton came to power just as subprime lending was gaining steam. The banking regulators under his watch saw problems brewing and tried to use their authority to head them off. In contrast, Congress passed only one law curbing subprime lending, the Home Ownership and Equity Protection Act of 1994 (HOEPA), which turned out to be ineffective for reasons we will explain later on.

Concerned legislators did file a handful of stronger anti-predatory lending bills in the House and the Senate. These bills had no real prospect of passage, however, given the implacable opposition of Senator Phil Gramm, the chair of the Senate Banking

Committee, who declared: "I don't know how we can hope to address the problem before we have decided what it is."[1] Gramm's ideological opposition and that of other senators, powerful lobbying by and financial contributions from banks, and the threat of a filibuster created an impasse in the Senate.

The executive branch was not so complacent. The Department of Housing and Urban Development, the Federal Reserve Board, and the Department of the Treasury issued various reports between 1998 and 2000 urging greater regulation of subprime lending.[2] In addition, the Federal Trade Commission and the Justice Department brought a string of well-publicized enforcement actions against bad subprime actors.[3] At the same time, under pressure from HUD secretary Andrew Cuomo, Fannie Mae and Freddie Mac amended their guidelines to prohibit purchases of predatory loans.[4]

The real action under President Clinton was happening at the federal agencies that regulated banks and thrifts, where concern was growing on two fronts. Regulators were alarmed about the risks that subprime lending and securitization posed to the soundness of depository institutions. They also voiced concern about the impact of predatory lending on borrowers.

Of the four federal banking regulators, Ellen Seidman, the Director of OTS, was the most outspoken about the dangers of subprime lending. Under Seidman, OTS actively used its power to deny charters to discourage subprime lenders from becoming federal thrifts. In one case, OTS suspended a charter application by one notorious subprime lender, Associates First Capital, and in another, it persuaded the questionable lender First Alliance to withdraw its application. Seidman also launched a full-scale review of OTS mortgage lending regulations to see whether the rules needed to be beefed up to fight predatory lending more aggressively. As part of that review, OTS sought public input on whether its own regulations were inadvertently boosting abusive lending.

Seidman also addressed growing evidence that lenders were offering people of color worse loan terms than comparably qualified white people. Adopting a model used to test for housing discrimination, in July 2000, Seidman's agency inaugurated a program to send mystery shoppers into thrifts to test for discriminatory lending.[5]

Seidman worked closely with her fellow bank regulators to step up compliance examinations for predatory lending. To improve the examination process, she and fellow regulators proposed collecting more information from banks and thrifts about their subprime operations. Toward the end of the Clinton administration, the regulators also proposed a new rule to increase oversight of risky subprime loans by banks and thrifts.

Donna Tanoue, chair of the FDIC, put subprime lending high on her agenda as well. The FDIC emphasized that the "models used to underwrite loans" were "untested in a recession," and, in a statement of the obvious, stressed that subprime borrowers were especially vulnerable to economic shocks. Tanoue also publicly worried that banks and thrifts were snapping up subprime lenders who would use insured deposits to fund subprime loans.[6]

Concerns about banks' roles in subprime lending came to a head during the fallout from the Asian financial crisis in 1998, when banks canceled credit lines to subprime lenders and securitization deals dried up. Scores of subprime lenders, unable to raise money on the bond markets, faced a cash crunch from which some of them never recovered. Among them were FDIC-insured banks and thrifts.[7] In a chilling premonition of the later credit crisis to come, regulators like Ellen Seidman warned that subprime lenders who relied on the bond markets for financing could face a liquidity crunch if investors lost confidence.

The Asian financial crisis also called into question the adequacy of subprime lenders' capital cushions. Not surprisingly, the FDIC found that the 150 insured banks and thrifts that were engaged in substantial subprime lending were twenty times more likely to become problem institutions than other banks and thrifts. In fact, between 1998 and 1999, six out of eleven bank and thrift failures were due to subprime lending run amok.

Two bank failures stand out because of their inadequate accounting of subprime mortgage-backed securities. During this period, lenders who made subprime loans for securitization typically retained the bottom (or residual) tranches of the securities carved from the loans they made, which, as readers may recall, meant they were holding the riskiest securities. The FDIC seized Pacific Thrift and Loan Company (PTL) in 1999 after finding that the bank had inflated its residual interests in subprime loans, leaving it insolvent. The more spectacular failure, that same year, was First National Bank of Keystone. Keystone had perpetrated a massive fraud to inflate the value of its holdings of subprime-backed securities. In the process, Keystone went so far as to bury key financial records to deceive OCC examiners.[8]

Savings and loan institutions managed to duck failures from subprime loans in the immediate wake of the 1998 credit crisis. Three years later, however, in July 2001, Superior Bank, FSB, became the first OTS institution to succumb to rash subprime lending. Superior had expanded aggressively into the origination and securitization of subprime mortgages beginning in 1993. Like PTL, Superior retained the first-loss position in its subprime securitizations. Eventually, these residual positions grew so large that Superior amassed a "high concentration of extremely risky assets."[9] Worse yet, Superior blatantly overvalued these residuals. When the OTS finally blew the whistle and forced Superior to write down its assets, the bank became "significantly undercapitalized" and was forced to close.[10]

Donna Tanoue took on the task of persuading the other federal banking regulators that subprime lending and the resulting securities subprime lenders were holding were a significant problem. Ultimately and after much effort, Tanoue prevailed and the regulators adopted a rule requiring banks and thrifts to hold more capital against their equity interests in subprime securitizations.[11]

In sum, once the Clinton-era regulators realized they had a problem, they attempted to put rules with teeth in place to prevent those problems in the future. One rule, on the capital treatment of securitized residuals, was adopted, but another, more important rule was not. That was the proposed rule to regulate subprime lending by banks and thrifts. But the Clinton years came to an end before the rule could be adopted in final form.

8

▷

# OTS and OCC Power Grab

With President Bush in the White House, curtailing subprime lending was not a priority, even though predatory lenders were sweeping the country. States and cities responded to Washington's inaction by passing anti-predatory lending laws of their own. Lenders, worried about potential liability, quickly organized a full-scale attack on the state and local initiatives. Lobbyists from the lending industry descended on statehouses and convinced legislators to water down or defeat proposed laws. When municipalities passed subprime lending ordinances, the American Financial Services Association and its allies challenged the constitutionality of those ordinances— and won.[1]

Lenders' most potent strategy lay in challenging the state and local laws under an obscure doctrine known as federal preemption. When a federal law "preempts" a state or local law, it overrides the application of that law, either in part or whole. Federal preemption proceeds from the idea that some policy areas demand one federal law, not fifty different state laws. When Congress or the executive branch invokes federal preemption, it is deciding that the country needs national uniformity in that area. Federal preemption can also mean that states lose authority to enforce their own laws in certain areas. The result is a shift in the balance of power, taking power away from the states and putting it in the hands of the federal government.

## FEDERAL PREEMPTION BY THE OTS AND OCC

In the early 1990s, all banks and thrifts had to obey state laws that were in effect on mortgages. Nonbank mortgage lenders had to comply with those laws as well. In 1996, however, that changed when the Office of Thrift Supervision (OTS) issued two preemption rules, declaring that state mortgage laws no longer applied to federal thrifts or their subsidiaries.[2] As a result, federal thrifts were able to operate under one set of laws wherever they did business across the nation.

By exempting federal thrifts from state mortgage laws, OTS took a level playing field and tilted it. Other lenders had to comply with state laws, but federal thrift institutions did not. At first, this competitive advantage for federal thrifts had relatively little bite. At the time, in the late 1990s, few states had laws restricting predatory lending and the laws that did exist were quite narrow. In addition, federal banking regulators were cracking down on abusive lenders and OTS was not using the OTS preemption rule as an escape from regulation.[3]

The climate changed with the election of President George W. Bush. In 2001, the Bush administration deep-sixed Seidman's proposal to institute new anti-predatory lending rules for depository institutions. It also decided to use OTS's preemption rule to halt state efforts to restrict unfair lending practices. Overnight, in the name of pre-emption, the OTS created a "safe zone" for federal thrifts.

In the meantime, the Office of the Comptroller of the Currency was hungrily eyeing the OTS, eager to give the same competitive advantage to national banks. As state anti-predatory lending laws proliferated, national banks lobbied the OCC for federal preemption privileges.[4] In 2004, the comptroller of the currency, John D. Hawke Jr., issued a preemption rule for national banks. The rule excused national banks and their subsidiaries from having to comply with state consumer protection laws related to mortgage lending.[5] Under a sister regulation, called the visitorial powers rule, the comptroller even barred the states from enforcing state laws that were not preempted—such as state lending discrimination laws—against national banks and their subsidiaries.[6]

The OCC rule sparked a firestorm of controversy. States had regulated consumer protection at national banks for over a century. With its preemption rule, the OCC toppled that tradition by disabling the states' ability to redress consumer protection violations by national banks. What is more, the OCC extended federal preemption to the nonbank subsidiaries of national banks, even though they were chartered by the states.

In the ensuing controversy, OCC officials went on the offensive, accusing states and consumer groups of bad faith. Questioning why states tried to apply their anti-predatory lending laws to banks, Comptroller Hawke asserted: "Surely there's a political dimension to it. Kicking banks around has been something of a national pastime since the days of Andrew Johnson." Julie Williams, the OCC's chief counsel and the architect of OCC preemption, upbraided those who opposed the rule, complaining that the OCC's "motives" had been "impugned" and that "allegation and innuendo" against the OCC was "standard fare." She even accused the states of fiscal irresponsibility, charging: "States are spending time and money that *could* be directed at practices by [nonbanks]."[7] Eventually, the validity of the OCC's preemption rule worked its way to the U.S. Supreme Court, which voted to affirm OCC preemption.[8]

The OCC preemption campaign played out against the backdrop of massive consolidation in the banking industry. During the late 1990s and throughout the subprime boom, the total number of depository institutions had steadily shrunk.

As the number of institutions dwindled, state and federal chartering authorities for banks and thrifts locked horns to preserve their turf. The best way for a regulator to preserve turf was to entice bigger institutions to its charter. And the best way to do that was to offer them a bigger menu of legally permissible banking activities and gentler regulation and laws.

Preemption helped alleviate two handicaps under which the OCC had labored. One, national banks pay higher fees on average than state banks, which can discourage

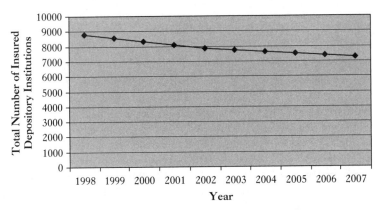

**FIGURE 8.1.**
Total number of insured depository institutions: 1998–2007. *Source*: FDIC Statistics on Depository Institutions.

institutions from becoming national banks.[9] Two, the federal thrift charter was the only charter at the time offering federal preemption. By offering preemption, the OCC hoped it could keep national banks from converting to thrift charters. It likewise hoped to attract state banks and nonbank lenders to the national bank fold. Because OCC preemption, like OTS preemption, provided uniform laws nationwide, it was especially attractive to large national banks with coast-to-coast operations that found it inconvenient to comply with fifty state laws.

## AN UNLEVEL PLAYING FIELD

By 2004, with OTS and OCC preemption firmly ensconced, competitive inequities became set in stone. National banks, federal savings associations, and their mortgage lending subsidiaries were regulated by federal banking regulators, but could ignore state laws. Independent mortgage lenders were free from federal banking regulation, but had to obey a patchwork of state laws, some of which were weak and some of which were strong. State banks, state thrifts, and their nondepository mortgage-lending subsidiaries were subject to both state and federal regulation.[10] The disparity was so severe that in 2005, under chairman Donald Powell, the FDIC flirted with its own preemption rule for state banks.[11]

Federal preemption created incentives for mortgage lenders to shop for the easiest regulators and laws. Even before the preemption rulings, lenders had the ability to pick their regulator. But preemption gave the OCC and OTS a powerful extra lure to entice lenders to their charters, in the form of relief from state anti-predatory lending laws.

Charter shopping was not a hypothetical concern. The story of Countrywide—back then the nation's number one mortgage lender—illustrates the corrosive effect of competition for laxity. From 1990 to 2007, Countrywide's parent company, Countrywide Financial Corporation, owned a national bank named Countrywide Bank, N.A. In 2005, Angelo Mozilo, the CEO of Countrywide, began to chafe under the OCC's regulation of its bank.[12] Hearing of Countrywide's discontent, OTS decided to try to persuade Countrywide Bank to turn in its national bank charter and become a thrift. In 2006, OTS staff, including Darrel Dochow, then the regional deputy director of the West Region of OTS, traveled to Calabasas, California, to meet with the executives at Countrywide's headquarters. There, according to the *Washington Post*, "OTS pitched itself as a more natural, less antagonistic regulator than OCC."[13] Among other things, OTS representatives reportedly portrayed OTS as more willing than the OCC or the Federal Reserve to allow loan officers to pick property appraisers.

The pitch succeeded. Not long after, Countrywide Bank, N.A., applied to convert to a thrift charter. It handily won approval and made the switch from a national bank to a federal savings association on March 12, 2007. The conversion was good for Countrywide, which was able to ditch the OCC and the Federal Reserve as regulators and replace them with OTS. The conversion was also good for OTS, which was able to collect fees from Countrywide covering about 3 percent of the agency's budget that year. And, in turn, the conversion was good for Darrel Dochow. Just six months later, in September 2007, John Reich, the director of OTS, promoted Dochow to be head of the West Region.[14]

Although landing Countrywide was a huge coup for OTS, the OCC was the biggest beneficiary of charter shopping after 2003. Within months after adopting the

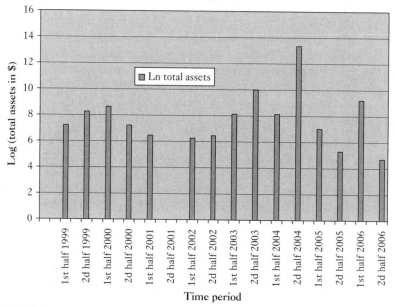

**FIGURE 8.2.**

Conversions from state bank to national bank charters, by log of total assets. *Note*: This chart shows the log of total assets due to the large size of JPMorgan Chase, which converted to a national bank charter in the second half of 2004. At the time, PJMorgan Chase had $649 billion dollars in assets. *Source*: FDIC Statistics on Depository Institutions.

preemption rule, Comptroller Hawke boasted that "the past several months have seen some notable movements of state banks into the national system."[15] JPMorgan Chase, HSBC, and the Bank of Montreal (Harris Trust) were the largest banks that converted from state bank to national bank charters in 2004 and 2005. Of the three, JPMorgan Chase and HSBC were major subprime lenders.

There is additional evidence of charter shopping. When we look at state bank conversions to national banks in terms of assets, the conversions peaked at two critical times: in 1999–2000, around the time that Congress passed the Gramm-Leach-Bliley Act that granted broader powers to national banks, and in 2003–2004, when the OCC proposed and then adopted its preemption rule.

Another way to track charter shopping is to compare the growth in total assets under supervision by the OCC to total assets supervised by state banking regulators. The growth in state bank assets largely tracked the growth in national bank assets until 2004, when their paths diverged. That year, the total assets of national banks surged, while the total assets of state banks dropped. It was a good time for banks to trade in their state charters for federal bank charters, which allowed them to avoid the growing body of state anti-predatory lending laws (also called "mini-HOEPA laws").

We can see a similar pattern around 2004 for state and federal thrifts, coinciding with the growth in state anti-predatory lending laws. OTS preemption was contin-uously in effect from 1997 through 2007 and beyond, but it was only when state anti-predatory lending laws multiplied that the number of federal savings associa-tions began increasing while state thrift charters dropped. And, like banks, the dollar amount of assets regulated by the OTS steadily increased.

From 2004 forward, national banks and federal savings associations attracted the lion's share of assets at the expense of state banks and thrifts. This suggests that the OCC and OTS successfully used preemption to boost the total amount of assets—and the fees levied on those assets—under their supervision. Relaxing regulation was the key to their success.

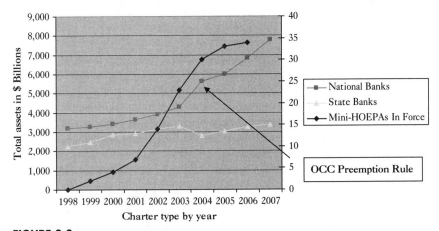

**FIGURE 8.3.**
Growth of mini-HOEPA laws by growth in total assets of state and national banks: 1998–2007. *Source*: FDIC Statistics on Depository Institutions.

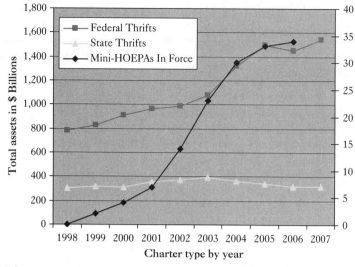

**FIGURE 8.4.**
Growth in mini-HOEPA laws by growth in total assets of state and federal thrifts: 1998–2007. *Source*: FDIC Statistics on Depository Institutions.

## PREEMPTION'S EFFECT ON CONSUMERS

OCC and OTS preemption had three harmful effects on borrowers, the first being inadequate redress. Most state anti-predatory lending laws allowed injured borrowers to sue their lenders for violations. However, in contrast, federal preemption prevented borrowers who received loans from national banks, federal savings associations, or their subsidiaries from suing their lenders for lending abuses under state laws. Borrowers could not even raise state law violations as defenses to foreclosure. Similarly, state attorneys general and other state officials could not protect borrowers by enforcing state laws prohibiting predatory lending against national banks and thrifts. Borrowers had to settle for complaining to federal regulators' call centers, whose first response was to tell customers, "If your case involves [a factual or contract dispute with the bank], consult an attorney for assistance."[16]

Second, federal preemption meant that affected borrowers with loans from national banks and federal thrifts had virtually no remedy because federal lending laws were extremely weak. This gap didn't bother federal regulators, like Hawke's successor as comptroller, John C. Dugan, who took the position that national banks shouldn't be subject to state laws even if they made sense. And, if there was a void, he and fellow regulators maintained, it was up to Congress to fill it.

Lastly, in response to the OCC and OTS preemption rules, state banks and thrifts lobbied state regulators for the same hands-off treatment so they would have competitive parity with their federally chartered counterparts. Some states acquiesced by not regulating subprime loans at all. Other states, like Georgia, waived their anti-predatory lending laws for state banks and thrifts. In these ways, preemption turned the playing field into one "with no rules."[17]

## JUDGING BY THE RESULTS

In defense of federal preemption, Comptroller Dugan maintained that the OCC's "comprehensive" supervision resulted in lower mortgage default rates.[18] You be the jury. The FDIC reported that among depository institutions, federal savings associations regulated by OTS had the worst default record for one- to four-family residential mortgages from 2006 through 2008. (See figure 8.5.) In 2007 and 2008, OCC-regulated national banks had the second-worst record. Both years, state thrifts had better default rates than either national banks or federal thrifts. State banks invariably had the lowest default rates of all.

Of these four types of charters, only national banks regulated by the OCC and federal thrift institutions regulated by OTS enjoyed federal preemption. State banks and state thrift institutions did not. Thus, at least when we compare depository institutions, federal preemption was associated with *higher* default rates, not lower ones, from 2006 through 2008. Those were the years when loan underwriting was at its worst and the credit markets experienced a meltdown.

These statistics have limitations. They do not tell us whether independent nonbank lenders had higher default rates than banks or thrifts. Similarly, we do not control for the credit quality of loan portfolios or other factors. Despite these limitations, however, the statistics refute the claim that federal preemption lowered default rates among mortgages by depository institution lenders. To the contrary, the best loan performance was at state banks and thrifts, which were subject to both state and federal regulation and did not enjoy preemption.

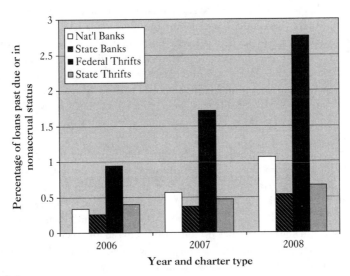

**FIGURE 8.5.**
Residential mortgages at least 30 days past due or in nonaccrual status, by charter type: 2006–2008. *Source*: FDIC Statistics on Depository Institutions.

## REGULATORY TOOLS

During the furor over federal preemption, the OCC and the OTS were mindful of charges that they were relaxing regulation. In response, both agencies went on the offensive, arguing that their brand of regulation was superior to state laws designed to restrict abusive lending.

States with anti-predatory lending laws regulated credit by restricting risky under-writing practices and harmful features in loan products. The laws were enforceable by state banking regulators, state attorneys general, and aggrieved borrowers. Federal banking regulators used an entirely different toolkit. Bank examinations and agency enforcement, not lawsuits, were the mainstays of banking supervision. By law, regulators had to examine banks and thrifts for safety and soundness every twelve months, or every eighteen months for smaller institutions in good condition. In addition, bank and thrift examiners reviewed institutions for compliance with consumer and fair lending laws.[19]

If examiners found a violation of law or a safety and soundness problem, they could write it up in their examination reports. In addition, agencies could take enforcement measures. Most banking regulators preferred *informal enforcement*, in part because it was comparatively congenial and cooperative in nature. Informal enforcement could range from resolutions or commitment letters signed by a bank's board of directors to supervisory directives and voluntary written agreements negotiated between the regulator and the bank. Depending on the agency, these voluntary agreements were known as supervisory agreements or memoranda of understanding (MOUs). In contrast, *formal enforcement* was usually harsher and could be imposed by an agency unilaterally, over management's objections. Regulators had a variety of formal enforcement techniques at their disposal, including safety and soundness agreements, cease-and-desist orders, civil money penalties, and orders removing management.[20]

Banking regulation depended on regulators, not consumers or elected officials, for enforcement. This regulatory structure put enormous discretion in regulators' hands. Zealous regulators could use their discretion in ways that were too harsh. Other times, regulators could do too little. Lax regulation was a particular concern because regulators often identified closely with the banks they supervised. There were different reasons for regulatory capture in the banking industry. Top regulators often were recruited from the ranks of bankers or lawyers for banks. Similarly, regulators wanted to keep their regulated institutions content to discourage them from converting to other charters.

If a regulator wanted to be lenient, there were lots of ways to do it. One was to delay examinations or forego them altogether. Another was to delay initiating enforcement actions. Still another was to refuse to ratchet up enforcement to formal action when an institution's condition was deteriorating but corrective steps had not been taken.

Regulators often shied away from formal action because informal enforcement was private and usually the product of consensus between the regulator and the bank. Informal enforcement, however, had major downsides. One was that bank management could drag its feet and try to water down a voluntary agreement during negotiations. Another was that some types of informal enforcement were not enforceable in court. If management eventually reneged on promises made during informal enforcement, regulators lost valuable time and losses could mount in the meantime. This scenario played out repeatedly during the 1980's savings and loan crisis, when foot-dragging by regulators and management of ailing thrifts alike multiplied the ultimate cost of the crisis to U.S. taxpayers. Finally, informal enforcement was secret, which allowed slack regulators to cover their tracks.[21]

In spite of, or perhaps of, the deficiencies in bank examinations, the OCC and OTS liked to plug banking supervision as the best way to detect and stop careless lending practices. John Reich, the director of OTS, often stressed the "seamless supervision" of thrifts and their holding companies as an advantage of the thrift charter. Similarly, John Hawke at the OCC argued strenuously that banking supervision was better than state anti-predatory lending laws in policing abuses:[22]

> We know that it's possible to deal effectively with predatory lending *without* putting impediments in the way of those who provide legitimate subprime credit. It's an unnecessary consequence because the approach that's been followed is an across-the-board, one-size-fits-all approach that applies to the good as well as the wrongdoers.
>
> We believe a far more effective approach would be to focus on the abusive practitioners, bringing to bear our formidable enforcement powers where we find abusive practices—after clearly articulating our expectations.

In Hawke's view, punishing wrongdoers after the fact was preferable to regulating underwriting practices up front.

## GUIDANCES OVER RULES

Federal regulators could have addressed abusive lending by adopting hard law in the form of binding rules prohibiting exploitative loan terms and careless underwriting of home mortgages, but they refused to take this step. Instead, during the Bush administration, all four federal banking regulators, including the OCC and OTS, addressed risky loans through advisory guidances and other types of soft law, not binding regulations. In fact, during this period, there was only one binding rule on abusive mortgage lending for loans not covered by HOEPA, and that rule was issued solely by the OCC.

The paucity of rules was, in part, due to regulators' aversion to dictating underwriting standards to lenders. In addition, they did not want to give independent nonbank lenders a competitive edge by imposing rules that would apply solely to depository institutions.[23] And finally, guidances gave regulators discretion to sit tight and *not* institute enforcement actions. As the OCC explained:[24]

> If a national bank fails to meet a standard prescribed by a regulation, the OCC must require it to submit a plan specifying the steps it will take to comply with the standard. If a national bank fails to meet a standard prescribed by a guideline, the OCC has the discretion to decide whether to require the submission of such a plan.

Guidances, thus, allowed for slack regulation and permitted lenders to argue that compliance was optional. Dugan encouraged this type of thinking when, in October 2006, he stressed what the guidance on nontraditional mortgages did not do: "It is *not* a ban on the use of nontraditional mortgage products. It does *not* impose a limit on the number of nontraditional mortgages that an institution may hold. And it does *not* impose any new capital requirements."[25]

In sum, with federal preemption came responsibility. Federal preemption displaced state and local law and gave the OCC and OTS sole enforcement power. Once those agencies asserted that power, they had a corresponding responsibility to protect people. If federal oversight was deficient—as it was under the OCC and OTS during the George W. Bush years--injured parties ended up with no legal redress against national banks, federally chartered thrifts, or their lending subsidiaries.

Federal preemption was a particularly toxic brew because it encouraged lenders to shop for legal regimes and charters. Because lenders that were not depository institutions could escape regulation in states with weak laws, that put pressure on federal banking regulators to relax their standards to give the entities they regulated a competitive advantage. A downward spiral in lending standards quickly resulted.

▷

# Put to the Test: OCC, OTS, and FDIC Oversight

The OCC and OTS not only instituted federal preemption and refused to adopt binding rules that would have mandated safe underwriting practices, but they also failed to take formal enforcement actions against troubled banks and thrifts. As the agencies turned a blind eye to unsafe loans, what began as a mortgage crisis turned into a banking crisis of catastrophic proportions.

Their sister regulator, the Federal Deposit Insurance Corporation, did not preempt state anti-predatory lending laws for the community banks it regulated. While a few FDIC-regulated banks got into trouble with subprime loans, for the most part FDIC institutions steered clear of those products. As a result, FDIC-regulated banks only had a small role in the unfolding subprime crisis.

## THE OFFICE OF THE COMPTROLLER
## OF THE CURRENCY

When it came to reckless lending, all three comptrollers of the currency after 2000 maintained that national banks were "*not* where the real problem exist[ed]."[1] Comptroller John C. Dugan asserted, for instance, that national banks made only 10 percent of subprime loans in 2006. In making this statement, Dugan picked his words carefully. He ignored the role that OCC preemption played in hastening a race to the bottom by federal regulators and the states. Furthermore, he conveniently failed to mention that national banks had moved aggressively into Alt-A low-documentation and no-documentation loans during the housing boom. These loans were ticking time-bombs. Indeed, according to the OCC's own statistics, by the first half of 2008, one of the two main drivers of new foreclosures was low-doc and no-doc loans.[2]

Dugan neglected to mention another big issue, which is that large national banks posed far more systemic risk than independent nonbank lenders. In September 2008, Wachovia Bank, N.A., one of the country's largest banks, suffered a run on deposits due to bad pay-option ARMs made by its affiliate. Federal regulators hastily engineered a rescue rather than let Wachovia fail. In contrast, when the New Century Financial

Corporation, a top subprime lender, but not a bank, failed and filed for bankruptcy in 2007, the federal government did not even consider throwing it a lifebuoy.

The OCC was not completely passive. In 2004, the agency adopted a rule banning unfair and deceptive acts and practices and mortgages made without regard to borrower's ability to repay.[3] At the time the OCC adopted the rule, the prospects for vigorous enforcement were not high because the rule was vague. It did not explicate what constituted an unfair or deceptive lending act or practice and, even though the OCC wrote the rule, the agency lacked the authority to define discrete practices that violated the rule.[4]

As for the ban on unaffordable mortgages, the rule allowed national banks to "use any reasonable method to determine a borrower's ability to repay, including, for example . . . credit history, or other relevant factors." This opened the door to such dubious practices as qualifying borrowers solely based on their credit scores for low-doc and no-doc loans. Almost by definition, such loans did not entail any assessment of borrowers' ability to repay. [5]

Oftentimes, OCC chiefs said "the right thing" when it came to subprime loans. Both Dugan and Julie Williams, the acting comptroller of the OCC before Dugan took the helm, routinely denounced risky lending practices. In spring 2005, Williams warned loan review professionals about the dangers arising from the proliferation of low-doc and no-doc loans at national banks. Three months later, in June 2005, an OCC survey of mortgage underwriting practices at the seventy-one largest national banks confirmed the problem, reporting a surge in "higher credit limits and loan-to-value ratios, lower credit scores, lower minimum payments, more revolving debt, less documentation and verification, and lengthening amortizations" in home mortgages. The report stressed that all of these practices "introduced more risk to retail portfolios."[6]

A few months later, in September 2005, Dugan gave a speech to the American Bankers Association, in which he warned of "looser underwriting standards" and questioned "how these loans will fare in the event of a rise in interest rates or a softening in house prices."[7] The following month, Dugan addressed OCC credit risk experts on the same problem.

In the fall of 2005, Dugan took the further step of spearheading an interagency guidance on nontraditional mortgage loans that eventually appeared in final form in September 2006.[8] The guidance looked strong at first glance, but it was incomplete in several respects. It did not cover subprime loans generally, only interest-only and pay-option ARMs. And, even for those products, the guidance placed no firm limits on low-doc and no-doc underwriting.

The subprime guidance was one of many examples of the OCC talking out of both sides of its mouth. At the same that the OCC was emphasizing the need for careful underwriting, it was limp-wristed when it came to supervision and enforcement. In 2004, Comptroller Hawke reassured the American Bankers Association that the OCC only used enforcement as a last resort:[9]

> It is our practice to identify and seek solutions for problems at an early stage, when there is still the prospect for effective improvement, to work constructively and calmly with our bankers to address concerns—and to escalate the

tone of our comments and our actions only where we are forced to do so because of management's unwillingness or inability to take corrective actions.

For her part, Julie Williams merely told bank risk managers to "manage" the risk of no-doc loans—through debt collection, higher reserves, prompt loss recognition, and testing for compliance with loan policies—instead of limiting or banning those loans outright.[10] In a speech in May 2005, she feebly called on community groups to defray the risk of no-doc loans through borrower counseling, foreclosure prevention hotlines, and buyers' broker services.[11]

Finally, in a 2005 speech to OCC credit risk experts, Dugan stopped short of instructing examiners to downgrade institutions making low and no documentation loans, even though these loans made it impossible for national banks to know whether borrowers could afford to repay. Instead, he just made vague admonitions to "evaluate the quality of loan underwriting, noting any weaknesses and deficiencies in the documentation and decision-making."[12]

### Reckless Lending by National Banks

It was in bank examinations that the OCC could act—or not act—to curtail questionable lending practices and loan terms. We do not know how often the OCC examined any given national bank because bank examinations are shrouded in secrecy. Nevertheless, we can gauge whether national banks and their subsidiaries made risky loans and what impact these lending practices had on banks' long-term viability.

#### National City Bank, N.A.

Exhibit A for dangerous low- and no-doc loans was National City Bank, N.A., in Cleveland. National City Bank owned First Franklin Mortgage, one of the nation's top subprime lenders, which was heavy into low-doc and no-doc loans. In December 2006, just before the subprime market tanked, National City had the foresight to sell First Franklin to Merrill Lynch. As part of the deal, however, Merrill Lynch made National City retain $10 billion of First Franklin's old "non-prime" loans.

That deal provision proved fatal to National City. Between year-end 2006, when National City Bank sold First Franklin, and September 30, 2008, the bank's delinquent loans ballooned, mostly thanks to bad First Franklin loans. National City Corporation reported net losses five quarters straight starting in the third quarter of 2007. By May 2008, National City Bank was deteriorating so fast that the OCC made it sign a secret memorandum of understanding to raise capital, boost risk management, and shed troubled loans. Matters worsened, though, and by late September, the turmoil surrounding Lehman Brothers' collapse threw National City into crisis. By then, the parent company's stock had plummeted 96 percent since year-end 2006, S&P had cut National City Bank's rating, and customers were withdrawing uninsured deposits in droves. Desperate to shore up its finances, National City Bank applied to the Treasury Department for a bailout from the Troubled Asset Relief Program. Treasury, however, turned it down as too weak to qualify. It took a rush takeover by PNC Financial Services Group in Pittsburgh in October 2008 to spare National City Bank from seizure by the FDIC.[13]

### The Five Biggest National Banks

The OCC also looked the other way as the top five national banks engaged in high-risk mortgage lending. All five of these banks posed systemic risk on a scale that made them "too big to fail" and later necessitated federal bailouts.

Bank of America, N.A., was the biggest U.S. bank in terms of assets in 2005. It made stated income and no-doc loans until August 2007, when the bond markets froze. How did these loans do? An Alt-A loan pool that Bank of America securitized in April 2007 gives us some idea. According to the prospectus, 72 percent of the loans in this securitization, known as the "Banc of America Alternative Loan Trust 2007-2," were low-doc or no-doc loans. Just eighteen months after the offering, over 15 percent of the loans in the loan pool were already delinquent, in foreclosure or foreclosed upon, or in bankruptcy.

The bank sustained large mortgage losses that, combined with the acquisitions of Countrywide and Merrill Lynch in 2008, left it in a weakened state. Despite an initial $25 billion federal capital infusion in October 2008, Bank of America Corporation reported a $15.31 billion net loss for the fourth quarter of 2008, requiring another $20 billion federal bailout in January 2009. At the same time, the federal government extended Bank of America protection against losses on $118 billion in loans and mortgage-backed securities.

JPMorgan Chase Bank, N.A., was the second largest U.S. bank in 2005. Its subsidiary, Chase Home Finance, became the fifteenth largest subprime lender in the nation in 2006. That same year, the OCC approved an asset purchase application by the bank over public objections about the bank's "substantial volume" of "no income, no asset," or "NINA," loans. The OCC said it was not concerned about those loans because the bank had proper "checks and balances" in place.[14] Later it came out that a Chase account representative reportedly sent an email titled "ZiPPY Cheats & Tricks," telling mortgage brokers how to inflate loan applicants' income to qualify them for low-doc loans from Chase. Tammy Lish, a former Chase account representative who sent the email, allegedly told *The Oregonian* that another Chase representative had sent her the tips along with other training documents, raising questions about the underwriting controls at Chase.[15] That did not stop the federal government from giving JPMorgan Chase $25 billion in Troubled Asset Relief Program funds in October 2008.

Similarly, in a blooper of major proportions, the OCC let Citibank, N.A., the third largest U.S bank in 2005, buy the subprime lender Argent Mortgage. Citibank bought Argent in September 2007, well after subprime lending had turned into a full-blown crisis. Argent had been an affiliate of the notorious subprime lender Ameriquest, which had agreed to a $295 million settlement for alleged predatory lending with forty-nine states and the District of Columbia in January 2006. Eager to ditch Argent's tarnished name, Citibank immediately renamed it Citi Residential Lending and announced that its new subsidiary would specialize in Alt-A and nonprime loans.

"Internally," according to the *New York Times*, "many Citi bankers [saw the purchase of Argent] as 'catching a falling knife.'"[16] The bankers were right. In a few short months, Citi Residential was ailing. By early May 2008, Citibank announced it was phasing out Citi Residential's lending operations. Undone by its penchant for risk, by fall 2008, Citigroup was on the ropes, needing not one, but two emergency federal bailouts totaling $45 billion. As part of that rescue, the federal government guaranteed up to $306 billion in bad Citigroup loans.[17] In January 2009, Citigroup announced an $8.29 billion net loss for the fourth quarter of 2008, putting pressure on the new Obama administration to shore up Citigroup again.

The OCC also dropped the ball regarding Wachovia Bank, N.A., which was big into residential mortgage lending through its two large mortgage subsidiaries, AmNet Mortgage and Wachovia Mortgage Corporation. Both had expanded into Alt-A loans as the credit boom progressed. A Wachovia loan submission form dated March 2007 told brokers that Wachovia Mortgage could offer them the following Alt-A products, notwithstanding the OCC's rule requiring ability to repay:

Stated Income/Stated Assets (SISA) loans
No Income, No Assets (NINA) loans
No Income, No Asset, No Employment (NINANE) loans

Wachovia expanded so aggressively into Alt-A territory that by the first half of 2007, Wachovia Bank was the twelfth largest Alt-A lender in the nation. By August 2007, however, investors pulled the plug on securitizations, and Wachovia abruptly stopped originating all Alt-A home loans. By May 2008, Fitch had downgraded tranches of securitized Wachovia Mortgage Alt-A loans dating from 2005 and 2006 and declared their prognosis "negative." Days before the third quarter ended in 2008, fears over the bank's condition ignited a silent run on Wachovia Bank and forced it into a shotgun marriage with Wells Fargo.

That takes us to Wells Fargo Bank, N.A., the fifth largest U.S. bank in 2005 and the seventh largest subprime lender in 2006. In a prospectus for one of Wells Fargo's Alt-A securitizations in 2007, the company reported that over 75 percent of the loans in the loan pool were low-doc or no-doc loans. Wells Fargo publicly admitted in the filing that it had loosened its underwriting standards in the second quarter of 2005 with knowledge that delinquencies and foreclosures could increase. Wells Fargo also revealed that it waited until after loan closings—when the money was already out the door—to verify whether the brokers who originated the weakest loans in the pool, the Alt A Minus loans, had followed the bank's underwriting rules. Worse yet, Wells Fargo admitted that it had financed loans through third parties—usually brokers— even though the brokers had not complied with Wells' underwriting standards.[18] This was a blatant violation of an OCC bulletin that required Wells Fargo to "implement an ongoing oversight program over" mortgage brokers' activities.[19]

Eventually, Wells Fargo had second thoughts about its lax underwriting and tight-ened its underwriting criteria for Alt-A Minus loans in February 2007. Later, in Octo-ber 2008, Wells Fargo received a $25 billion dole in TARP funds, courtesy of U.S. taxpayers.

## Small and Medium National Banks

Big national banks were not the only ones that plunged into risky no-doc loans. Smaller national banks did as well.

First Tennessee Bank, N.A., a medium-sized national bank that was headquartered in Memphis, made subprime, low-doc, and no-doc residential mortgages through its subsidiary, First Horizon Home Loans. When the subprime market crashed and investors refused to buy more securitized subprime loans, First Tennessee was stuck with bad loans in the pipeline. For 2007, its parent company reported a $170.1 million loss, largely due to losses on mortgage loans. The parent blamed a "significant increase in [home mortgage] delinquencies" for its 242 percent jump in nonperforming loans from year-end 2006 to year-end 2007.

First Tennessee was also loaded down with other types of past due loans that raised "serious doubts about the borrower's ability to comply with present repayment terms." First Tennessee finally threw in the towel in June 2008 and sold the bulk of its mortgage servicing and mortgage origination business to MetLife Bank. That did not resolve the bank's bad loans, though, because MetLife astutely refused to assume First Tennessee's subprime and Alt-A mortgages.[20] Largely because of these problems, Bankrate.com awarded First Tennessee only two out of five stars as of June 30, 2008, saying that the bank's loan "underwriting and appraisal standards . . . differ[ed] from normal bank guidelines" and its loan-to-value standards were "not in conformance with prudent underwriting requirements."[21]

At least First Tennessee Bank managed to survive. First National Bank of Nevada did not. The OCC closed the Nevada bank on July 25, 2008, after it found that "the bank's unsafe and unsound practices . . . seriously prejudiced the interests of the bank's depositors and the deposit insurance fund." The bank failed less than a month after it merged with the First National Bank of Arizona. The Arizona bank had made its mark as a subprime lender and a top twenty-five funder of Alt-A home loans in 2006. That year, high-cost subprime loans accounted for 33 percent of its first-lien home purchase loans and a whopping 75 percent of its junior-lien home purchase loans. The Arizona bank had relinquished underwriting control by outsourcing 81 percent of its residential loan originations to mortgage brokers. Subsequently, a Lehman Brothers investment trust sued the parent of the Arizona bank to force it to take back bad loans it had sold to Lehman, alleging that the bank had "misrepresented the values of properties, and the income, debt and employment" of certain borrowers. By March 31, 2008, 11 percent of the Arizona bank's loans were past due. The OCC finally took enforcement action against the bank on June 4 that year, but it was too late to stop the bank's fall.[22]

The public record shows only one time that the OCC banned reduced documentation loans at a national bank—Laredo National Bank, a medium-sized bank in Texas—before the mortgage meltdown began. Dugan used the occasion to give a tough-sounding speech to the Consumer Federation of America. After it issued the *Laredo* order in late 2005, the OCC did not publicly restrict low-doc or no-doc loans again until late 2007 and early 2008, when it entered consent orders prohibiting two more small banks—Ocala National Bank and First National Bank of Goodland, Kansas—from making no-income verification loans. By then, reckless no-doc loans were fomenting a financial crisis. As these examples show, the OCC's preferred enforcement method was to rattle the saber every couple of years by making an example of a local or regional bank while ignoring questionable lending by big national banks.

The OCC's laid-back stance towards enforcement was criticized by the Treasury Department's Inspector General in November 2008. In a report, the Inspector General evaluated the OCC's supervision of ANB Financial, N.A., a small national bank in Arkansas that failed on May 9, 2008 due to lax lending and too many brokered deposits. According to the Inspector General, OCC examiners "identified most of

ANB's problems in 2005" and even placed it on an OCC watch list. In 2006, OCC examiners found that ANB had not yet fixed these problems and its asset quality had deteriorated. Nevertheless, the OCC continued to sit on its hands. Although ANB's condition steadily worsened, the OCC delayed taking formal enforcement action against the bank until June 25, 2007. The Inspector General came down on the agency for dragging its feet, saying: "If OCC had acted more aggressively and sooner, ANB might have acted earlier or differently to address its problems." By the time the OCC sprung into action, the Inspector General concluded, "there was little that could be done to rehabilitate the bank."[23]

In response to the Inspector General's report, Comptroller Dugan conceded that "there were shortcomings in our execution of our supervisory process." Top officials at the OCC then convened a conference call with almost 1500 OCC examiners telling them to take formal enforcement action "while problems are still manageable." Nevertheless, in early 2009, another national bank failed – National Bank of Commerce in Berkeley, Illinois – with no prior public OCC enforcement action.[24]

What explained the OCC's reluctance to crack down on risky lending? One reason was the OCC's push to increase the short-term profitability of national banks. By 2002, fee income made up almost half the operating income of many commercial banks. To protect banks' fees, former comptroller John Hawke opposed state anti-predatory lending laws, complaining that the laws "hurt" the "legitimate business"[25] of banks. Julie Williams later acknowledged that "over the years the OCC . . . encouraged national banks to look to fee income as a way to diversify their income stream."[26] On the cost side of the profit equation, Hawke and Williams criticized consumer protections for saddling banks and regulators with burdensome expenses.[27]

The OCC, like the banks, also fell under the spell of securitization. The OCC prized securitization as a way for banks to offload the risk of exotic loans. In 2005, Dugan told OCC examiners: "Find out if your bank is originating these non-traditional mortgages, and, if so, whether they intend to hold them in their portfolios."[28] The message was that examiners could lower their guard so long as national banks securitized bad loans.

The OCC also believed in a "light touch" approach to risk management that stressed voluntary compliance over government intervention in credit markets. The OCC allowed banks to use their own judgment about hazardous loans so long as the benefits from good loans outweighed the risks from bad ones. Even when risky lending became too blatant to ignore, Dugan and Williams continued to oppose product controls and instead called for stronger "capital, liquidity, and risk management."[29]

Free market ideology also played a role. Regardless of party affiliation, comptrollers revered financial innovation and unfettered consumer choice as articles of faith, to be defended from encroaching consumer regulation. In September 2007, after the credit crisis was in full swing, Dugan remained categorically opposed to restrictions on financial innovations:[30]

> I, for one, would be quite reluctant to outlaw any particular product normally speaking . . . there are many different kinds of innovations that have led to positive things and sorting out which ones are the most positive and somewhat less positive is generally not something that the Federal Government is good at doing.

### Response to the Brewing Crisis

Dugan was not blind to the risks of lax loans. As early as 2005, he predicted the coming crisis: "If real estate prices decline—and there already is evidence of softening in some markets—[pay-option ARM] borrowers could face the bleak prospect of loan balances that exceed the value of the underlying properties."[31] Nevertheless, Dugan let the year pass with no new restrictions on credit. In October 2006, Dugan remarked that "competition among lenders appear[ed] to be intensifying, and, with some exceptions, that competition . . . extended to weaker underwriting standards." "Frankly," he told the American Bankers Association, "that concerns me." He still resisted clamping down on loan products or issuing a guidance on subprime loans. Instead, he called on banks to increase their loan loss reserves.[32] That was like telling someone playing with matches to keep a water bucket nearby.

In early 2007, the mortgage market became unglued. Only then did Dugan and his fellow federal banking regulators propose a subprime guidance with limits on low-doc and no-doc loans. The long delay in issuing the subprime guidance prompted Congressman Sherman, in a hearing before the House Financial Services Committee, to ask Dugan:

> After the hurricane hit, you decided to issue something saying they should be built to standard. You could have prohibited this practice 10 years ago. It was going on 10 years ago. Why did you not?

Dugan had no good answer.[33]

It was not until May 23, 2007, that Dugan gave his first major speech condemning stated income loans.[34] By October 2007, Dugan was finally calling for a federal statute requiring verification of the ability to repay on mortgage loans.[35] By then, however, the big national banks were staggering under the weight of billions of dollars in rash low-doc and no-doc home mortgages.

The history of OCC inaction is a tale of tunnel vision. In its rush to expand turf and boost the short-term profits of its client banks, the OCC undercut the ability of states to enforce their laws against abusive subprime loans. The OCC had the hubris to believe that it could "manage" the risk of imprudent loans by national banks in lieu of bans on reckless loan terms. The agency shrank from cracking down on loan underwriting, apart from advisory guidances and a solitary, vague rule that big national banks chose to ignore. In the meantime, the OCC encouraged national banks to securitize their noxious loans, which resulted in dumping the risk of those loans onto the financial system at large. Even so, enough bad loans and toxic mortgage bonds remained on national banks' books to bring some of the nation's largest banks to their knees. The behemoths were too big to fail, forcing U.S. taxpayers to foot the bill.

## OFFICE OF THRIFT SUPERVISION

The Office of Thrift Supervision was smaller than the OCC, but like its sister agency, OTS offered ironclad federal preemption to the federally chartered entities it regulated. Federal savings associations enjoyed certain unique advantages not shared by banks, including unlimited nationwide branching and consolidated regulation.[36] Thrifts labored, however, under a requirement that they invest at least 65 percent of their assets in consumer and small business loans such as home mortgages, education loans, loans to entrepreneurs, and credit card loans—or face stiffer regulation.[37]

The purpose of this requirement—known as the "qualified thrift lender" or QTL rule—was to channel thrift investments into home mortgages and other types of household loans. As a result, residential mortgages made up a much bigger portion of thrift portfolios, compared to banks. At the end of 2002, residential mortgages comprised 67.5 percent of thrift assets but only 27.3 percent of the assets at commercial banks. This made thrifts less diversified than banks and more exposed to the fortunes of the home mortgage market.[38]

This drawback to the thrift charter dampened the thrift industry's growth and made the thrift charter an obvious target for elimination. There were periodic calls to scrap the thrift charter and merge OTS with the OCC. Slow growth in the thrift industry also posed a budgetary challenge for OTS, because the agency received most of its operating budget from assessments on thrifts.[39]

By the late 1990s, with fee revenue down, OTS was in the red. James Gilleran took over the agency from Ellen Seidman in 2001 and was determined to balance the OTS budget. Around the same time, Charter One Bank FSB decided to give up its thrift charter and become a national bank—a move that cost OTS $4 million in fees and increased the pressure on Gilleran.

Gilleran, who came to be known as "Gut 'Em Gilleran," laid off sixty-nine OTS examiners, including 17.5 percent of its specialized consumer compliance examiners. He also scrapped separate examinations for consumer compliance, announcing that he expected thrifts to conduct compliance "self-evaluations" in advance of their safety and soundness examinations. When Congressman John LaFalce heard about Gilleran's actions, he dashed off an angry response. LaFalce accused Gilleran of "a complete abrogation of the mandate your agency has been given by Congress." LaFalce remarked, "The shortsighted reduction of examiners reminds me of the unfortunate safety-and-soundness experience of the 1980s."[40]

Gilleran also had a plan to boost OTS's fee income by increasing the revenue at thrifts. Changing business conditions made his task difficult. By 2004, rising interest rates were discouraging people from refinancing mortgages and many people could not qualify for fixed mortgages because of high monthly payments and rising home prices.[41] The solution was for OTS to permit thrifts to expand their ARM offerings to include some of the new products that reduced the qualification hurdles for borrowers. The thrift industry was already a major player in conventional ARMs, accounting for more than 45 percent of all ARMs in 2002, so introducing new ARM products did not seem like a stretch.[42] By providing a safe haven to thrifts to originate risky interest-only ARMs and pay-option ARMs, OTS could charge more fees and shore up its balance sheet.

At the same time, Gilleran carried the deregulation banner wherever he went. He was even more passionate about deregulation than his OCC counterparts. For instance, Gilleran stated that his goal as director of OTS was "to allow thrifts to operate with a wide breadth of freedom from regulatory intrusion."[43] At a press conference in summer 2003 to announce relief from regulatory red tape, other federal banking regulators arrived carrying garden shears; Gilleran showed up wielding a chainsaw.

In the fall of 2005, John Reich was appointed Gilleran's successor. John Reich was less colorful than Gilleran, but just as ardent about deregulation. A career community banker, Reich waxed eloquent about regulatory relief, calling it "his favorite topic" and something "near and dear to my heart."[44] As the head of a federal task force on regulatory relief, Reich boasted that he "raise[d] the issue of regulatory burden with almost every new regulation, process, or procedure." Throughout his tenure, Reich argued strenuously that "accumulated regulatory burden" was "suffocating the banking industry."[45] At one point, he downplayed the need for regulation by dismissing concerns about an overheated housing market, saying in March 2006: "Much of the hype about a housing bubble has subsided."[46]

As soon as he was appointed to OTS, Reich started traveling around the country touting interest-only ARMs and pay-option ARMs. In his speeches, Reich defended both types of products, asserting that "some thrifts have offered—and successfully managed—ARMs with negative amortization features for twenty years." As further support, he called the West Coast experience with these products "favorable."[47]

While being a cheerleader for pay-option ARMs, Reich was working behind the scenes to water down the interagency guidance on nontraditional mortgages that the OCC's Dugan had proposed. When the final guidance came out in September 2006, Reich refused to defend it. He even described the guidance as "extremely controversial" and not something that OTS "would have issued on [its] own."[48]

With Reich's patronage, thrifts became major players in subprime lending and captured much of the pay-option ARM and other Alt-A markets. Four of the top five originators of pay-option ARMs were thrift companies. The results were disastrous. Of the seven biggest depository institution failures in 2007 and 2008, five of them were thrifts supervised by OTS. Other big thrifts over that period were forced to merge to avoid failing. All told, in 2007 and 2008, thrifts with assets totaling $355 billion failed under OTS supervision. Most of them succumbed to pay-option ARMs or other types of hazardous home loans.

### IndyMac Bank

During the subprime crisis, the first major depository institution to fail was IndyMac Bank, FSB. IndyMac was the largest thrift in Southern California at the time and the tenth-biggest U.S. mortgage lender in 2007. It specialized in low-doc and no-doc loans, subprime loans, and jumbo mortgages. In 2006, the thrift's parent company, IndyMac Bancorp, became the nation's top Alt-A originator, surpassing even Countrywide, and it stayed in first place through the first half of 2007. OTS regulated both IndyMac Bancorp and IndyMac Bank.

In 2006 and 2007, IndyMac was busy digging its grave, with over half of IndyMac Bank's home purchase loans composed of higher-cost subprime loans. Statistics from an IndyMac subprime securitization from early 2007—known as the INABS 2007-A—reveal how poorly those loans performed. Half of the subprime loans in INABS 2007-A were low-doc loans. By December 2007—less than a year after the offering—a shocking 32 percent of the loans in INABS 2007-A were delinquent, in bankruptcy, or in or through foreclosure.

Eventually IndyMac's business model fell apart. By late 2007, after investors fled mortgage-backed securities, IndyMac was stuck with $11 billion in loans that it could not sell. Soon defaults on those loans soared. Still, when OTS examined IndyMac Bank in January 2008, the agency deemed it well capitalized and gave it a decent exam rating of 2 on a scale of 5, with a 1 being the highest.

But IndyMac's condition quickly plummeted. By June 30, 2008, IndyMac's total risk-based capital had slipped to a dangerously low 4.55 percent. Of IndyMac's loans, 10.47 percent, including 27.17 percent of its homebuilding loans, were noncurrent. As IndyMac's financial woes became known, customers instigated a $1.3 billion run on deposits. Not long after, on July 11, 2008, OTS was forced to close IndyMac Bank.

To regulators' consternation, even after IndyMac closed, FDIC insurance did not quell the public's panic. Instantly, IndyMac became the symbol of lost public confidence in FDIC insurance. Photos of panic-stricken depositors circulated on the Internet, sparking heightened withdrawals at other banks and a massive sell-off of bank stocks. Eventually, IndyMac's demise wiped out between $8.5 billion and $9.4 billion of the deposit insurance fund—almost 20 percent—and left the deposit insurance fund just one major bank failure away from insolvency.

At the time, IndyMac was the second largest bank failure in U.S. history and a huge blot on OTS's enforcement record. OTS had waited until June 20, 2008, to execute a voluntary enforcement agreement with IndyMac and did not impose formal enforcement orders against the company until July 1 and 3, just days before IndyMac failed. When the thrift collapsed on July 11, OTS lamely explained that it had been "finalizing a new set of enforcement actions" that were not yet in place.[49] Later, the Treasury Department's inspector general issued a damning indictment of OTS's multiple failures in overseeing IndyMac.[50]

But the story got worse. The Treasury Department accused a senior OTS official of outright misconduct in his handling of IndyMac. During a routine investigation in December 2008, the inspector general of the Treasury Department determined that Darrel Dochow, the director of the West Region of OTS, had helped manipulate IndyMac's capital status. This was the same Dochow who had been promoted to regional director of the West Region after he convinced Countrywide Bank to become a thrift.

According to the inspector general, Dochow participated in a conference call with Michael Perry, IndyMac's chief executive officer, on May 9, 2008. In the phone call, the inspector general reported, Dochow had given permission to IndyMac's parent company to infuse capital into IndyMac and to backdate $18 million of that capital contribution to March 31, 2008. Without the backdating, IndyMac would have dropped from well capitalized to adequately capitalized as of March 31. That, in turn, would have triggered statutory tripwires requiring IndyMac to get the FDIC's permission to continue to accept brokered deposits, which by no means was assured. At the time, brokered deposits made up 36 percent of IndyMac's deposits. Without these brokered deposits, IndyMac would have faced a severe liquidity crunch and probably would have closed. Although Reich demoted Dochow, he downplayed the incident "as a relatively small factor" in IndyMac's failure.[51]

It is well known that delaying the close of an ailing depository institution compounds the losses to the Deposit Insurance Fund.[52] During the savings and loan crisis of the 1980s, OTS's predecessor, the Federal Home Loan Bank Board, repeatedly delayed closing undercapitalized thrifts, a practice known as "forbearance." OTS engaged in similar forbearance at IndyMac. OTS had strong formal enforcement tools at hand to use against IndyMac, but it declined to use them until the bitter end. Instead, OTS wasted months dithering over a voluntary agreement. Similarly, the backdating incident was a blatant attempt by OTS to prolong IndyMac's life by making it seem better capitalized than it was.

Unfortunately, it appears that the backdating was not an isolated event. During the IndyMac investigation, the inspector general "also discovered that OTS had allowed other thrifts to record capital contributions in an earlier period than received."[53] The discovery eventually precipitated the departure of Reich's successor, acting OTS director Scott Polakoff.

### Washington Mutual Bank

IndyMac was just a taste of things to come. Two months after IndyMac tanked, Washington Mutual Bank (WaMu) collapsed on September 25, 2008, making it the largest U.S. depository institution to ever fail. WaMu had the distinction of being the country's largest savings and loan institution, boasting over $300 billion in assets. In a master stroke, the FDIC engineered an immediate sale of WaMu's deposits, assets, and some of its other liabilities to JPMorgan Chase for $1.9 billion, avoiding any loss to the deposit insurance fund or uninsured depositors. In turn, with WaMu in tow, JPMorgan vaulted to the top to become the largest U.S. bank in terms of deposits.

WaMu got into trouble partly because it had huge exposure to mortgages in California and Florida, where housing values had fallen the most. But there is more to the story. In 2004 and 2005, WaMu pushed heavily into subprime, low-doc, no-doc, and exotic mortgages because they paid more fees. WaMu made such large inroads into pay-option ARMs that on October 21, 2004, WaMu's CEO, Kerry Killinger, bragged to investors that pay-option ARMs were a "flagship product" for WaMu. By June 30, 2007, WaMu ranked fourth in the nation in Alt-A loan originations and sixth in subprime loan originations. Every year from 2004 through 2006, pay-option ARMs, subprime loans, and dicey home equity loans made up more than half of WaMu's total real estate loans.[54] When the joint guidance came out in 2006 telling banks and thrifts to qualify pay-option ARM borrowers at the fully indexed rate, WaMu ignored it and kept qualifying applicants for pay-option ARMs at the low, introductory rate until mid-2007.

At the same time that WaMu was expanding into questionable loan products, it was loosening its lending standards. A former senior mortgage underwriter at WaMu told the *New York Times:* "At WaMu it wasn't about the quality of the loans; it was about the numbers. They didn't care if we were giving loans to people that didn't qualify. Instead, it was how many loans did you guys close and fund?"[55]

From the last quarter of 2007 through the first two quarters of 2008, WaMu announced net losses of $6.6 billion due to rising defaults on mortgages. By June 30, 2008, 27.2 percent of WaMu's 2007 subprime mortgages were at least thirty days past due. Soon afterward, the FDIC started pressuring OTS to cut WaMu's exam rating to troubled status. According to the *Wall Street Journal,* OTS actively resisted downgrading the bank. Finally, on September 8, 2008, a little more than two weeks before the bank's failure, WaMu announced it had entered into a memorandum of understanding (MOU) with OTS to improve WaMu's risk management and compliance systems. In the MOU, WaMu agreed to provide OTS with "an updated, multi-year business plan and forecast for its earnings, asset quality, capital and business segment performance." WaMu stressed, however, that the agreement "did not require the company to raise capital, increase liquidity or make changes to the products and services it provide[d] to customers," giving the impression that the agreement was weak-kneed.

By then, analysts were telling the *Wall Street Journal* that WaMu's "financial position [was] among the worst of any major U.S. financial institution." On Thursday, September 11, Moody's slashed the holding company's credit rating to junk bond status and Standard & Poor's followed suit within days. September 15, when Lehman Brothers filed for bankruptcy, was the beginning of the end. WaMu's depositors got spooked and yanked $16.7 billion out of their accounts. To halt the run, on September 25, the FDIC was forced to put WaMu into receivership. At that point, fully one-sixth of the bank's assets—$52.9 billion—was in disastrous pay-option ARMs and another $16.1 billion was in subprime mortgages.[56]

Where was OTS during WaMu's downward spiral? WaMu was so enormous that OTS examiners were permanently on-site. Despite their presence, OTS never took formal enforcement action against WaMu for imprudent loans. OTS did institute formal sanctions against WaMu in October 2007, when the thrift was staggering under the weight of bad loans, but only for violations of anti-money-laundering laws and flood insurance regulations, not for credit losses. OTS was so cozy with WaMu, in fact, that the company boasted to its investors on June 11, 2008, that it was not the target of regulatory actions and "not currently in such discussions with any regulatory agency," including OTS.[57]

OTS had good reason to resist decisive action. WaMu was the nation's biggest thrift and accounted for the largest slice of the OTS budget. In fact, in 2008, assessments paid by WaMu supplied almost one-eighth—12 percent—of the agency's operating funds.[58] In a prophetic article in 2002, a banking consultant named Kenneth H. Thomas called WaMu "too big to regulate" because OTS could not afford to drive WaMu away and lose its fees. Thomas posed the question: "Does the OTS regulate Wamu, or does Wamu regulate the OTS?"[59]

## Downey Savings & Loan

The third biggest depository institution to fail in 2008 was Downey Savings & Loan, a thrift in Newport Beach, California. Downey, along with Golden West, Countrywide, WaMu, and IndyMac, was a top five originator of pay-option ARMs and, like them, it got burned. For the first nine months of 2008, Downey suffered $547.7 million in net losses, much of the loss coming on delinquent pay-option ARM loans. When Downey failed on November 21, 2008, pay-option ARMs made up half of its total assets. Other Downey losses came from soured subprime refinance loans, which Downey had loaded up on in 2006 and 2007.[60]

Downey's financial problems had been known for some time. The thrift had reported losses for five quarters straight, starting in the third quarter of 2007. By June 30, 2008, more than 14 percent of Downey's total assets were nonperforming, a sixfold increase in just twelve months. The following month, in July, Downey showed up on lists of ailing banks circulating on Wall Street. Soon after IndyMac was seized, the thrift experienced a run on deposits. On July 24, the board ousted Downey's top brass, including its eighty-three-year-old founder.[61]

Once again, OTS delayed instigating enforcement against Downey for bad loans until it was too late. In August 2007, as private-label securitizations were drying up, OTS was fiddling with a cease-and-desist order against Downey for anti-money-laundering violations, not for bad loans. By September 30 that year, Downey's nonperforming loans were 2.21 percent of total assets; by year-end 2007, they had mushroomed to a shocking 7.64 percent. Still, OTS did not wake up to Downey's sorry state until July 2008. It took a bank run on Downey for OTS to finally lower the thrift's exam rating and send it a confidential troubled condition letter. Later, the Treasury Department's inspector general criticized OTS for lax oversight and for dragging its feet in instituting strong enforcement.[62]

Even then, OTS waited until September 5, 2008, before consummating a voluntary cease-and-desist order with the thrift. Although the order required Downey to present OTS with a capital restoration plan, the agency still classified Downey as adequately capitalized. Downey pinned its hopes on a bailout from the Troubled Asset Relief Program, but the federal government turned it down. Downey's death vigil began, and on November 14, the FDIC seized the thrift.[63]

### Wachovia's Acquisition of Golden West and World Savings

In the fall of 2008, Wachovia Corporation became the largest bank holding company to topple to date. Technically, Wachovia Bank did not "fail"—in the sense of being seized by the FDIC—but that was only because the FDIC brokered the bank's sale to Wells Fargo through an unusual and controversial procedure known as "open bank assistance."

In October 2006, in an ill-timed move, Wachovia Corporation bought Golden West Financial Corporation (Golden West) and its two thrift subsidiaries. One of those thrifts was World Savings Bank, FSB, which at the time was the second largest entity regulated by OTS. OTS continued to oversee the thrift after it changed its name to Wachovia Mortgage, FSB, on December 31, 2007.[64]

Herb and Marion Sandler, who sold Golden West to Wachovia, had popularized pay-option ARMs on the West Coast. Golden West made the vast majority of its pay-option ARMs in the overheated California and Florida markets. Although Golden West insisted that it used stringent underwriting standards for pay-option ARMs, according to the Federal Reserve Board, Golden West "require[d] low- or no-documentation on ninety percent" of its loan applications.[65]

Wachovia Corporation shared Golden West's enthusiasm for risky pay-option ARMS. As late as 2007, Wachovia's chief executive officer, Ken Thompson, hailed pay-option ARMs as a "growth area" in a conference call to investors. It wasn't until June 30, 2008, nearly two years after the 2006 nontraditional mortgage guidance warned about the risks of those products, that Wachovia Corporation finally shut down its pay-option ARM machine.[66]

By early 2008, Wachovia Corporation was bleeding ink for an assortment of reasons, including a telemarketing scam, money-laundering charges, sour subprime bonds, charges over the sale of auction rate securities, alleged municipal bond bid-rigging, and bad construction loans. But Golden West was the straw that broke the camel's back. Golden West's $120 billion mortgage portfolio, which was mostly pay-option ARMs, made up nearly one-sixth of Wachovia's assets and explained almost the entire increase in Wachovia's nonperforming consumer loans.

Once again, OTS turned a blind eye. OTS failed to take any public enforcement action against any Wachovia entity to stop imprudent pay-option ARM loans. After the Wachovia acquisition, the only public enforcement action that OTS took was a $33,800 civil money penalty in late October 2007 for *flood insurance violations*, not unsafe loans—just like at WaMu that same month. By then, it was clear that the nation was in a mortgage crisis of catastrophic proportions. Yet OTS was fixated on flood insurance. In all likelihood, OTS did not want to upset Wachovia Mortgage, FSB, because it contributed a large chunk to the agency's operating budget and could easily have jumped to a national bank charter.[67]

It is no coincidence that so many thrift mishaps in 2008 involved institutions on the West Coast. Of course, housing values spiked in California and Nevada during the boom and fell the most when the market went bust. But that's not the only reason for the concentration of failed thrifts out west. All of those thrifts were supervised by one man: Darrel Dochow, the director of the West Region of OTS.

During the 1980s S&L crisis, Dochow had caught flak for delaying the closure of troubled thrifts. Back in 1989, Dochow had headed the Office of Regulatory Activities at OTS's predecessor, the Federal Home Loan Bank Board in Washington, D.C., where he oversaw the collapse of the notorious Lincoln Savings & Loan. According to the *Los Angeles Times*, Dochow had "balked at recommendations" that Lincoln be "shut down two years earlier."[68] For his role in Lincoln, the agency demoted Dochow, but he continued to be employed as an examiner at the newly formed OTS. Over the years, Dochow worked his way back up to the top post in the West Region. With Dochow at the helm, IndyMac, WaMu, Golden West, and Downey all failed. And once again, Dochow stood accused of delaying the closure of ailing thrifts. William Black, a former Federal Home Loan Bank Board lawyer who had blown the whistle on Dochow at FLHBB in the 1980s, marveled at the surreal turn of events: "It is astonishing that even [the Bush] administration would return him to power."[69]

## NetBank

In a remarkable show of consistency, OTS was as lenient with small thrifts as it was with the large ones.

One of the earliest thrift casualties in the subprime crisis was an Internet bank, NetBank, in Alpharetta, Georgia. NetBank was brought down by residential loans marred by lax underwriting, sloppy loan documentation, and weak internal controls. Among other things, NetBank expanded into subprime loans, low-doc and no-doc loans, interest-only ARMs, and pay-option ARMs. When the market for these loans began to soften, NetBank tried "to maintain high loan volumes at the expense of quality of loan originations."

OTS examiners first noticed a decline in NetBank's earnings in 2004. In 2005, agency examiners expressed concern to NetBank's managers about its mounting buy-backs of bad loans. By March 2006, OTS examiners had downgraded NetBank's overall exam rating to a 3 after NetBank's management failed to fix problems noted in earlier exams. In early summer 2006, NetBank required a capital infusion from its parent in order to stay well capitalized. This prompted OTS to issue a negative exam report on NetBank in June and to advise the bank to find a buyer as soon as possible. NetBank's condition continued to unravel, however, and examiners cut its overall rating to a 4 on November 2, 2006. Only then did the thrift consent to a written supervisory agreement, with OTS requiring it to raise capital and restore profitability. The agreement was too late to do any good. The bank failed within the year.[70]

The Treasury Department's inspector general performed an audit on NetBank that identified three problems with OTS's oversight.[71] One was that OTS examiners were not sufficiently aware of the risks from NetBank's mortgage banking operations and lacked adequate training and guidance. This finding is highly troubling, given that Reich liked to brag that OTS had special expertise "in regulating and supervising entities that are primarily mortgage lenders."[72] Contrary to that boast, the inspector general found that OTS allowed NetBank to expand into mortgage products that its own examiners did not understand.

The inspector general flagged another problem, which was that OTS examiners had viewed residential lending as a "low risk" activity. The examiners had also ignored the poor quality of the mortgage loans that NetBank sold to investors "because the loans were not going into NetBank's portfolio." They looked the other way even though NetBank sold the loans with recourse, meaning that NetBank had to buy back any loans that went into early default. Their blunder was not surprising, because the OTS Examination Handbook had no procedures for evaluating credit risk on loans that were sold.

Finally, the inspector general's report criticized OTS for not "react[ing] in a timely and forceful manner to certain repeated indications of problems in NetBank operations." In the IG's view, "OTS should have used enforcement actions sooner to address" NetBank's deteriorating business. According to the audit, as soon as OTS examiners realized that NetBank's management had not addressed the thrift's worsening condition, they should have initiated formal enforcement. Consequently, the inspector general recommended that OTS examiners should presume that formal enforcement action is necessary whenever they lower a thrift's overall exam rating to a 3.[73] Furthermore, the report stated, examiners who issue a 3 should document the reasons whenever formal enforcement action is not taken. In a written response, OTS concurred with the inspector general's criticisms and agreed to adopt his recommendations.

### All Talk, No Action

As the inspector general's report on NetBank demonstrated, OTS even had an aversion to voluntary enforcement agreements, let alone formal enforcement orders. While he was director of OTS, Reich publicly assured bankers that he preferred to work with them "in a collaborative partnership and not with the 'gotcha' mentality."[74] Consistent with that conciliatory approach, the most OTS required from NetBank, IndyMac, and WaMu were voluntary agreements that ultimately were of no value.

OTS did not even begin negotiating with WaMu about an MOU until four months after it had downgraded the thrift, and then the talks dragged on for two more months.[75] This was a pattern with OTS. When OTS discovered abusive loans at another thrift involved in subprime lending, AIG Financial Savings Bank, in May 2006, it did not procure a voluntary supervisory agreement until June 2007.[76]

Reich was averse to enforcement, but he was not blind to the risks of subprime lending. In November 2005, he gave a speech portraying the risks of interest-only and pay-option

ARMs and advised thrifts to "manage" those risks "successfully."[77] In April 2006, he stated publicly that thrifts were caving into pressure from sellers to buy loan participations without full documentation.[78] By fall 2006, Reich was seeing an uptick in troubled assets and in first payment and other early payment defaults. Despite these flags, all Reich had to say was that OTS was "proactively monitoring a number" of problem areas.[79]

### OTS's Response to the Crisis

Even in spring 2007, with the subprime market in flames, Reich was continuing his mantra that "the most important thing we can do in Washington [is] reducing regulatory burden on the industry." He vowed "to pursue additional regulatory relief, to develop support for eliminating as many additional items of regulation as is possible." As for the looming mortgage crisis, Reich promised "not to interfere where market solutions can be more effective and efficient—and [to] impose less regulatory burdens that run counter to the efficient allocation of credit in the housing markets."[80]

Reich went so far as to call greater regulation "extremist behavior," and he opposed even basic underwriting standards, telling a subcommittee of the House Financial Services Committee in March 2007:[81]

> I am a little reluctant to see Congress become so prescriptive as to proscribe [sic] underwriting standards for various types of loans. I feel the same way frankly about regulatory agencies becoming overly prescriptive. That takes away the creativity for bankers to do what they do best in devising solutions for particular borrowers.

The year 2007 was a watershed for Reich, as his natural instincts in favor of deregulation collided with public calls for greater regulation. Eventually he repositioned himself, calling for uniform federal underwriting standards for lenders and brokers. By the fall of 2007, after the private-label securitization market dried up and with NetBank approaching failure, Reich publicly admitted that some thrift institutions were experiencing liquidity problems and defaults on their mortgage portfolios. In a speech to the British Bankers' Association in October 2007, Reich declared the "turmoil in the recent U.S. mortgage markets is the direct result of not enough regulatory oversight in places where it was needed the most"—although mostly he was referring to the mortgage broker industry.[82] He also began to decry slipshod practices in the banking industry, declaring: "Bankers should never outsource their credit decisions to Wall Street or the investor community."[83] By October, he wailed: "What has become of Character, Collateral, Capacity, Capital and Conditions?"[84]

When news dribbled out about OTS's bungled oversight of IndyMac, OTS went into a defensive crouch. The agency overhauled its Web site the month after IndyMac was seized, expunging most of Gilleran's speeches and making it difficult to reconstruct the history of OTS enforcement actions. In the meantime, Reich stopped posting any of his new speeches on the Web site. On Election Day, it was clear that 2008 would be an *annus horribilis* for Reich and for OTS. Conceding defeat, Reich made an extraordinary statement of remorse, telling a group of bankers that he regretted not having curtailed no- and low-doc loans.[85]

The OTS saga parallels that of the OCC, but unlike the OCC, the story of OTS is marked by desperation and corruption. Acutely aware of the calls for its extinction,

OTS attempted to grow out of its problems by allowing thrift institutions to domi-nate the pay-option ARM market. The huge size of thrift companies like WaMu and Golden West and their importance to the OTS budget caused the agency to bend to their wishes. Meanwhile, the QTL rule made thrifts highly exposed to residential mortgages, placing them at heightened risk.

The result was a climate of laxity unmatched by any other federal banking agency. OTS adopted no binding rules on sound loan underwriting. Its director even tried to undermine an interagency guidance in public. Unlike the OCC, which at least attempted to inspire industry compliance through speeches, OTS had little use for moral suasion. Likewise, it had little use for enforcement. OTS delayed lowering exam ratings over the FDIC's objections, avoided even voluntary enforcement, and kept dying institutions on life support for as long as possible. Its examiners were green and its management corrupt. The irony is that OTS had been created to "clean up" the savings and loan disaster.

## THE FEDERAL DEPOSIT INSURANCE CORPORATION

The FDIC, which regulates state-chartered banks that are not members of the Federal Reserve System, appears to have taken its oversight responsibilities more seriously than the OCC or OTS. This is not to say that the FDIC had a flawless record. In 2001, an FDIC conservatorship went astray originating bad subprime loans. Later, two FDIC-regulated banks became deeply immersed in subprime lending and those activities contributed to their demise. Nevertheless, the FDIC's overall regulatory record during subprime's heyday trumped that of the OCC and OTS.

During the early years of the George W. Bush administration, under John Reich, who was then acting chairman, and his successor, Chairman Donald Powell, the FDIC became implicated in bad subprime loans while resolving the failed thrift Superior Bank, FSB. In 2001, OTS had closed down Superior. As conservator, the FDIC continued Superior's subprime lending business, originating $550 million of subprime loans while running the shop until the beginning of 2002. The FDIC sold a large number of Superior's loans to Beal Bank in Texas and Bank of America, about half of which the FDIC had originated after it took over Superior. When the FDIC sold the loans, it warranted that there had been no fraud or misrepresentations in the origination of the loans.[86]

In 2002, Beal sued the FDIC for breach of warranty, claiming that many of the loans that the FDIC sold the bank violated federal anti-predatory lending laws and others contained evidence of fraudulent appraisals and misrepresentations of borrow-ers' income. After Sheila Bair became chairman and six years after Beal filed the law-suit, the FDIC filed a report documenting that the FDIC's own expert had found that 19 percent of the loans sold to Beal breached the warranties. Six months later, the FDIC settled Beal's claim for $90 million.[87]

Later, during the housing bubble, two FDIC-regulated institutions became deeply involved in subprime lending. One was Fremont Investment & Loan, the fifth-ranked subprime lender in 2006 with nearly $13 billion in total assets. By the end of 2006, there were signs that the bank's residential loan portfolio was struggling. The per-centage of nonperforming loans had more than tripled over the course of the year.[88]

Because Fremont did not fail and therefore the inspector general was under no obligation to audit the bank, it is difficult to know whether the FDIC took any action in response to these signs of trouble. What we do know is that in March 2007, Fremont shut down its subprime unit in response to increased demands to repurchase nonperforming loans and pending sanctions by the FDIC.[89] A few days later, the FDIC issued a cease-and-desist order prohibiting the bank from marketing unsafe subprime ARMs. The order banned Fremont from engaging in a range of hazardous loan practices, including making low-doc and piggyback loans, requiring large prepayment penalties, engaging in misleading marketing, and lending without regard to borrowers' ability to repay.[90]

The FDIC was not the only one knocking at Fremont's door. In June 2007, the Commonwealth of Massachusetts brought suit against the bank, alleging that it made loans that borrowers could not afford to repay in violation of the Commonwealth's consumer protection laws.[91] Fremont's troubles continued. In 2008, the FDIC issued an order to recapitalize the bank. Unable to meet the FDIC's demands, Fremont General, Fremont's parent, sold most of the bank's assets and liabilities to CapitalSource. The parent then filed for bankruptcy.[92] In the final chapter, Fremont General settled Massachusetts's consumer protection lawsuit for $10 million and an agreement that it would not foreclose on any loans in Massachusetts without approval from the state attorney general.[93]

The other heavily implicated FDIC-regulated bank was Houston's Franklin Bank, S.S.B., which went down in 2008 after going too deep into high-risk subprime lending. Franklin's failure was noteworthy in that the bank was founded by Lewis Ranieri, the Wall Street icon credited with developing mortgage-backed securities. Franklin Bank had concentrated in risky products, including interest-only, stated-income, pay-option, and high-loan-to-value loans. It made loans to borrowers with low credit scores containing multiple layers of risk. By July 2008, 82 percent of the residential loans in the bank's portfolio were low-doc or no-doc loans. The Bank's high-risk lending, coupled with weak risk management, prevented it from weathering the economic downturn in 2007. The following year, the state regulator closed Franklin.[94]

There was ample evidence of a downward slide in the quality of Franklin Bank's loans. By 2003, the bank's examiners reported that Franklin's loans were concentrated in high-risk locations. They also noted that Franklin was making hybrid ARMs, interest-only, subprime, and Alt-A loans. These risks began to materialize in the spring of 2006, when the percentage of bank-held loans that were past due began creeping up. The situation worsened in 2007, when the percentage of nonperforming loans increased almost tenfold. Despite this evidence, the FDIC did not downgrade the bank's examination rating until October 2007, when it gave the bank a rating of 3, down from 2, which the bank had had for the prior three years.[95]

In reviewing the FDIC's supervision of Franklin, the agency's inspector general criticized the FDIC for not checking for compliance with the 2006 guidance on nontraditional mortgages during its examinations of Franklin. According to the IG, the FDIC failed to oversee Franklin's high-risk lending effectively:

Had the FDIC encouraged Franklin to adequately identify, measure, monitor and control its nontraditional and subprime loan portfolio, the level of loss incurred by the bank due to the economic decline could have potentially been reduced. In addition, both bank management and examiners could have more effectively assessed and managed/supervised the risk associated with the bank's nontraditional and subprime mortgage loan products.[96]

The IG also faulted the FDIC for not encouraging Franklin to engage in thorough due diligence review of the loans that the bank purchased. As a result of this laxity, neither Franklin nor the FDIC was aware that Franklin was buying first-lien loans that had been coupled with piggyback loans held by other investors.[97]

Franklin and Fremont were both substantial subprime originators, and both bear some of the responsibility for the subprime crisis, along with their federal regulator, the FDIC. Those institutions, however, appeared to be isolated instances of involvement by FDIC-supervised institutions in subprime. Other FDIC-regulated banks failed during the credit crisis, but generally those institutions capsized because of large portfolios of commercial real-estate loans or development loans, not subprime loans. Almost all of these failures took place after the housing and credit markets collapsed and the recession was under way. As businesses failed, commercial real estate rentals declined and sales of commercial real estate froze. Small community banks felt the squeeze on their balance sheets and, by 2009, bank closure rates mirrored the decline in the economy. Thus, these failures were, in part, extensions of the subprime virus.[98]

## LESSONS LEARNED

In August 2008, the *Wall Street Journal* asked the four federal banking regulators for statistics on their memoranda of understanding with banks in 2008 to date. The OCC said it had instituted 9, the Federal Reserve 32, and the FDIC 118. OTS, however, stonewalled and "refused to disclose its data," even when confronted with a Freedom of Information Act request.[99] This metric of enforcement orders is one sign of the commitment—or lack thereof—the regulators had to checking abusive and risky lending.

The OCC and OTS experience provides several vivid lessons, the first being the danger of mixing federal preemption with charter competition. When regulators must compete to attract institutions and retain them, federal preemption becomes an invitation to participate in a race to the bottom. The sorry enforcement record of both federal agencies serves as a reminder of the risk of concentrating enforcement power over a class of entities in one agency's hands. This is even truer when the agency is prone to capture by the entities it regulates. Through federal preemption, the OCC and OTS denied the states and individual consumers the power to bring their own enforcement actions against national banks, federal thrifts, and their mortgage lending subsidiaries for abusive loans. Instead, the sole discretion to investigate and levy sanctions was held by the OCC and OTS. With no outside investigations to prod the two agencies into enforcement, discretion too often devolved into inaction.

The OCC and OTS also suffered from a silo mentality that blinded them to the larger risk of standing by idly. Their laissez-faire attitude to questionable loans, combined with their fondness for securitization, pumped unnecessary risk out of banks and into the global financial system. The OCC and OTS were also cavalier about their duty to rein in moral hazard at institutions that were too big to fail or manage. If any national bank that was too big to fail became needlessly mired in bad mortgages, it was one bank too many. Likewise, OTS ignored the fact that the failure of a massive thrift could have potential domino effects, including public panic over the safety of deposits and a blow to the reputation of sister banks.

In the final analysis, the OCC and OTS were in a state of denial about the grave nature of bank and thrift involvement in reckless lending and the equally grave nature of their own failure to supervise. Whatever the size of banks' and thrifts' involvement, it was big enough to require hundreds of billions of dollars in public bailouts to banks, undermine public trust in federal deposit insurance, and plunge the U.S. and world economies into recession. Had the OCC and OTS done their job, at least some of this could have been avoided.

10

▷

# Blind Spot: Greenspan's Federal Reserve

During the housing boom, the OCC, OTS, and FDIC were not the only federal banking cops on the block. There was also the Federal Reserve Board. In fact, of the federal banking regulators, the Fed had the most power to regulate home mortgages. That is because Congress invested the Fed with the sole authority to police abuses across the entire mortgage market, including banks and thrifts, nonbank lenders, and mortgage brokers. Alan Greenspan, the chairman of the Fed for almost twenty years, refused to exercise those powers. Only when Ben Bernanke assumed the chairmanship did the Fed eventually adopt binding rules to crack down on reckless mortgages. Even then the Fed's efforts were "too little, too late."

Of the top federal banking regulators during the subprime era, Greenspan had the longest tenure bar none. Greenspan took office in 1987, before subprime loans ever took off, and he presided over the housing bubble until January 2006, when he retired. As the longest serving Fed chairman except for William McChesney Martin Jr., Greenspan put his distinct ideological imprint on the Fed. Nowhere was this more evident than in mortgage lending.

## GREENSPAN'S AVERSION TO REGULATION

When one reads Greenspan's pronouncements over the years, what stands out is his aversion to regulation. This hostility first emerged in the 1950s, when Greenspan was a young economist coming of age during the backwash of New Deal regulation. Early on, he rejected Keynes's premise that governments need to intervene to correct market failures. By the 1960s and 1970s, Greenspan was so disenchanted with New Deal regulation that he concluded that the U.S. economy had "lost its way."[1]

Greenspan's lifelong distrust of regulation was rooted in the writings of the philosophers John Locke, Adam Smith, Joseph Schumpeter, and Ayn Rand. Greenspan was attracted to them for their thinking on "the shortest, straightest path to prosperity." Locke, for example, regarded private property as intrinsic to prosperity because it allowed individuals to reap the rewards from their labor in improving the land.

Based on Locke, Greenspan considered the core function of government to provide "a system of laws that protects individual rights, especially the right to own property." Conversely, he reasoned, other regulation should be shunned when possible because it "impinges on the exercise of a property right." Unless property rights were secure, Greenspan argued, people would "not exert the effort to accumulate the capital necessary for economic growth."[2]

Adam Smith and his invocation of the "invisible hand" likewise had a profound influence on Greenspan. Smith argued that wealth flourishes best when individuals can pursue their self-interest with minimal government interference. So long as the government exercises restraint, Smith held, each individual will be "led by an invisible hand to promote an end which was no part of his intention. By pursuing his own interest, he frequently promotes that of society more effectually than when he really intends to promote it."[3] Greenspan took this as a prescription for government to "provide[] stability and freedom and otherwise stay[] out of the way."[4]

Greenspan's dedication to increased prosperity further attracted him to the idea of "creative destruction," as expounded by the Harvard economist Joseph Schumpeter. Through creative destruction, Schumpeter contended, new technologies continually replace the old, improving productivity and thereby causing living standards to rise. As a corollary, Greenspan believed that regulation and union contracts slowed the growth of wealth by creating obstacles to creative destruction.[5]

Schumpeter was not the only contemporary who garnered Greenspan's attention. As a young economist in New York in the early 1950s and 1960s, Greenspan was drawn into the inner circle of Ayn Rand. While he was attracted to Rand for championing laissez-faire capitalism, she shaped a further belief of his: that government regulation squelches private responsibility and initiative. Rand, who was born in 1905 in Russia and experienced the Russian Revolution firsthand, fled to the United States after the Soviets seized her father's store. The experience left her deeply suspicious of state control in the daily lives of citizens. Rand had many reasons for her objections to state interference, but one was that state control undermined the free will that enabled individuals to choose the moral principles that guide their actions. In Rand's worldview, government intervention was abhorrent not only because it crushed personal initiative, but also because it destroyed moral autonomy.

Rand's fierce antiregulatory stance had a lasting effect on Greenspan. Indeed, in Greenspan's words, Rand was such "a stabilizing force" in his life that he chose her to stand at his side at the White House when he took the oath of office as Chairman of the Council of Economic Advisers. In keeping with Rand's teachings, Greenspan made it a point to seize "opportunities to dismantle policies that contribute to unnecessary rigidity" while heading the council.[6]

Later, upon his appointment as chair of the Federal Reserve Board, Greenspan was acutely aware that his aversion to regulation was in tension with the Fed's role as "a major bank regulator and the overseer of America's payments system." He claimed that having sworn to uphold the Constitution and federal laws, he would put aside his personal stance on regulation. "Since I was an outlier in my libertarian opposition to most regulation," he later recalled, "I planned to be largely passive in such matters and allow other Federal Reserve governors to take the lead."[7]

**FIGURE 10.1.**
Greenspan testifies on monetary policy report. (Mark Wilson/Getty Images News/
Getty Images).

Flexibility, which was a codeword for deregulation, was central to Greenspan's macroeconomic conception of the world. In his view, deregulation was "the Ford administration's great unsung achievement," which "set the stage for an enormous wave of creative destruction in the 1980s."[8] Flexibility also governed his approach to potential economic shocks. In this vein, Greenspan opposed regulation designed to prevent financial crises and believed that flexibly responding to such crises was the preferable approach. In his mind, flexibility allowed for "a faster response to shocks and a correspondingly greater ability to absorb their downside consequences and recover from their aftermath."[9]

Greenspan's antipathy toward regulation was not just a matter of healthy skepticism, but was taken to an extreme. This is evident in his stance on federal deposit insurance. In past crises, federal deposit insurance has successfully halted bank runs. At the same time, federal deposit insurance has a well-known downside, which is the phenomenon of moral hazard. Federal deposit insurance encourages banks to take unreasonable risks because they can keep the profits if they win and the federal government will absorb the losses if they fail. Many economists take the position that the government must regulate banks to counteract the moral hazard from deposit insurance. Greenspan vehemently disagreed with this assertion. To him, bank regulation made moral hazard worse by discouraging personal integrity and lulling bankers and depositors into complacency about instituting precautions to ensure a bank's safety.

To minimize the moral hazard arising from deposit insurance, Greenspan called instead for a radical shift in regulatory philosophy. Most important, Greenspan advocated scrapping binding rules and prohibitions in favor of risk management tools that "attempt to stimulate . . . what markets alone might do." His goal, in the process, was to give "market forces . . . free rein."[10]

### Greenspan's Captivation with Private Risk Management

While he was chairman, one of Greenspan's overriding objectives was to replace the old command-and-control model of bank regulation with oversight designed to bolster private risk management by banks. Greenspan considered risk management techniques "far better suited to policymaking" than rules. While Greenspan was the first to admit that "reckless gambling rarely pays off in the end," he trusted bankers to avoid excessive risk in the interest of self-preservation. If regulators could "gain greater confidence in a bank's operating procedures and in its own evaluation of risk," he maintained, "we should be able to reduce our oversight role." Consequently, Greenspan made it his mission to minimize government oversight by outsourcing risk management to banks.[11]

Greenspan was the first to acknowledge that risk management models suffer from a variety of possible flaws, including rear-view vision, false assumptions, and "fragmentary evidence."[12] He was no stranger to lax lending, having witnessed the 1980s savings and loan debacle. Nevertheless, he was sanguine that the errors of the 1980s would not be repeated. In his judgment, recent advances in risk management laid worries about a replay of the savings and loan crisis to rest. This was largely because banks' ability to quantify risk meant risk managers had better data. Armed with that data, Greenspan predicted, risk managers would gain new power over marketing departments and loan officers to nix reckless loans. He went so far as to call private risk management a "revolution" with "real potential" for reducing lending booms and busts.[13] Citigroup later revealed the folly of Greenspan's views, when company representatives allegedly told the SEC that the bank had not taken into account the possibility that subprime mortgages would default when conducting risk analyses.[14]

Greenspan embraced private risk management in many arenas. For instance, he spearheaded a successful campaign to allow the largest U.S. banks to calculate their minimum capital using their own internal risk models. Similarly, Greenspan was captivated by financial innovations to spread and hedge risk. He heaped praise on mortgage-backed securities, collateralized debt obligations, and credit default swaps for allowing "the largest and most sophisticated banks . . . to divest themselves of much credit risk by passing it on to institutions" such as insurance companies, pension funds, and hedge funds. "As a result," he argued, "not only have individual financial institutions become less vulnerable to shocks from underlying risk factors, but also the financial system as a whole has become more resilient."[15]

### Greenspan's Naïveté

Greenspan's fascination with risk management also made him an advocate for subprime loans. Over the years, Greenspan became a cheerleader for more consumer credit and more subprime loans in particular. To him, subprime lending was a technological marvel, one where credit-scoring models permitted lenders to "efficiently judge the risk" of loan applicants with blemished credit. Because he had faith in those models, he was willing to allow banks to expand credit to weaker borrowers, so long as they "knowingly [chose] their risk profiles and price[d] that risk accordingly."[16]

Greenspan's stress on the importance of property ownership to a strong democracy also explained his enthusiasm for subprime loans. The "expansion of ownership," he believed, "gave more people a stake in the future of our country and boded well for the cohesion of the nation."[17] He praised subprime loans for producing record homeownership rates, especially for lower income families, Hispanics, and blacks.

Greenspan was likewise upbeat about people's ability to manage high debt. In 2004, he acknowledged that household debt was at a "record high," but dismissed it as a concern. He knew that bankruptcy rates were on the rise and that some subprime borrowers were "highly leveraged." On balance, however, rising family debt burdens did not bother Greenspan because "ever-wealthier households" had an "increased capacity . . . to service debt." In fact, he viewed higher household debt as an affirmative good, saying: "Rising debt goes hand in hand with progress."[18]

During the credit boom, Greenspan was well aware of the run-up in housing prices, but discounted concerns about a housing price bubble throughout his chairmanship. Why did Greenspan miss the bubble? He simply did not believe that housing prices could decline across the nation. According to his research, there was "no national housing market in the United States" because "nominal house prices in the aggregate ha[d] rarely fallen and certainly not by very much." High levels of home equity gave him even more reason for reassurance. "It would take a large, and historically most unusual, fall in home prices," Greenspan opined, "to wipe out a significant part of home equity."[19]

In August 2005, as concerns about a housing bubble started surfacing in the press, Greenspan took to the hustings to tamp down those concerns. In a widely heralded speech, he announced there were "signs of froth" in some local housing markets "where home prices seem[ed] to have risen to unsustainable levels." He assured audiences that "we were facing not a bubble but a froth—lots of small, local bubbles."[20]

At the same time that Greenspan was trying to mute rumblings about a bubble, he conceded that the "apparent froth in housing markets may have spilled over into mortgage markets." Greenspan acknowledged the "dramatic increase" in "more-exotic forms of adjustable-rate mortgages," including interest-only ARMs and pay-option ARMs, and admitted that if home prices cooled, these loans could lead to "significant losses." But instead of restricting dicey loans, his response was to raise interest rates. The interest rate hikes failed to halt the bubble.

Only later, after the financial system imploded, did Greenspan have second thoughts about what happened under his tenure at the Fed. In testimony before the House Oversight Committee, he admitted that the "modern risk management paradigm [that had] held sway for decades . . . collapsed." He described himself as "in a state of shocked disbelief" upon realizing, contrary to his faith in the self-protective instincts of banks, that lenders "did not have the incentive to evaluate the credit quality of what they were selling." When committee chairman Henry Waxman asked Greenspan whether "your ideology pushed you to make decisions that you wish you had not made?" Greenspan replied:[21]

MR. GREENSPAN   . . . [Y]es, I found a flaw, I don't know how significant or permanent it is, but I have been very distressed by that fact.

CHAIRMAN WAXMAN   You found a flaw?

MR. GREENSPAN   I found a flaw in the model that defines how the world works, so to speak.

CHAIRMAN WAXMAN   In other words, you found that your view of the world, your ideology, was not right, it was not working.

MR. GREENSPAN   Precisely. That's precisely the reason I was shocked, because I had been going for 40 years or more with very considerable evidence that it was working exceptionally well.

## THE FEDERAL RESERVE BOARD'S POWER TO REGULATE RECKLESS MORTGAGES

By 2005, Greenspan knew that making poor-quality loans was unsustainable if there was a housing bubble. In spite of this, he continued to resist meaningful mortgage regulation, rationalizing his inaction as a way of giving lenders economic flexibility to absorb the shock of any drop in housing prices. There was a lot riding on his decision to stay his hand, because the Fed was the only federal agency with the statutory power to crack down on lax mortgages by originators of every stripe.

In 1994, Congress gave the Federal Reserve Board the power to curb unfair or deceptive loans for virtually every mortgage originator in the country. Under Greenspan, however, the board consistently refused to exercise that power. The board did not change course until July 2008, after Greenspan had retired and Ben Bernanke had replaced him. By then the floodgates were open.

The story of mortgage regulation by the Fed starts in 1968, when Congress passed the Truth in Lending Act (TILA).[22] TILA standardized the disclosures given to consumers about the price of their home mortgages. In TILA, Congress gave the Federal Reserve Board the job of carrying out the act by designing disclosures and adopting rules for disclosures. The Fed did not want this responsibility and made that very clear to Congress. The Vice Chairman of the Board of Governors, J. L. Robertson, told a Congressional subcommittee that the Fed was not familiar with mortgage loan practices and did not have staff who were skilled at detecting TILA violations. Robertson further argued that having to enforce TILA would distract the Board from making monetary policy and he hoped that Congress would assign TILA regulation and enforcement "to an agency better suited to perform the function."[23]

Originally, TILA was just a disclosure statute, and it remained just that for the first quarter-century of its existence. In the early 1990s, however, the subprime market took off, and Congress got an earful about new types of abusive mortgages. Its response was to amend TILA in 1994 to prohibit abusive terms or practices in home mortgages. The amendments, known as the Home Ownership and Equity Protection Act of 1994 (HOEPA),[24] were Congress's sole effort to address problems in the fledgling subprime market.

HOEPA applied to most home loan originators and had two parts. The first part required the Fed to regulate certain "high-cost" residential mortgages. This was known as the high-cost loan provision of HOEPA because it only applied to home mortgages with exorbitant interest rates or fees. If a loan qualified as high cost, HOEPA subjected it to numerous restrictions, including limitations on prepayment penalties, balloon clauses, and negative amortization.[25]

A loan was high cost if it exceeded certain "triggers" for the interest rate or fees. HOEPA defined a loan as high cost if (1) the total points and fees exceeded 8 percent of the total loan amount or $400, whichever was greater; or (2) the first mortgage had an annual percentage rate (APR) at least eight percentage points higher than the comparable Treasury bond. For second mortgages, the APR had to exceed the comparable Treasury bond by ten percentage points or more to qualify as high cost. Under this test, for example, a thirty-year first-lien mortgage made on October 27, 2006, needed an APR of 12.8 percent or more to qualify as a high-cost loan. To give some idea of how expensive that was, the same month, APRs on thirty-year fixed-rate prime mortgages were running just under 7 percent.

HOEPA's high-cost loan provision covered only a tiny fraction of loans because the triggers were so high that few subprime loans met them. Furthermore, the provision only applied to refinance loans, not to loans to buy a home, reverse mortgages, or home equity lines of credit. For these reasons, lenders found it easy to get around the high-cost loan provision by charging interest rates and fees that were slightly below HOEPA's triggers and by expanding into subprime home purchase loans.[26]

The second part of HOEPA required the Federal Reserve Board to prohibit two things: (1) unfair or deceptive mortgage practices; and (2) refinance loans that involved abusive practices or were otherwise not in the interest of the borrower.[27] This part of HOEPA was known as the "UDAP" provision because it prohibited unfair and deceptive practices. The UDAP provision was much broader than the high-cost loan provision of HOEPA. For one thing, it covered both purchase loans and refinance loans. And, it prohibited unfair or deceptive practices regardless of interest rates or fees.

There was only one catch with the UDAP provision: it was not self-executing. In other words, the Federal Reserve Board had to issue a rule or order to activate the UDAP provision. When HOEPA passed, Congress instructed the Fed to implement the UDAP provision, but Alan Greenspan was dead set against obeying that Congressional mandate so long as he was chairman. This became apparent as early as 1998, when the Fed, in a joint report with the Department of Housing and Urban Development, dissented from a HUD recommendation proposing a federal UDAP standard for home mortgages.[28]

There was one member of the Federal Reserve Board of Governors who supported a UDAP rule. Edward Gramlich, the chair of the board's Committee on Consumer and Community Affairs, was an anomaly on the board. Appointed by President Clinton, Gramlich was a liberal Democrat who had studied the economics of poverty during his earlier academic career. At the Fed, Gramlich regularly gave speeches denouncing abusive loans and criticizing the disproportionate effect of subprime foreclosures on minority groups and neighborhoods.[29]

By 2000, predatory lending was dominating the headlines, putting pressure on the Fed to respond. Under the glare of the press, Gramlich successfully pushed Greenspan and the other Fed governors to amend the Fed's rules to expand the reach of the high-cost loan provisions of HOEPA in late 2001.[30] The Fed spilled a lot of ink over the 2001 amendment, but ultimately it had little if any effect. Even with the amendment, HOEPA's triggers were still so high that they only covered 1 percent of all subprime loans.[31]

If the Fed was going to seriously address risky subprime loans, it would have to activate HOEPA's UDAP provision. Starting in 2000, Gramlich attempted to persuade Greenspan to implement the provision to address the entire subprime market. Although Greenspan says he vowed to let "other Federal Reserve governors . . . take the lead" on regulatory matters,[32] this time he put his foot down. Gramlich later reminisced that Greenspan "was opposed to it, so I didn't really pursue it."[33]

Instead, Greenspan insisted on less rigorous means of addressing subprime abuses, limited to speeches,[34] consumer literacy, bank examinations, and guidances without binding effect.[35] Subsequent events raised serious questions about the efficacy of these methods. In any case, neither bank examinations nor guidances applied to independent nonbank mortgage lenders. Only a Fed UDAP rule would have had industry-wide effect.

In January 2006, Greenspan reached the end of his fourth term and retired from the Federal Reserve Board, succeeded by Ben Bernanke. Within months, starting in June 2006, the governors began acknowledging growing signs of distress, including the cooling of the housing market, a sharp deterioration in lending standards, an uptick in subprime delinquencies, and increased home speculation by investors. Still, the board clung to its standard approach of addressing loose underwriting through nonbinding guidances and moral jawboning.[36]

By January 2007, the surge in subprime delinquencies had become glaringly apparent to the board. To their consternation, the governors saw the latest crop of subprime loans, made in 2005 and 2006, going into default at an accelerated rate. Investors were starting to flee the subprime securitization market. In March 2007, consistent with their preference for guidances over regulations, the Fed and fellow banking regulators proposed yet another guidance on subprime mortgages.[37]

By the spring, calls for stronger medicine became more insistent. In May, Bernanke started giving active consideration to exercising the Fed's UDAP power and instructed his staff to hold hearings on possible new rules to ban unfair and deceptive mortgages. Still, Bernanke did not appear unduly troubled. He assured the public in June 2007 that subprime woes were not a threat to the larger economy.[38]

The hearings and drafting process on the new UDAP rules dragged on for months, during which the crisis deepened. It was not for another year—until July 30, 2008— that the board finally issued a binding rule under HOEPA's UDAP provision banning specific types of risky loans.[39] Even then, the rule was largely limited to higher priced mortgages. Most of the new rule was confined to first mortgages costing at least 1.5 percentage points above the prime rate for similar loans, or 3.5 percentage points above for second-lien loans. Although less pricey nontraditional loans had helped fuel the credit crisis, the rule left those loans—plus prime loans—mostly untouched.[40] The new rule, while badly needed, was one more instance where the board delayed taking action and then proceeded too cautiously.

## DISCLOSURE

For many decades, Truth in Lending Act disclosures were the main form of mortgage regulation at the Fed. If the government has to regulate, many economists—including economists at the Fed—prefer mandatory disclosures of loan terms to substantive regulation. They contend that disclosures allow parties to strike any agreement they want because disclosures make it possible for all the parties to know the risks and benefits.[41] Or so the theory goes.

When subprime lending began in the 1990s, the Fed's TILA rules were already showing their age. The last time the Fed had revamped the disclosure rules in any major way was in 1981. Back then, a lender offered a loan product at one price and the loan applicant either qualified for that loan or did not. With the advent of subprime loans and risk-based pricing, lenders could offer loans with an array of interest rates and terms. Later, in the 2000s, the market underwent further changes as exotic ARMs took off, with their high potential for payment shock.

The Fed's truth-in-lending disclosures, which had worked fairly well for traditional prime loans, were not well designed to produce accurate, timely disclosures for loans with risk-based pricing. Similarly, the Fed's rules did not require clear disclosures to borrowers who had hybrid ARMs, interest-only ARMs, and pay-option ARMs about how high their monthly payments could go.

For refinance loans, the Fed's TILA rules allowed lenders to wait until closing to tell borrowers their highest possible monthly payment in dollar terms. Even then, the Fed allowed lenders to bury the amount in the payment schedule, which was somewhere in a big stack of documents presented to the borrower at closing.[42] In the rush to sign those documents, many borrowers with exotic ARMs never noticed how high their payments could go.

The Fed started focusing on the problem of inadequate TILA disclosures in the fall of 2005, but proceeded at a snail's pace. The first move was a guidance that exhorted lenders in vague terms to tell consumers the highest possible monthly payments on their loans. Next, the Fed held some hearings, which took place in the summer of 2006. Eventually, in 2007 and the spring of 2008, the Fed and fellow regulators came out with a new consumer brochure plus some sample disclosures about the payment shock on exotic ARMs. True to form, however, the guidances and sample disclosures were couched as advice, not as binding rules.

The Fed did not get around to adopting a binding rule on payment shock disclosures until July 30, 2008. All the rule did was move up delivery of the payment schedule closer to the date of application, before consumers paid most fees. The Fed refused to make the payment shock disclosures more visible, saying it needed more time for testing.[43] By then, Congress was fed up with the Fed's foot-dragging. In a sharp rebuke, Congress enacted a statute on the very same day that the Fed issued its rule, requiring lenders to disclose payment shock in a format that was easy to understand and conspicuous.[44]

The Fed's disclosure rules had other major flaws.[45] During the housing bubble, the Fed allowed subprime lenders to hawk rates that were reserved only for their best customers. Borrowers with poorer credit were reeled in by these advertisements, even though they did not qualify for the advertised rates. This problem was compounded by the fact that under the Fed's rules, lenders usually did not have to provide firm price quotes to customers until closing, when it was too late for borrowers to shop for a better deal. As a result, lenders could attract consumers by advertising their lowest rates, collect a nonrefundable application fee, and then jack up the rate at the closing, usually without advance notice. The effect was to open the door to rampant bait-and-switch schemes.

The Fed had been aware of these problems for years. In fact, in 1998, the Fed and the Department of Housing and Urban Development had issued a report concluding that TILA disclosures did not come early enough in the loan application process to permit informed comparison shopping. In that report, HUD recommended requiring mortgage originators to provide binding price quotes before taking loan applications. The Fed refused to endorse the proposal, however, and it never gained traction.[46]

As of this writing, the Fed still allows ads to tout a lender's most competitive rates even when those rates aren't available to most borrowers. Similarly, the board still does not require binding price quotes for closed-end home loans at the point of application. In its July 30, 2008, rule, the board refused to even institute a modest proposal by consumer advocates to require lenders to correct inaccurate interest rate disclosures a few days before closing. The Fed refused to take this step even though it supposedly was concerned about "bait and switch tactics."[47] In a second rebuke to the Fed, Congress, in its bill requiring stronger disclosures, mandated that lenders provide borrowers with corrected disclosures at least three business days before the loan closing if there are any changes in the annual percentage rate.[48]

## SUPERVISION OF LENDING INSTITUTIONS BY THE FED

The Fed's tools were not limited to promulgating rules to curb reckless underwriting or improve disclosures. The Fed was also the overseer of bank holding companies and their subsidiaries (except for subsidiaries owned by an intermediate bank or thrift), which at times included several of the nation's largest subprime lenders. The Fed also supervised state-chartered banks that were members of the Federal Reserve System, as well as their subsidiaries. For all of these entities, the Fed could have addressed problems with subprime loans through examinations and enforcement.

The 900 or so state-chartered member banks overseen by the Fed[49] were generally small- to medium-sized community banks. As of year-end 2008, only three of the banks that the Fed supervised had failed during the credit crisis.[50] All three were located in parts of the country with the steepest housing price declines, and they mostly got in trouble because of bad commercial real estate and construction loans, not home loans. With the onset of the recession, more Fed-supervised banks failed in 2009, but subprime lending did not seem to play a major role in their failures. Whatever the merits of the Fed's examination and enforcement at those banks, it does not appear that the Fed's supervision of state member banks precipitated the subprime crisis.

Where the Fed fell down was in its supervision of bank holding companies and certain of their nonbank mortgage subsidiaries,[51] including HSBC Finance (the number one subprime lender in 2006), Countrywide Financial Corporation (number three that year), and CitiFinancial (number eleven).[52] Just before Governor Gramlich died of cancer in 2007, a colleague delivered a tell-all speech on his behalf to the assembled dignitaries of the Federal Reserve System in Jackson Hole, Wyoming, in which he revealed a bombshell. The Fed, according to Gramlich, had not regularly examined the nonbank mortgage lending subsidiaries under its supervision. Together, those lenders made 17.7 percent—almost one-fifth—of higher-priced loans in 2007.[53]

One ostensible argument for the Fed's inaction was that Congress in the Gramm-Leach-Bliley Act of 1999 said that the Fed could not examine subsidiaries of bank

**FIGURE 10.2.**
Federal Reserve Board Governor Edward M. Gramlich. (Bloomberg/ Getty Images).

holding companies unless their activities could have a materially adverse effect on the safety and soundness of any of their sister bank or thrift affiliates.[54] It doesn't appear that this provision was what motivated the Fed's refusal to examine subsidiaries. In fact, the evidence suggests that the Fed's failure to conduct routine examinations of subsidiaries during the subprime boom was a matter of discretion, not a dictate of the law. In the summer of 2007, the Fed reversed course and initiated a pilot project to evaluate the underwriting practices of nonbank mortgage lenders owned by bank holding companies.[55] Two years later, the Fed announced it was setting up a consumer compliance supervision program for all the subsidiaries under its purview.[56] In neither instance did the Fed question its authority to examine subsidiary lenders.

### HSBC Finance

In 2003, the British banking giant HSBC Holdings bought Household Finance Corporation, a discredited subprime lender with major legal woes. Household had recently shelled out $484 million to state attorneys general to resolve predatory lending claims. After the acquisition, HSBC dubbed Household "HSBC Finance" to give it a new lease on life. By 2006, HSBC Finance was at the top of the subprime charts, with almost 8 percent of the market.

HSBC Finance had two mortgage divisions: a wholesale channel, Mortgage Services, and a retail channel, Consumer Lending. In 2008 and 2009, after a string of multi-billion-dollar losses from improvident home loans, HSBC closed both mortgage lending operations. Mortgage Services was the first to go, felled by an aggressive product line and poor quality control over its brokers and correspondents. Stated-income loans were a big reason for Mortgage Services's demise. The division had stepped up stated loans in 2005 and 2006 and by the end of 2006, these loans made up a fourth of Mortgage Services's portfolio. At that point, HSBC Finance held $11.8 billion in stated-income loans on its books. Greedy for more, HSBC Finance originated another $7.9 billion in stated-income loans in 2007. HSBC finally put the kibosh on stated-income loans on New Year's Eve 2007, long after their risks were known and almost six months after federal regulators came out against stated-income loans.

The Consumer Lending division had a somewhat better product mix and default record than Mortgage Services, but it, too, ran aground. HSBC Finance described the division's business as "focused on subprime customers who rely on drawing cash against the equity in their homes to help meet their cash needs." By 2008, this business model had failed. Seriously delinquent first-lien mortgages by Consumer Lending rose 212 percent in 2008, generating a $2.7 billion net loss for HSBC Finance that year. Two months later, in February 2009, HSBC Finance threw in the towel and closed down mortgage originations by Consumer Lending.[57] Ultimately, Mike Geoghegan, the group chief executive of HSBC Holdings, issued a damning indictment of HSBC's purchase of Household when he told investors in March 2009: "With the benefit of hindsight the Group wishes that it hadn't made [the] investment" in Household.

HSBC's predicament was of its own making. Take, for example, a pool of loans that HSBC Finance securitized in May 2007.[58] Fully 24 percent of the loans in the pool were made to borrowers who owed more on their homes than their homes were worth. On top of that, more than half of the borrowers in the loan pool had a track record of not paying their bills. Not surprisingly, by the end of January 2009, 14 percent of the loans in the pool (measured in dollars) had gone into default or been restructured. This pool had a high rate of default even though it consisted of supposedly safe, fixed-rate, fully amortizing loans.

Despite these problems, the Fed never took public enforcement action against HSBC Finance or its holding company for unsafe and unsound loans. In fact, one searches in vain through the Fed's Web site for any evidence of mortgage oversight of HSBC Finance.[59]

### Countrywide

Under the Fed's eye, Countrywide grew into the nation's number one mortgage lender and one of the top three lenders in subprime mortgages. The Fed obtained jurisdiction over Countrywide in 2001, when Countrywide applied for permission to become a bank holding company. From then until March 2007, the Fed supervised Countrywide's holding company and its main lending arm, Countrywide Home Loans. Countrywide's "book" included piggyback loans and exotic ARMs, too often with reduced documentation. Countrywide also adopted the practice of qualifying borrowers for subprime hybrid ARMs based on their loan's initial interest rate, not the fully indexed rate. At the height of the subprime market, in 2005, Countrywide was originating more than $41 billion in home mortgages every month, including $3.7 billion in nonprime loans.

Countrywide continued to slash its underwriting standards in 2005 and 2006 to hold on to market share. By 2006, Countrywide was one of the nation's biggest originators of pay-option ARMs, the second-largest originator of interest-only loans, and the third-largest originator of low-doc and no-doc loans. Countrywide had a special fondness for stated-income loans because it could process them in as little as thirty minutes, allowing the company to churn out more loans and generate more fees. Countrywide continued making risky loans well into 2007, long after wiser lenders had exited the business. It did not stop making no-doc loans with less than 5 percent down until February 23, 2007. It did not halt piggyback second mortgages until March 16 that year. It did not close its subprime operation until November 2007.[60]

While Countrywide was spewing out hundreds of billions of dollars in toxic loans, where was the Fed? For the most part, the Fed's oversight of Countrywide was confidential and thus hidden from view. But we know three things. First, the Fed did not regularly examine the nonbank mortgage lenders under its authority, raising the question whether it ever examined Countrywide Home Loans. Second, the Fed never took formal enforcement action against Countrywide. Third, the Fed did not halt Countrywide's disastrous lending, even though it had full authority to do so.

The Fed's inaction is of even more concern given that, in 2004, New York attorney general Andrew Cuomo uncovered evidence that Countrywide charged blacks and Hispanics more than comparable whites for mortgages. Countrywide settled with New York in 2006. According to Cuomo, the discrimination arose from "racial and ethnic differences in the discretionary components of pricing."[61] Nevertheless, there is no evidence that the Fed investigated Countrywide's commission structure for its race effect or that it looked more generally into Countrywide's loan terms and lending practices.

Maybe the Fed was cowed because Countrywide lodged vehement protests against even mild attempts at regulation. Countrywide astutely hired a former senior attorney from the Fed, Mary Jane M. Seebach, to press the Fed to preserve the status quo. For instance, in late 2005 when federal regulators proposed the guidance recommending that lenders underwrite pay-option ARMs and interest-only ARMs to the fully indexed rate, Countrywide's business model was threatened. Seebach wrote to the Fed on March 27, 2006, calling for outright "withdrawal of the Proposal," defending Countrywide's right to qualify borrowers for interest-only ARMs solely "based on the interest only payment." If the Fed tightened that standard, Seebach complained, it "would significantly reduce the number of borrowers that could qualify for this product." What she didn't say was that the guidance would hurt Countrywide's profits.[62] In the end, Countrywide lost the battle over the guidance on nontraditional mortgages, which came out in October 2006.

The dispute over underwriting non-traditional loans put Countrywide on notice that more guidances could be on the way: if federal regulators wanted pay-option ARMs and interest-only ARMs underwritten to the fully indexed rate, subprime hybrid ARMs couldn't be far behind. That, in turn, would put another big dent in Countrywide's originations. As Seebach later admitted in a May 7, 2007, letter to OTS, in fourth quarter 2006, "almost 60% of [Countrywide] borrowers who obtained subprime hybrid ARMs would not have qualified at the fully indexed rate."[63] Seebach conceded, moreover, that almost 25 percent of Countrywide's subprime hybrid ARM borrowers that quarter did not qualify for any other product.[64]

It was impossible for Countrywide to avoid the guidances altogether, but it could reduce the risk of regulatory interference by going with the weakest regulator. That meant escaping supervision by the Fed and the Office of the Comptroller of the Currency and applying to the Office of Thrift Supervision to become a savings and loan holding company—a step Countrywide took less than two months after the final guidance on nontraditional mortgages came out.[65] OTS was happy to oblige and approved Countrywide's application in March 2007.

Countrywide's freedom from Fed supervision proved short-lived. When Bank of America agreed to purchase Countrywide in January 2008, the Federal Reserve had to approve the deal. In order to win approval for the merger, Bank of America pledged to stop making subprime and pay-option ARM loans. It further promised to "offer[] customers loan products for which they qualify," implying that Countrywide had not done that to date. By April 27, 2009, Bank of America had retired the Countrywide name, and the storied lender was history.

### Citigroup and CitiFinancial

Citigroup and its subprime mortgage subsidiary, CitiFinancial, were regulated by the Fed as well. In late 2000, Citigroup bought the shady subprime lender, Associates First Capital Corporation, and renamed it CitiFinancial Credit Company. Thereafter, Citigroup did its subprime lending through CitiFinancial, which grew to become the eleventh largest subprime lender in 2006.

CitiFinancial was constantly in the public eye because Citigroup engaged in frequent acquisitions and had to regularly apply to the Fed for merger approvals. Every time Citigroup submitted a merger application, members of the public would file protests against subprime lending by CitiFinancial. The Federal Trade Commission was also on Citigroup's back. In 2001, the FTC brought a deceptive and abusive acts and practices claim against Citigroup, CitiFinancial, and Associates. The case ultimately settled for $215 million in September 2002, but in the meantime, the suit put considerable pressure on the Fed to ensure that Citigroup stamped out the culture of questionable lending and fraud by Associates.[66]

In September 2001, in an order approving Citigroup's acquisition of European American Bank, the Fed announced that it was opening an examination into charges of predatory lending and lending discrimination by CitiFinancial and CitiFinancial Mortgage.[67] The Fed ordered Citigroup to make quarterly reports on litigation and compliance involving the company's subprime lending.[68] CitiFinancial offered to stop making subprime balloon loans and loans with negative amortization in order to pave the way for approval of future Citigroup acquisitions. CitiFinancial also agreed to clean up its credit insurance sales practices and refer customers with strong credit to Citigroup's prime lender.

The Fed's examination dragged on for two-and-a-half years. Eventually, in May 2004, the Fed announced that it was levying a $70 million civil money penalty against Citigroup for abusive subprime loans.[69] In the consent order, the Federal Reserve Bank of New York stated that it found "violations and deficiencies" by CitiFinancial, including lending discrimination, unsafe and unsound lending, and—disturbingly—attempts to mislead examiners. Citigroup agreed to institute reforms and to make restitution to injured borrowers. Later, while under close Fed scrutiny in 2005, Citigroup made a corporate decision to refrain from making hybrid ARMs and interest-only subprime mortgages to customers with less than prime credit scores. The Fed terminated the 2004 consent order in June 2006.

After the Fed terminated the consent order, problems started to surface in Citigroup's mortgage-lending operations. In 2006, credit losses started to creep up and interest revenues dropped. Citigroup tried to compensate for these problems by increasing its home loan originations. At first, the strategy seemed to work, with Citigroup boosting its mortgage originations 8 percent in 2006 compared to 2005.

The problem was that Citigroup pumped up its loan volumes by resorting to a litany of hazardous practices. The company increased loans to subprime borrowers with low down payments and piggyback second mortgages. It also expanded its low-doc and no-doc lending and increased home loans to investors. It further boosted volumes by lending to people lower down the credit spectrum. In the process, Citigroup increased its mix of subprime loans from 10 percent of total first mortgages in 2005 (totaling $2.4 billion) to 19 percent in 2007 (totaling $6.7 billion). To ramp up subprime loans, Citigroup relied heavily on bulk purchases of loans from correspondent lenders in 2006 and 2007. By all appearances, the Fed had relaxed its oversight of CitiFinancial.

The consequences were disastrous. On November 4, 2007, Citigroup went public with the news that it was buried under $55 billion in radioactive subprime loans that were stuck in the securitization pipeline and toxic CDOs and other derivatives backed by subprime loans, all of which the bank acquired while the Federal Reserve was overseeing its operations. The news worsened in 2008. Almost all of CitiFinancial's loans to subprime borrowers with low credit scores—below 620—were first mortgages. By 2008, 11.77 percent of those borrowers were at least ninety days past due, compared to an overall default rate of 5.71 among the subsidiary's first-lien borrowers. Among subprime mortgages with loan-to-value ratios over 90 percent, 25.4 percent were ninety days past due or more. The default rates on Citigroup mortgages made in 2006 and 2007 were twice as high as those made in 2004 and 2005, which was not surprising, given that Citigroup had slashed its lending standards in 2006 and 2007.

At the same time Citigroup was ramping up bad loans, the Fed allowed it to shave its loan loss reserves. In the run-up to the crisis in 2006, Citigroup had reduced its loan loss allowance for consumer loans from $8.3 billion in 2004 to $6.0 billion. Later, in 2007, after the housing market cratered, the company was forced to double its loan loss reserves for consumer loans to $12.3 billion. In 2008, Citigroup had to increase that loan loss reserve once again, to $22.3 billion.

Citigroup's story illuminates both the weaknesses and strengths in the Fed's oversight of the nonbank mortgage originators under its aegis. The 2004 order against Citigroup and CitiFinancial showed that the Fed was capable of strong enforcement when it chose to use its powers. In contrast, after the Fed terminated the consent order, it simply watched silently as CitiFinancial pursued an ultimately ruinous strategy. In the process, the Fed put the entire financial system at risk.

## OTHER FED ENFORCEMENT ACTIONS AFFECTING MORTGAGE LENDING

When we examined the Fed's other public enforcement actions during the housing bubble, a clear pattern emerged. The Fed was strict when it came to mortgage lending by state member banks. It took at least twenty-two enforcement actions between 2003 and 2007 aimed at weak home mortgage underwriting by small community banks. The Fed's orders almost always included a requirement that borrowers' repayment source and ability to repay be consistently documented in all future loans.

The opposite was true for the nonbank lending subsidiaries of bank holding companies. Apart from the Citigroup case, the Fed did not enter a single public enforcement order from 2003 through 2007 for lax home mortgage underwriting by a nonbank mortgage lender under its purview or its parent corporation.[70] The Fed's enforcement patterns suggest that where the law required the Fed to examine an entity regularly[71]—as it did for state member banks—the Fed detected hazardous lending practices and often instituted crackdowns. Conversely, where the law did not require the Fed to routinely examine an entity—as was true for nonbank mortgage subsidiaries—the Fed ignored its responsibilities and, as a result, did not catch major problems. It is hardly surprising, then, that there was a dearth of Fed enforcement actions for the nonbank mortgage lenders on its watch.

## THE FEDERAL GOVERNMENT'S COLLECTIVE BLAME

As the collapse of the financial system unfolded in 2008, what had started as the subprime crisis came to be known as the "banking crisis." One major bank failure came to light that year after another, making painfully obvious that the largest commercial banking companies—all of which were supervised by federal banking regulators—were deeply implicated in the origination and securitization of bad mortgage loans, whether through the banks themselves or their nonbank affiliates.

Some federal banking regulators blamed the subprime fiasco on independent subprime lenders that were regulated by states. The evidence contradicts these claims. For 2006—the last full year of the subprime boom—fully twelve of the fifteen largest subprime lenders were regulated by federal banking regulators. Together, these twelve lenders controlled 50 percent of the subprime market. By the end of 2008, almost all of those lenders were operating under a death warrant or were out of business. The pervasive federal supervisory power over most of the top subprime originators makes clear that the federal government bears strong collective responsibility for the subprime crisis and the enormous financial harm it inflicted on ordinary Americans.

One reason for the regulatory failure was a "silo approach" that infected federal regulators and the statutes under which they operated. This silo approach was not just a matter of turf wars, but was the result of actual legislation. In the Gramm-Leach-Bliley Act of 1999, Congress designated the Federal Reserve as the super-regulator for financial holding companies[72] because they posed heightened risks to the country's financial health. In so doing, however, Congress tied the Federal Reserve's hands. For example, Congress told the Fed to rely on bank and thrift examination reports by other state and federal banking regulators to the fullest extent possible instead of having the Fed examine those banks and thrifts itself. As a result, the Fed could not directly obtain the information it needed to assess the risks that large firms were creating.[73]

The silo approach to regulation carried another risk. It allowed federal regulators to slough off moral responsibility for their contribution to the crisis. By confining federal regulators to different silos and keeping each regulator's silo off limits to other regulators, Congress encouraged federal officials to shrug at their counterparts' lapses. Early on, one could see intimations of this mentality in bank merger decisions, where the Fed downplayed public complaints about destructive subprime lending because the banks or thrifts in question were supervised by federal regulators other than the

**TABLE 10.1.**
Top subprime lenders in 2006, by federal banking regulator.

| RANK IN 2006 | NAME OF LENDER | FEDERAL BANKING REGULATOR |
|---|---|---|
| 1 | HSBC Finance | FRB |
| 2 | New Century Financial Corp. | * |
| 3 | Countrywide Financial Corp. | FRB |
| 4 | WMC Mortgage Corp. | OTS |
| 5 | Fremont Investment and Loan | FDIC |
| 6 | Option One Mortgage Corp. | OTS |
| 7 | Wells Fargo Home Mortgage | OCC |
| 8 | First Franklin Financial | OCC |
| 9 | Washington Mutual Bank | OTS |
| 10 | Ameriquest Mortgage Corp. | * |
| 11 | CitiFinancial | FRB |
| 12 | GMAC-RFC | OTS |
| 13 | Accredited Home Lenders | * |
| 14 | BNC Mortgage Inc. | OTS |
| 15 | Chase Home Finance | OCC |

* Independent lender not subject to federal banking regulation.
*Sources*: www.americanbanker.com; Padilla (2008).

Fed. Later, this lack of moral responsibility resurfaced in a much more vicious way, as the OCC and OTS labored desperately—but not persuasively—to shift blame to the states.

**CONCLUSION**

In 2002, Alan Greenspan prophesied the regulatory failure that would happen on his watch. During an asset boom, he said, federal regulators tend to relax their guard: "Ever less attention is paid to potential problems as the cautious voices appear curiously quaint and have little quantitative support because all the recent news and facts are favorable." "Even the supervisors and policymakers," he continued, "tend to be caught up by the process." He went on to say: "Their voices of caution are rarely raised because they, too, find it difficult to make a case for restraint because the quantitative indicators do not support caution until too late in the lending expansion."[74]

Years later, in September 2008, a senior Fed official turned to one of us and said: "All of you were warning us about subprime loans, but we didn't listen back then because everything seemed to be doing fine." For once, Greenspan was right.

▷

# Wall Street Skirts Regulation

Without Wall Street financing of subprime mortgages, there would have been no housing bubble and no contagion. The credit boom was a supply-side phenomenon, driven by the clamoring of investors for high-yield mortgage-backed securities and CDOs peddled by Wall Street. Consequently, it is necessary to ask, who regulated the finance side of the equation and what did they do wrong?

Just as deregulation fed risk in mortgage lending, it gave Wall Street firms carte blanche to manufacture dizzying levels of risk and to pump that risk into the global financial system, until the entire system collapsed. The Securities and Exchange Commission (SEC) and federal banking regulators allowed the nation's largest banks to reduce their capital and reserves to dangerously low levels. Capitol Hill and federal regulators declined to regulate large swaths of the financial system, including credit derivatives, hedge funds, private bond offerings, and credit-rating agencies. What resulted was a shadow financial system trillions of dollars in size, with scant federal oversight.

Congress laid the groundwork back in 1999 and 2000, when it deregulated over-the-counter credit default swaps, which ultimately became pathways of contagion. The SEC for its part looked the other way while banks issued droves of subprime bonds and CDOs marred by shoddy due diligence, skimpy disclosures, and inflated credit ratings. Then federal banking regulators sealed the financial system's fate by allowing commercial banks to load up on toxic mortgage-backed securities. Having magnified financial risk many times over, the federal government sat by while the country's financial institutions spun out of control.[1]

## LEVERAGED TO THE HILT

The rampant speculation that characterized the housing boom occurred in part because the big financial houses, including investment banks, commercial banks, and their holding companies, were overleveraged to an extreme. Punch-drunk on debt, these giants had too little of their own money at stake to exercise caution. This over-leveraging was expressly countenanced by the SEC and federal banking regulators.

To grasp why leverage matters, it is useful to think about leverage in both its narrow and its broad sense. Leverage, in its narrow sense, means the percentage of a company's operating money that comes from borrowed funds instead of cash contributed by shareholders. For example, if a bank's balance sheet shows $9 million in borrowed funds and $1 million in shareholders' equity, the bank has a leverage ratio of nine. In its broad sense, leverage refers to the fact that the more a company borrows, the more shareholders will make on their investment if the company's business strategy pans out.

It is easy to see this when buying and selling a home. Let's say you bought a home for $200,000. Some years later, you sell it for $220,000. If you originally paid all cash for your home, your return on your investment—or your return on equity, in finance talk—is $20,000 divided by $200,000 or 10 percent. But let's assume that you only put $20,000 down when you bought the house and took out a zero-percent, no-cost mortgage for the rest. Later, when you sell it, your return on equity is $20,000 divided by $20,000 or 100 percent. In this way, leverage works like a gear: by borrowing 90 percent of the purchase price, you boosted your return tenfold. That, in short, is the power of leverage.

Shareholders like leverage because it magnifies their returns. At the same time, leverage has real dangers. It makes shareholders more prone to gamble on big risks, because they will capture all the profits if they win but have little at stake if they lose. Leverage also makes companies more dependent on debt for their survival, which can jeopardize those companies if creditors refuse to advance funds. Companies that depend on short-term debt are especially vulnerable if they suffer major losses; lenders can suddenly lose confidence and deny the company more credit, putting the company in immediate peril of bankruptcy.

Because of these concerns, financial regulators have long regulated the capital levels of banks, brokerage houses, and insurance companies. These rules—known as maximum leverage or capital adequacy rules—are designed to ensure that financial firms have an adequate safety cushion against losses. The rules are also meant to deter financial companies from taking excessive risks.

## INVESTMENT BANKS AND THE SEC

The year 2008 spelled the demise of the free-standing Wall Street investment bank. The "Big Five" Wall Street houses had storied histories, having survived wars, panics, and the Great Depression. Morgan Stanley was the youngest of the pack, spun off from J.P. Morgan in 1935. Bear Stearns was founded in 1923 and Merrill Lynch in 1914. Goldman Sachs dated back even earlier, to 1869. Lehman Brothers, the most venerable of all, predated the Civil War, having been founded in 1850. Yet within six short months in 2008, Lehman Brothers failed, Bear Stearns and Merrill Lynch were taken over, and Goldman Sachs and Morgan Stanley became bank holding companies in a desperate bid for access to the Fed's discount window. All five banks suffered from excessive leverage, and when the piper sought to be paid, they simply did not have enough capital.

Why did the Securities and Exchange Commission let the five big solo Wall Street firms get away with so little skin in the game? One part of the answer traces its history to 2004, when the SEC adopted the "alternative net capital rule." Until then, the SEC had imposed maximum leverage ratios on all brokerage houses, allowing broker-dealers to borrow only $15 for every $1 in capital they held.[2] Under the "alternative net capital rule," the largest investment banks, with $5 billion in assets or more, became exempt from the maximum leverage ratio of fifteen. Instead, the rule allowed the Big Five firms to set their own leverage ceilings, using their internal mathematical models. The Big Five were the only independent investment banks that qualified for this loophole. That comes as no surprise because they were the ones that lobbied for the rule.[3]

What ensued was a free-for-all, as the Big Five lobbed their leverage into the stratosphere. They took billions of dollars out of their capital reserves and invested those funds in mortgage-backed securities and CDOs. The week Bear Stearns sank, its leverage ratio hit 35, meaning that for every $1 in tangible equity capital, it had borrowed $35. Later that month, on March 31, Lehman Brothers' ratio stood at 31.7. Meanwhile, in 2007, Morgan Stanley's ratio had also hit 35, while Merrill Lynch and Goldman Sachs had topped out at 31.9 and 28. In contrast, the biggest global commercial banks had leverage ratios of around 11.[4]

When the SEC agreed to the alternative net capital rule, the commission fooled itself into thinking it had gotten a quid pro quo. Under federal securities laws, Congress only gave the SEC formal authority to regulate registered broker-dealers, not the holding companies of investment banks. Before 2002, that suited the Big Five perfectly fine. But in 2002, the European Union adopted its Financial Conglomerates Directive, which put the Big Five in a bind. Under the directive, the European Union threatened to impose heavy regulation on the European operations of the Big Five firms—including higher capital requirements—unless the SEC regulated the holding companies. The EU directive contained an "out," however, for foreign companies subject to "equivalent" regulation by their home country regulator. In order to take advantage of this exception, the Big Five brought a proposal to the SEC for consideration. What they proposed was this: Allow us to compute our own leverage caps company-wide and we will submit our holding company and all other unregulated affiliates to voluntary SEC examination and supervision. The SEC hastily agreed. Thus, the Big Five swapped looser leverage requirements for "consolidated" SEC supervision to escape EU oversight of their European operations.[5]

Four years later, in 2008, the SEC disbanded its consolidated supervised entity (CSE) program after the agency's inspector general issued a report in September of that year finding that the consolidated oversight "program failed to carry out its mission in its oversight of Bear Stearns."[6] The whole point of the CSE program had been to prevent financial or operational weaknesses at the Big Five firms that could place "the broader financial system at risk." But after the Bear Stearns fiasco, it was "undisputable," in the words of the SEC inspector general, that the CSE program had failed.[7]

The inspector general detailed a litany of holes in the CSE program's oversight. The SEC had ignored warning signs at Bear Stearns even after two of its hedge funds failed in June 2007. Among them were red flags that Bear Stearns was increasing its holdings of risky mortgage securities to "new highs," sometimes exceeding the company's own internal limits. The SEC stood back while Bear gorged itself on mortgage-backed securities, even though its risk managers lacked expertise in mortgages. By spring 2007, turnover had left Bear Stearns's risk management unit in "disarray," giving its "trading desks more power over risk managers." Similarly, the SEC knew that Bear Stearns was using "outdated models that were more than ten years old" to value mortgage derivatives.[8] Yet the agency did not force Bear to update its models.

The SEC was also lackadaisical about Bear Stearns's stress tests. Incredibly, through early 2007, Bear Stearns's stress test models for mortgages did not take falling house prices, consumer credit scores, or patterns of default rates into account. The previous fall, Bear Stearns had briefed the SEC on rising subprime delinquencies and the extreme risks posed by its subprime residuals. Still, the agency did not force Bear Stearns to "add a meltdown of the subprime market to its risk scenarios." Furthermore, the SEC assumed that Bear Stearns would have access to financing in a financial crisis. The SEC was wrong.[9]

The inspector general's report revealed other irregularities in the SEC's handling of the CSE program. In violation of its own procedures, the SEC had lifted its net capital rule for Bear Stearns and three other Big Five firms before its staff had completed a required inspection process. The agency also let the Big Five firms use their own, internal auditors to check their risk management control systems even though the SEC had a rule requiring independent, outside auditors to do that work.

Part of the problem was that the SEC just didn't have the staff to regularly examine the Big Five firms and their empires spanning the globe. Badly outgunned, the SEC assumed that the Big Five would keep their leverage in check. What was supposed to be a substitute for vigilant EU oversight deteriorated into industry self-regulation.[10] In a damning admission before the Senate Banking Committee in September 2008, former SEC chairman Christopher Cox later conceded that "voluntary regulation doesn't work."[11]

The experience with the CSE program also reflected the SEC's hostility to regulation. In a speech in 2004, for example, SEC commissioner Paul S. Atkins criticized the federal government for what he called its "intrusive involvement in the markets during the Great Depression." In Atkins's view, "the danger" was "that politicians and regulators" would "go too far . . . by enacting regulations that supplant the market's judgment."[12] Atkins continued his attack in a 2006 speech: "We must not allow the American economy to be encumbered by a web of excessive regulations that fail the cost/benefit test."[13]

Later on, the SEC attempted to obscure evidence of its lapses. As late as June 2010, the CSE program report that the SEC inspector general had posted on its Web site was heavily "redacted to delete information that SEC believe[d] [was] nonpublic and confidential."[14] According to Bloomberg News, the inspector general redacted the report at the request of the SEC's Division of Trading and Markets, which supervises Wall Street. A full version of the report posted by Senator Charles Grassley revealed that the redacted material included not only material specific to Bear Stearns, but language directly critical of the SEC. The redactions smacked not only of an SEC cover-up (a clumsy one at that), but called the independence of the SEC's inspector general into doubt.[15]

## CAPITAL REGULATION OF BANKS

Securities brokers are not the only companies that are supposed to keep their leverage in check. Bank holding companies and commercial banks and thrifts have to meet minimum capital requirements, too. These requirements are supposed to serve as a shock absorber if a bank is hit by unexpected losses. With adequate capital, a bank or thrift should be able to absorb its losses while continuing to make loans and safeguard the funds of its depositors.

From the height of the housing boom in 2005 through 2008, however, capital levels steadily dwindled at FDIC-insured banks and thrifts. For the banking industry as a whole, core capital shrank from 8.25 percent in 2005 to 7.48 percent in 2008. Over that same period, the percentage of unprofitable banks and thrifts increased nearly fourfold. By the end of 2008, almost one-fourth of all FDIC-insured institutions were unprofitable, a shocking number by any account.[16]

On top of capital, banks are expected to maintain loan loss reserves as a buffer against expected loan losses. During the housing boom, however, major banking companies slashed their loan loss reserves. Citigroup, for example, cut its loan loss reserves almost one-fifth, from $13.2 billion to $10.6 billion, between 2003 and 2005. The same trend was evident throughout the banking industry. (See figures 11.1 and 11.2.)

While banks were playing with fire, why didn't the regulators step in? Part of the answer involves the history of capital regulation in the United States. When the credit crisis hit, the United States was in its third generation of capital rules, each more "sophisticated" than the last. During the first generation, pre-1999, capital was calculated in a straightforward way, by dividing shareholders' equity by average total assets. In 1999, however, federal banking regulators switched to a new capital method known as "Basel I risk-based capital," at the instigation of the Federal Reserve. The idea behind Basel I was to allow banks and thrifts to hold less capital against assets that were considered "safer." Under that approach, institutions sorted their assets into four pigeonholes according to risk, each assigned a different weight. The amount of the assets in each pigeonhole was then multiplied by the appropriate weight and the weighted products were added together to calculate a bank's total risk-weighted assets. Banks had to maintain capital of at least 8 percent of their risk-weighted assets.[17]

Basel I was not foolproof. Even as it was being implemented in the United States, critics were challenging the risk weights for home mortgages and mortgage-backed

**TABLE 11.1.**
Core capital, all FDIC-insured institutions: 2005–2008.

|  | 2005 | 2006 | 2007 | 2008 |
|---|---|---|---|---|
| Core capital (leverage) ratio (%) | 8.25 | 8.22 | 7.97 | 7.48 |

*Source*: FDIC Statistics on Depository Institutions.

**TABLE 11.2.**
Percentage of unprofitable FDIC-insured institutions: 2005–2008.

|  | 2005 | 2006 | 2007 | 2008 |
|---|---|---|---|---|
| Percentage of unprofitable institutions | 6.22 | 7.94 | 12.07 | 24.41 |

*Source*: FDIC Statistics on Depository Institutions.

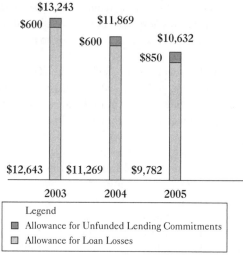

**FIGURE 11.1.**
Citigroup's loan loss reserves in millions of dollars: 2003–2005.

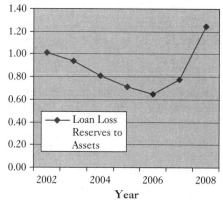

**FIGURE 11.2.**
U.S. banking industry, total loan loss reserves to total assets: 2002–2008.

securities as too low. There were also concerns that banks could understate their capital requirements by using securitization or SIVs to move risky assets off their balance sheets.

Under Basel I, lenders did not have to reserve full capital against assets that they transferred off their balance sheets. Later, subprime loans and related assets came back to haunt banks, either via recourse clauses requiring them to buy back loans or because banks had guaranteed the debts of SIVs, sometimes informally. As a result, many banks suffered losses in excess of their capital reserves. As one commentator astutely observed, these "off-balance-sheet strategies hid risks instead of reducing them."[18]

In the early 2000s, the Federal Reserve launched a new capital initiative called "Basel II" to further reduce capital levels. In the Greenspan tradition, Basel II was yet another gambit to swap government regulation for private risk management. With exceptionally poor timing, federal regulators unveiled the "advanced approach" of Basel II in December 2007, just in time for the subprime crisis.

From the moment of its debut, Basel II came under attack. The new capital standards relied on ratings by the rating agencies to set risk weights; this was folly. Worse yet, Basel II allowed the largest internationally active banks—that is, banks posing the most systemic risk—to compute their own minimum capital levels according to their internal risk models. The message was, "Make up your test and tell us how you are doing."[19] There was no requirement that banks take account of low points in the business cycle. Nor did they have to factor in "tail events," which are like tsunamis: highly unlikely yet possible.[20] And like a tsunami, if a tail event is a "fat tail event," the losses can be disastrous. The credit crisis was just such a fat tail event.

Basel II had another Achilles heel, which is that it did not require banks to quantify interest-rate risk, liquidity risk, or systemic risk. Interest-rate risk sparked the savings and loan crisis in the 1980s; liquidity risk and systemic risk were drivers of the credit crisis of 2007 and 2008. Timothy Geithner observed: "Basel II is too confident that a firm can adjust to protect itself from its own mistakes without adding to downward pressure on markets and takes too little account of the risk of a flight to safety—a broad-based, marketwise rush for the exits as the financial system as a whole de-leverages and tries collectively to move into more liquid and lower risk assets of government obligations."[21]

Banks took advantage of Basel II's permissive approach and developed models that served their own purposes. One professor of quantitative finance described conferences on risk models under Basel II, saying "All the time I'm sitting in the audience thinking that these models are far too simplistic and based on countless unrealistic assumptions. I tell people that these instruments are dangerous, that no one understands the risks. But no one cares."[22] Another analyst claimed that banks dumbed down their models to boost short-term returns. He was quoted saying, "There was a willful designing of the systems to measure the risks in a certain way that would not necessarily pick up all the right risks. . . . [Investment banks] wanted to keep their capital base as stable as possible so that the limits they imposed on their trading desks and portfolio managers would be stable."[23]

Banks were not operating in a regulatory vacuum. Basel II put the onus on regulators to weed out the bad models from the good. Whether the regulators had the expertise or the backbone to recognize rigged models and overhaul them is an open question. The evidence suggests they had neither.

With banks having carte blanche to develop self-serving models, it is no surprise that in December 2008 Moody's found that almost all banks using the Basel II standard had cut their capital levels. SEC chairman Christopher Cox eventually told Congress: "Neither the Basel I nor Basel II standards as then in force were adequate. Each had serious need of improvement."[24] It was sweet vindication for Sheila Bair, who had refused to sign off on Basel II without keeping the old ratio (that is, shareholders' equity to total assets) as a backstop, over vehement protests by the other federal banking regulators. Evidence like this led the FDIC's Sheila Bair to muse, "If [Basel II] says banks need less capital at the height of a global banking crisis, imagine the financial leverage it would encourage during good times."[25]

## SKIMPY DISCLOSURES TO INVESTORS

By loosening leverage and capital rules, federal regulators gave banks and Wall Street firms a much bigger appetite for excessive risk. The resulting subprime crisis would not have been so disastrous if investors had grasped the enormity of the risks they were undertaking. Their ability to gauge those risks, however, depended on accurate and complete disclosures about the mortgage-backed securities and CDOs they were buying. It was the Securities and Exchange Commission's job to adopt disclosure rules with teeth so that investors could make educated decisions.

The SEC's disclosure requirements for asset-backed bonds fell short of the mark. For most of the housing bubble, the SEC had no rule in place requiring disclosures that were specifically tailored to mortgage-backed securities or CDOs. The SEC's Regulation AB,[26] adopted in 2005, attempted to address that gap; however, Reg AB did not go into effect until January 1, 2006, after most private-label offerings backed by subprime bonds had been sold.

Reg AB had two critical flaws: (1) it suffered from limited coverage; and (2) when it did apply, the rule failed to give investors the information they needed to seriously analyze an offering. Reg AB governed only "asset-backed securities," which were narrowly defined to exclude many types of structured finance products. Furthermore, the rule only applied to public offerings, that is, offerings that were marketed to the general public. An investment bank could simply bypass Reg AB by structuring an issue as a private offering that was limited to big institutional investors. In these private offerings, SEC disclosures were lighter or left to private negotiation, based on the notion that institutional investors had the clout and sophistication to demand the information they needed to make informed and smart choices. Not surprisingly, Wall Street took full advantage of this loophole. In particular, CDOs were "almost always" sold through private offerings with seriously deficient disclosures.[27]

Even when Reg AB did apply, the disclosures were too skimpy to be of use. The SEC designed Reg AB as a "principles-based rule,"[28] meaning that its substance was deliberately vague. In addition, the commission modeled many of Reg AB's disclosures on the reporting requirements for corporate issuers. Corporations usually have track records so securities disclosures for those issuers focus on the firms' performance. In contrast, past performance was irrelevant for most offerings of mortgage-backed securities and CDOs because the issues were backed by new mortgages with scarce payment histories.[29] In essence, Reg AB put the wrong information under the microscope.

Investors in subprime securities needed standardized information on the risk characteristics of the individual loans backing the bonds because the loans were the main source of payment for the bonds. Information on the loan-to-value ratio, debt-to-income ratio, property location, and payment shock ratio for each of the loans was the only way investors could know with confidence what they were getting into. Reg AB did not mandate disclosure of that level of detail. The rule did encourage investment banks to make tapes with loan level data available to investors, but it did not require them to provide this information. All Reg AB mandated was a summary of the aggregate characteristics of the loan pool. That made it difficult to discern whether the riskiest loans were going to the strongest or to the weakest borrowers in the loan pool.[30]

Leaving disclosure of individual loan characteristics to Wall Street's discretion turned out to be a big mistake. In 2009, the Committee on Capital Markets Regulation conducted a sample of the data tapes that issuers had voluntarily filed on the SEC's Web site and found that "numerous data fields considered essential by investors were simply not available to them."[31] The data fields on the tapes, moreover, were not standardized and varied all over the lot.[32] In the case of CDOs, drilling down to the individual loans supporting the bond payments was impossible.

Similarly, Reg AB did not make investment banks disclose the due diligence reports they commissioned from outside firms, even when those reports contained evidence of deteriorating lending standards. As we discussed earlier, too often investment banks swept those reports under the rug, withholding them from investors and ratings agencies.[33] Reg AB also dropped the ball when it came to tracking the quality of new loans that were added to revolving loan pools after an offering closed.[34]

Reg AB failed investors in another respect, by not requiring ongoing disclosure of performance information. The rule required data on loan performance for the first year following the offering, but not for the life of the loans.[35] Even during the first year, issuers' web sites containing payment histories were "scattered and hidden." Many of the web sites only made "limited loan-level data" available on the payment history of a loan pool and the data that was reported "var[ied] widely across servicers and deals."[36]

All told, there was a dearth of useful publicly available information on the loan pools underlying private-label mortgage bonds and CDOs. The problem was so severe that the trade association for mutual funds—many of whom were large institutional investors in subprime bonds—complained that "our members . . . do not receive the same amount of information from issuers as is received by" the rating agencies, "regardless of whether the offering is subject to Regulation AB, and despite the fact that the [SEC] had indicated that a determination to provide information to a credit rating agency should be considered in determining whether such information is material to investors."[37]

The SEC disclosure scheme for subprime mortgage-backed securities and CDOs was so misbegotten and riddled with exceptions that the securities operated in a fact-free zone. Investors and analysts who wanted to conduct serious due diligence could not obtain the facts they needed to figure out the true risk associated with the underlying loans. Without those facts, investors often overpaid for those securities. Worse yet, investors could not police the market through decisions about whether to buy securities and at what price.

## SEC ABDICATION OF ENFORCEMENT

Under federal securities law, disclosures in Wall Street offerings of mortgage-backed securities and CDOs have to be truthful, under pain of enforcement for securities fraud.[38] Moreover, federal securities law has a capacious conception of the "truth." It is not enough for Wall Street firms to refrain from affirmative lies when drafting prospectuses and offering circulars. They must also avoid misleading half-truths, otherwise known in securities parlance as "misleading omissions of material fact." Just like in the courtroom, Wall Street firms in securities prospectuses must tell the truth, the whole truth, and nothing but the truth.

Without strong enforcement, however, these antifraud provisions lack teeth. The SEC had that enforcement authority. On the front end, the SEC had the ability to review public subprime bond offerings for truthfulness and to halt offerings involving misleading or missing disclosures. On the back end, the SEC had the authority to investigate suspected securities fraud and to bring wrongdoers to justice through civil or criminal enforcement.

Despite the threat of SEC enforcement, disclosures made in subprime offerings were not always accurate. A pervasive problem was the prevalence of exception loans, which we discussed earlier in connection with securitization. Prospectuses and offering memoranda for subprime mortgage-backed securities usually set forth the lender's underwriting standards in detail, followed by a general disclaimer that the lender reserved the right to make exceptions to the guidelines. Rarely did the issues reveal the extent of the exceptions or the quality of the loans that deviated from the lenders' promised standards. In a 2006 offering document, for instance, the lender Aegis declared that it could make exceptions to its underwriting guidelines if[39]

the application reflects compensating factors, such as: low loan-to-value ratios; stable ownership; low debt ratios; strong residual income; a maximum of one 30-day late payment on all mortgage loans during the last 12 months; and stable employment or ownership of current residence of four or more years.

Aegis was silent, though, about the extent of its exception loans. The fact that subprime bonds were marketed with such deficient disclosures on exception loans suggests that the SEC was asleep at the switch.[40]

The SEC was similarly remiss when it came to enforcement. From 2000 to 2007, the number of SEC investigations culminating in Justice Department prosecutions for securities fraud plummeted 87 percent, from sixty-nine down to nine. Even more alarming was what the SEC missed over that period, ranging from the ongoing problems at Bear Stearns to alleged Ponzi schemes, including one for $8 billion by Texas financier Robert Allen Stanford and another for $1 billion by PEMGroup and its founder, Jerry Pang.

The biggest Ponzi scheme to elude the SEC was Bernard Madoff. In May 2000, an experienced derivatives expert and private fraud investigator named Harry Markopolos presented the SEC with a written analysis questioning the consistently glowing returns on Madoff's funds. Markopolos showed that Madoff could not have earned constant positive returns for seven years straight given his purported investment strategy. Markopolos also considered it suspicious that Madoff did not allow any large international outside accounting firms to audit his company. Markopolos concluded, "Combining the discrepancies I've noted . . . with the hearsay I've heard, [the evidence] seems to fit in with the patterns commonly found in Ponzi Schemes."

Markopolos did not stop there. In 2001 and 2005 he submitted more detailed reports with evidence on Madoff to the SEC.[41] It was not until 2006, however, that the SEC finally opened an investigation into Madoff and his firm. In a hapless performance, the agency closed that inquiry in 2008 after finding "no evidence of fraud."[42]

As the Madoff incident showed, the SEC was ill-equipped to uncover fraud or even recognize major tips. According to the SEC's inspector general, the SEC lacked effective, uniform procedures for processing tips, and whatever procedures did exist were generally ignored.[43] Part of the problem was that most of the SEC's examiners were too young, inexperienced, and poorly paid to grasp the industries they were examining. Markopolos criticized them for huddling in corporate conference rooms looking at documents that management fed them, instead of roaming the trading floors or barging into portfolio managers' offices to question company personnel. Furthermore, most SEC examiners were not trained on Bloomberg terminals. Markopolos termed Bloomberg terminals "the lifeblood of the industry," with "much of the data an SEC staffer would need for any fraud analysis of a company." "If everyone in industry is using Bloombergs except for the SEC," he mused, "it is little wonder the SEC can't find fraud."[44]

The SEC liked to blame underfunding and staff cuts for its poor track record. While both were problems,[45] there were larger forces at work. For one thing, the Madoff affair raised serious questions about the SEC's independence from the securities industry. Madoff was exalted in the securities industry, having served as the chairman of the NASDAQ Stock Exchange starting in 1990. Indeed, he was so respected in the agency's inner circles that SEC commissioners sought him out for advice and the commission appointed him to its advisory committee on market information in 2000.[46]

The Madoff scandal put a spotlight on the commission's hostility to strong securities oversight. Under the leadership of Chairman Christopher Cox, the commission took deliberate steps to disable the SEC's enforcement apparatus and impede its enforcement lawyers from doing their job. For example, in 2006, Chairman Cox instituted a new policy prohibiting the agency from assessing civil money penalties against corporations except in "egregious" cases. To keep the SEC's lawyers on a short leash, Cox issued a further decree requiring the agency's lawyers to get prior approval from the full commission before they could negotiate civil money penalties against public issuers. The results were disastrous. Three years later, a brand-new SEC commissioner, Luis Aguilar, looked at the results of this "pilot program," and reported that "penalty amounts in SEC cases against corporate issuers . . . plummeted" 85 percent between 2003 and 2008. That, according to Aguilar, was "not the way to run an aggressive and robust enforcement program." Not long after, the *New York Times* reported that "demoralized [SEC] staff members had been watering down proposed settlements in enforcement cases out of the fear that the commission would reject them."[47]

Christopher Cox further tied his staff's hands by prohibiting them from opening formal investigations or issuing subpoenas without advance approval by the full commission. Even worse, Cox shelved investigation requests from the staff unless the commission gave unanimous consent. Not surprisingly, Aguilar later noted, the result was a "logjam."[48] These seemingly mundane rules had a profoundly chilling effect on SEC enforcement.

The SEC's hostility to tough securities enforcement under Chairman Cox was just one chapter in a protracted campaign by the securities industry, accounting firms, and conservatives to dismantle securities regulation. This agenda took flight in the 1980s with the ascendance of the efficient capital market hypothesis, which holds that securities prices "self-correct" rapidly in response to new information. Its corollary—at least according to some—is that strong securities disclosures and enforcement are not needed because markets maintain their equilibrium.

Consistent with this laissez-faire mind-set, Congress pushed through a series of laws in the 1990s that undercut strong securities fraud enforcement. The opening salvo was the Private Securities Litigation Reform Act of 1995, which made it easier for private securities fraud class actions to get thrown out of court. The following year, Congress set its sights on state securities regulators in the National Securities Markets Improvement Act of 1996. In that act, Congress stripped the states of the power to scrutinize two types of securities offerings for fraud: private offerings and public offerings of shares traded on NASDAQ and the New York Stock Exchange. Two years later, Congress targeted private securities fraud plaintiffs again, banning state law securities fraud class actions in the Securities Litigation Uniform Standards Act of 1998.[49]

The SEC was also a powerful advocate for management interests in the courts. Starting in the late 1980s and accelerating in later years, the agency filed a series of briefs in the Supreme Court and lower courts successfully arguing for a stingy reading of the federal securities laws, to the detriment of investors. In fact, SEC commissioner Atkins went so far as to issue an invitation to trade groups in 2006, saying: "If you think there are ripe issues on which the Commissioner should be participating as an Amicus in particular cases, I invite you to tell us. The Commission will not shy away from a good fight if it makes sense!" The commission's "friend of the court" briefs resulted in a string of court victories that narrowed the class of wrongdoers who could face liability for securities fraud and raised new hurdles for injured investors to get to trial on securities fraud claims.[50] In the process, the SEC shed its role as a protector of investors "into a mechanism for protecting financial predators with political clout from investors."[51]

## THE UNDERREGULATED CREDIT-RATING INDUSTRY

The SEC's lax regulation was matched by the federal government's failure to regulate the credit-rating agencies. Until 2006, three firms—Moody's, Standard & Poor's, and Fitch, which together held 80 percent of the credit-ratings business—were virtually free from regulation.[52] All three firms were key players in the shadow banking system, responsible for the reliability of billions of dollars in bonds but accountable to no one.

The rating agencies had gotten in trouble well before their ratings of subprime bonds became an issue. Back in 2001, they were implicated in the Enron crisis,[53] which led Congress to enact the Credit Rating Agency Reform Act in 2006.[54] As we discussed earlier in the chapter on securitization, the SEC had the power to confer Nationally Recognized Statistical Rating Organization (NRSRO) status on individual credit-rating agencies. In the new act, Congress placed rating agencies seeking NRSRO status under SEC oversight. The primary thrust of the act was SEC registration, record-keeping, disclosure, and a ban on coercive practices that could only be enforced by the SEC. There was no requirement that rating agencies do a good job making rating decisions. Indeed, the act expressly prohibited the SEC and the states from "regulat[ing] the substance of credit ratings or the procedures and methodologies by which any" NRSRO "determines credit ratings." The act also left the "issuer pays" system intact, instructing rating agencies just to disclose their conflicts of interest and "manage" them.[55]

In light of the fact that the government's NRSRO designation helped rating agencies generate business and sent a signal to investors that the agencies' ratings were trustworthy, the government should have vigorously overseen the rating agencies much earlier. Instead, when Congress finally decided that some regulation was needed, it came up with a wholly ineffectual law.

## CREDIT DEFAULT SWAPS

Credit default swaps linked three extraordinary events in 2008—the federal government's bailout of Bear Stearns, its life buoy to AIG, and its decision to let Lehman Brothers fail. All three companies owed hundreds of billions of dollars in potential credit default swap (CDS) liabilities to other major financial players.

### Credit Default Swaps 101

Credit default swaps became common in the early 1990s, when JPMorgan touted them as a way to hedge credit risk and reduce capital requirements.[56] As we explained earlier, credit default swaps are guarantees that protect investors if a company or a bond defaults.

In general, sellers of CDS are large, global insurance companies and banks operating in London and New York. Banks were the biggest buyers of CDS, and they bought them for several purposes. CDS enabled banks to protect themselves from default by specific companies, such as Lehman Brothers. Banks also bought swaps to hedge the risk of default on subprime mortgage-backed securities and collateralized debt obligations (CDOs). CDS were attractive hedges because they enabled banks to reduce their capital requirements.[57] In addition, speculators bought CDS as bets that securities would default, without owning the securities themselves.

All three uses of CDS can magnify financial risk. For example, when credit default swaps are used as hedges, they almost always introduce speculation into the financial system because one party to the swap is a hedger and the other party is a speculator.[58] In addition, credit default swaps make buyers of hedges bullish about their ability to manage risks. For banks, the ability to hedge with swaps—and the favorable capital treatment that resulted—gave some of them confidence to shift their investments from boring, liquid assets into risky, illiquid assets offering higher potential yields. CDS boosted the incentives of banking companies, like Citigroup, to make rash mortgages and invest in massive portfolios of illiquid subprime bonds.[59] In the process, these swaps fueled the supply of lax credit and, with it, the housing bubble.

Credit default swaps can also create multilateral exposure through daisy chains of liability, in which one swap seller's ability to meet its CDS obligations to a buyer depends on another seller's solvency down the line. This is because a seller, who is concerned about the liability it has taken on, can turn around and buy a CDS to cover its liability. It can do this because it does not need to own the bond being hedged in order to buy a CDS.[60] This practice became so common that by 2008, fully 90 percent of outstanding CDS were such naked swaps.[61]

To illustrate, say, for instance, a thrift institution, Thrifty, bought a AAA subprime bond. To hedge against a possible default on the bond, Thrifty bought an over-the-counter credit default swap from a CDS dealer called Jamestown. Jamestown was now on the hook if Thrifty's AAA subprime bond missed payments. To protect itself, Jamestown then bought a CDS from another dealer, Reserve, to hedge the risk on Thrifty's AAA subprime bond.

Next let's assume the AAA subprime bond owned by Thrifty went into default. Thrifty would demand payment from Jamestown under the original CDS. In turn, Jamestown would demand payment from Reserve under the second CDS. If Reserve was insolvent and could not make the promised payment, then Jamestown would have to pay off Thrifty without any reimbursement from Reserve. If the liability was too large, it could force Jamestown into bankruptcy. Then Thrifty would be stuck with the loss on its AAA subprime bond, eroding its capital. In this way, a CDS default by a seller such as Reserve could trigger a domino effect of failures at other firms down the line. This domino effect is more likely in a recession, when investment portfolios go sour, making it harder for CDS sellers to honor their promises to provide protection. It is even more likely if a seller is a big player in the swaps market, with exposure to many large buyers.[62]

The potential for contagion with CDS resulted from the way over-the-counter CDS were traded. Over-the-counter swaps result from private negotiation between two parties, usually with a dealer between. Unlike with an exchange, in the OTC market, there was no central clearinghouse to post prices, to keep records of who owns what, or to settle a trade gone bad.[63] The lack of an exchange or central clearinghouse increases systemic risk. With no central clearing party, buyers in OTC deals are forced to depend on the creditworthiness of remote, unknown parties. In a privately negotiated OTC transaction, the buyer looks to the creditworthiness of the seller for assurance of protection. The buyer, however, does not know how much total CDS exposure the seller has or how much that exposure will increase in the future. Similarly, the buyer does not know if the seller will buy protection from someone else to defray its CDS obligation to the buyer and whether that someone else is good for the money. Unwittingly, then, the buyer may be forced to rely on someone it never knew or dealt with to hedge its risk.

The lack of an exchange also means that there is no central place where prices of OTC swaps are posted, which makes it impossible to establish a "market price" or other method of valuing swaps. In addition, because OTS CDS contracts are not necessarily standardized, CDS can be harder to trade and unwind. For all of these reasons, Warren Buffett called derivatives "financial weapons of mass destruction, carrying dangers that . . . are potentially lethal."[64]

The inability to net customized swaps spawned additional risk. For a buyer that is stuck with a questionable bespoke swap, often it is easier to hedge that swap by buying a new swap from someone else than to unwind the original swap. In the process of the new swap transaction, the buyer creates a new counterparty, which expands the total counterparty risk in the system. This problem prompted Buffett to muse that "like Hell," derivatives "are easy to enter and almost impossible to exit."[65]

## CDS Escape Regulation

Credit default swaps posed catastrophic risk to the financial system. At year-end 2007, the total notional amount of outstanding CDS stood at $62 trillion, which exceeded the world's gross domestic product.[66]

The risk from swaps was not unknown to regulators. Just a decade earlier, the United States had experienced a near-meltdown involving other types of swaps. In 1998, swaps sent the U.S. financial system into a tailspin when the nation's largest hedge fund, Long-Term Capital Management, imploded. Swaps had been LTCM's "instrument of choice," which is how LTCM amassed "a $1.45 trillion off-balance-sheet position" that culminated in its failure.[67]

Where were Congress and the regulators? In 1998, the chair of the Commodity Futures Trading Commission (CFTC), Brooksley E. Born, began warning about the dangers of unregulated CDS. That May, things came to a head when the CFTC, at Born's initiative, solicited public comment on whether to regulate over-the-counter derivatives, including CDS. When the CFTC's notice came out, the bond markets, joined by Congress, Greenspan, Treasury secretary Robert E. Rubin, and SEC chairman Arthur Levitt, immediately launched an all-out offensive to defeat the CFTC's proposal. Within months, Congress enacted a law placing a six-month moratorium on CFTC regulation of the derivatives market. Defeated, Born resigned in May 1999.[68]

Later in November 1999, Greenspan, Levitt, and Larry Summers, Rubin's successor as Treasury secretary, issued a formal report endorsing congressional deregulation of credit default swaps. Senator Phil Gramm of Texas, an ardent force for deregulation, seized on the report to carve out a broad exemption from regulation for credit default swaps. First, in the Gramm-Leach-Bliley Act of 1999, he convinced Congress to amend the securities statutes to exempt CDS from most aspects of federal securities law apart from the antifraud provisions. As a result, the SEC could not regulate the trading of CDS or require firms to file reports on who traded CDS when and in what amounts.[69] Next Gramm persuaded Congress to amend the Commodity Exchange Act to exempt over-the-counter CDS entirely from commodities regulation, including from the antifraud provisions.[70]

Gramm also did his utmost to ensure that states did not tread on the swaps market. To accomplish this purpose, he inserted a clause in Gramm-Leach-Bliley that prohibited states from regulating swaps under their laws proscribing gambling and fake exchanges.[71] The latter provision did not resolve whether credit default swaps were insurance for purposes of state insurance law.

For their part, states took a hands-off stance toward CDS in the years leading up to the credit crisis. One might have expected New York State to step to the fore, since New York City, along with London, is the mecca of swaps trading. The New York Insurance Department declared in a 2000 opinion, however, that naked CDS—swaps where the buyer did not own the underlying bond—were not insurance because the buyer had no "insurable interest" in the bond. The opinion was silent on the question whether covered CDS, where the buyer owned the bond, were regulated as insurance. In 2004, New York State nailed the coffin shut by amending its Insurance Code to state that credit default swaps are not insurance. Later, in 2008, New York insurance superintendent Eric Dinallo recalled the New York history thus: "In . . . 2000, as a society we chose not to regulate credit default swaps."[72]

### Case in Point: AIG Financial Products

In September 2008, the international insurance conglomerate American International Group (AIG) became the poster child for the ability of credit default swaps to spread contagion. Improbably, the Office of Thrift Supervision had previously acquired jurisdiction over AIG's subsidiary, AIG Financial Products, which was the biggest provider of CDS. But just as OTS failed to supervise thrifts, it failed to oversee AIG's swaps activity.

OTS ended up being AIG's regulator because AIG owned a savings and loan institution called AIG Federal Savings Bank. That put the holding company and the thrift under OTS supervision beginning in 2000.[73]

Normally, the London headquarters of AIG Financial Products would have been under United Kingdom supervision. However, AIG Financial Products successfully maneuvered to escape stricter U.K. regulation with the assistance of OTS. After years of negotiations, OTS hammered out an agreement with the French regulator Commission Bancaire in January 2007 that designated OTS as the consolidated regulator of AIG's European operations, including Banque AIG in France. This agreement sprang from the same EU directive as the SEC's failed consolidated supervisory entity program and replaced European Union officials with OTS as the regulator for AIG's European operations. Under EU law, since one EU regulator—the Commission Bancaire in France—had already signed off on consolidated OTS oversight, AIG Financial Products could operate in London free from U.K. regulation.[74]

Although CDS were not regulated as securities or commodities, OTS did have jurisdiction to make sure that AIG Financial Products, including its swaps operations, operated safely. A "handful of [OTS] officials were always on the scene at an A.I.G. Financial Products branch office" in Wilton, Connecticut, according to the *New York Times,* and could have seen warning signs of trouble at AIG Financial Products as early as 2004.[75] Instead, OTS sat on its hands until 2008.

On February 22, 2008, AIG notified the Securities and Exchange Commission that it was substantially writing down its super senior credit default swaps portfolio. A week later, on February 29, AIG's outside auditor, PricewaterhouseCoopers, publicly announced that AIG's internal controls over the valuation of its swaps portfolio had a weakness that could cause "a material misstatement" of AIG's annual financial statements. AIG's management concurred with that announcement and announced that the holding company's controls over AIG's CDS portfolio had not been "effective."

It took February's revelations to spur OTS into action. On March 10, 2008, C. K. Lee, the managing director of Complex and International Organizations at OTS, wrote AIG stating that the holding company's "oversight of AIG Financial Products . . . lack[ed] elements of independence, transparency, and granularity." The agency expressed concern that AIG Financial Products had overvalued its super senior CDS and had blocked access to "key" internal risk managers who raised concerns about those valuations. In the absence of "effective risk management," OTS said, it no longer had faith in AIG's "accounting and financial reporting disclosures."[76]

On March 10, OTS dropped AIG's examination rating and required it to submit a corrective action plan within thirty days.[77] When AIG missed the deadline, OTS did not take formal enforcement action.[78] Meanwhile, Lee resigned his post in April 2008 to become the director of the OTS regional office in Dallas. The same month, OTS disbanded its Complex and International Organizations unit.[79] In the shuffle, the corrective action plan requirement fell by the wayside.

Later, after AIG's near-death experience, the press asked Lee why OTS had not grasped the enormous risks that AIG presented. Lee answered that he and his unit had not "recognized the . . . risk" from AIG's credit default swaps. OTS viewed those swaps as "fairly benign products" because the underlying CDOs had top credit ratings, AIG had a huge capital base, and management had assured OTS that any added risk from CDS was "manageable." In the process, Lee conceded, "We missed the impact" of the collateral call triggers. It was the triggers—not actual credit losses on the company's credit default swaps—that ultimately brought AIG down.[80]

## SEARCHING FOR A SYSTEMIC RISK REGULATOR

In retrospect, one agency should have been tasked with the power and responsibility to oversee systemic risk and contain it. Unfortunately, this crucial detail fell between the cracks. Congress never gave any agency sufficient authority to monitor systemic risk and address it when it designed the financial system's regulatory structure.

Congress withheld statutory power from the SEC to oversee investment bank conglomerates and the financial system as a whole. Nominally, OTS did have the power to supervise one sector—thrift holding company conglomerates like AIG—for systemic risk, but it lacked the sophistication, commitment, and know-how to exercise that power competently. While Congress did designate the Federal Reserve Board as the umbrella supervisor for bank holding companies in the Gramm-Leach-Bliley Act of 1999, it tied the Fed's hands in crucial respects.

In Gramm-Leach-Bliley, Congress was concerned about the burden from forcing the insurance, securities, and commodities subsidiaries of financial holding companies to report to multiple regulators. To minimize this burden, Congress decreed that the Fed, whenever possible, had to accept reports by those subsidiaries to their primary regulators in lieu of direct reporting to the Fed.[81] Congress also banned the board from examining the securities, commodities, and insurance subsidiaries except when their activities posed a materially adverse effect on the safety and soundness of a sister bank or thrift.[82] Similarly, the Fed lacked systemic oversight authority over entities that were outside of bank holding companies, such as hedge funds and independent investment banks. It was thus that the financial system steamed full speed ahead toward calamity in early 2008, with no captain at the bridge.

# Part IV

▷

# Solutions

If the subprime crisis taught us anything, it was that the country puts itself at risk when it ignores consumer protection. Early attention to basic consumer protections would have halted disastrous subprime loans in their tracks.

In July 2010, Congress and President Obama tackled consumer financial protection and systemic risk in the Dodd-Frank Wall Street Reform and Consumer Protection Act (the Dodd-Frank Act or Dodd-Frank).[1] The new law dramatically alters the financial playing field, but a great deal of uncertainty remains. The real strength of the law will depend on the regulators charged with writing and enforcing new rules under the law. In the worst case, regulators could refuse to write rules, as Greenspan did while heading up the Fed, or draft rules that are concessions to industry. Or, if they fully do their job, they will adopt rules designed to protect consumers, encourage industry innovation, and prevent another economic crisis.

▷

# Consumer Protection

No one has lived through the subprime crisis unscathed. Both the country and individual citizens have paid an extreme price to learn that consumer protection and systemic risk are joined at the hip. In 2010, Congress finally acknowledged this reality. In this chapter, we evaluate whether the Dodd-Frank Act achieves the goals that are critical to consumer protection.

## A NEW CONSUMER FINANCIAL PROTECTION AGENCY

The subprime crisis showed that federal banking regulators cannot be relied on to put consumer safety over the interests of regulated banks. When subprime was king, our system of fragmented regulation drove lenders to shop for the easiest legal regime. The ability of lenders to switch charters put pressure on regulators to relax credit standards. In the process, federal banking regulators sacrificed consumer protection for the short-term profitability of banks. Meanwhile, non bank lenders mushroomed out of control.

Until the Dodd-Frank Act, banking regulators had primary responsibility for consumer compliance examinations and enforcing consumer laws against depository institutions. The FTC had authority over nondepository institutions. Each agency had discretion about the extent to which it enforced the law and no government agency was charged with consumer financial protection across the board.

The Dodd-Frank Act remedies this situation by transferring most of the responsibility for consumer financial protection from federal banking regulators to a new, dedicated agency called the Consumer Financial Protection Bureau (the CFPB). The consumer protections established under Dodd-Frank and the regulations that the CFPB issues to implement the act will apply equally across the mortgage industry regardless of the type of institution.

The new structure also puts an end to fragmented supervision of mortgages. With one exception, the CFPB will have supervisory and enforcement authority over everyone who originates, brokers, or services mortgage loans.[2] Thus, Dodd-Frank levels the playing field and reduces the incentives for lenders to switch charters in search of the easiest regulator. Even OCC preemption was pruned; the new rule restricts preemption to situations in which the application of a state law would favor state-chartered banks over national banks or federal thrifts.[3]

Dodd-Frank empowers the CFPB to establish rules for many aspects of mortgage lending. In addition, it allows the states to protect consumers over and above the standards set by federal law.[4] In other words, the Dodd-Frank Act functions as a floor, not a ceiling. This approach provides an important safeguard against the possibility that the CFPB might adopt unduly weak rules or fail to update its rules over time. It also recognizes that states are closer to local conditions, often are more responsive to emerging problems and may be better able to protect their citizens. Lastly, by giving latitude to states to adopt stricter standards, the law preserves the states' key role as laboratories of experimentation.

## REGULATING MORTGAGES

The Dodd-Frank Act contains general and specific provisions governing mortgage loans. The general provision gives the CFPB the authority to issue rules to ensure that consumers have access to "fair, transparent, and competitive" markets for consumer financial products and services. Other sections of the law prohibit specific terms in mortgage loans.[5] In this section, we discuss the protections that people need when they take out mortgages and evaluate whether Dodd-Frank provides these protections.

### Requiring Proof of Ability to Repay

For well over a decade before the financial crisis, consumer advocates tried to convince Congress to prohibit loans that borrowers could not afford. These efforts were trumped by industry arguments that borrowers should have an unfettered choice of loan terms. While lenders chanted the mantra of choice, their real motive was short-term profits. They could collect more fees and boost their quarterly reports if they could disregard borrowers' ability to repay.

The Dodd-Frank Act now requires that lenders ensure that borrowers can afford their loans. Creditors cannot make loans unless they make "a reasonable and good faith determination based on verified and documented information that, at the time the loan is consummated, the consumer has a reasonable ability to repay the loan." This means a lender has to consider an applicant's income, debt, credit history, employment status, and other factors specified in the statute.[6]

The new affordability requirements also address how creditors go about calculating borrowers' anticipated loan payments. When pay-option ARMs, interest-only ARMs, and hybrid ARMs were all the rage, lenders too often underwrote them based solely on a borrower's initial minimum monthly payment. When interest rates on those loans reset, many borrowers faced a financial crisis unless they could refinance. The Dodd-Frank Act avoids a repeat scenario by requiring lenders to assess the affordability of

ARMs based on the maximum interest rate a borrower would have to pay in the first five years of the loan.[7]

In the past, lenders made loans appear affordable by excluding homeowners' insurance and real-estate taxes from borrowers' projected monthly payments. By omitting these costs, lenders put an artificially rosy glow on borrowers' ability to pay, giving them false confidence that they could afford the loans. Dodd-Frank addresses this issue by requiring creditors to take taxes and insurance into account when calculating whether borrowers can afford loans. In addition, lenders must escrow taxes and insurance for the first five years of a loan. Both steps will lead to more reliable underwriting and reduce the chance that borrowers will be surprised by tax and insurance bills.[8]

The downside of these provisions is that when the mandatory five-year period for escrow accounts expires, the risk of surprise returns. Borrowers, who may not have cash on hand when tax bills for thousands of dollars arrive in their mailbox, could be forced into tax foreclosure. This is an area where borrower choice does not make sense for borrowers or their neighborhoods. For this reason, we advocate mandatory escrow accounts for the life of all home loans.

Dodd-Frank also spells the end of low-doc and no-doc loans by requiring creditors to verify the information that they rely on when determining affordability.[9] The practice of underwriting loans with little or no information on borrowers' creditworthiness is now illegal, and there are serious sanctions for violating these prohibitions.

Affordability requirements met resistance, in the past, on the grounds that a one-size-fits-all approach means that one size fits none. This is a legitimate concern. If every loan had to be manually underwritten, we would lose many of the efficiencies and cost savings that automated underwriting made possible. Through what is known as a "safe harbor" provision, the Dodd-Frank Act obviates the need for creditors to conduct manual assessments of borrowers' ability to repay. Instead, if loans meet specific requirements, such as income verification, debt-to-income ratios below caps set by the CFPB and points and fees no higher than 3 percent of the loan amount, the law presumes that the loans are affordable.[10]

## Preventing Nasty Surprises

Mortgage regulation should foil efforts by lenders to ambush borrowers. There are enough unforeseen events that homeowners cannot prevent, like pipes that suddenly burst. In contrast, many nasty surprises in mortgages can be avoided.

One hidden surprise is escalating payments caused by rate resets. Our approach would be to restrict loan terms with the potential for payment shock. Dodd-Frank places some limits on surprises by, for example, banning balloon payments on high-cost loans. Borrowers with hybrid ARMs must also receive a detailed notice six months before any rate adjustment.[11] These provisions are not enough, however. We would also recommend a cap on the size of individual interest rate adjustments and maximum rate adjustments over the life of loans.

Prepayment penalties can also provide a nasty surprise. When penalties are buried in the closing documents, borrowers are often shocked to find they cannot refinance into cheaper loans. This can hinder borrowers' ability to refinance before their rates reset, which increases the risk they will default.

The Dodd-Frank Act severely limits the duration and size of prepayment penalties as well as the types of loans in which such penalties are permitted. Adjustable-rate loans cannot contain them at all. For fixed-rate loans, such penalties are allowed only in "qualified loans" (as defined by the statute) that are subject to interest rate caps. Even in qualified loans, the prepayment penalty cannot exceed 3 percent of the loan amount during the first year of the loan and must expire by the end of the third year. Finally, to give consumers a choice, Dodd-Frank bans lenders from offering borrowers loans with prepayment penalties unless they also offer loans without those penalties.[12]

## Better Disclosures

Disclosures cannot eliminate surprises in loans, primarily because mortgage documents with dozens of pages of legalese are impenetrable to most borrowers. This does not mean that we should abandon disclosure as a tool for protecting borrowers. Instead, disclosures should supplement substantive rules and increase borrowers' understanding.

The Dodd-Frank Act permits the CFPB to require disclosures that help consumers "understand the costs, benefits, and risks" of loans. The act also aims to consolidate disclosures so that borrowers receive a single document that spells out their loan terms, instead of the multiple disclosures they received in the past.[13] What the new disclosures will look like remains to be seen. In framing new disclosure templates, the CFPB needs to employ consumer testing of prototypes and keep disclosures up to date in response to market changes and new learning about consumer behavior.

There is another disclosure issue that we hope the CFPB will place high on its rule-making agenda: lenders and brokers must be required to provide binding quotes when customers submit their loan applications.[14] Without binding quotes for closing costs and interest rates and fees, borrowers have no assurance they are shopping for loans on realistic terms. In 1998, the Department of Housing and Urban Development concluded that binding quotes at application were already possible, so surely they are possible now.[15]

## Eliminating the Mortgage Confusopoly

The home mortgage market is a confusopoly—a term Scott Adams of *Dilbert* fame coined to refer to "a group of companies with similar products who intentionally confuse customers instead of competing on price."[16] Home mortgages made during the peak in lending had so many moving parts that it was difficult or impossible for borrowers to comparison shop. One lender might offer a 2/28 ARM with a 6 percent initial interest rate and a lifetime cap of 13 percent, but no points or fees. If a consumer shopped that loan to another lender in search of a better interest rate, the second lender might say that the same product wasn't available, but offer a 3/27 with a 5 percent initial interest rate, a lifetime cap of 15 percent, and one point. This level of complexity made comparisons virtually impossible and allowed lenders to avoid competing on price.[17]

One way to increase price competition would be to harness the Internet to help borrowers identify the types of loans that best suit their needs at the lowest price. For example, the government could sponsor a Web site to allow consumers to explore products and lenders to bid for their business. Customers could use the Web site to research different types of loans to serve their needs. To get advice on appropriate loans, consumers would enter traditional underwriting information, such as their job and income and how long they plan to live in their home (because loans with no points or fees make more sense if borrowers plan to move soon). The computer program would winnow down customers' choices to a short list of possible loan products. Then people could seek binding "bids" from lenders for each of those products. Lenders and brokers would quote their best combination of interest rates and fees, based on the underwriting information that the consumers had entered. The system, of course, would need strong privacy safeguards, and bids would be subject to verification of the applicants' qualifications.

A Web-based bidding process would have many benefits. By allowing consumers to get binding quotes up front, it would make comparison shopping truly possible. In the process, it would fuel market competition and bring down prices. Psychologically, it would shift borrowers away from thinking of brokers and loan officers as their agents and friends. It would also guard against information overload by giving borrowers less information to process, which would help them make better decisions.

The Dodd-Frank Act does contemplate employing information systems to improve consumer decision-making. In a part of the law on credit counseling, Congress stated that the secretary of HUD "shall provide for the certification of various computer software programs for consumers to use in evaluating different residential mortgage loan proposals."[18]

There is another way to help borrowers make informed decisions: require that lenders and brokers offer all borrowers a "plain vanilla," no points, no fee, fixed-rate loan. This would make comparison shopping remarkably easy. With a simple option in front of them, borrowers would be more inclined to compare the trade-off between the relative safety of a fixed-rate product and the possibly lower costs of an adjustable-rate loan. Congress considered a plain vanilla requirement, but ultimately took the path of least resistance after fierce lobbying by the financial industry and neither imposed nor rejected that option. The possibility remains that the CFPB could impose such a requirement.

### Reining in Rogue Behavior

As we discussed earlier, compensation practices in the mortgage industry harmed borrowers while reaping huge profits for exploitative and fraudulent mortgage brokers, loan officers, and appraisers, among others. These compensation schemes encouraged rogue practices, and the law did not deter them. Yield spread premiums rewarded brokers who arranged costly loans even when borrowers qualified for cheaper products. A similar compensation structure awarded loan officers at many banks. The Dodd-Frank Act forcefully takes on this practice by banning yield spread premiums altogether. Loan originators can no longer be compensated based on any loan term except the size of a loan.[19] Dodd-Frank also tackles the problem of appraisers who lined their pockets by inflating property valuations to please the brokers and lenders who gave them business. The new law has strong provisions to ensure that appraisers do not have such conflicts of interest.[20]

While Dodd-Frank addresses the carrots that could lure loan originators and appraisers into unfair practices, it does not strengthen the stick that can be wielded against them. For the most part, brokers and appraisers who are not employed by large companies have little in the way of assets. This often means that they are judgment-proof if borrowers sue them, which in turn reduces incentives for them to behave ethically and denies recovery to injured borrowers in the event of wrongdoing. Our recommendation is for the federal government to impose minimum capitalization requirements on brokers and appraisers. Congress could have made this move when writing the Dodd-Frank Act. Instead, the law leaves out capitalization mandates for appraisers and simply provides that the CFPB "may prescribe rules" imposing bonding or other financial requirements on brokers.[21]

## ENSURING ACCESS TO AFFORDABLE CREDIT

Although we advocate a return to careful underwriting, we don't endorse a return to the era when credit was only available to people with substantial resources. Increased consumer protection under the Dodd-Frank Act, together with the recent contraction in credit markets, will affect access to private sources of credit for people with modest incomes and weak credit histories. Thus, it is critical for the government to step in and facilitate safe, sustainable loans where credit is scarce, especially given the importance of homeownership as an asset-building tool.

Often, lower-income people don't qualify for loans that could be sold to Fannie Mae or Freddie Mac because they don't meet the credit score or debt-to-income ratio requirements, both of which have become more stringent. Their alternative, the FHA loan program, has lower down-payment requirements but requires an upfront mortgage insurance premium of 1.5 percent of the loan amount. The key to helping cash-constrained people buy homes is savings programs where they can accumulate money for down payments, FHA insurance premiums, and unexpected expenses like home repairs. The government should finance a matched savings program for lower-income households. In addition, the government should give tax credits to people in lower tax brackets who salt away money in special home ownership funds.

Private savings programs have gained traction and could also help people amass down payments or emergency funds. For example, the nonprofit Doorways to Dreams has harnessed people's fascination with the lottery to create a "save to win" program. On average, households spend $479 each year on lottery tickets, and as much as 80 percent of lottery sales are from households with incomes under $50,000. Participants in the "save to win" program put the money they would have spent on lottery tickets into a credit union account, and every month they have a chance to win prizes, like a laptop or MP3 player. In the first seven months of "save to win," participants saved $4.67 million.[22]

The Dodd-Frank Act takes a small step in this direction by authorizing programs designed to help low- and moderate-income people set up bank accounts.[23] Much more is needed. The government needs to make a stronger policy and financial commitment to savings programs and credit for people of modest means.

## DATA LIMITATIONS

To date, private industry has controlled the key data on mortgage lending. The industry has selected who has access to its data, on what terms, and at what cost (which almost always has been prohibitive). Furthermore, the government has had no say in what information is collected or how it is organized, and has had no way of assessing the reliability of the data.

Until recently, government efforts to collect home mortgage data were minimal and the data were not very useful. Lenders did not have to report borrowers' credit scores, the terms of their loans, or the compensation paid to loan originators.[24] No federal agency had responsibility for identifying and reviewing new loan products as they came on the market. Similarly, until recently, the government did not track the performance of different types of mortgages, which made it difficult to understand the relationship among subprime loans, underwriting, and defaults.

When subprime loans began to flood the market, researchers within and outside the government sought to analyze the loans' hazards, but data limitations hampered their efforts. Likewise, as policy proposals emerged, researchers could not fully assess the implications of those proposals because they did not have enough information. With the subprime crisis, the government suddenly saw the value in collecting data and began gathering loan performance data from servicers. Had the government been tracking loan terms and performance all along, the crisis might have been averted.

The Dodd-Frank Act opens the door to more extensive data collection, which should allow policymaking that is better informed. The law amends the Home Mortgage Disclosure Act to mandate reporting of information such as credit scores, points and fees paid, prepayment penalties, rate reset features in adjustable-rate mortgages, and property values.[25] In addition, a new national database will track loans in default and foreclosure.[26]

Although obtaining this information is certain to help government agencies analyze mortgage markets and detect emerging problems, the data-reporting requirements in the law are incomplete. Some provisions simply suggest data fields that the CFPB could require if deemed appropriate. Others leave open the form in which the data are supplied. And, importantly for nongovernmental researchers, the law defers to the CFPB to determine who has access to the data. The CFPB needs to make sure that mortgage data are not locked up in government and industry hands, leaving the public with anecdotes and no meaningful information.

## MAKING PRIVATE-LABEL SECURITIZATION SAFE

No reform of mortgage origination can be complete without addressing the role of Wall Street. Private-label mortgage securitization will inevitably return in one form or another. Just as surely, investors will eventually forget the lessons of the crisis. To avoid repeating the mistakes of the past, we must put private-label mortgage securitization on a sound footing. The Dodd-Frank Act transforms securitization by increasing oversight, reducing conflicts of interest, and forcing industry actors to retain more risk. We laud these efforts, but urge the law to go further.

### Improved Due Diligence by Investors

A critical reform is giving investors the ability to conduct meaningful due diligence before purchasing private-label, mortgage-related bonds. To accomplish this task, there must be transparency, simplification, and standardization, plus rating agency reform.

### Transparency

The Dodd-Frank Act addresses transparency by charging the SEC to adopt regulations requiring that the issuers of asset-backed securities disclose loan-level data so investors can assess the risks of securitized mortgages. In the act, Congress also required that the SEC write rules mandating that the rating agencies disclose the accuracy of their initial credit ratings on asset-backed securities and make public any changes to those ratings.[27] This will help investors assess the reliability of ratings. However, the law still does not require rating agencies to conduct routine updates of their ratings of securities. As a result, investors will not know whether the initial ratings were predictive until long after they bought their securities.

### Product Simplification and Standardization

The government should encourage simpler, standardized securitization products, whether through the tax rules or rules governing permissible investments by insured banks and thrifts. Similarly, the government should explore ways to build a liquid secondary trading market in private-label RMBS and other bonds. The Dodd-Frank Act falls short in these areas.

### Rating Agency Reform

Although the Dodd-Frank Act did strengthen oversight of credit rating agencies, the act omitted the most needed reform: a ban on the "issuer pays" system, in which issuers pay for ratings. As long as that system persists, rating agencies will work for issuers, not investors. In addition, we need to fix grade inflation for mortgage-backed finance by creating a new, different ratings scale for mortgage bonds to distinguish it from the ratings scale for corporate bonds. As recent events showed, a AAA-rated RMBS or CDO did worse on average than a AAA-rated corporate bond. Finally, NRSRO designations should be abolished.[28]

## Protecting Borrowers and the Financial System

Reforms that help investors police lenders and arrangers do not guarantee that investors will exert their influence to curtail abusive lending. If profits are high—even if they are ultimately short-lived—investors will often throw caution to the wind. For this reason, the law should create incentives for investors to avoid financing abusive lending.

### Assignee Liability Provisions

To give teeth to minimum federal underwriting standards, injured borrowers must be able to raise claims as well as defenses if they are sued for foreclosure. As the law currently stands, if lenders or brokers violate the law when making loans, borrowers can typically sue them for relief. Alternatively, borrowers can refuse to pay their loan, and defend their failure to pay on grounds that the loans were illegal.[29] This path is available only if the original lender still owns the loan.

Once loans are sold up the lending food chain, it is investors who foreclose on borrowers. Paradoxically, in most states borrowers cannot defend foreclosures brought by investors on grounds that their loans were illegal. Similarly, most borrowers cannot bring affirmative claims against investors who were not the loan originators. The reason for this limitation on borrowers' rights is a legal doctrine called the *holder in due course* (HDC) rule. The HDC rule prevents borrowers from asserting most claims and defenses based on illegal origination practices against subsequent owners of their loans so long as the owners paid a fair price and were unaware of the wrongdoing.[30]

The HDC rule has arbitrary and unfair consequences for borrowers. As soon as a loan is sold, borrowers lose important legal rights even though they do not have the power to prevent the sale of their loans and are not compensated for the loss of their rights. Why should borrowers lose the ability to challenge an illegal or fraudulent loan just because the loan was sold? We contend that the law should not be complicit in granting foreclosures on illegal loans.

The HDC rule has another perverse effect that contributed to the financial crisis. As a result of the HDC rule, no one who purchases a loan has enough incentive to "police" lenders to be sure the loans comply with the law.[31] In fact, the opposite is the case. Purchasers have an incentive *not* to investigate the loan origination or loan terms because an investigation could reveal wrongdoing at origination, in which the case the owner could lose its status as a holder in due course. Eliminating the HDC rule would eliminate the unfairness it imposes on borrowers, increase due diligence, and reward careful underwriting.

When the owners of securitized loans, which are literally securitization trusts but effectively are the investors in the securities, bear some of the burden of wrongdoing in the origination of loans, the legal term of art is *assignee liability*. Imposing liability on assignees is not a new idea. In consumer loans for goods and services, there is already assignee liability. In addition, several states impose assignee liability, as does the federal Home Ownership and Equity Protection Act, for a slice of high-cost mortgages.

Some argue that broad assignee liability would reduce access to credit. With a team of economists, we examined that question by looking at the effect of nine state assignee liability laws on the availability of subprime credit. Our study found "no definitive effect of assignee liability on the likelihood of subprime originations, even when the [assignee] liability provisions are in their strongest form." Subprime originations actually rose in six of the nine states that had assignee liability. Results were mixed in the other three states, depending on how subprime lending was defined. No state with assignee liability reported a consistent drop in subprime originations.[32]

In short, assignee liability is not likely to impede access to credit. To the contrary, relief for borrowers will provide needed incentives for originators, Wall Street, and investors to securitize only those loans that borrowers can repay. It will further ensure that the courts are not used to enforce loans that were illegal out of the gate.

The Dodd-Frank Act does adopt limited assignee liability. In a foreclosure or collection action, a borrower can defend the action if there was any violation of the provisions of the law governing yield spread premiums or affordability. This holds true even if an assignee owns the loan and is the one suing the borrower. Successful borrowers can have the amount they owe the assignee reduced according to a damages scheme specified in the statute.[33]

Effective assignee liability provisions must expand beyond this narrow scope. If assignees sue on illegal contracts, borrowers should be able to defend nonpayment based on the illegality. In addition, they need the right to collect from assignees if originators engaged in unlawful practices or made their loans on unlawful terms. Investors have the power to police lenders; assignee liability will give them the incentive to exercise that power.

### Arranger Liability

So far, our proposal for imposing liability on entities in the lending food chain has not touched on arrangers. The only ways arrangers can be liable to injured borrowers under current law is if they were involved in or aware that lenders were making illegal loans. If the goal of legal reform is to increase scrutiny of loan terms and lending practices, arrangers need skin in the game too.

The financial reform bill does put some onus on arrangers by requiring that they retain 5 percent of the credit risk of any security backed by residential mortgage loans.[34] This risk retention provision is not a panacea. Depending on the profits arrangers make, 5 percent may be too low a number, especially given that people with unlawful loans may refinance their way out of the loans and thus never expose arrangers to any credit losses. To keep arrangers vigilant, we recommend that they also be liable for unlawful lending if the broker, lender, or other responsible party is insolvent. This legal liability will increase arrangers' commitment to overseeing both the loans and the parties involved at loan origination.

### Remove Artificial Barriers to Cost-Effective Loan Modifications

Too many distressed loans needlessly went into foreclosure when property values crashed, despite the availability of cost-effective loan modifications. Not only did these foreclosures oust borrowers from their homes, they needlessly depressed home values for everyone else. It is time to cut this Gordian knot.

Most securitized loan pools are created as Real Estate Mortgage Investment Conduits, or REMICs, under the federal tax code. Any securitization vehicle that qualifies for REMIC treatment is exempt from federal income taxes. Congress or the Internal Revenue Service should amend the REMIC rules to disqualify future mortgage pools from favored REMIC tax treatment unless pooling and servicing agreements and related deal documents are drafted to give servicers ironclad incentives to participate in large-scale loan modifications when specific triggers are met.[35]

Dodd-Frank takes bold steps toward protecting consumers, with the ultimate effect of reducing the threat of systemic risk. The consumer protection reforms do not, however, eliminate that threat altogether. Rather, as we discuss next, interventions are needed at every link in the financial system to contain systemic risk.

# 13

▷

# Containing Contagion

By resolving the subprime crisis with bailouts, the federal government put us at increased danger of more severe financial crises in the future. Its job now is to avert those crises going forward.

Bear Stearns, Fannie Mae, Freddie Mac, AIG, GM, and Chrysler were the most obvious beneficiaries of the government's largess. What is less well understood is the extent to which policymakers bailed out entire financial sectors. The Fed gave investment banks unheard-of access to discount window loans and domestic auto suppliers got massive bailouts. In an astonishing number of instances—witness the markets for commercial paper, housing finance, and asset-backed securities—the federal government became the lender of first resort after private market mechanisms broke down. Uncle Sam even issued blanket guarantees on money market funds and Fannie Mae and Freddie Mac obligations in order to keep the money market and housing industries afloat.

These crisis interventions reached their apex with respect to commercial banks. Before 2008, banks and thrifts got federal subsidies in the form of access to the Fed's discount window plus deposit insurance guarantees of $100,000 per depositor. These subsidies looked positively quaint, however, compared to the subsidies federal regulators handed out in the fall of 2008. At that point, the FDIC upped the deposit insurance cap 150 percent to $250,000 and lifted it altogether for business checking accounts. Both actions were supposed to be temporary, but Congress made the $250,000 cap permanent in the Dodd-Frank Act.[1] The FDIC also guaranteed senior debt issued by banks and over 700 banks took capital infusions under TARP. Meanwhile, the Fed eased access to its discount window, which meant banks could borrow funds without sending a signal that they were in desperate financial straits.[2]

Absent at least some of these interventions, the world's financial order would likely have collapsed, resulting in global depression and incalculable human toll. In the process, however, the government sowed the seeds of future financial instability by sending businesses a message that they can pursue senseless strategies in search of higher yields because shareholders will reap the profits and Uncle Sam will absorb any losses if firms are too big to fail.[3] The result of the bailouts was moral hazard.

A disclosure by the mutual fund company Dodge & Cox provided a telling illustration of the potency of moral hazard. In a 2008 quarterly report to investors, the Dodge & Cox Stock Fund defended its decision to hold onto stock in Fannie Mae, AIG, and Wachovia, saying that it had relied on the fact that federal regulators had "provid[ed] banks with breathing room and flexibility needed to overcome temporary challenges" during the last two banking crises.[4] In choosing its investments, Dodge & Cox proceeded on the assumption that if Fannie Mae, Wachovia, and AIG became insolvent, the federal government would bail out shareholders to avoid damage to the financial system and thus protect Dodge & Cox investors.

In 2008 and 2009, the United States made the too-big-to-fail problem worse in four critical ways. It singled out nine financial giants to receive $125 billion in TARP funds, sending an unmistakable message that those firms were too big to fail. It brokered emergency mergers of Countrywide with Bank of America, Bear Stearns with JPMorgan Chase, Merrill Lynch with Bank of America, and Wachovia with Wells Fargo, causing the resulting institutions to swell in size. It encouraged investment banks like Goldman Sachs and Morgan Stanley to become bank holding companies to allow them to tap insured bank deposits and the discount window. Later, during the stress tests, the Fed anointed still more large institutions as too big to fail.

The *New York Times* columnist Floyd Norris astutely said, "If an activity is important enough to justify a government nationalization to prevent a default, it is important enough to be regulated."[5] For this reason, too-big-to-fail firms need to be reined in in three essential ways. First, the law should require federal regulators to put failing financial giants into receivership before stabilizing them with federal aid. The Dodd-Frank Act contains landmark provisions to this effect. Second, the nation needs a systemic risk regulator to track and address looming systemic risks. Dodd-Frank tackles this issue as well, albeit in an abstruse and clumsy manner. Finally, swaps need to be moved onto exchanges as much as possible, and swaps that bet on the performance of assets owned by others should be banned. Here, Dodd-Frank's new provisions for swaps regulation fall seriously short of the mark.

## HOLDING INVESTORS AND MANAGERS RESPONSIBLE

Government promises of "no more bailouts" will not eliminate moral hazard. Rather, the government has to forge a no-bailout policy that is credible and holds investors and managers responsible for their actions. When financial companies fail, shareholders must lose their investments and managers must lose their jobs. We can no longer allow shareholders, like those at Bear Stearns, to extract concessions if the government lends a hand. The only way that shareholders and managers will manage their companies responsibly is if their investments and jobs depend on the company's health.

For a "no bailout" message to be credible, the government must force failing financial megafirms into receivership. The purpose of special receivership procedures is to allow the federal government to seize insolvent financial giants, fire their managers, and wipe out their shareholders. After a company goes into receivership, the federal government then needs the power to stabilize the company to halt any spillover effects that could damage the larger economy. Following that, the government would liquidate the company or sell it to private investors.

This idea is hardly new. The United States has used federal conservatorship and receivership procedures for years to resolve failed banks and thrifts. Every time the FDIC seizes a depository institution, it invokes those procedures. The FDIC's resolution process has had remarkable success in quelling panics surrounding bank failures. Often the FDIC is able to sell the good parts of a failed bank immediately upon seizure; even a six-month delay is rare. In addition, once a firm is put into receivership, the government can seize its toxic assets and hold them, if necessary, for later resale when market conditions improve. That way, toxic assets can be removed from a failed bank's books without requiring parties to reach agreement on a sales price during a period of market turmoil (which was the fatal flaw of the original toxic assets plan under TARP).

Until the Dodd-Frank Act, the FDIC's receivership authority extended only to failed banks or thrifts, not to their holding companies or other types of financial firms. That is why, when Bear Stearns and AIG faced collapse, the government could not put them into receivership and ended up bailing them out instead, with the attendant moral hazard.

Now, under Dodd-Frank, the federal government has the power to put an insolvent financial company that poses a significant risk to the financial stability of the United States—whether it is a bank holding company, investment bank, insurance conglomerate, hedge fund, or other financial firm—into FDIC receivership.[6] The FDIC must liquidate the company by selling off the company's assets and liabilities to satisfy creditors, according to their priority for payment.[7]

### Why Isn't Bankruptcy Enough?

At this point, one might ask, why not just force failing financial giants into bankruptcy? That is what the government did with Lehman Brothers and it could have forced AIG and Bear Stearns into bankruptcy, too. As the events of 2008 showed, however, bankruptcy is not always the right solution.

The central problem is this: bankruptcy proceedings do not stop financial contagion from spreading to other firms. Bankruptcy is designed to address competing claims for a failed company's assets, not the risk of a domino effect endangering other, solvent firms. While bankruptcy procedures work well for the vast majority of failing companies, they do not work well for banks or other systemically important financial firms during times of economic crisis. As the fallout from the Lehman Brothers bankruptcy demonstrated, putting a major financial player into bankruptcy can ignite financial panic and threaten the solvency of other financial firms. This is, in part, because bankruptcy trustees lack the power to maintain key financial activities, such as payments, settlements, securities trading, brokerage accounts, and sensitive derivatives obligations.[8] If payment or settlement systems are disrupted, the wheels of commerce and finance can quickly grind to a halt. This is why Congress created separate resolution procedures for failed banks.

At the same time, in crafting Dodd-Frank, Congress did not want regulators to invoke federal receivership unless a failing financial firm actually jeopardized the nation's financial system. Consequently, Dodd-Frank states that the federal government cannot put an insolvent financial firm into receivership unless at least two-thirds of the governors of the Federal Reserve Board and the members of the board of the FDIC find that the country's financial stability is at risk and recommend receivership.[9] Once they make this decision, the Treasury secretary, in consultation with the president, must agree that the firm threatens the larger economy, at which point the secretary can initiate receivership proceedings. If the ailing company's directors oppose receivership, the secretary must go to federal court for an order appointing the FDIC as receiver. In that proceeding—which is "strictly confidential" and must occur within twenty-four hours—the court has to decide whether the company is actually a financial company and on the verge of failure. Unless all of these preconditions are satisfied, bankruptcy is the only route available for resolving insolvencies among financial companies that are not banks or insurance companies.[10]

### Who Should Face Market Discipline?

As we mentioned, a financial giant's failure can cause financial paralysis unless the receiver keeps key financial systems afloat. With a firm like Bear Stearns or Lehman Brothers, the government will likely need to furnish short-term guarantees to overnight lenders and derivatives counterparties to preserve the company's liquidity and unwind the company's assets in an orderly manner. It may also need to segregate brokerage accounts to discourage anxious hedge funds from moving their prime brokerage accounts to other firms. Dodd-Frank provides the FDIC with these and other powers to keep financial systems smoothly operating while a failed financial firm is winding up.[11]

FDIC guarantees and other methods of reassuring creditors solve the problem of financial disruption but create another problem. They undermine market discipline. A basic tenet of market discipline is that a company's unsecured creditors—whether they are bondholders, or other holders of the company's unsecured debt—should absorb their share of any losses. The thinking is that the prospect of losses gives short-term unsecured creditors an incentive to police the parties to whom they extend credit. When a firm is insolvent, however, there is the risk that short-term creditors will simply head for the exit, triggering a liquidity run that could widen into contagion. For this reason, Michael Krimminger, an FDIC policy advisor, has noted that while making creditors whole "is not the optimal approach to control moral hazard," it "may be a necessary trade-off for continued functioning of critical settlement and payment processes."[12]

The Dodd-Frank Act includes a clever solution to this problem by allowing the FDIC to make emergency guarantees or payments to outside creditors during the first critical days of a receivership. The agency then has five years to assess creditors for all guarantees or other payments that exceeded their share of recovery.[13] This allows the FDIC to halt contagion during the initial fallout from the receivership, but requires it to collect any windfall to creditors once the financial crisis has subsided.

### Who Should Pay and When?

A separate issue is whether the cost of receivership should be funded in advance by financial institutions, akin to FDIC deposit insurance, or paid for *ex post* through special assessments on the financial industry. Under an *ex post* system, special assessments could be stretched out over time to avoid overtaxing institutions during times of economic stress.

Proponents of advance funding argue that requiring giant firms to pay premiums for the systemic risk that they create will force them to internalize that risk. Opponents claim that creating a standing fund by charging premiums will lead to moral hazard, just as the existence of the Deposit Insurance Fund arguably lulls managers, shareholders, and creditors of some banks into taking imprudent risks. This latter claim finds support in empirical research that shows that explicit deposit insurance systems do, in fact, create moral hazard compared to funding after the fact.[14]

An *ex post* system has an undeniable downside. In an *ex post* system, the receiver lacks a dedicated fund to draw on to stabilize a failed firm. This creates the danger that the agency will delay putting an insolvent company into receivership because it does not have funds on hand. Consequently, if an *ex post* system is adopted, it will only work if the agency has assurance of immediate access to sufficient funds, with no strings attached, to finance receivership operations until the special assessments kick in. Requiring the receiver to negotiate with the Treasury Department for funds could undermine the system. Requiring the receiver to go to Congress for an appropriation would be disastrous. Unless an immediate, unconditional funding mechanism was in place, an *ex post* system would be tantamount to no resolution system at all.

Congress resolved this issue in Dodd-Frank by adopting an *ex post* funding mechanism that will likely turn into a standing fund over time. Whenever a financial company is put into federal receivership, the FDIC can raise cash for receivership expenses by selling obligations to the secretary of the Treasury, which the secretary may resell to the public in the form of Treasury bonds. The obligations are subject to a dollar cap, and the FDIC cannot issue them without agreeing with the Treasury secretary on a repayment plan. Dodd-Frank requires the FDIC to repay these obligations in sixty months, first by collecting any overages from the creditors who received them and then by levying risk-based assessments on companies presenting systemic risk.[15]

While the statute did not create a standing fund at the outset, a standing fund will eventually come to pass because Dodd-Frank requires the FDIC to deposit the proceeds from the sale of the obligations, along with the assessments, interest earnings, and repayments, into a new "Orderly Liquidation Fund." Two of the law's provisions seem to contemplate an ongoing fund once it is created. For one thing, the law permits the fund to invest any excess cash beyond the FDIC's current needs in Treasury bonds. For another, Dodd-Frank provides that the fund will be available to pay for current and future receiverships, as well as to retire debt.[16]

This setup avoids exacerbating moral hazard for the moment by postponing creation of the Orderly Liquidation Fund until the first financial company is put into receivership. But once the fund comes into being, its presence will layer a new source of moral hazard on top of that already created by the Deposit Insurance Fund. To some extent, this moral hazard will be mitigated by a risk-based assessment requirement, which will help make megabanks internalize the costs of the systemic risk they create. The experience with risk-based assessments in deposit insurance suggests, however, that such assessments help reduce moral hazard from a standing fund but do not eliminate it.

## Minimizing the Risk of Bailouts

An effective and believable "no bailout" message must include prohibitions on giving federal aid to ailing megafirms unless they are in receivership.[17] This means prohibiting the executive branch and other federal agencies from giving financial support in the form of cash infusions, government guarantees, discount window loans, or government-assisted mergers to financial firms that face imminent collapse, but are not yet in receivership. Likewise, the Federal Reserve Board should not be allowed to use its "unusual and exigent circumstances" power under Section 13(3) of the Federal Reserve Act to shore up insolvent firms. Section 13(3) should be strictly limited to relief to viable firms or for industry-wide relief during times of financial crisis and only with the written consent of the Treasury Department. In addition, Congress should prohibit the FDIC from invoking its special authority to bail out distressed banks when there is systemic risk.[18] Without these restrictions on federal bailouts of megafirms, the receivership procedures will not ensure "no more bailouts."

Dodd-Frank is replete with provisions aimed at banning bailouts. The legislation sternly states, for example, that "no taxpayer funds shall be used to prevent the liquidation of any financial company" through FDIC receivership.[19] Congress stripped the FDIC of its power to bail out distressed banks or thrifts because of systemic risk. Similarly, the federal government cannot dip into the Deposit Insurance Fund or Federal Reserve facilities under Section 13(3) to avoid putting a dying financial firm into bankruptcy or receivership. Once a financial firm goes into FDIC receivership, all funds spent to liquidate it must come from the failed company's assets or the financial sector; by law, taxpayers shall not bear any of those losses.[20]

These provisions look good on paper. The question is whether the executive branch, the Federal Reserve, and Congress will observe them in the heat of future financial crises. The historical evidence is mixed. On the plus side, when the Federal Reserve invoked its extraordinary bailout powers under Section 13(3) in 2008, it did stay within the law (though pushing the law's outer limits). On the minus side, during the savings and loan crisis of the 1980s and the events of 2008, regulators—in order to avoid political controversy or retain turf—delayed using the powers they already had to put failing banks and thrifts into receivership. Similarly, the TARP legislation showed that Congress is capable of legislating mammoth bailouts at taxpayer expense when the financial pressure becomes unbearable. Just as Congress could enact TARP, it could repeal the no-bailout provisions in Dodd-Frank.

Ultimately, whether these provisions survive comes down to political will. While the past is not encouraging, there is some reason for hope. By and large, federal regulators attempt to operate within the law—often creatively, but within the law nevertheless. By making it illegal to tap potential major sources of bailout funds, the "no bailout" provisions in Dodd-Frank put pressure on regulators to initiate timely receivership proceedings. The new receivership procedures also give regulators an alternative to bailouts and bankruptcy that they did not have in 2008. And the procedures do so in a way that permits the federal government to disburse funds (subject to future recovery) to halt a ripple effect at other financial firms.[21]

## A SYSTEMIC RISK REGULATOR

Before the passage of the Dodd-Frank Act, there was no regulator tasked with detecting mounting risks in the financial system and defusing them. Dodd-Frank's response is to create not one systemic risk regulator, but two. Under the law, the Federal Reserve Board has expanded powers to supervise large nonbank financial firms for systemic risk. In addition, the statute creates a new Financial Stability Oversight Council made up of state and federal regulators. The Council has responsibility for deciding which nonbank financial companies are subject to systemic risk oversight by the Fed. The Council is further charged with monitoring systemic risk, recommending stricter prudential standards, and resolving turf wars among federal financial regulators.[22]

### Early Warning System

Previously, no U.S. agency had the data to pinpoint the location and size of risks to the financial system. Likewise, there was no way to assess who was threatened by contagion if a major financial player failed. Sources of this information were fragmentary and incomplete. SEC and bank regulatory reporting systems focused on the financial condition of individual institutions, not on interdependencies among those firms. Worse, hedge funds and private equity firms were exempt from registration and reporting despite their potential systemic risk.

As late as 2010, twelve years after the Fed had to avert a financial meltdown by Long-Term Capital Management, hedge funds and investment banks were still able to shroud themselves in secrecy from the Fed. No one knew for sure where toxic assets were hidden or who the key counterparties were. That is why, when the Federal Reserve Board was pressed to rescue Bear Stearns, it did not know the company's condition. Similarly, the credit markets crashed in September 2008 because no one with cash to lend could tell who was a good credit bet.

The Dodd-Frank Act is filled with new reporting requirements designed to lift this veil of darkness. The act creates a new Office of Financial Research to collect data on systemic risk from banks and nonbank financial firms. These data include information on financial companies' counterparty exposures, capital and leverage, funding sources, credit concentrations, and aggregate positions. The Council has full use of the data to analyze emerging financial risks. In addition, the Federal Reserve Board may impose its own reporting requirements on the nonbank financial companies within its jurisdiction. Hedge funds are also, for the first time, required to report data on systemic risk. Lastly, the law contains expanded reporting requirements for home mortgages and asset-backed securities.[23]

In the derivatives area, Dodd-Frank spearheads new market mechanisms to make mandatory reporting possible. Its major innovation is to require real-time reporting of data on all swap transactions to a centralized swap data repository or SEC or the Commodity Future Trading Commission. The data must include the volume and the price of swaps trades. Each repository will make data on individual transactions available to regulators on a confidential basis. In addition, the statute promotes price competition by requiring exchanges, clearinghouses, and other swap-trading facilities to publicly disclose the terms and conditions of every swap transaction that is cleared and settled, including volume and daily settlement prices.[24]

The result is a wealth of new financial information that the Council and the Fed can use to track the movement of investors into specific asset classes, the spread of risky investment strategies, mounting leverage, and the rapid growth of swaps liability at any one counterparty like AIG. Dodd-Frank does not give the Council or the Fed, however, the full power they need to collect data on systemic risk. Instead, Congress instructed both bodies to rely, "to the fullest extent possible," on reports made to other regulators, on publicly available information, and on audited reports.[25] Even for foreign companies, Congress told the Council to rely, whenever possible, on information collected by foreign regulators that is translated into English.[26] Here, Congress made a mistake If the Council and the Fed use these instructions as an excuse to rely on fragmentary reports from sister regulators, the government has little hope of obtaining an overarching view of the financial universe.

## Supervision and Regulation

It is not enough for the Council and the Fed to know of developing risks. When systemic threats appear, the Fed and the Council need to take action. Capital regulation and reducing the size of firms are two key tools to reducing the threat megafirms pose to the economy.

### Capital Regulation.

In theory, capital regulation should discourage firms from spawning systemic risk by reducing their dependence on debt financing and raising the cost of concentrating in highly risky activities.

Basel I was a failed attempt at risk-weighted capital regulation. Basel I's capital standards encouraged the reckless growth of subprime mortgages and private-label securitization and failed to stop the top U.S. banking companies from becoming undercapitalized during the housing bubble. Basel II intensified these problems by allowing megabanks to gauge their own capital levels using internal models.

Given the flaws in the existing risk-based capital rules, the better approach is the older, traditional minimum capital requirement from commercial banking regulation in tandem with risk-based measures and the imposition of higher capital requirements when systemic risks grow. (This traditional requirement is also called the leverage ratio and is different from the leverage ratio in securities regulation.) The historical leverage ratio has a number of virtues, not the least of which is simplicity. To compute it, you divide total shareholders' equity by average total assets. This ratio is harder to game than risk-based ratios, and it is easy for regulators to monitor.

The Dodd-Frank Act embraces many of these ideas, but not all. The act requires federal banking agencies to establish minimum leverage capital (the traditional ratio) and risk-based capital requirements for insured banks and thrifts, their holding companies, and nonbank financial companies supervised by the Fed. The law further forbids regulators from reducing these minimum capital requirements below set numeric floors. Other provisions in the law mandate that bank regulators take account of the risks institutions pose to "other private and public stakeholders." These risks include significant volumes of derivatives, securitization, financial guarantees, securities borrowing, repo lending, and overconcentration in a firm's market activities.[27]

Dodd-Frank further allows the Council and the Fed to raise minimum capital requirements as systemic risk increases—an idea advanced by the economist Alice Rivlin.

If a financial firm's risk profile or the economy overheats, the Council and the Fed may crank up capital requirements. This power extends to a wide range of financial companies, among them investment banks, swaps providers, hedge funds, and private equity funds, not just commercial banks. Furthermore, capital requirements for the largest bank holding companies (with $50 billion or more in total assets) and for non-bank financial companies that are supervised by the Fed must now take into account off-balance-sheet liabilities.[28]

In another wise move, Dodd-Frank mandates annual stress tests like those performed on large banks in the spring of 2009 to test financial megafirms' ability to withstand different types of crises. The legislation requires publicizing the results of these exercises to the public and the press. This is another way of broadcasting the government's commitment to avoiding future bailouts.[29]

Where the capital provisions of Dodd-Frank fall short is in not requiring financial megafirms to mark their assets to market. Mark-to-market accounting would make the traditional capital ratio more accurate by reflecting the market value of a firm's assets. A mark-to-market approach would also give the Council and the Fed more reliable notice when systemically important companies are approaching insolvency. This, in turn, would increase the likelihood that the government could put financial companies into receivership while their net worth was still positive, which would reduce spillover effects.

## Breaking Up Big Firms?

During the financial crisis, policymakers floated a controversial proposal to give the systemic risk regulator the power to break up financial giants. Former Federal Reserve chairman Paul Volcker argued, for example, in favor of reinstating the Glass-Steagall Act's ban on joint corporate ownership of investment banks and commercial banks. He also sought to prohibit commercial banking concerns from owning or sponsoring hedge funds and private equity funds. According to Volcker, breaking up financial conglomerates was the only serious way to contain systemic risk because the largest financial firms typically evade other forms of regulation.[30]

Throughout the long slog leading to the passage of the Dodd-Frank Act, most pundits doubted Volcker's ability to secure enactment of his ideas. To the amazement of almost everyone, he prevailed in two major respects. First, Volcker persuaded Congress to give the Council and the Federal Reserve joint authority to force financial megafirms to cap their growth or downsize if they pose a "grave threat" to the financial stability of the United States.[31] He also convinced Congress to curtail commercial banks' and bank holding companies' ability to engage in proprietary trading (using their own money to make bets on the market) and restricting their ownership stakes in hedge funds and private equity funds.[32]

There are other ways the Dodd-Frank Act encourages downsizing of firms. The most straightforward is a provision that allows the Council and the Fed to assess financial megafirms a higher capital charge than smaller firms to defray their added risk to the financial system.[33] Another section of the law empowers the Fed to force megafirms to unload assets and engage in divestiture as a last resort if firms hit certain triggers. The last critical piece of the law that relates to the size of firms gives the Federal Reserve Board the authority to limit the growth of megafirms by denying them approval to buy other companies that have total consolidated assets of $10 billion or more.[34]

Congress could have taken an added step to reduce the size of firms: subject top executives at the biggest financial conglomerates to stricter executive compensation rules that favor long-term returns over short-term profits. The urgency with which banks rushed to repay their TARP bailouts to avoid TARP's restrictions on executive compensation suggests that executive pay restrictions are powerful motivators. With pay limits, firms would have a choice: downsize to escape pay restrictions and attract the best talent, or observe pay limits and stay big.

### Searching for the Ideal Systemic Risk Regulator

During the debate over Dodd-Frank, there were several possible candidates for the job of systemic risk regulator, including the SEC, the Federal Reserve Board, some new agency, or a council of federal banking regulators. In the end, Congress took a dual approach, by dividing systemic risk oversight between the Council and the Fed, with the added overlay of the Office of Financial Research as chief data collector.

The Dodd-Frank Act assigns the day-to-day job of systemic risk regulation to the Federal Reserve Board. For financial megafirms that fall within the Fed's jurisdiction, Congress gave the Fed broad powers to implement enhanced regulation and supervision, including reporting requirements, examinations, and enforcement. Doing so ensures that the Fed can act nimbly and fast. It also helps make the Fed accountable for its actions.

Among the contenders for the job, the Federal Reserve Board was clearly the best suited. From its discount window operations to its historic purview over bank holding companies, the Fed has a view from the top that no other financial regulator enjoys. In addition, the Fed already engages in consolidated entity regulation and has permanent examiners on-site at every major bank holding company. Beyond its examiners, the Fed has economists, lawyers, and policy analysts on board that are unrivaled by any other federal financial regulator. Finally, only the Fed has the monetary tools at hand to intervene instantly to stabilize viable banks when systemic threats arise.[35] That is why the Fed, not the SEC, took the lead in stabilizing investment banks during the crisis with Bear Stearns.

Where Dodd-Frank goes wrong is in giving the Financial Stability Oversight Council sole power to decide which financial megafirms to subject to systemic risk oversight by the Fed. The decision which firms to regulate is the linchpin of the systemic risk regulatory scheme and should have been entrusted to a body that could act swiftly and decisively. The makeup of the Council suggests that it will be anything but swift and decisive. Nine of its ten voting members are powerful federal financial regulators with a long history of agency infighting. In all likelihood, the Council will be prey to the same rivalries and delays that plague interagency rulemaking. Indeed, federal banking regulators could not even agree on an effective guidance on subprime mortgages—let alone binding regulation—until spring 2007, well after the crisis was under way.

Having adopted the cumbersome Council model, the Dodd-Frank legislation makes it worse by requiring two-thirds of the Council (including the Treasury secretary) to agree before subjecting a nonbank financial giant to systemic risk regulation. This stiff supermajority requirement is a recipe for inaction, particularly in a body made up of warring agencies. Making matters worse, Dodd-Frank's test for whether a nonbank financial company could jeopardize financial stability is extremely vague.[36] Together, these factors raise serious doubt whether all nonbank financial megafirms that need systemic risk regulation will receive it.[37]

There is another flaw in the systemic regulator provisions of Dodd-Frank. In establishing the Council, Congress missed an opportunity to use the Council as a backstop in case the Fed shirks at its job. Although the Council has expansive powers, it does not have the authority to order the Fed to institute enforcement actions if a financial giant under the Fed's aegis goes astray. The Council cannot step in and examine those companies or sanction them if the Fed sits on its hands. By not giving the Council these powers, Congress passed up a valuable tool for prodding the Fed into action. By now, it is quite apparent that the Fed was lax in its oversight of bank holding companies during the run-up to the credit crisis. Without someone nipping at its heels, the Fed could once again fail to fulfill its mandate.

## COUNTERACTING THE VIRAL EFFECT OF CREDIT DEFAULT SWAPS

In Dodd-Frank, Congress had to grapple with the explosive growth in credit default swaps that mutated into worldwide financial contagion. Dodd-Frank's swaps provisions, however, are so technical, dense, and laden with loopholes that serious questions remain whether the new regulatory scheme will really rein in contagion from swaps.

### Solving the Problem of Multilateral Exposure

The potential contagion from swaps trading stems from one key problem in the CDS market. That problem is that trading in over-the-counter credit default swaps results in multilateral rather than bilateral exposure.

By definition, trading on the over-the-counter market is not conducted on centralized exchanges. Rather, an end user will buy a derivative from a dealer. The dealer will want to get the exposure off its hands, and so it will typically buy an offsetting derivative from another dealer or end user who agrees to assume the risk. That protection seller, in turn, may enter into a third derivatives contract with a fourth party to offset its own risk. This daisy chain is how OTC swaps trading results in multilateral exposure. If the first dealer defaults and inflicts losses on its protection buyer, the losses may force the protection buyer to default on its derivatives obligations down the line, causing losses to cascade.[38]

Looking at the difference between the notional size and gross size of the OTC swaps market gives some sense of the degree to which OTC trading magnifies potential exposure. OTC swaps obligations are not netted at inception, so the market's notional size dwarfs its gross size. (Netting takes traders' swap obligations with one another and cancels them out to calculate a final net liability. The notional amount of swaps activity refers to the amount of outstanding swaps before they are netted.) In June 2008, at the height of the market, the total notional amount of outstanding OTC swaps worldwide stood at $638 trillion. The total gross value that month was only $20 trillion, just 3 percent of the total notional amount. Given the significant risk that the OTC swaps market generates, a critical task of financial reform is to cabin multilateral exposure whenever possible or, barring that, put it on safer footing.[39]

## Centralized Trading Platforms

One of the most compelling proposals to curb multilateral exposure from swaps trades is to move as many OTC trades as possible onto centralized platforms. The Dodd-Frank Act seeks to accomplish this by requiring swaps contracts to be cleared through central clearinghouses, subject to certain exceptions.[40]

Centralized clearing shifts counterparty risk from end users to a central clearinghouse that assumes the risk. Let's assume that Hannah and Eden enter into a derivatives trade. If they clear it through a clearinghouse, they eliminate their credit exposure to each other. Instead of Eden, Hannah's counterparty becomes the clearinghouse, which guarantees the performance of the contract. The clearinghouse also becomes the counterparty for Eden and for all other derivatives trades that it accepts for clearing. Then it nets the obligations, which reduces its total exposure to any one firm.

Centralized clearing offers several advantages. First, centralized platforms help reduce exposure from multilateral trading by collapsing strings of multilateral exposures into one set of bilateral, netted exposures to the clearinghouse. If a big trader like AIG collapses, no one who did swaps business with that trader will sustain a loss except the clearinghouse. In the process, clearinghouses make big financial institutions less interdependent. Clearinghouses also help stabilize large banks with trading operations by removing some swaps trades from their books. Finally, a timely reporting system for trades can benefit customers by publicly reporting prices for all cleared transactions on a real-time basis, thus giving important information about the market value of CDS and the assets they reference.

Centralized clearing has its drawbacks. If a large clearinghouse failed, it could be a catastrophe for the financial system. For that reason, Dodd-Frank subjects clearinghouses to stringent regulation to assure their solvency. As part of that regulation, clearinghouses must be deeply capitalized and maintain substantial funds to absorb any losses. Under the law, a clearinghouse must have enough capital to absorb all losses from the failure of its biggest counterparty and still operate properly without having to assess its members for additional capital.[41] Dodd-Frank also requires clearinghouses to have robust risk management systems and makes traders post initial margins.[42]

In moving to centralized platforms, Congress created major exceptions to the mandatory clearing requirement. The big dealers opposed a mandatory clearing rule because it would make prices more transparent and take a bite out of their bid-ask spreads.[43] After much debate (and lobbying), Congress punted, giving the Commodity Futures Trading Commission and the SEC full authority to exempt certain swaps or categories of swaps from mandatory clearing. Similarly, Congress exempted many commercial end users of swaps, like utility companies and grain companies, from mandatory clearing even though they buy swaps from major dealers in daisy-chain transactions that spawn systemic risk.[44] Finally, customized swaps escape centralized clearing entirely.

## The Conundrum of Customized Swaps Contracts

It is easy to see the value and efficiency of a clearinghouse for swaps, particularly if OTC swaps are standardized and, thus, can be easily traded and cleared through a central platform. The majority of OTC trades, however, are customized swaps that are not suitable for centralized clearing or for exchange trading.

Customization has the salutary effect of allowing buyers to tailor swaps to the exact risks they seek to manage. At the same time, customized swaps are illiquid by definition, which makes them difficult to trade and difficult to price. Even if the law sought to push all customized swaps onto centralized trading platforms, it is doubtful that those trading platforms could accommodate them. Centralized clearinghouses are reluctant to handle customized swaps because they would need market data to model the risks associated with the swaps and would have to compute daily gains and losses on positions. These data usually do not exist for bespoke CDS.

For similar reasons, customized swaps are rarely suitable for trading on exchanges. This is because exchanges require a continuous stream of parties seeking to trade. Without a ready supply of willing and able buyers and sellers, exchanges cannot offer liquidity.[45] This is not a hypothetical problem. Worldwide, the volume of swaps traded on exchanges is positively dinky compared to the volume of OTC swaps trades.[46]

Dodd-Frank attempts to address the impediments to exchange trading by requiring many swaps that exchanges reject for trading—but not all—to be executed on less regulated electronic trading systems known as "swap execution facilities." Like the centralized clearing requirement, the centralized trading requirement is riddled with loopholes. For example, swaps are exempt from centralized trading altogether if no swap execution facility will accept them. In another exception, swaps that are exempt from the central clearing requirement can also escape centralized trading so long as an "eligible contract participant"—statutory jargon for a financial end user—is on one side of the trade. This exception is the size of the proverbial Mack truck.[47] That is why, before Dodd-Frank's passage, Commodity Futures Trading Commission chairman Gary Gensler spoke out against this loophole, saying that 60 percent of standardized swaps—which could easily be cleared and traded on a centralized platform—would remain unregulated.[48]

The loophole for financial end users was a major victory for the five largest U.S. derivatives dealers, that is, JPMorgan Chase, Bank of America, Goldman Sachs, Morgan Stanley, and Citigroup, which reportedly handle up to 90 percent of derivatives trades. During the fight over the Dodd-Frank legislation, their trade association opposed transparency in the trading positions and price of over-the-counter swaps by resisting centralized trading of swaps bought by financial end users. The association's stance came as no surprise because its members were the largest derivatives traders, and they reap billions of dollars in fees from opaque trades. Taken together, these loopholes mean that Dodd-Frank's centralized clearing and exchange provisions will leave the majority of swaps trading untouched.

Irrespective of the loopholes, customized swaps pose gnarly problems for processing through clearinghouses and trading on exchanges. Dodd-Frank may make the problem worse by creating incentives for more customized swaps. To the extent that standardized swaps operate under one set of rules and customized contracts operate under another set with less transparency, there is a danger that swaps trading will migrate into the less regulated market with end users designing financial instruments to be nonstandard to avoid having to use a clearinghouse or exchange. At the end of the day, the daisy chain problem will likely live on despite Dodd-Frank's heralded passage.[49]

## Capital and Margin Requirements for Customized OTC Swaps

Swaps that are not cleared or centrally traded pose substantially higher risk to the financial system. Congress tried to address the problems posed by customized swaps by mandating higher margin and capital requirements for swaps dealers and major end users.[50] We have doubts whether these requirements alone are sufficient to prevent OTC swaps from becoming Warren Buffett's "weapons of mass destruction."[51] For one thing, the Dodd-Frank Act does not require sellers of OTC CDS to mark their exposures to market and adjust their margins on a daily basis. In addition, customized swaps have no ready resale market and no trading prices, so the capital and margin requirements for those derivatives will always rely on values generated by the same internal models that failed so miserably during the credit crisis.[52] Even if we set aside the inherent biases and limitations of these models, we have to ask whether regulators have the acumen and skill to assess the surfeit of internal valuation models and to fix their flaws. The answer, regrettably, is no.

## Other Regulatory Approaches to the OTC Market

If we do not have confidence in Dodd-Frank's capital and margin requirements as the failsafe for customized swaps, then what is to be done? Christopher Whalen, an experienced industry analyst, has called for the outright abolition of all OTC derivatives unless they are based on cash instruments. Whalen advances that proposal because of his concerns about murky valuation. If adopted, Whalen's proposal would result in the elimination of most CDS, private-label mortgage-backed securities, and CDOs.[53]

Law professor Roberta Karmel would not ban OTC swaps outright, but would restrict them to instruments that received advance governmental approval. Her proposal is not new. As she points out, before 2000, the Commodity Futures Trading Commission could not approve trading of credit default swaps on commodity exchanges "until these instruments were tested for their intrinsic merit and [it was] shown that they had an economic purpose and [were] not ... contrary to the public interest."[54] Congress abolished that advance approval procedure in 2000.

Although the advance approval proposal is intriguing, it would not work for customized CDS. Customized swaps are inherently unique and time-sensitive. Imposing an advance testing system would function as a ban.

We support an alternative, more modest path that takes a leaf from insurance law.[55] In insurance law, insurance policies are only enforceable in court when the insured has an "insurable interest." In other words, the insured must have a direct economic interest in the risk being insured to be able to collect payment. This rule prevents such situations as someone taking out life insurance on a stranger on the bet that the person will die.[56]

Speculation using CDS raises similar concerns. In a true hedging transaction, at least one of the parties to the deal has a direct economic interest in the asset or event being referenced. The party with the direct interest benefits from the trade by hedging that risk. In contrast, when neither trader has a direct interest in the reference, the trade is a zero-sum game. When someone buys a credit default swap on another company's debt without having an ownership interest in that debt, the buyer is not allocating its own risk of loss. Instead, the swap creates new losses for whomever loses the bet. The party to the other side of the trade will emerge the winner, but only by inflicting additional losses on its counterparty and on society. And if the loser becomes insolvent and cannot pay its swap obligation, a simple default can morph into contagion.[57]

The problem of speculation is not trifling. Consider that the total notional amount of CDS outstanding at year-end 2008 was $67 trillion, while the total market value of outstanding U.S. corporate bonds was just $15 trillion.[58] The fact that the underlying bond market was less than one-fourth of the total notional amount of swaps is a strong indication that the majority of credit default swaps were used for speculation.

For these reasons, we would limit the use of swaps to transactions where they strictly serve as hedges (in other words, where one or both of the parties to the trade has a direct economic interest in the asset being referenced). Prohibiting purely speculative CDS would help constrain systemic risk in two important respects. First, it would substantially reduce the total notional amount of swaps outstanding. Second, it would address systemic risk directly by eliminating transactions that increase losses throughout the system.

Despite its obvious flaws, the Dodd-Frank Act represents a tremendous effort to tackle systemic risk in the future. The creation of federal receivership proceedings for insolvent financial giants—with the associated ban on federal bailouts for failing firms outside receivership—are the legislation's biggest achievement in curbing systemic risk. Assuming that those two provisions are honored in future years, the federal government's "no bailout" slogan will gain a credibility it never had before.

Dodd-Frank further advances the cause of systemic safety by anointing the Federal Reserve as systemic risk regulator, in tandem with two new agencies, the Financial Stability Oversight Council and the Office of Financial Research. The new authority in the Fed and in the two new entities is breathtaking in scope and gives the Council and the Fed ample power to oversee the financial system and systemically important firms. The biggest concern is whether the Council, which is by design clumsy and ridden with rivalries, will promptly put nonbank financial firms that pose a systemic threat under Federal Reserve regulation. Past experience also gives rise to worries that the Council and the Fed will be overly cautious when ordering private firms to report data on systemic risk and instead will rely on fragmentary reports from other regulators. Similarly, Dodd-Frank lacks any meaningful mechanism to prod the Fed into taking vigorous enforcement before a systemically important firm spirals into insolvency. In sum, Dodd-Frank may do a better job addressing what to do with insolvent financial megafirms than preventing those insolvencies in the first place.

Dodd-Frank's rules on swaps are the most problematic of all. To its credit, Dodd-Frank subjects swaps to regulation, whereas they were exempt from oversight before. Within that convoluted regulatory scheme, however, a large percentage of the most dangerous swaps—customized swaps—evade centralized clearing, which is the most effective way of eliminating contagion from multilateral exposure. For swaps that escape centralized platforms, Dodd-Frank relies instead on minimum capital and margin requirements, licensing of market participants, and data reporting. Recent events do not give confidence, however, in the efficacy of those tools in cabining contagious effects of OTC swaps trading.

Ultimately, Dodd-Frank is a mixed bag, containing some failures and some successes. Its effectiveness will hinge on whether regulators consistently exercise their newfound powers. As we have outlined in earlier chapters, regulators' failure to exercise their authority brought us to the point of crisis. The robust exercise of that authority is one of the core challenges in financial regulation and the one that is hardest to ensure.

# Epilogue

As we finish this book in October 2010, two years have passed since Lehman Brothers filed for bankruptcy. The conflagration that followed set off one of the world's biggest financial cataclysms. Worldwide, financial institutions wrote down $3.4 trillion in assets.[1] Here in the United States, millions of people lost their jobs and even more had wrecked pensions and underwater mortgages.

After a drawn-out fight, the Obama administration attained a landmark achievement with the passage of the Dodd-Frank Act. With the law in place, it remains to be seen whether federal regulators will use their newfound powers to protect the financial system and consumers or cater to the financial industry.

## MONEY TALKS

As we gaze into the crystal ball to gauge the success of financial reform, one thing is certain: the lobbying might of banks. Wall Street and commercial banks made full use of their power to delay Dodd-Frank's passage and secure concessions. The bill that emerged was littered with compromises that lobbyists and legislators on both sides of the aisle extracted along the way.

In 2009 and 2010, the banking industry pelted members of the Senate Banking Committee with campaign contributions, with the senior members of the committee enjoying the biggest share of the bounty. Some of the committee's members received campaign contributions from commercial banks that were ten times larger than the contributions that banks made to Congressman Barney Frank, chairman of the House Financial Services Committee, who pushed stricter banking reforms and vowed to protect consumers.[2]

The year 2009 similarly set a record for lobbying expenditures by banks. Faced with the threat of stringent regulation, commercial banks paid over $50 million to lobbyists to beat back legislative reforms. The American Bankers Association led the pack, spending almost $9 million on lobbying, followed by JPMorgan Chase ($6.1 million) and Citigroup ($5.5 million). They were joined by a hit parade of other commercial banks that had accepted billions of dollars in TARP bailouts from tax-payers the year before.[3] Then, in an early 2010 decision, the Supreme Court boosted lobbyists' firepower by ruling that corporations have a First Amendment right to pay for ads calling for a political candidate's defeat.[4] Within weeks, the *New York Times* reported that executives at JPMorgan Chase and other big banks were threatening to withhold campaign contributions from Democrats who supported strong financial reforms.[5] This lobbying was business as usual. Back in 2009, when the Senate was considering the bankruptcy cram-down legislation, lobbyists had descended on the Senate and convinced key Democrats to oppose the Obama administration's proposal, at which point Senator Dick Durbin threw up his hands and charged that banks "own" the Senate.[6]

In the ensuing fight over financial reform, the banking industry exerted influence in fighting off consumer protection measures. From the day the Obama administration proposed a new agency to protect consumers, the banking industry geared up for bat-tle. The banks knew that they could not oppose consumer protection outright. Instead, they adopted a game plan of burying consumer protection authority within one of the federal banking regulatory agencies and then clipping its wings.

The industry's war cry was "no independent consumer protection agency." Banks exploited fears of even more financial crises in the future by arguing that an indepen-dent agency would jeopardize the safety of the banking system by imposing rules that would destroy profitability. The argument was ludicrous, since federal banking regu-lators had done a fine job all by themselves of capsizing the banking system during the housing bubble. Nevertheless, the Senate Banking Committee toed the industry line. By late November 2009, rumors started circulating that Senator Christopher Dodd, the chairman of the Senate Banking Committee, had struck a deal with Senate Republicans to nix an independent agency.

The final legislation was a compromise. The Consumer Financial Protection Bureau sits inside the Federal Reserve, but has an independent head appointed by the president with confirmation by the Senate, and statutory safeguards against interfer-ence by the Fed. In addition, the CFPB is financially independent and will not have to rely on congressional appropriations for its budget.

At the same time, the Dodd-Frank Act, in some respects, keeps the new bureau on a short leash. It gives federal banking regulators the unprecedented right to appeal consumer protection rules issued by the bureau to the Financial Stability Oversight Council, made up in part of federal banking regulators. The Council can overturn any final rule by the CFPB by a two-thirds vote, upon finding that the rule puts the safety and soundness of the U.S. financial system at risk. Thus, although the CFPB has expansive powers, any federal banking regulator who is industry captive can challenge the bureau's rules or water them down just by threatening to file an appeal.

## A SECOND BITE AT THE APPLE

Senator Dodd and Congressman Frank scored a big win with passage of their name-sake law, but another battle looms for which the industry has already begun preparing. Throughout the new law, Congress legislated in generalities, leaving it to federal reg-ulators to flesh out the details of financial reform through regulations. By one law firm's count, Dodd-Frank calls for 243 separate rulemakings.[7] Similarly, the law gives federal regulators the discretion to create exceptions to what otherwise appear to be hard-and-fast rules and to exempt companies and products from regulation. Examples of both of these maneuvers appear in the swaps provisions.

As a result, the financial services industry will get another bite at the apple to weaken financial reform during the rulemaking proceedings, and, if that fails, the industry will find ways to fall within the law's exemptions. Already financial lobbyists are lining up and recruiting onetime government regulators to aid their cause. Since 2009, close to 150 former financial regulators have filed forms to register as lobbyists.[8] In all likelihood, the lobbying campaign will dwarf the one that culminated in the Dodd-Frank bill—and have far less visibility.

## MINDING THE MINDERS

Dodd-Frank's legacy raises another, related question, which is whether the law adequately addresses the danger of agency inaction of the sort that allowed subprime products to grow to crisis proportions. The legislation gives copious powers to federal regulators to adopt rules and institute enforcement. The question is whether they will use those powers effectively.

Agency capture and inaction are always a concern. The Federal Trade Commission had a vigorous enforcement record on mortgage abuses during the Clinton administration but a lackluster record under George W. Bush. OCC and OTS preemption raised concerns about industry capture as well. Even in the absence of industry capture, every agency has periods of drift and inaction. Not every agency head will be a Ben Bernanke or Sheila Bair.

If the credit crisis teaches us anything, it is that multiple avenues of oversight and enforcement—via other federal regulators, private citizens, and the states—are key to counteracting industry capture and lethargy. Designating someone to mind the minder gives government officials or affected citizens the power to act (or at least exert pressure) when the lead regulator fails to take action.

So how does the Dodd-Frank Act stack up in this regard? Its record is uneven. Kudos go to Congress for giving the Financial Stability Oversight Council the power to recommend stricter standards for financial companies to the Federal Reserve Board and other federal financial regulators. If regulators fail to adopt the stricter standards, they must within ninety days explain why they declined to do so.[9] Dodd-Frank, however, falls short by not giving the Council backup authority to order enforcement actions to curb systemic risk if the Fed falls down on the job. .

When it comes to ensuring checks and balances in the area of consumer financial protection rule-making, the act relies on states. By allowing states to adopt consumer protection laws that exceed the federal floor, Dodd-Frank ameliorates the risks that could arise if the CFPB becomes lax. The law does not, however, entirely eliminate the possibility of OCC preemption of state laws for national banks and federal thrifts.

The CFPB's enforcement authority has explicit backup provisions. For large banks, with assets of $10 billion or more, the CFPB has primary authority and banks' primary banking regulators serve as the backups. For nonbank lenders, enforcement is by the CFPB and the FTC, depending on how the two agencies negotiate enforcement. Our hope is that however the CFPB and the FTC allocate their authority both agencies will have enforcement powers, whether concurrent or as primary and back-up enforcers. The story is different for smaller banks. There, Dodd-Frank vests sole enforcement power in the banks' primary regulators but gives no backup authority to the bureau.

Litigation by state attorneys general serves as a critical added check if the federal government fails to fulfill its consumer protection mandate. Under Dodd-Frank, state attorneys general can sue banks of all sizes for violations of CFPB regulations unless OCC preemption applies. The states have even broader authority over non-bank lenders.[10] In sum, the strength of checks and balances in the area of consumer financial protection in Dodd-Frank depends in large part on the size and nature of the institutions.

What's missing from the bill is a private right of action against loan originators for engaging in unfair or deceptive acts and practices (UDAP) under federal law.[11] By not allowing borrowers to bring claims for deceptive acts and practices—outside of the explicit prohibitions under Dodd-Frank and pre-existing federal laws--Congress bypassed an important opportunity to give consumers the role of backup enforcers.

## MEANWHILE, BACK IN CLEVELAND

A lot rides on the success of Dodd-Frank's financial reforms. If reforms fail and excessive risk-taking propels the country into financial disaster again, Main Street will be the loser. As we near the end of 2010, over 7 million homeowners are delinquent on their mortgage loans or in foreclosure; fully one-quarter no longer have any equity in their homes.[12] People are facing rising monthly payments on adjustable-rate mortgages and credit cards. The unemployment rate is stuck on "high". Workers who spent years saving for their futures have seen their wealth go up in smoke as their property values have fallen and their retirement accounts have slumped.

The fallout from the subprime crisis blanketed entire neighborhoods and communities. Back in Cleveland, graffitied buildings and weed-strewn lots litter the landscape. Once-proud homeowners watch rodents and drug dealers take over their neighborhoods. The city is trying its best to keep up, but it just can't. Armed with plywood to board up empty homes and demolition equipment to take down those that can't be saved, the city struggles to fight the devastation from abusive loans. Meanwhile, residents are fleeing, driving down tax revenues and property values. Some blocks look like a neutron bomb hit. The grimmest statistic of all: by June 2008, over 40 percent of bank-owned, foreclosed homes in the Cleveland area sold for $10,000 or less.[13]

No one knows the harm from reckless loans better than Jim Rokakis, the treasurer of Cuyahoga County, where Cleveland is located. Rokakis grew up in Cleveland with his six siblings and parents—immigrants from Greece—in a modest 1,350-square-foot home. Rokakis, with degrees from Oberlin College and Cleveland-Marshall College of Law, could have gone anywhere, but he chose to stay in Cleveland and try to improve the city. He was a force in Cleveland's revitalization in the 1990s and knew firsthand how fragile the city's renaissance was. Later, when abusive lending threatened to undo the strides that Cleveland had made, Rokakis did everything he could to get the attention of the Federal Reserve, the state capitol in Columbus, and Washington, D.C., but he was rebuffed at every turn.[14]

Rokakis wasn't alone. Harold Jackson, a city council member and later mayor of Cleveland, worked to pass an antipredatory lending ordinance in 2002. Eventually, though, the courts struck down the ordinance after the financial services industry brought a legal attack.[15] More recently, Cleveland sued Wall Street firms, seeking damages for the harm they caused the city by financing loans that residents could not afford. As we write, the federal appellate court has rejected the city's claims. A parallel case is still pending in state court.

Cleveland's story is not unique. It was one of the first regions to show signs of stress from abusive lending, but its story has been repeated many times since. Two foreclosures in particular epitomize the link between Cleveland and other, far-off towns. In Cleveland, Jim Rokakis's childhood home went into foreclosure and sold for $15,250.[16] Hundreds of miles away in Dillon, South Carolina, the same fate befell the home where Federal Reserve chairman Ben Bernanke grew up.[17]

The avarice of lenders and Wall Street reversed the efforts of cities like Cleveland to revitalize their communities. Aided by bank regulators, those financiers pushed communities across the country to the breaking point. We cannot afford to let this happen again. Local officials and individuals simply do not have the power to safeguard themselves alone. The federal government must make sure that what's good for Wall Street is good for Main Street too.

# Notes

CHAPTER 1

1. The proposal appeared in print in 2001 and in fuller form in 2002. Engel and McCoy (2001); Engel and McCoy (2002).

2. Federal Trade Commission (2003).

3. Heller and Garver (2000), at 1 ("As the regulators themselves admit, there is no definition of predatory lending. I don't know how we can hope to address the problem before we have decided what it is").

4. General Accountability Office (2004), at 6.

5. Associated Press (2007a).

6. Greenspan (2004).

7. Avery, Canner, and Cook (2005), at 385–87.

8. Engel and McCoy (2007); Engel and McCoy (2004).

9. Donald Powell, the FDIC's chairman at the time, floated the proposal. His successor, Chairman Sheila Bair, put that proposal on ice.


CHAPTER 2

1. For a detailed description of home mortgage regulation during this period, see McCoy and Renuart (2008).

2. Freddie Mac, "30-Year Fixed-Rate Mortgages Since 1971."

3. Balloon loans feature a final lump sum payment of tens of thousands of dollars that comes due after a specific number of years. In interest-only loans, the borrowers only pay interest and no principal for an initial period. In reverse mortgages, homeowners borrow against the equity in their homes but do not have to pay principal or interest until they move out or die, at which time the debt is paid off or the lenders take the home.

4. Depository Institutions Deregulation and Monetary Control Act of 1980, Pub. L. No. 96-221; Alternative Mortgage Transactions Parity Act of 1982, Pub. L. No. 97-320.

5. Browning (2007).

6. Dungey (2007b).

7. In 1968, Congress transferred responsibility for the securitization of FHA loans to Ginnie Mae.

8. Fannie Mae (2008a), at 3–5.

9. Schumer and Maloney (2007), at 20.

10. Chomsisengphet and Pennington-Cross (2006), at 40.

11. ElBoghdady and Cohen (2009).

12. Greenspan (2007), at 229.

13. Story (2008b).

14. Morgenson (2008a); Patterson (2008).

15. Morgenson (2007a).

16. Williams (2004b).

17. Shear (2009), at 1.

18. Olson and Aslanian (2008); Bailey (1997).

19. Rath (2000).

20. Morton (2000).

21. Seidman (1999), at 6.

22. Henriques and Bergman (2000).

23. Rath (2000); Henriques and Bergman (2000).

24. Hevesi (2002).

25. Henriques and Bergman (2000).

26. Rath (2000).

27. Kane (2008); Karp (2007).

28. Hevesi (2002); Kane (2008).

29. Hudson (2003).

30. Podelco (2001).

31. Hevesi (2002).

32. Reddy (2002); Hudson (2003).

33. Henriques and Bergman (2000).

34. Hevesi (2002).

35. Henriques and Bergman (2000).

36. Bradley and Skillern (2000).

37. Boylon (2002).

38. Hudson (2003).

39. Arnold (2008a).

40. Dough (1998).

41. Lubove (1999).

42. Murray (2008b).

43. Berman (2007).

44. Fuld (2008), at 145–46.

45. Lord (2005).

46. Grollmus (2005).

47. Grollmus (2005).

48. *California v. Countrywide Financial Corp., et al.* (2008), at 7, par. 28; Tully (2003); Morgenson and Fabricant (2007); Reuters (2008).

49. Mildenberg and Freifeld (2008).

50. Apgar et al. (2007), at 7, citing Inside Mortgage Finance, "Top Subprime Mortgage Market Players & Key Subprime Data 2005" (Bethesda, Md.: Inside Mortgage Finance Publications, 2005).

51. Guttentag (2004), at 133.

52. Smith et al. (2006), at 6; Dugan (2006a); Mishel and Bernstein (2007).

53. Streitfeld and Morgenson (2008); Bailey (2005).

54. Stone (2008); Morgenson (2008a).

55. *California v. Countrywide Financial Corp., et al.* (2008), at 29, pars. 115–17; Reckard and Hudson (2005).

56. Stone (2008).

57. Lord (2005).

58. Brooks and Simon (2007).

59. Morgenson (2007a); Hevesi (2002).

60. Goldstein and Son (2003), at 2–4.

61. Quercia et al. (2005), at 26.

62. Carr (2009), at 9; Mayer and Pence (2008), at 12; Calem et al. (2004), at 401.

63. *Mayor and City Council of Baltimore v. Wells Fargo Bank, N.A.* (2009b), at pars. 5, 8, and 10–11.

64. *Mayor and City Council of Baltimore v. Wells Fargo Bank, N.A.* (2009a), at 10, par. 27.

65. Woodward (2008), at 46.

66. Engel and McCoy (2008), at 81–108.

67. Woodward (2008), at 48–49.

68. Immergluck (2008), at 3.

69. Fitch Ratings (2007), at 6.

70. Caniglia and Heider (2002).

71. Arnold (2008a).

72. Arnold (2008a).

73. Morgenson (2008d).

74. Swecker (2004), at 6.

75. Mason and Rosner (2007a), at 9.

76. Reckard and Hudson (2005).

77. Efrati (2007b).

78. *Provident Bank v. Community Home Mortgage Corp.* (2007).

79. Markon (2008).

80. *Ricci et al. v. Ameriquest Mortgage Co. et al.* (2007).

81. Henriques and Bergman (2000).

82. Credit scores rank-order consumers based on the likelihood they will repay their debts. Scores are between 300 and 850. Credit scores are derived from complex algorithms that take into account factors such as consumers' record of making timely payments, their level of debt, the length of their credit history, and the types of credit they use. A score of 720 is usually the minimum required for a prime mortgage. People with scores above 720 qualify for prime loans unless they cannot meet the minimum income required for the mortgage or do not want to provide the paperwork supporting the information on their applications.

83. Brooks and Simon (2007); Craig (2008); Woodward (2008), at 10.

84. Brooks and Simon (2007); Arnold (2008a).

85. Jackson and Berry (2002), at 8.

86. Ernst et al. (2008), at 14–16. For another study documenting the high cost to borrowers of loans with YSPs, see Woodward (2008), at 70.

87. *Mayor and City Council of Baltimore v. Wells Fargo Bank, N.A.* (2009a), at 4, par. 12.

88. Haurin and Rosenthal (2005), at vii.

89. Pelley (2009).

90. Tully (2003).
91. *In Re New Century TRS Holdings, Inc.* (2008), at 131.
92. Federal Deposit Insurance Corporation (2006).
93. McCoy et al. (2009); Federal Deposit Insurance Corporation (2006).
94. Office of the Attorney General of Illinois (2007); *America's Housing Market: Cracks in the Façade* (2007); Brinkmann (2008), at 4.
95. Cagan (2006); Fratantoni (2005); Shenn (2006); Simon (2006).
96. Fishbein and Woodall (2006).
97. McCoy (2007b).
98. Cagan (2006).
99. *California v. Countrywide Financial Corp.* (2008), at 31, par. 125.
100. Simon (2008b).
101. *S.E.C. v. Mozilo et al.* (2009), at 28–29, par. 68.
102. Simon (2008b).
103. Demyanyk and Van Hemert (2008), at 7–8; Danis and Pennington-Cross (2008), at 77.
104. Mason and Rosner (2007a), at 14.
105. *Securities and Exchange Commission v. Mozilo et al.* (2009), at 21, par. 50.
106. Simpson and Hagerty (2008); Danis and Pennington-Cross (2008), at 78–79; *America's Housing Market: Cracks in the Façade* (2007); Haughwout (2008), at 12; McCoy et al. (2009), at 507, figure 5.
107. Pelley (2009).
108. Sharick et al. (2006), at 12.
109. Fitch Ratings (2007), at 1.
110. Goodman and Morgenson (2008).
111. Simpson and Hagerty (2008).
112. Associated Press (2008).
113. Morgenson (2007a); Schloemer (2006).
114. Gerardi et al. (2009), at 515–16.
115. T2 Partners LLC (2009) at 5 and 66; Chomsisengphet et al. (2008), at 1.
116. Haviv and Kaiser (2007); Reckard (2007).
117. *California v. Countrywide Financial Corp.* (2008), at 35, par. 140.
118. Morgenson (2007c).
119. *In re Washington Mutual, Inc.* (2008), at 135, par. 387.
120. Goldfarb and Klein (2008).
121. Reckard and Hudson (2005).
122. Goodman and Morgenson (2008).
123. Swecker (2004), at 8–9.
124. *In re Washington Mutual, Inc.* (2008), at 26, par. 70; 138, par. 395; and 115, par. 331.
125. *In re Washington Mutual, Inc.* (2008), at 140–43; Morgenson (2008d).
126. Cho (2007).
127. *In re Washington Mutual, Inc.* (2008), at 143, par. 413.
128. Fitch Ratings (2007), at 1, 4, and 6.
129. Shear (2009), at 17.
130. Federal Housing Administration (2009).
131. Smith et al. (2006), at 7.
132. Office of Federal Housing Enterprise Oversight (2007); Dodd (2007), at 16–17; ElBoghdady and Cohen (2009).

133. Simpson and Hagerty (2008).

134. Duhigg (2008b).

135. *In Re New Century TRS Holdings, Inc., et al.* (2008), at 114.

136. "FICO" refers to credit scores produced by the Fair, Isaac and Company. FICO scores are a common industry benchmark for borrowers' creditworthiness.

137. Keys et al. (2008), at 19–20.

138. Berndt and Gupta (2008), at 5.

139. Purnanandam (2009), at 29.

140. McCoy (2007b), at 137–38; Sylvan (2007).

141. Essene and Apgar (2007), at 19; Australian Government Productivity Commission (2008), at 385, quoting economist Peter Earl; Fannie Mae (2003), at 7.

142. Stango and Zinman (2006), at 5 and 12.

143. McCoy (2005), at 731–32.

CHAPTER 3

1. Merriam-Webster (1981).

2. Bajaj and Anderson (2008).

3. Bethel et al. (2008), at 18.

4. Arnold (2008b).

5. Bajaj and Anderson (2008).

6. Rucker (2007).

7. Cho (2007).

8. Arnold (2008b).

9. Kelly et al. (2008).

10. Engel and McCoy (2007a), at 2047; American Securitization Forum (2009), at 2–3.

11. Drew (2008); Dunbar and Donald (2009).

12. Securities and Exchange Commission (2008), at 18.

13. Bajaj and Anderson (2008).

14. White (2007), at 49.

15. Fitzpatrick and Sagers (2009).

16. Richardson and Lucchetti (2008); Norris (2009b).

17. Lucchetti and Ng (2007).

18. Lowenstein (2008).

19. Securities and Exchange Commission (2008), at 12.

20. Morgenson (2008g).

21. Securities and Exchange Commission (2008), at 9.

22. Waxman (2008), at 6.

23. Morgenson (2008g).

24. Lucchetti (2008a).

25. Calomiris (2008).

26. Woellert and Kopecki (2008).

27. Lucchetti and Ng (2007).

28. Egan (2008), at 27.

29. Scannell and Solomon (2007); Raiter (2008), at 23.

30. Lowenstein (2008).

31. Securities and Exchange Commission (2008), at 32.

32. Lucchetti and Ng (2007).
33. Securities and Exchange Commission (2008), at 24–25.
34. McDaniel (2007).
35. Lucchetti (2008b).
36. Lucchetti (2008a); Morgenson (2008g).
37. Securities and Exchange Commission (2008), at 13–19.
38. Lewis and Einhorn (2009).
39. Laby (2009), at 32; Cox et al. (2009), at 120; Levine (2007), at 60.
40. Pulliam et al. (2008).
41. Dash and Creswell (2008b).
42. Dungey (2007a); Morgenson (2007c).
43. Berman (2007); Securities and Exchange Commission (2008), at 9.
44. Laing (2007); Mason and Rosner (2007b), at 72.
45. Securities and Exchange Commission (2008), at 7.
46. Securities and Exchange Commission (2008), at 7; "At the Risky End of Finance" (2007); Jickling (2008), at 4.
47. Lowenstein (2008).
48. Morgenson (2008e); Dash and Creswell (2008b); Pulliam et al. (2008).
49. Blundell-Wignall (2007), at 45.
50. Norris (2007).
51. Jickling (2008), at 3; Keoun (2009); Read (2009).
52. Norris (2007).
53. Greenberger (2008).
54. Eggert (2009), at 1268.
55. Osinski (2009).
56. Gerding (2009), at 3–4; Nocera (2009a).
57. Overbye (2009).
58. "Professionally Gloomy" (2008).
59. Nocera (2009a).
60. Dash and Creswell (2008b); Krugman (2001); Gerding (2009), at 52.
61. Securities and Exchange Commission (2008), at 21; Calomiris (2008).
62. Raiter (2008), at 24.
63. Partnoy (2006), at 79.
64. Partnoy (2009), at 263.
65. Bajaj (2007a).
66. Fremont General Corp. (2006).
67. *California v. Countrywide Financial Corp. et al.* (2008), at 8–9, pars. 32–35.
68. Levine (2007), at 60–61.
69. Levine (2007), at 60–61.
70. Business Wire (2005); Levine (2007), at 60-64.
71. Levine (2007), at 60–64.
72. Morgan Stanley (2007).
73. Morgenson and Fabricant (2007).
74. Gregory (2000), at 2.
75. *California v. Countrywide Financial Corp. et al.* (2008), at 7, par. 28.
76. Insurance Information Institute (2009), at v.
77. Anderson (2006).
78. Cho (2007).

79. Benmelech and Dlugos (2009), at 20.

80. Leonnig (2008); Shenn (2008).

81. Shepard (2005), at 8.

82. Greenspan (2005b).

83. Kaufman (2007).

84. Ng et al. (2007).

85. Wessel (2008).

86. *Securities and Exchange Commission v. Mozilo et al.* (2009), at 9–10, par. 21, and 40–41, par. 103.

87. Financial Stability Board (2008), at 8; Anderson and Bajaj (2008); Howley (2007); Paulson (2008a), at 10.

88. Drew (2008).

89. "Ruptured Credit" (2008).

90. Schwarcz (2008), at 380–81.

91. Duhigg and Dougherty (2008).

92. Demyanyk and Van Hemert (2008), at 32–33.

93. *In Re New Century TRS Holdings, Inc., et al.* (2008), at 112.

94. Garcia (2004), at 2.

95. Lehman Brothers (1999).

96. Federal Trade Commission (2002).

97. Dunbar and Donald (2009), at 6.

98. Board of Governors of the Federal Reserve System and Department of Housing and Urban Development (1998).

99. Department of Treasury and Department of Housing and Urban Development (2000), at 24 and 79–80.

100. Appelbaum and Nakashima (2008).

101. Becker et al. (2008).

102. Stecklow (2009).

103. Mason and Rosner (2007a), at 5.

104. Nocera (2009a).

105. Hagerty (2008).

106. Duhigg (2008a).

107. Nocera (2009a).

108. Shepard (2003), at 2.

109. Lowenstein (2008).

110. Waxman (2008), at 6.

111. Dennis and O'Harrow (2008).

112. American International Group (2007b).

113. Consumer Affairs (2001).

114. Berenson (2001).

115. Consumer Affairs (2001).

116. Norris and Berenson (2002).

117. Currie (2007).

118. Pate et al. (1998), at 30.

119. Becker et al. (2008).

120. Tanoue (2000b).

121. Henriques and Bergman (2000).

122. Hudson (2007).

CHAPTER 4

1. In spring 2006, loan buybacks had previously caused two other subprime lenders—Merit Financial and Acoustic Home Loans—to fail, followed by the failure of Meritage Mortgage (a NetBank affiliate) and Axis Mortgage and Investment in November 2006.

2. Lucchetti and Ng (2007); Lowenstein (2008).

3. Bajaj and Haughney (2007); Gosselin (2007a).

4. Reed (2006).

5. Bernasek (2007); Leonhardt and Bajaj (2007).

6. Board of Governors of the Federal Reserve System (2008a), at 6; Board of Governors of the Federal Reserve System (2008b); Board of Governors of the Federal Reserve System, Table Data for Mortgage Delinquency Rates, 2001–07.

7. Creswell (2007a).

8. Anderson and Bajaj (2007b); Board of Governors of the Federal Reserve Board System (2007b); England (2008), at 28; International Financial Services London (2009).

9. Kanef (2007), at 23, 32; Tillman (2007), at 23–24.

10. Berry (2007).

11. Bernanke (2007b).

12. Becker et al. (2008).

13. Bajaj (2007b); Morgenson (2008g); Bloomberg News (2007a).

14. Anderson and Bajaj (2007a); Reuters (2007).

15. Onaran (2007).

16. Alster (2007).

17. Dinallo (2008), preliminary transcript at 17.

18. Dennis and O'Harrow (2008); Bajaj and Landler (2007).

19. Morgenson (2008b).

20. Dennis (2009); Dennis and O'Harrow (2008); Morgenson (2008b); Dinallo (2008), preliminary transcript at 68 and 143.

21. Glater (2008).

22. "American International Group Investor Meeting – Final" (2007).

23. Lanman (2009).

24. Bloomberg News (2007c); Dash (2007a); Morgenson and Anderson (2007); Bernanke (2007c); Dugan (2007d).

25. Bookstaber (2007b).

26. Dash (2007b); Norris and Dash (2007); Uchitelle (2007).

27. Bernanke (2007c).

28. Bernanke (2007d).

29. Dugan (2007d), at 3.

30. Bernanke (2007c).

31. Walsh (2007), at 1.

32. That same day, the Federal Open Market Committee voted to set up foreign exchange swaps with the European Central Bank and the Swiss National Bank, also to ease pressure in the money markets.

33. Sengupta and Tam (2008).

34. Bernanke (2007c); Dugan (2007d); Walsh (2007).

35. BBC News (2007a).

36. Gallagher (2007).

37. Bernanke (2007c); Dash (2007c).

38. Strott (2007).

39. Sengupta and Tam (2008).

40. Bair (2007a); Bair (2007b); Dash (2007c).

41. Wighton (2007).

42. Bajaj and Landler (2007); Bloomberg News (2007b); Clark (2007); González-Páramo (2009).

43. BBC News (2007b).

44. Fouché (2008).

45. Onaran (2008); Bauerlein (2007); Dash and Creswell (2008b); Stoll (2008); Stempel (2008a); Berman (2008); Associated Press (2007a); Bajaj (2007a).

46. Reddy (2007); Hagerty and Simon (2007b).

47. Hagerty and Simon (2007b); Fannie Mae (2008b).

48. Insurance Information Institute (2008), at 172.

49. Berner (2008); Moellenkamp (2008); Sidel (2008b); Simon (2008a); Hagerty and Simon (2007b); Stoll (2008); Tomsho and Hechinger (2008).

50. McCracken and Zuckerman (2007); Sidel (2008a); Bernanke (2007c); Heath (2007).

51. Andrews (2008a).

52. Andrews (2008a); Andrews and Uchitelle (2008); Brinkman (2008), at 3.

53. Grow et al. (2009).

54. Andrews (2007).

55. Reichman (2007).

56. Reichman (2007).

57. Corkery (2008b).

58. The PEW Charitable Trust (2008), at 33.

59. Office of the Comptroller of the Currency and Office of Thrift Supervision (2008a), at 7; Hope Now (2008).

60. Grow et al. (2009); Congressional Oversight Panel (2009a), at 31.

61. Terris (2007).

62. Morgenson (2007c).

63. Kane (2009b).

64. Morgenson (2007c).

65. Federal Trade Commission (2008).

66. Clark and Barron (2009), at 13–14.

67. In Re Foreclosure Cases (2007), at *3.

68. Stutt (2008).

69. Irwin (2008).

70. Ishmael et al. (2008).

71. Ishmael et al. (2008).

72. "SOS—'Save Our Stocks': A Look Back at a Year of Bailouts, Underwater Investors and Sunken Hopes" (2009).

73. Economic Stimulus Act of 2008, Pub. L. No. 110-185.

74. Lucchetti and Ng (2008).

75. Becker et al. (2008).

76. Pilling et al. (2008).

77. Burrough (2008).

78. Bank for International Settlements (2008), at 3.

79. Between March 7 and March 11, the Fed increased its swap lines with the European Central Bank and the Swiss National Bank and created a new, $100 billion repurchase program designed to accept subprime bonds from primary dealers as collateral. It also upped the Term Auction Facility, created in December 2007, to $100 billion and extended its term.

80. For a comprehensive account of Bear Stearns's collapse, see Cohan (2009).

81. Scannell (2008a).

82. Boyd (2008).

83. Scannell (2008a); Sidel et al. (2008).

84. Guerrera and Sender (2008).

85. Bernanke (2008).

86. Fettig (2008).

87. Grynbaum (2008).

88. Ng and Craig (2008).

89. Later, on July 7, 2008, the Fed reached an agreement with the SEC to share the supervision of large investment banks. That agreement, however, did not give the Fed the full panoply of powers that a direct supervisor would possess.

90. White and Guerrera (2008).

91. Cohan (2009).

92. Department of the Treasury (2008a).

93. Specifically, the price for the nearby-month gold contract. The nearby month is the option delivery month with the soonest expiration date.

94. Simpson (2008); Simpson and Hagerty (2008).

95. Guerrera and White (2008).

96. Tomsho (2008b). In late April, Congress had authorized these measures in the Ensuring Continued Access to Student Loans Act of 2008, Pub. L. No. 110-227, passed with broad bipartisan support and signed by President Bush on May 7, 2008.

97. Paulson (2008b).

98. Meinero and Rooney (2008).

99. Scholtes (2008).

100. Kamalakaran and Miller (2008).

101. Labaton and Weisman (2008).

102. Pub. L. No. 110-289.

103. Goldfarb (2008b); Marsh (2008); Razzi (2008); ElBoghdady (2008); Department of Housing and Urban Development (2009a); Flitter (2008).

104. Johnson (2008).

105. Moore (2008a).

106. Guerrera and Bullock (2008).

107. Specifically, the Fed extended the Primary Dealer Credit Facility—providing discount window loans to investment banks—and the Term Securities Lending Facility through January 30, 2009. The Fed also unveiled a new program offering auctions of options on $50 billion worth of loans through the TSLF. Finally, it increased its dollar swap line with the European Central Bank to $55 billion.

108. Kennedy (2008).

109. Chung et al. (2008); Guerrera et al. (2008).

110. Onaran and Pierson (2008).

CHAPTER 5

1. BBC News (2008).
2. Gunther (2008).
3. Paulson (2008c).
4. Morgenson and Duhigg (2008).
5. Duhigg et al. (2008).
6. Federal Housing Finance Agency (2009). Banks that held Fannie and Freddie stock had to deduct the net unrealized losses on those securities from their capital. At least one bank, the National Bank of Commerce in Berkeley, Illinois, failed because of the loss of value in its GSE preferred stock.
7. Federal Housing Finance Agency (2009).
8. The same privilege was extended to the Federal Home Loan Banks.
9. Paulson (2008c).
10. Paulson (2008c).
11. DeMarco (2009), at 4-5; Demarco (2010), at 2.
12. Associated Press (2007a); Corkery (2008a); Schwartz (2007); Streitfeld (2008); "Shutting Up Shop" (2008).
13. Millman (2008).
14. Naughton (2009); Karmin (2009).
15. Sorkin (2009).
16. Eavis (2008).
17. Fitzpatrick (2009); Craig (2009); Story (2009a); Story (2009b).
18. Fitzpatrick (2009).
19. Dash and Sorkin (2008).
20. Andrews (2008b).
21. Karnitschig et al. (2008).
22. Turner (2008).
23. As of October 2009, the interest rate on AIG's loan was three-month LIBOR plus 3 percent, an interest rate reduction of 5.5 percent from the original terms of the loan.
24. Government Accountability Office (2009b).
25. Wilczek (2009).
26. Bajaj (2008b).
27. Sloan (2008).
28. Later, on October 21, 2008, the Federal Reserve announced yet another program under Section 13(3) to prop up money market funds: the Money Market Investor Funding Facility. In that program, the New York Fed agreed to provide senior secured funding to special purpose vehicles created by the money market industry. In turn, U.S. money market funds could sell short-term commercial paper, banknotes, and certificates of deposit issued by fifty highly rated North American and European financial institutions to the SPVs, which would allow them to meet a surge in redemption requests and buy newly issued commercial paper.
29. Becker et al. (2008).
30. Barnes et al. (2008).
31. Pub. L. No. 110-343.
32. Emergency Economic Stabilization Act, Pub. L. No. 110-343, sec. 3(9).
33. Paulson (2008d).
34. Fox (2008); Stein (2009).

35. Corkery (2008b); Fox (2008); Berry (2009b); Levitan (2009).

36. Merle (2008).

37. Duhigg (2008c).

38. The previous day, October 6, the Federal Reserve Board had exercised its new powers under EESA to pay interest on reserves held by depository institutions at the Federal Reserve, effective immediately. This was one more way in which the Fed injected liquidity into the system.

39. This measures the spread of LIBOR over the price for overnight indexed swaps.

40. Landler (2008).

41. Landler and Dash (2008). The dividend on the preferred shares would rise to 9 percent after five years, to give companies an incentive to repay their TARP funds promptly. In addition, the government took warrants for common stock equaling 15 percent of its initial capital infusion. The executive compensation limits included a clawback of any bonus based on earnings that later were restated, a ban on golden parachutes, and a $500,000 cap on company tax deductions for salaries paid executives.

42. Paulson (2008f).

43. Bank of America received a second installment of $10 billion on January 9, 2009, to consummate the Merrill Lynch acquisition.

44. CNN (2008).

45. Mortgage Bankers Association (2009d).

46. Bernanke (2009), at 2–4.

47. Bailey (2008).

48. In September 2009, Bank of America paid the U.S. government an exit fee to terminate the guarantee on the $118 billion asset pool. The guarantee was never drawn on.

49. Story (2009a).

50. Warsh (2008).

51. Morgenson (2008f).

52. Goldfarb (2008b).

53. Luhby (2008a).

54. Merle (2009a); Luhby (2008a); Gomstyn (2008); Hopkins (2008b); Duhigg (2008c); ElBoghdady (2008); Appelbaum (2008a). US Bancorp adopted the IndyMac program as part of its agreement with the FDIC when it acquired two California banks that had gone under.

55. Mortgage Bankers Association (2009a); Schoen (2009); Palmeri (2008); Merle (2009b).

56. Streitfeld (2008); Hoak (2009).

57. Center for Responsible Lending (2007), at 2–3; Demyanyk (2009), at 92; Calem et al. (2009), at 3–4.

58. CNN (2008).

CHAPTER 6

1. "Senate Confirms Geithner to Head Treasury" (2009).

2. Originally, that number was reported at 598,000, but later it was revised upward. Geithner (2009c).

3. Bartlett (2009).

4. Pressley (2009).

5. Hagerty and Simon (2009).

6. Barkley (2007); Goldfarb (2008a); Merle (2009d).

7. Pub. L. No. 111-5.

8. In November 2009, Congress extended the credit through April 30, 2010, raised its income limits, and created a new $6,500 tax credit for many repeat homebuyers.

9. Government Accountability Office (2009c), Highlights.

10. Government Accountability Office (2009c), Highlights.

11. Pub. L. No. 111-25.

12. Simon (2008e); Simon (2008d).

13. Adelino et al. (2009), at 3.

14. White (2009), at 8.

15. Simon (2008e).

16. Credit Suisse (2008a), at 6.

17. Office of the Comptroller of the Currency and Office of Thrift Supervision (2009), at 7.

18. Carter (2007).

19. Goodman (2009b).

20. Grow et al. (2009).

21. Adelino (2009), at 6.

22. Nocera (2009b).

23. Nocera (2009b).

24. Grow et al. (2009).

25. Williamson and Simon (2009); Fox (2008).

26. Berry (2009a); Credit Suisse (2008a), at 6; Seidenberg (2009).

27. Department of the Treasury (2009b); Andrews (2009a). In July 2009, HUD expanded the Home Affordable Refinance Program, which was the loan modification program for loans owned or guaranteed by Fannie and Freddie that were underwater by up to 125 percent. Department of Housing and Urban Development (2009b). Even with this expansion of eligible borrowers, HARP had only refinanced 116,677 loans as of September 2009. Streitfeld (2009b).

28. Department of the Treasury (2009b); Andrews (2009a); Donovan (2009), at 2.

29. Department of the Treasury (2009b); Andrews (2009a).

30. Department of Housing and Urban Development (2009b). There were special incentives for modifying loans of borrowers who were current on their loans but at imminent risk of default. For these modifications, mortgage holders received $1500 and servicers, $500. Department of Housing and Urban Development (2009b).

31. Department of the Treasury (2009b).

32. Yoon (2009).

33. Office of the Attorney General, State of California (2009).

34. Merle (2009a).

35. Freddie Mac (2009a); Stout, D. (2009).

36. Adler (2009); www.mortgagebankers.org; Kulikowski (2009); Mollenkamp (2009); Corkery (2009).

37. Goodman and Healy (2009).

38. Cordell et al. (2008), at 16 and 23; Dietz (2009).

39. Dietz (2009); Seidenberg (2009); Rudolf (2009).

40. Thompson (2009), at 40; Terris (2008); Goodman (2009b); Dungey (2007a); Grow (2009); White (2009), at 24–25.

41. Goodman (2009b).

42. Another hurdle had been contract terms that prohibited loan modifications unless the borrowers were in default or certain to default. These provisions were, in part, necessary to ensure that trusts avoided incurring certain tax liabilities. In response to these concerns and in light of the foreclosure crisis, in late 2007 the IRS issued a statement that permitted modifications of troubled loans without running afoul of tax rules. Internal Revenue Service (2007); Thompson (2009), at 12–13.

43. Pinedo and Baumgardner (2009), at 4; Thompson (2009), at 38–39.

44. Grow (2009); Cordell et al. (2008), at 22.

45. Cordell et al. (2008), at 12.

46. Thompson (2009), at 18; Associated Press (2007b); Terris (2007); Geanakoplos and Koniak (2008).

47. Adelino et al. (2009), at 25.

48. Pub. L. No. 110-289, sec. 1403.

49. Helping Families Save their Homes Act of 2009, Pub. L. No. 111-22, sec. 201.

50. Merle (2009c); Christie (2009); Pinedo and Baumgardner (2009), at 8; Holzer (2009b).

51. Christie (2009).

52. Holzer (2009b).

53. Department of Housing and Urban Development (2009e).

54. Holzer (2009a).

55. Seidenberg (2009); Cordell et al. (2008), at 4; Morgenson (2009b).

56. Simon (2009b).

57. Adler (2009); Nocera (2009b); Office of the Comptroller of the Currency and Office of Thrift Supervision (2009), at 6; Donovan (2009).

58. Goodman (2009c); Credit Suisse (2008b), at 2; Department of the Treasury (2009d), at 2.

59. Hagerty (2009a); Office of the Comptroller of the Currency and Office of Thrift Supervision (2009), at 26; Simon (2009e); Merle (2009e); Nocera (2009b).

60. Goodman (2009c).

61. Department of Housing and Urban Development (2009e).

62. Simon (2009c); Simon (2009d).

63. Leland (2009); Schoen (2009).

64. Goodman (2009a).

65. Goodman (2009a).

66. Goodman (2009a).

67. Lawder (2009); Schoen (2009).

68. Goodman (2009a).

69. Dunbar (2009).

70. Timiraos and Solomon (2009); Enrich (2009); Story (2009b).

71. Streitfeld and Story (2009); Timiraos and Solomon (2009); Hogberg (2009); ElBoghdady (2009).

72. Engel (2009), at 4.

73. Office of the Inspector General, Department of Housing and Urban Development (2009), at 1–2.

74. American Express, BB&T, Bank of New York Mellon, Capital One, Goldman Sachs, JPMorgan Chase, MetLife, State Street, and US Bancorp.

75. Among them was Citigroup. In late February 2009, Citigroup had asked for and received permission to convert $25 billion of Treasury's preferred stock in the company into common shares to improve its capital ratios.

76. Banks have to satisfy capital requirements for two different categories of capital, Tier 1 and Tier 2. Tier 1 contains higher quality capital, compared to the types of capital that qualify for Tier 2. During the stress test, the examiners measured whether each institution could maintain a Tier 1 risk-based ratio of at least 6 percent and a Tier 1 common risk-based ratio of at least 4 percent at year-end 2010 under a variety of downturn scenarios.

77. Enrich et al. (2009).

78. Fitzpatrick and Paletta (2009).

79. Elliott (2009). Elliott estimated that if "the tests mis-estimated the value of the [nineteen banks'] assets at the end of 2010 by just 3%, it would require another $300 billion of capital." Elliott (2009), at 10.

80. Enrich et al. (2009).

81. Under the legacy loan program, investors would bid to buy pools of distressed loans. Six-sevenths of the purchase price would come from borrowed money, backed by an FDIC guarantee. The last seventh would consist of equity, half from the winning investor's own funds and half from TARP funds. The investor would service the loans in the pool and manage their disposition. Under the legacy securities program, Treasury would match each dollar of private equity, while the Federal Reserve under TALF would lend the investor an amount equal to the amount of private equity (or even double) to buy troubled securities.

82. Some eligible securities that sold for 30 cents on the dollar in March 2009 were selling for 65 cents on the dollar by fall 2009.

83. Financial Accounting Standards Board (2009a); Financial Accounting Standards Board (2009b). Under the ruling, a bank could hold troubled assets at book value under two conditions: first, the bank planned to hold the assets indefinitely; and second, market prices were unavailable or based on distress sale prices. In a sister ruling, FASB added that any permanent impairment due to market conditions would not reduce earnings or regulatory capital so long as the bank planned to hold the assets indefinitely. In contrast, if a bank sold a troubled asset, FASB required it to mark the asset to market and absorb any resulting hit to earnings and capital.

84. Separately, starting in 2008, the FDIC sold several billion dollars in distressed loans, acquired through bank receiverships, outside of the PPIP program. The FDIC placed these loans in limited liability companies. The FDIC was the majority owner of the companies and private investors held the remaining stakes. The limited liability companies then sold the loans and distributed the proceeds.

85. Federal Deposit Insurance Corporation (2009b), at 13.

86. For third quarter 2009, the Deposit Insurance Fund had $38.9 billion in contingent loss reserves, which absorb the first hit when a bank fails. Once the contingent loss reserve was taken into account, the fund had total reserves of $30.7 billion for the quarter. Federal Deposit Insurance Corporation (2009d). In addition, the FDIC separately held $23 billion in cash and U.S. Treasury securities. Federal Deposit Insurance Corporation (2009c).

87. Bel Bruno (2009).

88. Craig and Solomon (2009).

89. Banks that received assistance under the regular capital injection program would be subject to one-size-fits-all guidelines. Under a "say on pay" provision, executive compensation plans had to be put to a shareholder vote. In addition, the guidelines expanded the ban on golden parachute payments and the clawback provisions for senior executives who knowingly falsified the company's financial statements.

90. No restricted stock could be sold, moreover, unless performance targets were met and the company repaid its TARP funds with interest. Feinberg also imposed new restrictions on executive perks and golden parachute packages.

91. Engel (2006).

92. T2 Partners LLC (2009), at 23–24.

93. Miroff (2008).

94. Margolies (2008).

95. ElBoghdady and Cohen (2009).

96. ElBoghdady and Cohen (2009); Kane (2009a).

97. Haughney (2008).

98. Kane (2009a).

99. Margolies (2008); Kane (2009a).

100. Casey (2009).

101. Corkery and Simon (2008).

102. http/cgi.ebay.com, October 28, 2009.

103. Saulny (2009); Kane (2009a).

104. Pelletiere (2009), at 7–8.

105. Pelletiere (2009), at 6–7; Osterman (2008); Miroff (2008); Evans (2007).

106. Goldfarb (2008a); Fannie Mae (2009); Freddie Mac (2009a); Freddie Mac (2009b).

107. Helping Families Save Their Homes Act of 2009, Public Law No. 111-22.

108. Schumer and Maloney (2007), at 3; Christie (2007); Sword and Cormier (2007); Eaton et al. (2009).

109. PEW Charitable Trust (2008), at 12.

110. Department of Housing and Urban Development (2009c).

111. Immergluck (2008), at 12–13. A report of the Joint Economic Committee put the cost to neighbors from the spillover effect of foreclosures at $32 billion for the thirty-month period between mid-2007 and the end of 2009. Schumer and Maloney (2007), at 3.

112. Gerardi and Willen (2008), at 13.

113. Smith and Duda (2009), at 7.

114. Carr (2009), at 7.

115. Carr (2009), at 9; Lovell and Isaacs (2008), at 1; Eckholm (2009).

116. Pouliot (2009); Trexler (2008).

117. Bureau of Economic Analysis (2009); Geithner (2009c); Krueger (2009).

118. Department of the Treasury (2009c), at 8.

119. Department of the Treasury (2009c), at 10; Federal Deposit Insurance Corporation (2009c).

120. Department of the Treasury (2009c), at 13. In June 2009, the Fed reduced the size of auctions under the Term Auction Facility, and by September of that year, demand for those auctions had fallen from their peak by more than half. TAF was the Fed's best-used special crisis program by far, accounting for 84 percent of total average daily balances under all of those programs. Department of the Treasury (2009c), at 11. Later that year, the Fed curtailed activities under the Term Securities Lending Facility, the Primary Dealer Credit Facility, and the Asset-Backed Commercial Paper Money Market Mutual Fund Liquidity Facility after new borrowings dropped to zero. Federal Reserve System (2009a), at 9, 12, 26, 28. The Fed left the Commercial Paper Funding Facility intact as of late 2009, while noting that its use had substantially declined. Department of the Treasury (2009c), at 2; Geithner (2009c).

121. Baker (2010).

122. Luo and Thee-Brenan (2009).

123. Acs (2009), at 1; Carr (2009), at 7; DeParle (2009); DeParle and Gebeloff (2009); Murray (2009); Simon and Hagerty (2009); ElBoghdady and Cohen (2009).

124. Streitfeld (2009a).

125. Simon (2009a).

126. Hagerty (2009b).

127. Department of the Treasury (2009c), at 2–4, 12, 15.

128. Andrews and Sanger (2009).

129. Department of the Treasury (2009c), at 2; Geithner (2009c); Shrivastava (2009).

130. Department of the Treasury (2009c), at 12.


CHAPTER 7

1. Heller and Garver (2000), at 1; Predatory Lending Consumer Protection Act of 2000, H.R. 4250 and S. 2415; Predatory Lending Deterrence Act, S. 2405. In a defensive move, conservative Republicans Schakowsky and Ney introduced watered-down legislation in the House. Anti-Predatory Lending Act of 2000, H.R. 3901; Consumer Mortgage Protection Act of 2000, H.R. 4213.

2. Board of Governors of the Federal Reserve System and Department of Housing and Urban Development (1998); Department of the Treasury and Department of Housing and Urban Development (2000).

3. Department of Justice, Civil Rights Division (2001); Federal Trade Commission (2000), at 5–7 (describing settlements with Delta Funding Corporation, Fleet Finance, Inc., The Money Tree, Tower Loan, and seven other subprime lenders); *Federal Trade Commission v. Capital City Mortgage Corp.* (1998) (alleging that asset-based lending violated the Federal Trade Commission Act); Federal Trade Commission (2005).

4. Fannie Mae (2000); Freddie Mac (2000).

5. Board of Governors of the Federal Reserve System et al. (2000b); Office of Thrift Supervision (2000a); Office of Thrift Supervision (2000b); Office of Thrift Supervision (2000c); "GMAC Seeks Thrift Charter" (1998); Heller (2000), at 1; "OTS Suspends Associates' App" (1998). While Seidman was pushing for binding rules, she and fellow banking regulators adopted the first of a string of federal interagency guidances on subprime mortgages and securitization. Federal Deposit Insurance Corporation (1999a); Federal Deposit Insurance Corporation (1999b).

6. Federal Deposit Insurance Corporation (1999c); Tanoue (1999).

7. Federal Deposit Insurance Corporation (1999c).

8. Office of Inspector General, Department of the Treasury (2000); Office of Inspector General, Federal Deposit Insurance Corporation (2000).

9. General Accounting Office (2002).

10. General Accounting Office (2002).

11. Department of the Treasury et al. (2001); Board of Governors of the Federal Reserve System et al. (2000a); Collins (1999); "FDIC Says Banks Undercapitalized for Subprime Lending" (2000), at 2; Tanoue (1999); Tanoue (2000a); Whiteman (1999), at 1.


CHAPTER 8

1. See, *e.g.*, *American Financial Services Ass'n v. City of Toledo* (2006) (overturning Toledo's law); *American Financial Services Ass'n v. City of Cleveland* (2006) (overturning Cleveland's ordinance); *American Financial Services Ass'n v. City of Oakland* (2005)

(overturning Oakland's ordinance); *Mayor of the City of New York v. Council of the City of New York* (2004) (AFSA won judgment overturning the New York City ordinance); Berner and Grow (2008), at 36; *American Financial Services Ass'n v. Burke* (2001) (successfully challenging state law prohibiting mandatory arbitration clauses in high-cost mortgages as violating the Federal Arbitration Act).

2. Office of Thrift Supervision (1996a) (codified at 12 U.S.C. sec. 560.2); Office of Thrift Supervision (1996b) (codified at 12 C.F.R. sec. 559.3(h)); Gilleran (2003).

3. Bostic et al. (2008a), at 140; Office of Thrift Supervision (2000b), at 17814–17816.

4. National City Corporation, the parent of National City Bank, N.A., and a major subprime lender, spearheaded the campaign for OCC preemption. "Predatory Lending Laws Neutered" (2003); Berner and Grow (2008), at 36.

5. Office of the Comptroller of the Currency (2004b) (codified at 12 C.F.R. secs. 7.4007–7.4009, 34.4).

6. Office of the Comptroller of the Currency (2004a) (codified at 12 C.F.R. sec. 7.4000). For the OTS counterpart of the visitorial powers rule, see *Fidelity Fed. Sav. & Loan Ass'n v. de la Cuesta* (1982).

7. Hawke (2003b); Williams (2003b) (emphasis in original).

8. *Watters v. Wachovia Bank, N.A.* (2007); Peterson (2007); Wilmarth (2004). The *Watters* case only upheld OCC preemption. Later, the Supreme Court affirmed a challenge to the OCC visitorial powers rule by Andrew Cuomo, the Attorney General of New York. *Cuomo v. Clearing House Ass'n et al.* (2009).

The OCC and the OTS left some areas of state law untouched, namely, state criminal law and state law regulating contracts, torts, homestead rights, debt collection, property, taxation, and zoning. Both agencies, though, reserved the right to declare that any state laws in those areas are preempted in the future. For fuller discussion, see McCoy and Renuart (2008), at 120–21.

9. Comptroller Hawke stated, for example, that the average national bank paid two and a quarter times more in supervisory fees than the average state bank. Office of the Comptroller of the Currency (2002b).

10. Some states, such as Georgia, created exemptions in their anti-predatory lending laws for state banks, state thrifts, and their mortgage lending subsidiaries. See, e.g., Ga. Code Ann. sec. 7-6A-12. Those institutions, however, otherwise remained subject to state and federal banking regulation.

11. Federal Deposit Insurance Corporation (2005). After Sheila Bair succeeded Donald Powell as chairman of the FDIC, the agency did not pursue the proposal any further.

12. Office of the Attorney General of the State of New York (2006b); Appelbaum and Nakashima (2008).

13. Appelbaum and Nakashima (2008).

14. Appelbaum and Nakashima (2008); "A System That Invited Bankers to Make Bad Loans" (2009); Enrich (2008).

15. Hawke (2004).

16. U.S. Government Accountability Office (2006); Wilmarth (2007); Dugan (2007a); Gilleran (2003).

17. Apgar et al. (2007); Berner and Grow (2008), at 36; Stein (2008).

18. Dugan (2007b).

19. 12 U.S.C. sec. 1820(d).

20. McCoy (2000), secs. 13.02–13.03.

21. McCoy (2000), secs. 13.02–13.03.

22. Reich (2007d); Hawke (2003a) (emphasis in original).

23. The chief national bank examiner testified to Congress in 2007 about why the OCC had left subprime hybrid ARMs out of the September 2006 guidance on nontraditional mortgage products: "We [were] also concerned about the possibility of an 'unlevel regulatory playing field' if already highly-regulated, federally-regulated institutions [were] subject to stricter standards on subprime mortgage lending, but state-licensed nonbank lenders [were] not." Rushton (2007).

24. Office of the Comptroller of the Currency (2005), at 6330 (emphasis in original); Department of the Treasury et al. (2006); Department of the Treasury et al. (2007a); Department of the Treasury et al. (2007b); Department of the Treasury et al. (2008); Office of the Comptroller of the Currency (2000); Office of the Comptroller of the Currency (2002a); Office of the Comptroller of the Currency (2003).

25. Dugan (2006c) (emphasis in original).

CHAPTER 9

1. Hawke (2003a) (emphasis in original); Hawke (2003b) ("there is no evidence that federally regulated banks—national or state—are a serious part of the [predatory lending problem]"); Williams (2004a) ("Clearly, there is a real problem with abusive lending practices in this country, but national banks and federal thrifts are not the breeding ground").

2. "Bank Regulator Pressures Lenders to Aid Troubled Borrowers" (2007); Office of the Comptroller of the Currency and Office of Thrift Supervision (2008b); Dugan (2008).

3. Office of the Comptroller of the Currency (2004b).

4. Magnuson-Moss Warranty—Federal Trade Commission Improvement Act, Pub. L. No. 93–637, codified at 15 U.S.C. sec. 57a(f)(1); Dugan (2007d).

5. Dugan (2007c) (emphasis in original).

6. Office of the Comptroller of the Currency (2005).

7. Dugan (2005a).

8. Dugan (2005a); Dugan (2005b); Department of the Treasury et al. (2006).

9. Hawke (2004).

10. Williams (2005b).

11. Williams (2005c).

12. Dugan (2005b).

13. Fitzpatrick et al. (2008); Jackson (2007b); Moore (2008b); Murray (2008a); Paletta (2008a).

14. Office of the Comptroller of the Currency (2006a), at 17–19.

15. Office of the Comptroller of the Currency (2006a); Manning (2008). According to *The Oregonian*, the email contained the following text:

"ZiPPY Cheats & Tricks . . .

If you get a "refer" or if you DO NOT get Stated Income / Stated Asset findings. . . . Never Fear!! ZiPPY can be adjusted (just ever so slightly)

Try these steps next time you use Zippy! You just might get the findings you need!!

• Always select "ALTERNATE DOCS" in the documentation drop down.
• Borrower(s) MUST have a mid credit score of 700.

- First time homebuyers require a 720 credit score.
- NO! BK's OR Foreclosures, EVER!! Regardless of time!
- Salaried borrowers must have 2 years time on job with current employer .
- Self employed must be in existence for 2 years. (verified with biz license)
- NO non-occupant co borrowers.
- Max LTV/CLTV is 100%

Try these handy steps to get SISA findings . . .

(1) In the income section of your 1003, make sure you input all income in base income. DO NOT break it down by overtime, commissions or bonus.
(2) NO GIFT FUNDS! If your borrower is getting a gift, add it to a bank account along with the rest of the assets. Be sure to remove any mention of gift funds on the rest of your 1003.
(3) If you do not get Stated/Stated, try resubmitting with slightly higher income. Inch it up $500 to see if you can get the findings you want. Do the same for assets. It's super easy! Give it a try!

If you get stuck, call me . . . I am happy to help!"

16. Dash (2008b).
17. Dash (2007d); Dash (2008a); Dash (2008c).
18. BCAPB LLC Trust 2007-AB1 (2007).
19. Office of the Comptroller of the Currency (2004c).
20. "MetLife Buys Residential Mortgage Assets" (2008).
21. Bankrate.com (2008).
22. Adler (2008); Edwards (2008); Finkelstein (2008); Reagor (2007); Sidel and Paletta (2008).
23. Office of Inspector General, Department of the Treasury (2008b).
24. Office of Inspector General, Department of the Treasury (2008b); Paletta (2009).
25. Hawke (2003b).
26. Williams (2003a).
27. Hawke (2004); Williams (2003a); Williams (2004a); Williams (2005a).
28. Dugan (2005b).
29. Williams (2005b); Dugan (2005a); Rushton (2007).
30. Dugan (2007d).
31. Dugan (2005c).
32. Dugan (2006b).
33. Dugan (2007d).
34. Dugan (2007c).
35. Dugan (2007d).
36. "Consolidated regulation" refers to the fact that OTS regulates the parent companies of many thrifts as well as the thrifts themselves. In contrast, many banks have a different federal regulator than their parent holding companies, which are regulated by the Federal Reserve.
37. Home Owners Loan Act of 1933, Pub. L. No. 101-73, codified at 12 U.S.C. secs. 1464(c)(2), 1467a(m).
38. Gilleran (2003). In part because of these concerns, OTS director John M. Reich petitioned Congress to liberalize the qualified thrift lender test, but he did not succeed. Reich (2006a).

39. Reich (2006b).

40. Blackwell (2002); Blackwell and Garver (2002); Heller (2002); Linder (2003); "NPA Members Give OTS Chairman the Pink Slip" (2002); Office of Thrift Supervision (2002). A biography penned by Gilleran posted on the SEC's Web site stated that when he arrived as director of OTS, the agency "was in a turnaround situation as the Agency was in a deficit financial position and there were rumors that it would be merged with another agency." Gilleran (2008).

41. Gilleran (2004).

42. Gilleran (2004); Reich (2006b); Reich (2007b).

43. Gilleran (2004).

44. Reich (2006a); Reich (2006b).

45. Reich (2006b).

46. Reich (2006b).

47. Reich (2005).

48. Reich (2006e).

49. Bajaj (2008b); Chang et al. (2008); ElBoghdady and Merle (2008); Hagerty and Karp (2008); Kristof and Chang (2008); Lueck (2008); Reckard and Chang (2008); Schmitt (2008).

50. Office of Inspector General, Department of the Treasury (2009a).

51. Appelbaum (2008b); Thorson (2008).

52. White (1991), at 139–42, 232–35.

53. Thorson (2008).

54. DeSilver (2008); Fitch Ratings (2008a).

55. Morgenson (2008f).

56. Curran (2008); Fitzpatrick (2008); Fitzpatrick and Lattman (2008); Ivry and Shen (2008); Luhby (2008b); Paletta (2008b); Sidel et al. (2008); Simon (2008c).

57. Appelbaum and Nakashima (2008); Davidson (2007); Fitch Ratings (2008c).

58. Hopkins (2008a).

59. Thomas (2002).

60. Heisel and Hsu (2008); Pollock (2008).

61. Heisel (2008); Petruno and Heisel (2008); Reckard and Chang (2008).

62. Office of Inspector General, Department of the Treasury (2009b).

63. Muir and Gittelsohn (2008).

64. Stewart (2008).

65. Board of Governors of the Federal Reserve System (2006).

66. Bauerlein (2008b); Bauerlein and Simon (2008); Enrich (2007); Hagerty and Simon (2007a); Wachovia Corporation at Citigroup 2007 Financial Services Conference—Final (2007).

67. In 2006, WaMu, Golden West, and Citibank, FSB, were the three largest thrift companies, and together they paid about a quarter of OTS's total assessments. Kaper and Rehm (2006).

68. Schmitt (2008).

69. Schmitt (2008); Appelbaum and Nakashima (2008); Adams (1990); Black (2008).

70. Bauerlein and Paletta (2007); "Online Bank Fails, and Regulators Shut It" (2007); Paul (2007).

71. Office of Inspector General, Department of the Treasury (2008a).

72. Reich (2008).

73. Specifically, the report recommended formal enforcement action when any of the following facts exists: (1) management is weak; (2) uncertainty exists whether management and the board are able or willing to take appropriate corrective measures; (3) conditions are quickly deteriorating; or (4) the thrift had a rating of 3 for two consecutive examinations after it agreed to an informal enforcement action, unless the thrift observed that action and there are no new grounds for initiating a formal action.

74. Compare Reich (2007a) with Reich (2007c). In his first major speech on OTS's enforcement philosophy in September 2007, Reich described the agency's approach as such: "Our strategy in these cases is to try first to gain compliance by an institution voluntarily and through informal supervisory efforts. This strategy is typically effective. But in other cases, a formal enforcement action may be needed." Reich (2007g).

75. Office of Thrift Supervision (2008b).

76. Almost two-thirds of that thrift's residential loans in 2005 had been high-cost loans. "Bank Regulator Pressures Lenders to Aid Troubled Borrowers" (2007); Office of Thrift Supervision (2007).

77. Reich (2005).

78. Reich (2006c).

79. Reich (2006f).

80. Reich (2006a); Reich (2006b); Reich (2006f); Reich (2007a); Reich (2007b); Reich (2007e).

81. Subprime and Predatory Lending: New Regulatory Guidance, Current Market Conditions, and Effects on Regulated Financial Institutions, at 33; Reich (2007b).

82. Reich (2007g).

83. Reich (2007d); Reich (2007f).

84. Reich (2007h).

85. McGreer (2008).

86. Maremont (2008).

87. Maremont (2008).

88. This information is from the FDIC's Institution Database at http://www2.fdic.gov/idasp/main2.asp.

89. Jackson (2007a).

90. *In the Matter of Fremont Investment*, 3–4.

91. Office of the Attorney General of Massachusetts (2009).

92. McKay and Paletta (2008).

93. Levitz (2009).

94. Levy (2008b); Office of the Inspector General, Federal Deposit Insurance Corporation (2009), at 3–5.

95. Office of the Inspector General, Federal Deposit Insurance Corporation (2009), at 17 and 23. Some of this information is from the FDIC's Institution Database at http://www2.fdic.gov/idasp/main2.asp.

96. Office of the Inspector General, Federal Deposit Insurance Corporation (2009), at 12–13.

97. Office of the Inspector General, Federal Deposit Insurance Corporation (2009), at 13.

98. Vekshin (2009). Other information in this paragraph is from the FDIC inspector general's Web site at http://www.fdicig.gov/index.htm.

99. Paletta and Enrich (2008).

CHAPTER 10

1. Greenspan (2004a).
2. Greenspan (2004b); Greenspan (2007), at 250–52.
3. Smith (1776); Greenspan (2007), at 260–66.
4. Greenspan (2007).
5. Greenspan (2004a); Greenspan (2007), at 48–51, 268–69.
6. Greenspan (2002); Greenspan (2004a); Greenspan (2004d); Greenspan (2005c); Greenspan (2007), at 71, 255.
7. Greenspan (2007), at 373.
8. Greenspan (2007).
9. Greenspan (2004a); Greenspan (2005c).
10. Greenspan (2001a); Greenspan (2007), at 374.
11. Greenspan (2001b); Greenspan (2003b); Greenspan (2007), at 273.
12. Greenspan (2002).
13. Greenspan (2002).
14. Dash and Creswell (2008b).
15. Greenspan (2001b); Greenspan (2002); Greenspan (2004a); Greenspan (2004e). The new capital rules were known as the Basel II minimum capital rules.
16. Greenspan (2002); Greenspan (2005a).
17. Greenspan (2007), at 229–30, 232–33.
18. Greenspan (2004d); Greenspan (2007), at 346–47, 359–60.
19. Greenspan (2003a); Greenspan (2004d); Greenspan (2004f).
20. Greenspan (2007), at 230–31.
21. U.S. House of Representatives, Committee on Oversight and Government Reform (2008), Preliminary Transcript at 36–37.
22. Truth in Lending Act, Pub. L. No. 90-321, codified at 15 U.S.C. secs. 1601–1693r.
23. Budnitz (2010), at 11.
24. Riegle-Neal Community Development and Regulatory Improvement Act of 1994, Pub. L. No. 103-325, codified at 15 U.S.C. secs. 1601, 1602(aa), 1639(a)–(b).
25. Riegle-Neal Community Development and Regulatory Improvement Act of 1994, Pub. L. No. 103-325, codified at 15 U.S.C. secs. 1602(aa)(1)–(4), 1639(a)-(k); 12 C.F.R. secs. 226.32, 226.34. The $400 figure was adjusted annually for inflation.
26. Riegle-Neal Community Development and Regulatory Improvement Act of 1994, Pub. L. No. 103-325, codified at 15 U.S.C. sec. 1602(i), (w), (bb); 12 C.F.R. sec. 226.32(a)(2); Gramlich (2007b), at 28.
27. Riegle-Neal Community Development and Regulatory Improvement Act of 1994, Pub. L. No. 103-325, codified at 15 U.S.C. sec. 1639(*l*), (2).
28. Board of Governors of the Federal Reserve System and Department of Housing and Urban Development (1998), at 67–68, 74–75.
29. Gramlich (2001); Gramlich (2002); Gramlich (2003); Gramlich (2004).
30. Board of Governors of the Federal Reserve System (2001) (codified at 12 C.F.R. secs. 226.1, 226.32, 226.34). The 2001 amendment liberalized HOEPA in three ways. First, it broadened HOEPA's coverage by lowering the interest rate trigger from 10 percent to 8 percent for first-lien mortgages and by including premiums for optional credit life insurance in the points and fee trigger. Second, it beefed up the disclosures for HOEPA loans. Lastly, the rule banned or limited several more abuses in HOEPA loans, including due-on-demand clauses, certain refinancings that were not in the borrower's interest, and

any pattern and practice of making HOEPA loans without regard to borrowers' ability to repay.

31. Gramlich (2007b), at 28.

32. Greenspan (2007), at 373.

33. Ip (2007); U.S. House of Representatives, Committee on Oversight and Government Reform (2008), at 35, 37–38. Greenspan told the House Oversight Committee in 2008:

> Well, let's take the issue of unfair and deceptive practices, which is a fundamental concept to the whole predatory lending issue.
> The staff of the Federal Reserve ... say[] how do they determine as a regulatory group what is unfair and deceptive? And the problem that they were concluding ... was the issue of maybe 10 percent or so are self-evidently unfair and deceptive, but the vast majority would require a jury trial or other means to deal with it.

U.S. House of Representatives, Committee on Oversight and Government Reform (2008), at 89.

34. Starting in 2005, for instance, Fed governor Susan Schmidt Bies gave a series of frank and detailed speeches outlining the dangers of interest ARMs, option ARMs, and other risky products and underwriting practices. Bies (2005); Bies (2006a); Bies (2006b); Bies (2006d); Bies (2007a).

35. Greenspan (2003c). In contrast, Gramlich's views evolved over time. In 2001, for example, he called consumer education "the very best defense against predatory lending." Gramlich (2001). By 2003, however, he was calling for a more "nuanced" approach combining financial literacy with compliance examinations and enforcement. Gramlich (2003). By 2004, Gramlich had rejected financial literacy as a panacea, instead asserting that a "good defense against predatory lending, perhaps the best defense society has devised, is a careful compliance examination for banks." Gramlich (2004).

36. Bies (2006c); Bies (2006d); Bernanke (2006); Mishkin (2007a); Bernanke (2007a).

37. Department of the Treasury et al. (2007a).

38. Bernanke (2007b); Bernanke (2007a); Bies (2007a); Mishkin (2007a); Mishkin (2007b).

39. Board of Governors of the Federal Reserve System (2008c).

40. Board of Governors of the Federal Reserve System (2008c), at 44536. The board set those triggers with the intention of covering the subprime market, but not the prime market. See Board of Governors of the Federal Reserve System (2008c), at 44536–37.

41. Bernanke (2005).

42. 12 C.F.R. sec. 226.19(b)(2)(viii)(A)–(B), (ix)(A)–(B) (2006). In addition, lenders had to describe the payment shock on a hypothetical $10,000 mortgage and let borrowers do the math. Not surprisingly, in 2004, the Consumer Federation of America found that over one-third of people who preferred ARMs could not calculate this number. That percentage was even higher—between 43 and 50 percent, depending on the group—for young adults, Hispanics and blacks, low-income individuals, and people lacking a high school degree. Consumer Federation of America (2004).

43. Department of the Treasury et al. (2006), at 58616–58618; Department of the Treasury et al. (2007b), at 37572, 37574; Department of the Treasury et al. (2007c); Department of the Treasury et al. (2008); Board of Governors of the Federal Reserve System (2008f), at 44524, 44584, 44588, 44590–44591, 44600–44601, 44607, 44593–44594; Bies (2007b); Kroszner (2007).

44. Housing and Economic Recovery Act of 2008; Board of Governors of the Federal Reserve System (2008d).

45. For other problems with the Fed's interpretation of the Truth in Lending Act, see Renuart and Thompson (2008).

46. Board of Governors of the Federal Reserve System and Department of Housing and Urban Development (1998), at iv–v, 28–29, 39–43, 63–64.

47. Board of Governors of the Federal Reserve System (2008f), at 44594.

48. Housing and Economic Recovery Act of 2008, Pub. L. No. 110-289.

49. Board of Governors of the Federal Reserve System (2005), at 12.

50. The banks were Riverside Bank of the Gulf Coast in Cape Coral, Florida, with $539 million in assets, County Bank in Merced, California, with $1.7 billion in assets, and First Georgia Community Bank in Jackson, Georgia, with $237.5 million in assets.

51. In addition to state member banks, the Fed supervised bank holding companies and their nonbank mortgage subsidiaries (except for lending subsidiaries owned by an intermediate bank or thrift). For example, suppose a bank holding company owned two subsidiaries: a nonbank lender and a national bank and the national bank had its own separate subsidiary, which, too, was a nonbank lender. The Federal Reserve oversaw the bank holding company and the nonbank lender that the holding company directly owned. The OCC supervised the national bank and its lending subsidiary.

52. Data from *American Banker;* Ip (2007).

53. Avery et al. (2008), at A124.

54. Gramm-Leach-Bliley Act of 1999, Pub. L. No. 106-102, codified at 12 U.S.C. sec. 1844(c)(2)(C).

55. Gramlich (2007a), at 8–9; Board of Governors of the Federal Reserve Board (2007a).

56. Federal Reserve System (2009b).

57. Norris (2009a); HSBC (2009).

58. The securitization in question was HSBC Home Equity Loan Trust (USA) 2007–2.

59. The Fed did enter into a written agreement with HSBC Bank USA on April 30, 2003, on compliance with the Bank Secrecy Act. That agreement, however, did not address mortgage lending practices.

60. Morgenson (2007b).

61. Office of the Attorney General of the State of New York (2006a), at 3. Two years later, Countrywide paid $8.4 billion, a record settlement at the time, to settle predatory lending charges lodged by state attorneys general. Morgenson (2008c).

The Cuomo case was not the first time that lending discrimination charges were lodged against Countrywide. When Countrywide applied to the Fed to become a bank holding company in 2001, members of the public alleged that the lender targeted minorities for higher cost loans. Undeterred, the board approved Countrywide's application after referring the charges to other federal agencies. Nothing ever became of the charges.

62. Seebach (2006).

63. Seebach (2007), at 6.

64. Seebach (2007), at 6.

65. The OCC had supervised Countrywide Bank, N.A., a national bank subsidiary of Countrywide Financial Corporation. Following the conversion, Countrywide Bank gave up its national bank charter to become a federal savings bank.

66. Federal Trade Commission (2002).

67. Originally, the Fed supervised CitiFinancial Mortgage. In May 2004, however, Citicorp Trust Bank, FSB, acquired CitiFinancial Mortgage, and thereafter it was supervised by the Office of Thrift Supervision. deV. Frierson (2004). CitiFinancial Credit Company, however, remained under oversight by the Fed.

68. Citigroup (2001a) (EAB order); Citigroup (2001b) (Banamex order). In 2002, the Fed required Citigroup to also make quarterly reports on its success in implementing its lending reform commitments. Citigroup (2002).

69. Citigroup (2004).

70. The Fed did reach written agreements on St. Patrick's Day 2006 with three Puerto Rican bank holding companies that each owned nonbank mortgage subsidiaries. The three cases involved R&G Financial Corp. in San Juan, First BanCorp in Santurce, Puerto Rico, and Doral Financial Corp. in San Juan. Those agreements, however, addressed the accounting treatment of the companies' mortgage securitization deals, not the underwriting quality of their loans.

71. In 1991, Congress required federal banking regulators, including the Fed, to examine the banks they supervised every twelve months. Congress allowed the Fed to conduct routine examinations in alternate years if a state banking regulator examined a state member bank in the off year. In addition, by law, some small banks could go eighteen months between regular examinations if they were well capitalized. Financial Services Regulatory Relief Act of 2006, Pub. L. No. 109-473, codified at 12 U.S.C. sec. 1820(d).

72. Financial holding companies are a type of bank holding company on steroids that can own insurance underwriters and full-service investment banks on top of commercial banks. Congress first authorized financial holding companies in Gramm-Leach-Bliley.

73. Gramm-Leach-Bliley Act of 1999, Pub. L. No. 106-102, codified at 12 U.S.C. sec. 1844(c)(2).

74. Greenspan (2002).

CHAPTER 11

1. Foley (2008); Lewis (2008); Scannell and Craig (2008).

2. The net capital rule is located at 17 C.F.R. sec. 240.15c3-1. Under that rule, broker-dealers must either maintain (1) a debt-to-net capital ratio of 15 or less; or (2) net capital no less than $250,000 or 2 percent of aggregate debit items (i.e., the debt owed to them on margin accounts), whichever is greater. For a fuller explanation, see Poser (2009), at 12.

3. Alternative Net Capital Requirements for Broker-Dealers That Are Part of Consolidated Supervised Entities (2004), at 34,428, 34,434–34,451 (codified at 17 C.F.R. pts. 200 and 240); Inspector General, Securities and Exchange Commission (2008), at 19; Labaton (2008a). Under this program, the Big Five firms had to have "tentative net capital" of $1 billion or more. In addition, they had to alert the SEC any time their tentative net capital fell below $5 billion. Inspector General, Securities and Exchange Commission (2008), at 11.

4. Boyd (2008b); Hilsenrath et al. (2008), at A1; Karmel (2009), at 28; Pulliam et al. (2008), at A1; Office of Inspector General, Securities and Exchange Commission (2008), at 5 n. 40 and appendix IX; Story (2008a), at C1.

5. Alternative Net Capital Requirements for Broker-Dealers That Are Part of Consolidated Supervised Entities (2004); Council Directive 2002/87; Cox (2008a) ("The merger of Bear Stearns and J.P. Morgan highlighted the inherent problems with the lack

of any statutory authority for the SEC, or indeed any government agency, to regulate investment bank holding companies"); Office of Inspector General, Securities and Exchange Commission (2008), at v, 2–4; Labaton (2008a). JPMorgan Chase and Citigroup, Inc., also participated in the SEC's Consolidated Supervised Entity program. Because both were financial holding companies, however, their umbrella supervisor was not the SEC, but the Federal Reserve Board. Office of Inspector General, Securities and Exchange Commission (2008), at i–v.

6. Office of Inspector General, Securities and Exchange Commission (2008), at viii.

7. Office of Inspector General, Securities and Exchange Commission (2008), at viii.

8. Office of Inspector General, Securities and Exchange Commission (2008).

9. Office of Inspector General, Securities and Exchange Commission (2008), at 15, 17–18, 20–27, 31–33.

10. Coffee (2008); Office of Inspector General, Securities and Exchange Commission (2008), at 34, 37–38, 49; Coffee and Sale (2008).

11. Cox (2008b); Office of Inspector General, Securities and Exchange Commission (2008); Labaton (2008a).

12. Atkins (2004).

13. Atkins (2006).

14. Compare http://www.sec-oig.gov/Reports/AuditsInspections/2008/446-a.pdf with http://finance.senate.gov/press/Gpress/2008/prg092608i.pdf.

15. Pittman (2008).

16. Federal Deposit Insurance Corporation (2009a), table I-A.

17. The discussion of the capital adequacy requirements is taken from McCoy (2000), sec.§ 6.03; Hu (2001), at 117.

18. Taylor (2009); Deng (2008).

19. Hopkins (2009) (quoting Karen Shaw Petrou).

20. Glacy (2008), at 38–39. Under something known as "Pillar II" of Basel II, banks were supposed to set aside extra capital for systemic risk. However, they did not need to project the size of that set-aside in their quantitative models.

21. Geithner (2008).

22. Wilmott (2008).

23. Hansell (2008).

24. Cox (2008b).

25. Bair (2009a). The Basel Committee on Banking Supervision similarly concluded that the advanced approach of Basel II would lower capital levels in the G10 nations, particularly for "retail mortgage exposures." Basel Committee on Banking Supervision (2006), at 1–2.

26. 17 C.F.R. secs. 229.1100—1123.

27. Technical Committee of the International Organization of Securities Commissions (2008), at xvi; Investment Company Institute (2009), at 7–8, n. 13. Most often, these private offerings consisted of Regulation D offerings to institutional accredited investors, Rule 144A offerings for qualified institutional buyers, and offshore offerings under Regulation S of the Securities Act of 1933.

28. Securities and Exchange Commission (2009), at 6495.

29. Borod et al. (2009), at 47; Mendales (2009), at 36.

30. Investment Company Institute (2009), at 9–10; Moody's Investors Service (2009), at 12–13; President's Working Group on Financial Market Developments (2008), at 12.

31. Committee on Capital Markets Regulation (2009), at 147.

32. Mason (2008), at 9.

33. Rucker (2007).

34. Borod et al. (2009), at 48–51.

35. Under Section 15(d) of the Securities Exchange Act of 1934, the disclosures could be suspended one year after a particular offering if there were less than 300 holders of the bonds in that offering.

36. Committee on Capital Markets Regulation (2009), at 147–48; Mason (2008), at 10; Stevens (2009).

37. Investment Company Institute (2009), at 8, n. 17; Securities and Exchange Commission (2009), at 6495.

38. Securities Act of 1933; Securities Exchange Act of 1934.

39. Soundview Home Loan Trust 2006-3 (2006).

40. Not surprisingly, private class actions for false SEC disclosures in subprime offerings surged in 2008, giving some sense of the size of the problem. Cornerstone Research (2009), at 2–4, 9, 21–22.

41. Markopolos (2009).

42. Securities and Exchange Commission (2007b); Donohue (2009), at 13; "You Mean That Bernie Madoff?" (2008).

43. Office of Inspector General, Securities and Exchange Commission (2009), at iv–v, 25–32.

44. Markopolos (2009), at 45–49.

45. Between 2005 and 2007, the SEC enforcement division lost 10 percent of its lawyers. Enforcement teams were whittled down from fifteen lawyers to often only seven or eight. The number of SEC examiners remained flat between 2002 and the 2008 crisis, even though the number of investment advisers grew by 50 percent. Karmel (2009), at 43; Aguilar (2009); Turner (2008), preliminary transcript at 91–92.

46. Burrows (2008); Labaton (2008b); Labaton (2008c); Williamson and Scannell (2008).

47. Labaton (2009a); Aguilar (2009); Schapiro (2009).

48. Securities and Exchange Commission (2006); Walter (2009), at 29–30; Goldfarb (2009); Labaton (2009a); Morgenson (2009a); Smith and Scannell (2008); Aguilar (2009); Schapiro (2009).

49. Ropp (2009), at 6; Coffee and Sale (2008), at 2–3, 36–37.

50. Atkins (2006). For a cogent analysis of this trend, see Poser (2009), at 21–28. Examples include *Shearson/American Express, Inc. v. McMahon* (1987) (where the SEC argued that form contract arbitration clauses that prevented injured investors from suing in federal court were enforceable); *Dura Pharmaceuticals, Inc. v. Broudo* (2005) (arguing for a heightened proof requirement in order for securities fraud plaintiffs to show loss causation); *Tellabs v. Makor Issues & Rights* (2007) (supporting a strict reading of the heightened standard for plaintiffs to plead securities fraud); *Credit Suisse Securities (USA) LLC v. Billing* (2007) (urging the Court to grant investment banks an implied immunity from the antitrust laws for initial public offerings).

51. Lewis and Einhorn (2009).

52. Partnoy (2006), at 64; Hill (2004), at 44, 56–57, 60–63.

53. Moody's had rated Enron's debt investment grade until four days before Enron filed for bankruptcy. "Judge Clears Deal for Enron Unit" (2002), at E02.

54. Pub. L. No. 109-291.

55. Pub. L. No. 109-291, codified at 15 U.S.C. sec. 78o-7(c)(2), (m)(2). Subsequently, in three separate rulemakings, the SEC was forced to water down its rules implementing

the act because of strong pushback by the rating agencies. During those proceedings, the commission dropped two of its bolder proposals: one, to adopt different rating symbols for structured finance products and traditional corporate bonds and, two, to end the use of NRSRO credit ratings in SEC rules. In the first rulemaking, under Christopher Cox, the commission adopted some tepid rules in June 2007, when the credit crisis was first unfolding. Securities and Exchange Commission (2007a). The 2007 rules established requirements on SEC registration, record-keeping, annual financial reports, disclosure and management of conflicts of interest, and prohibitions on insider trading and coercive acts. 12 C.F.R. secs. 204.17g-2 through g-6.

A year later, the SEC published an examination report of the three largest rating agencies that identified other unsolved problems. Securities and Exchange Commission (2008). The Obama administration responded with new rules adopting a harder stance. In February 2009, the commission adopted a new regulation banning ratings analysts from participating in structuring deals. The new rule also required disclosure of the performance of credit ratings over a ten-year period and disclosure of the downgrade histories of 10 percent of issuer-paid ratings. Later, in December 2009, the commission expanded the disclosure of ratings histories to all issuer-paid ratings that were initially determined after June 25, 2007 after a twelve-month time lag. The SEC further required arrangers and any rating agency they hired to provide other NRSROs with the data provided to the hired firm to do the rating on a real-time basis. Securities and Exchange Commission (2009a); Securities and Exchange Commission (2009b). The purpose of the ratings history rule was to provide users with raw data to enable them to pick the rating agencies with the most accurate ratings. The last provision was intended to spur competition by providing rating agencies that are not hired with the information they need to offer unsolicited ratings.

56. Philips (2008), at 46.

57. Heyde and Neyer (2008), at 2.

58. Karmel (2009), at 12, n. 42.

59. Dash and Creswell (2008a); Heyde and Neyer (2008), at 2–3, 15–17, 27–28; Hu (1993), at 1476–95; Parlour and Winton (2008); Partnoy and Skeel (2007), at 1033.

60. Sirri (2008).

61. Dinallo (2008a), at 18, 28, 67–68.

62. Heyde and Neyer (2008), at 3, 24–28; Thompson (2008), at 1.

63. Faiola et al. (2008), at A01; Dinallo (2008a), at 30; Murawski (2002), at 2.

64. Berkshire Hathway Inc. (2003a), at 14–15.

65. Berkshire Hathaway Inc. (2003a), at 13; Overdahl (2008). Our thanks to Joshua Swift for bringing this point to our attention.

66. International Swaps and Derivatives Association, Inc. (2007) (worldwide GDP for 2007 was $54.584 trillion).

67. Greenspan (2005b); Greenspan (2007), at 370–71.

68. Commodity Futures Trading Commission (1998); Faiola et al. (2008), at A01; Leising (2008).

69. Gramm-Leach-Bliley Act of 1999, Pub. L. No. 106-102, codified at 15 U.S.C. secs. 77q, 78i(a), 78j(b), 78o(c)(1), 78p(b), 78t(d); Sirri (2008).

70. Gramm-Leach-Bliley Act of 1999, Pub. L. No. 106-102, codified at 7 U.S.C. secs. 1a(13), 2(c)–(h), 27a–27f and 15 U.S.C. sec. 78c(a)(55); Gkonos and Cawley (2009); Karmel (2009); Lipton and Labaton (2008), at 1.

71. Gramm-Leach-Bliley Act of 1999, Pub. L. No. 106-102, codified at 7 U.S.C. sec. 27f(c). State laws against fraudulent exchanges are also known as "bucket shop" laws.

72. Dinallo (2008b); Office of the General Counsel, New York Insurance Department (2000); Gkonos and Cawley (2009); N.Y. Ins. Law sec. 6901(j-1). In 2009, after the AIG debacle, New York flip-flopped, first issuing a circular suggesting that covered CDSs were insurance, then putting that announcement on indefinite hold pending the federal government's development of a central CDS exchange. New York Insurance Department (2008a), at 7; New York Insurance Department (2008b).

73. AIG Federal Savings Bank also goes by the moniker "AIG Bank."

74. Morgenson (2008b); Northedge (2009); Office of Thrift Supervision (2007a).

75. Morgenson (2008b), at A1.

76. Lee (2008), at 1.

77. Lee (2008), at 1–3.

78. Lee (2008).

79. Lee (2008).

80. Gerth (2008); American International Group (2009).

81. Gramm-Leach-Bliley Act of 1999, Pub. L. No. 106-102, codified at 12 U.S.C. sec. 1844(c)(1)(B).

82. In addition, the Fed could do an examination to ascertain compliance with a narrow set of laws.

CHAPTER 12

1. Dodd-Frank Wall Street Reform and Consumer Protection Act of 2010, Pub. L. No. 111-203.

2. The exception is that the CFPB has limited supervisory authority and no enforcement authority over depository institutions and credit unions with assets under $10 billion. For these institutions, their prudential regulators will have lead examination authority and will also be responsible for enforcing any federal consumer protection laws. Dodd-Frank Act, secs. 1025–26.

3. Dodd-Frank Act, sec. 1043.

4. Dodd-Frank Act, sec. 1041(a)(2).

5. Dodd-Frank Act, sec. 1021.

6. Dodd-Frank Act, sec. 1411.

7. Dodd-Frank Act, sec. 1411.

8. Dodd-Frank Act, sec. 1411.

9. Dodd-Frank Act, sec. 1411.

10. This presumption is rebuttable. Dodd-Frank Act, sec. 1412.

11. Dodd-Frank Act, sec. 1418.

12. Dodd-Frank Act, sec. 1414.

13. Dodd-Frank Act, sec. 1032.

14. Lenders could subsequently deny borrowers who were not qualified.

15. Board of Governors of the Federal Reserve System and the Department of Housing and Urban Development (1998), at 28–29, 39–42.

16. Adams (1998), at 159–63.

17. Engel and McCoy (2002), at 1273–98.

18. Dodd-Frank Act, sec. 1443.

19. Dodd-Frank Act, sec. 1403.

20. Dodd-Frank Act, sec. 1472.

21. Dodd-Frank Act, sec. 1024.

22. Maynard (2009).

23. Dodd-Frank Act, sec. 1204.

24. Avery et al. (2007), at 373.

25. Dodd-Frank Act, sec. 1094.

26. Dodd-Frank Act, sec. 1447.

27. Dodd-Frank Act, sec. 932.

28. The Dodd-Frank Act did eliminate some statutes and rules that required the use of ratings from NRSROs. For example, see sec. 939.

29. This is only true in states that require lenders to use the judicial process to foreclose. In states where the foreclosure process happens outside the court system, borrowers have to bring affirmative claims for damages or equitable relief, such as injunctions to stop foreclosures.

30. Engel and McCoy (2007), at 2053–54, 2079.

31. Investors still have an incentive to police for default and prepayment risks.

32. Bostic et al. (2008b).

33. Dodd-Frank Act, sec. 1413.

34. The law also provides a safe harbor for loans that are "qualified" and meet specific underwriting criteria. Dodd-Frank charges the federal banking agencies, the Securities and Exchange Commission, the secretary of Housing and Urban Development, and the director of the Federal Housing Finance Agency with defining "qualified loans." Dodd-Frank Act, sec. 941.

35. Barr and Feldman (2008).


CHAPTER 13

1. Dodd-Frank Act, sec. 335.

2. The Federal Reserve Board's plan was to explore making its Term Auction Facility permanent. Federal Reserve System (2009a), at 26.

3. These interventions also left a mound of national debt, the consequences of which economists will debate for years to come. In December 2009, when interest rates were low and certain to rise eventually, the national debt surpassed $12 trillion. The significance of that number was subject to debate. Fiscal conservatives pointed to Obama administration estimates that once interest rates reached normal levels, service on the national debt would rise from $202 billion in 2009 to more than $700 billion in 2019. Andrews (2009b). Other economists argued that the expenditures were necessary to avert disaster and the majority would be recouped, some immediately and others in a few years. Mark Zandi predicted, for example, that of the $12 trillion committed by the federal government and the $4 trillion paid out as of July 2009, the final cost of the crisis would approach $1.2 trillion. Zandi (2009), at 1. Still others argued that the nation's projected debt service in 2019 would only reach the level hit by the first President Bush around 1990, which would give the Federal Reserve time to control inflation. Krugman (2009); Krugman (2010); Greenspan (2009); Zandi (2009), at 1–2, 11–12.

4. Dodge & Cox (2008), at 1. The two crises were the failure of Continental Bank in 1984 and the 1980s savings and loans debacle.

5. Norris (2008b).

6. Dodd-Frank Act, title II.

7. Under the receivership procedures in Dodd-Frank, a failed financial company's unsecured creditors are to be paid off in the following priority: (1) administrative expenses of the receiver; (2) amounts owed to the United States; (3) wages, salaries, or commissions of the firm's employees (except for the company's senior executives and directors), subject to cap; (4) past contributions owed to employee benefit plans, subject to cap; (5) most other general or senior liabilities of the company; (6) subordinated obligations; (7) wages, salaries, and commissions owed to the company's senior executives and directors; and (8) obligations to shareholders or other equity holders. Dodd-Frank Act, sec. 210(b).

8. Krimminger (2008), at 15, 17.

9. Dodd-Frank Act, sec. 203(a)(1). The voting procedures are somewhat different for broker-dealer companies and insurance conglomerates. For broker-dealers or financial companies whose largest U.S. subsidiary is a broker-dealer, at least two-thirds of the Federal Reserve Board's governors and two-thirds of the members of the Securities and Exchange Commission must vote to approve the systemic risk determination. For insurance companies or financial companies whose largest U.S. subsidiary is an insurer, the determination requires approval by two-thirds of the Fed governors and the director of the Federal Insurance Office, in consultation with the FDIC. Dodd-Frank Act, sec. 203(a)(1).

10. Dodd-Frank Act, secs. 201(a)(1), 201(a)(8), 201(a)(11), 201(b), 203(a), 203(b), 203(e), 204(a). Failed insurers go into state receivership instead of bankruptcy.

11. Dodd-Frank Act, secs. 205, 210.

12. Krimminger (2008), at 15; Cochrane (2009), at 3.

13. Dodd-Frank Act, sec. 210(*o*).

14. Hovakimian et al. (2002), at 13–15; McCoy (2008).

15. Dodd-Frank Act, secs. 210(n), 210(*o*). Any nonbank financial company supervised by the Fed and bank holding companies and other financial companies with total consolidated assets of $50 billion or more are subject to those assessments. Dodd-Frank Act, sec. 210(*o*).

16. Dodd-Frank Act, sec. 210(n).

17. If the government can resolve the situation by brokering a private sale without federal aid in lieu of receivership or bankruptcy, that would also be satisfactory. If federal aid or guarantees are necessary to facilitate a takeover, however, then the government should be required to put the failing firm into receivership.

18. In the Federal Deposit Insurance Corporation Improvement Act of 1991, Congress prohibited the FDIC from making bank bailouts (also known as "open bank assistance") except in instances posing systemic risk. In general, under what is known as the least-cost rule, the FDIC can only use the resolution technique that results in the least cost to the Deposit Insurance Fund. But under the systemic risk exception, the FDIC could assist an ailing bank regardless of cost in order to avoid or mitigate systemic risk, so long as it procured sign-offs by the secretary of the Treasury (in consultation with the president), the FDIC's board of directors, and the Federal Reserve Board (approved by no less than two-thirds of each body's members). Former 12 U.S.C. sec. 1823(c)(4)(G)(i).

The FDIC invoked the systemic risk exception three times in the fall of 2008: in its decision to resolve Wachovia Bank, N.A., using open bank assistance; in its decision on October 14, 2008, to remove deposit insurance caps on business checking accounts; and in its decision that same day to guarantee interbank lending on a temporary basis.

19. Dodd-Frank Act, sec. 214(a).

20. Dodd-Frank Act, secs. 210(n)(8), 212(a)–(b), 214(b)–(c), 1101(a), 1105–6.

21. In a similar vein, Dodd-Frank requires financial megafirms to prepare "living wills" describing how their companies could be best dismantled in an economic crisis so as to minimize spillover effects. Dodd-Frank Act, sec. 115(d)(1). This is a huge, expensive process that will have to be regularly revised because companies alter their business strategies all the time. Given the uncertain payoff, we rank living wills lower on the list of effective tools to resolve failing megafirms and curb systemic risk than other measures.

22. Dodd-Frank Act, secs. 111–17, 119–20, 161–62, 164–66. The voting members of the Council include the secretary of the Treasury (who serves as the chair), the chairman of the Federal Reserve Board, the Comptroller of the Currency, the director of the Consumer Financial Protection Bureau, the chairman of the Securities and Exchange Commission, the chairman of the FDIC, the chairman of the Commodity Futures Trading Commission, the director of the Federal Housing Finance Agency, the chairman of the National Credit Union Administration, and an independent member with insurance expertise. The nonvoting members include the director of the Office of Financial Research, the director of the Federal Insurance Office, a state insurance commissioner, a state banking supervisor, and a state securities commissioner.

23. Dodd-Frank Act, secs. 111, 116, 151–55, 161(a), 165, 404, 942, 1094, 1447, 1493; Bookstaber (2009); Group of Thirty (2009), at 41.

24. Dodd-Frank Act, secs. 725(c), 727, 729, 733, 735(b), 763(a), 763(i).

25. Dodd-Frank Act, secs. 111(d)(3), 116, 161(a)(2).

26. Dodd-Frank Act, sec. 111(d)(3).

27. Dodd-Frank Act, sec. 171. Many of these same concepts are embraced by the new Basel III risk-based capital initiative, unveiled in September 2010.

28. Dodd-Frank Act, secs. 2(12), 115, 120, 165. For Rivlin's proposal, see Rivlin (2009), at 5–6; Bair (2009b), at 12.

29. The stress test requirement applies to all bank holding companies with total assets of at least $50 billion and all nonbank financial companies under Federal Reserve oversight. Dodd-Frank Act, sec. 165; Stern (2009); Stern and Feldman (2009), at 112–16.

30. Volcker (2009), at 10–11; Johnson (2009). In the Gramm-Leach-Bliley Act of 1999, Congress repealed that part of Glass-Steagall.

31. This provision applies to bank holding companies with $50 billion or more in total assets and to nonbank financial companies under Federal Reserve Board supervision. Dodd-Frank Act, sec. 121.

32. Under the Volcker provision, commercial banks and bank holding companies cannot invest more than 3 percent of their capital in hedge funds and private equity funds. Similarly, under Dodd-Frank's so-called pushout provisions—championed by Senator Blanche Lincoln—commercial banks must spin off their riskiest trading operations (including derivatives linked to equities, below-investment-grade credit default swaps, and derivatives tied to commodities, energy, agriculture, and certain metals) into separate affiliates. Commercial banks can retain their other swap-trading activities, however, including interest rate swaps, foreign exchange swaps, gold and silver derivatives, investment-grade CDS, and other transactions used to hedge risk. All credit default swaps traded by banks have to be cleared through central clearinghouses. Dodd-Frank Act, secs. 619, 716.

33. Dodd-Frank Act, secs. 115, 120.

34. Dodd-Frank Act, secs. 115, 120, 163(b), 165(b), 165(d)(5), 166.

35. In Dodd-Frank, Congress prohibited the Fed from using monetary tools to bail out ailing institutions. Dodd-Frank Act, sec. 1101. But the Fed still has the

ability—appropriately so—to use the discount window and other monetary tools to stabilize liquidity at healthy firms.

36. To trigger regulation by the Fed, the Council must find that "material financial distress at the U.S. nonbank financial company, or the nature, scope, size, scale, concentration, interconnectedness, or mix of the company's activities could pose a threat" to the financial stability of the United States. In making that determination, the Council is required to take a sum total of eleven statutory factors into account. Dodd-Frank Act, sec. 113(a).

37. The Fed has independent power under Dodd-Frank to subject large, interconnected bank holding companies and most of the largest TARP recipients to enhanced systemic oversight. Dodd-Frank Act, secs. 115(a)(1), 115(c), 117(a)–(b).

38. Stulz (2009), at 3–4.

39. Bank for International Settlements (2009), at table 19; Stulz (2009), at 8 and n. 6.

40. Subject to exceptions, the act also requires all swaps contracts to be executed on exchanges or electronic trade execution systems that are regulated by the SEC or the Commodity Futures Trading Commission. Dodd-Frank Act, secs. 723, 763.

41. Dodd-Frank Act, secs. 725, 740, 763(a); Stulz (2009), at 9–19.

42. Dodd-Frank Act, secs. 731, 736.

43. Whalen (2009), at 2.

44. Dodd-Frank Act, secs. 723(a), 763(a). Under the law, if the swaps activities of a commercial end user create systemic risk, it will lose the exemption.

45. Stulz (2009), at 4.

46. Bank for International Settlements (2009), at table 23A.

47. Dodd-Frank Act, secs. 723, 763.

48. Bowley (2010); Chan (2010); Gensler (2010); OCC (2009), at tables 1–2.

49. Dodd-Frank Act, secs. 723(a), 727, 729, 763(a).

50. Dodd-Frank Act, secs. 721, 731, 736, 761, 764.

51. Berkshire Hathaway Inc. (2002), at 15.

52. Whalen (2009), at 3.

53. Whalen (2009), at 4.

54. Karmel (2009), at 34 (citing 17 C.F.R. sec. 40.2).

55. Lynn Stout aired this idea under a somewhat different rubric. Stout, L. (2009). Gary Gensler, the chairman of the Commodity Futures Trading Commission, also alluded to this approach when he testified that "any clearing exception for end users should be very narrowly defined to only include nonfinancial entities that use swaps incidental to their business to hedge actual commercial risks." Gensler (2009), at 9.

56. Kimball-Stanley (2008–9).

57. Whalen (2009), at 5–6.

58. Stout, L. (2009), at 33.

EPILOGUE

1. International Monetary Fund (2009), at 5.

2. Center for Responsive Politics (2010).

3. Center for Responsive Politics (2010).

4. *Citizens United v. Federal Election Commission* (2010).

5. Kirkpatrick (2010).

6. Grim (2009).

7. See, e.g., Lichtblau (2010).

8. See, e.g., Lichtblau (2010).

9. Dodd-Frank Act, secs. 115, 120.

10. State attorneys general can bring claims against nonbank lenders for violations of the act's ban on unfair, deceptive, or abusive conduct as well as violations of CFPB regulations.

11. The extent to which consumers can use Dodd-Frank as the basis for UDAP claims under state law and the extent to which the CFPB will use its UDAP authority to expand the list of unlawful practices for which borrowers could bring claims is uncertain.

12. Streitfeld (2010); Timiraos (2010).

13. Colton, Schramm and Hirsh (2008), at 3.

14. Trickey (2007).

15. *American Financial Services Association v. City of Cleveland* (2006).

16. Trickey (2007).

17. Phillips (2009).

# Bibliography

*Note:* In addition to the sources listed in this bibliography, other, uncited data on the institutions and other companies discussed in this book come from statistics, filings, press releases, and orders of federal banking regulators and the Securities and Exchange Commission; rating agency reports; press releases and other web materials by the companies mentioned; the *American Banker*; and financial press reports.

GENERAL SOURCES

"A System That Invited Bankers to Make Bad Loans." *USA Today.* January 5, 2009.

Acs, Gregory. *Poverty in the United States, 2008.* Report. Washington, D.C.: The Urban Institute, September 10, 2009.

Adams, James Ring. "How to Win Friends and Influence Regulators; The Delayed Closing of Lincoln Savings Cost the Taxpayers $1 Billion." *National Review.* March 19, 1990.

Adams, Scott. *The Dilbert Future: Thriving on Business Stupidity in the 21st Century.* New York: Harper Paperbacks, 1998.

Adelino, Manuel, Kristopher Gerardi, and Paul S. Willen. "Why Don't Lenders Renegotiate More Home Mortgages? Redefaults, Self-Cures and Securitization." Public Policy Discussion Paper No. 2009–4, Federal Reserve Bank of Boston. July 2009.

Adler, Joe. "Declaring a Failure: When Should It Happen?" *American Banker.* August 7, 2008.

Adler, Lynn. "U.S. Foreclosures at Record High in First Half 2009 Despite Aid." TheStreet.com. July 15, 2009. http://www.thestreet.com/story/10586042/banks-foreclosure-pain-worsens-with-us-job-losses.html.

Aguilar, Luis A. Commissioner, U.S. Securities and Exchange Commission. "Empowering the Markets Watchdog to Effect Real Results." Speech. January 10, 2009. http://www.sec.gov.

Allen, Franklin, and Elena Carletti. "Credit Risk Transfer and Contagion." *Journal of Monetary Economics* 53 (2006): 89–111.

Alster, Norm. "Signs of Weakness in a Sector Known for Its Strength." *New York Times.* August 12, 2007.

"Alternative Net Capital Requirements for Broker-Dealers That Are Part of Consolidated Supervised Entities." *Federal Register* 69 (June 21, 2004): 34428–34472.

"America's Housing Market: Cracks in the Façade." *The Economist.* March 22, 2007.

*American Financial Services Association v. Burke,* 169 F. Supp.2d 62 (D. Conn. 2001).

*American Financial Services Association v. City of Cleveland,* 112 Ohio St.3d 170 (2006).

*American Financial Services Association v. City of Oakland,* 34 Cal.4th 1239 (2005).

*American Financial Services Association v. City of Toledo,* 112 Ohio St.3d 323 (2006).

American International Group. "The AIG Financial Crisis: A Summary." *Addendum to Testimony by Edward M. Liddy before the House Financial Services Subcommittee on Capital Markets, Insurance and Government-Sponsored Enterprises.* March 18, 2009.

"American International Group Investor Meeting—Final." *FD (Fair Disclosure) Wire.* December 5, 2007.

American Securitization Forum. The Impact of Forborne Principal on RMBS Transactions. Discussion Paper, American Securitization Forum. June 18, 2009.

Anderson, Jenny. "Goldman Chief Gets Record $53.4 Million Bonus." *New York Times.* December 20, 2006.

Anderson, Jenny, and Vikas Bajaj. "Lehman Is Shutting Loan Unit." *New York Times.* August 23, 2007. [2007a].

Anderson, Jenny, and Vikas Bajaj. "Wary of Risk, Bankers Sold Shaky Mortgage Debt." *New York Times.* December 6, 2007. [2007b].

Anderson, Jenny, and Vikas Bajaj. "Loan Reviewer Aiding Inquiry Into Big Banks." *New York Times.* January 27, 2008.

Andrews, Edmund L. "In Washington, Measuring a Lifeline." *New York Times.* August 28, 2007.

Andrews, Edmund L. "A 'Moral Hazard' for a Housing Bailout: Sorting the Victims From Those Who Volunteered." *New York Times.* February 23, 2008. [2008a].

Andrews, Edmund L. "A New Role for the Fed: Investor of Last Resort." *New York Times.* September 18, 2008. [2008b].

Andrews, Edmund L. "U.S. Sets Big Incentives to Head Off Foreclosures." *New York Times.* March 5, 2009. [2009a].

Andrews, Edmund L. "Wave of Debt Payments Facing U.S. Government." *New York Times.* November 23, 2009. [2009b].

Andrews, Edmund L., and David E. Sanger. "U.S. Is Finding Its Role in Business Hard to Unwind." *New York Times.* September 13, 2009.

Andrews, Edmund L., and Louis Uchitelle. "Rescues for Homeowners in Debt Weighed." *New York Times.* February 22, 2008.

Apgar, William, Amal Bendimerad, and Ren S. Essene. "Mortgage Market Channels and Fair Lending: An Analysis of HMDA Data." Working paper, Joint Center on Housing Studies, Harvard University. April 25, 2007. http://www.jchs.harvard.edu/publications/finance/mm07-2_mortgage_market_channels.pdf.

Appelbaum, Binyamin. "FDIC Seizes Three Banks, Expanding Loan-Relief Effort." *Washington Post.* November 22, 2008. [2008a].

Appelbaum, Binyamin. "Senior Federal Banking Regulator Removed." *Washington Post.* December 22, 2008. [2008b].

Appelbaum, Binyamin, and Ellen Nakashima. "Banking Regulator Played Advocate Over Enforcer." *Washington Post.* November 23, 2008.

Arnold, Chris. "Ex-Subprime Brokers Help Troubled Homeowners." National Public Radio. April 9, 2008. http://www.npr.org/templates/story/story.php?storyId=89505982. [2008a].

Arnold, Chris. "Auditor: Supervisors Covered Up Risky Loans." National Public Radio. May 27, 2008. http://www.npr.org/templates/story/story.php?storyId=90840958. [2008b].

Ashcraft, Adam B., and Til Schuermann. "Understanding the Securitization of Subprime Mortgage Credit." Working paper. December 17, 2007.

Associated Press. "Land America to Cut 1,100 Jobs." August 28, 2007. [2007a].

Associated Press. "Investors Resist Modifying Mortgages." September 11, 2007. [2007b].

Associated Press. " 'Liar Loans' Threaten to Prolong Mortgage Mess." August 18, 2008.

"At the Risky End of Finance." *Economist.* April 19, 2007.

Atkins, Paul S. Commissioner, U.S. Securities and Exchange Commission. "Speech before the Securities Traders Association." October 7, 2004. http://www.sec.gov.

Atkins, Paul S. Commissioner, U.S. Securities and Exchange Commission. "Speech before the U.S. Chamber Institute for Legal Reform." February 16, 2006. http://www.sec.gov.

Augstums, Ieva M. "Bank of America Plans to Exit Consumer Mortgage Wholesale Business by 2008." Associated Press. October 25, 2007.

Australian Government Productivity Commission. *Review of Australia's Consumer Policy Framework.* Vol. 2. Final Report. Melbourne, 2008.

Avery, Robert B., Glenn B. Canner, and Robert E. Cook. "New Information Reported under HMDA and Its Application in Fair Lending Enforcement." *Federal Reserve Bulletin* 91, no. 3 (Summer 2005): 344–394.

Avery, Robert B., Kenneth P. Brevoort, and Glenn B. Canner. "Opportunities and Issues in Using HMDA Data." *Journal of Real Estate Research* 29, no. 4 (October-December 2007): 351–379.

Avery, Robert B., Kenneth P. Brevoort, and Glenn B. Canner. "The 2007 HMDA Data." *Federal Reserve Bulletin* (December 2008): A107–A146.

Bailey, Deborah P. Email from Deborah P. Bailey to Mac Alfriend and Roger Cole Regarding BAC. December 20, 2008. Federal Reserve Documents. *Bank of America and Merrill Lynch: How Did a Private Deal Turn Into a Federal Bailout? Part II, Hearing Before the House Committee on Oversight and Government Reform.* June 25, 2009. http://oversight. house.gov/images/stories/documents/20090625093832.pdf.

Bailey, Jeff. "A Man and His Loan: Why Bennie Roberts Refinanced 10 Times." *Wall Street Journal.* April 23, 1997.

Bailey, Jeff. "Mortgage Maker vs. the World." *New York Times.* October 16, 2005.

Bair, Sheila C. Chairman, Federal Deposit Insurance Corporation. "Remarks to American Community Bankers Annual Meeting." November 9, 2007. http://www.fdic.gov. [2007a].

Bair, Sheila C. Chairman, Federal Deposit Insurance Corporation. "Remarks before the Nikkin 18th Special Seminar on International Finance." November 14, 2007. http://www.fdic.gov. [2007b].

Bair, Sheila C. Chairman, Federal Deposit Insurance Corporation. "Remarks to the Institute of International Bankers Annual Washington Conference, Washington, DC." March 2, 2009. http://www.fdic.gov. [2009a].

Bair, Sheila C. "Statement of Sheila C. Bair, Chairman, Federal Deposit Insurance Corporation, on Systemic Regulation, Prudential Measures, Resolution Authority and Securitization before the Financial Services Committee, U.S. House of Representatives." October 29, 2009. [2009b].

Bajaj, Vikas. "A Cross-Country Blame Game." *New York Times.* May 8, 2007. [2007a].

Bajaj, Vikas. "Rate Agencies Move Toward Downgrading Some Mortgage Bonds." *New York Times*. July 11, 2007. [2007b].

Bajaj, Vikas. "Creators of Credit Crisis Revel in Las Vegas." *New York Times*. February 8, 2008. [2008a].

Bajaj, Vikas. "The Downfall of a California Dreamer." *New York Times*. July 29, 2008. [2008b].

Bajaj, Vikas. "Credit Markets Suffer, and Borrowing Costs Threaten Businesses." *New York Times*. September 18, 2008. [2008c].

Bajaj, Vikas, and Jenny Anderson. "Inquiry Focuses on Withholding of Data on Loans." *New York Times*. January 12, 2008.

Bajaj, Vikas, and Christine Haughney. "More People With Weak Credit Are Defaulting on Mortgages." *New York Times*. January 26, 2007.

Bajaj, Vikas, and Mark Landler. "Mortgage Losses Echo in Europe and on Wall St." *New York Times*. August 10, 2007.

Baker, Mike. "Bankruptcies Jump 32% to 1.4 Million in 2009." *USA Today*. January 4, 2010.

Bank for International Settlements. "International banking and financial market developments." *BIS Quarterly Review* (March 2008): 1–29.

Bank for International Settlements. "Semiannual OTC Derivatives Statistics at End-June 2009." http://www.bis.org/statistics/derstats.htm.

"Bank Regulator Pressures Lenders to Aid Troubled Borrowers." *Mortgage Line*. August 22, 2007.

Bankrate.com. "Memorandum on Findings: First Tennessee Bank National Association Memphis as of June 30, 2008."

Barkley, Tom. "Existing-Home Sales Tumble 8%." *Wall Street Journal*. October 24, 2007.

Barnes, Robert, Michael D. Snear, and Peter Baker. "McCain: Fundamentals of Economy are 'Strong' but 'Threatened.'" *Washington Post*. September 15, 2008.

Barr, Michael S., and James A. Feldman. "Issue Brief: Overcoming Legal Barriers to the Bulk Sale of At-Risk Mortgages." Center for American Progress. April 2008.

Bartlett, Bruce. "The Harsh Impact on Consumption of Lost Home Equity." *Forbes*. February 6, 2009. http://www.forbes.com/2009/02/05/spending-housing-equity-opinions-columnists_0206_bruce_bartlett.html.

Basel Committee on Banking Supervision. *Results of the Fifth Quantitative Impact Study (QIS 5)*. Basel: Bank for International Settlements, June 16, 2006. http://www.bis.org/bcbs/qis/qis5results.pdf.

Bauerlein, Valerie. "BofA's Wall Street Retreat." *Wall Street Journal*. October 25, 2007.

Bauerlein, Valerie. "New Chief Plots Wachovia Overhaul—Dumping Loans Among Possibilities." *Wall Street Journal*. July 11, 2008.

Bauerlein, Valerie, and Damian Paletta. "NetBank's Failure Shows Online Limits." *Wall Street Journal*. September 29, 2007.

Bauerlein, Valerie, and Ruth Simon. "Wachovia to Discontinue Option-ARMs." *Wall Street Journal*. July 1, 2008.

BBC News. "Moody's to Widen its Debt Review." December 3, 2007. http://news.bbc.co.uk/2/hi/business/7125235.stm. [2007a].

BBC News. "Lenders 'Must Prepare for Worst.'" December 4, 2007. http://news.bbc.co.uk/2/hi/business/7127534.stm. [2007b].

BBC News. "US Bank 'To Fail Within Months.'" August 19, 2008. http://news.bbc.co.uk/2/hi/7569903.stm.

BCAPB LLC Trust 2007-AB1. *Prospectus.* July 19, 2007. http://sec.gov/Archives/edgar/data/1405863/000091412107001743/0000914121–07–001743-index.htm.

Becker, Jo, Sheryl Gay Stolberg, and Stephen Labaton. "White House Philosophy Stoked Mortgage Bonfire." *New York Times.* December 21, 2008.

Bel Bruno, Joe. "Failed Banks Weighing on FDIC." *Wall Street Journal.* August 17, 2009.

Benmelech, Efraim, and Jennifer Dlugosz. "The Alchemy of CDO Credit Ratings." Working Paper No. 14878, National Bureau of Economic Research. April 2009.

Berenson, Alex. "Boom Built Upon Sand, Gone Bust." *New York Times.* November 25, 2001.

Berkshire Hathaway Inc. *2002 Annual Report.* 2003. http://www.berkshirehathaway.com/2002ar/2002ar.pdf. [2003a].

Berkshire Hathaway Inc. "Letter to the Shareholders of Berkshire Hathaway Inc. 2003." http://www.berkshirehathaway.com/letters/2002pdf.pdf. [2003b].

Berman, Dennis K. "Why Street Bankers Get Away with Repeating Old Mistake." *Wall Street Journal.* November 6, 2007.

Berman, Dennis K. "Grim Reaper of Jobs Stalks the Street: Layoffs as High as 20% Are Predicted as the Banking Downturn Widens; Self-Reinforcing Cycle of Risk-Taking." *Wall Street Journal.* March 11, 2008.

Bernanke, Ben S. Governor, Board of Governors of the Federal Reserve System. "Remarks at the Annual Meeting of the American Economic Association." January 7, 2005. http://www.federalreserve.gov.

Bernanke, Ben S. Chairman, Board of Governors of the Federal Reserve System. "Remarks before the National Italian American Foundation." November 28, 2006. http://www.federalreserve.gov.

Bernanke, Ben S. Chairman, Board of Governors of the Federal Reserve System. "Speech At the Federal Reserve Bank of Chicago's 43rd Annual Conference on Bank Structure and Competition." May 17, 2007. http://www.federalreserve.gov. [2007a].

Bernanke, Ben S. Chairman, Board of Governors of the Federal Reserve System. "The Housing Market and Subprime Lending." Speech before the 2007 International Monetary Conference. June 5, 2007. http://www.federalreserve.gov. [2007b].

Bernanke, Ben S. Chairman, Board of Governors of the Federal Reserve System. "The Recent Financial Turmoil and its Economic and Policy Consequences." Speech before the Economic Club of New York. October 15, 2007. http://www.federalreserve.gov. [2007c].

Bernanke, Ben S. Chairman, Board of Governors of the Federal Reserve System. *The Economic Outlook: Testimony before the Joint Economic Committee of the United States Congress.* November 8, 2007. http://www.federalreserve.gov. [2007d].

Bernanke, Ben S. Chairman, Board of Governors of the Federal Reserve System. *Developments in the Financial Markets: Testimony before The U.S. Senate Committee on Banking, Housing, and Urban Affairs.* April 3, 2008. http://www.federalreserve.gov.

Bernanke, Ben S. *Statement of Ben S. Bernanke, Chairman, Board of Governors of the Federal Reserve System, before the Committee on Oversight and Government Reform, U.S. House of Representatives, Washington, D.C.* June 25, 2009. http://www.federalreserve.gov.

Bernasek, Anna. "When Does a Housing Slump Become a Bust?" *New York Times.* June 17, 2007.

Berndt, Antje, and Anurag Gupta. "Moral Hazard and Adverse Selection in the Originate-to-Distribute Model of Bank Credit." Working paper. October 24, 2008.

Berner, Robert. "A Credit Card You Want to Toss." *BusinessWeek.* February 7, 2008.

Berner, Robert, and Brian Grow. "They Warned Us." *BusinessWeek.* October 20, 2008.

Berry, John M. "Market Volatility Won't Affect Fed's Decision." Bloomberg.com. July 30, 2007. http://www.bloomberg.com/apps/news?pid=20601039&sid=a.kPZnsSdS58&refer=columnist_berry.

Berry, Kate. "Why Some Say Cramdowns Good for Banks." *American Banker.* February 3, 2009. [2009a].

Berry, Kate. "Bankruptcy Bill Seen Forcing Losses on High-Rated MBS." *American Banker.* February 13, 2009. [2009b].

Bethel, Jennifer E., Allan Ferrell, and Gang Hu. "Law and Economic Issues in Subprime Litigation." Discussion Paper No. 612, Harvard Law School. March 2008.

Bies, Susan Schmidt. Governor, Board of Governors of the Federal Reserve System. "Remarks at the North Carolina Bankers Association 109th Annual Convention, Kiawah Island." June 14, 2005. http://www.federalreserve.gov.

Bies, Susan Schmidt. Governor, Board of Governors of the Federal Reserve System. "Speech at the Financial Services Institute." February 2, 2006. http://www.federalreserve.gov. [2006a].

Bies, Susan Schmidt. Governor, Board of Governors of the Federal Reserve System. "Speech at the Bank Administration Institute Treasury Management Conference." May 4, 2006. http://www.federalreserve.gov. [2006b].

Bies, Susan Schmidt. Governor, Board of Governors of the Federal Reserve System. "Speech at the Mortgage Bankers Association Presidents Conference." June 14, 2006. http://www.federalreserve.gov. [2006c].

Bies, Susan Schmidt. Governor, Board of Governors of the Federal Reserve System. "Speech at the American Bankers Association Annual Convention." October 17, 2006. http://www.federalreserve.gov. [2006d].

Bies, Susan Schmidt. Governor, Board of Governors of the Federal Reserve System. "Speech at the National Credit Union Administration 2007 Risk Mitigation Summit." January 11, 2007. http://www.federalreserve.gov. [2007a].

Bies, Susan Schmidt. Governor, Board of Governors of the Federal Reserve System. "Speech at the Eller College of Management Distinguished Speaker Series." January 18, 2007. http://www.federalreserve.gov. [2007b].

Black, William K. "The Moral Quandaries of a Government Whistleblower." http://www.scu.edu/ethics/publications/submitted/black/whistleblower.html.

Blackwell, Rob. "Reeling from Defection, OTS Now Scraps Thrift Powers Plan." *American Banker.* January 10, 2002.

Blackwell, Rob, and Rob Garver. "OTS Likes One-Exam Model, Cuts Examiners." *American Banker.* April 2, 2002.

Bloomberg News. "Ratings Cut Near For Debt Products." July 12, 2007. http://www.nytimes.com/2007/07/12/business/12mortgage.html. [2007a].

Bloomberg News. "Chinese Bank Has $9 Billion in Subprime-Backed Securities." *New York Times.* August 24, 2007. [2007b].

Bloomberg News. "Commercial Paper Market Shrinks the Most in Seven Years." *New York Times.* August 24, 2007. [2007c].

Blundell-Wignall, Adrian. "Structured Products: Implications for Financial Markets." *Financial Market Trends* no. 2 (2007): 27–57.

Board of Governors of the Federal Reserve System. "Truth in Lending; Final Rule." *Federal Register* 66 (December 20, 2001): 65604–65622.

Board of Governors of the Federal Reserve System. *Purposes & Functions.* 9th ed. Washington, D.C., 2005.

Board of Governors of the Federal Reserve System. Order approving the application of Wachovia Corporation, Charlotte, North Carolina, to acquire all the voting shares of Golden West Financial Corporation ("Golden West"), Oakland, California, and thereby acquire World Savings Bank FSB, Oakland, California, and World Savings Bank FSB (Texas), Houston, Texas, and the other nonbanking subsidiaries of Golden West. September 29, 2006. http://www.federalreserve.gov.

Board of Governors of the Federal Reserve System. "Federal and State Agencies Announce Pilot Project to Improve Supervision of Subprime Mortgage Lenders." July 17, 2007. http://www.federalreserve.gov/newsevents/press/bcreg/20070717a.htm. [2007a].

Board of Governors of the Federal Reserve System. "Monetary Policy Report to the Congress." July 18, 2007. http://www.federalreserve.gov. [2007b].

Board of Governors of the Federal Reserve System. "Monetary Policy Report to the Congress." February 27, 2008. http://www.federalreserve.gov. [2008a].

Board of Governors of the Federal Reserve System. "2007 Annual Report to Congress." April 2008. http://www.federalreserve.gov. [2008b].

Board of Governors of the Federal Reserve System. "Truth in Lending: Final rule; official staff commentary." *Federal Register* 73 (July 30, 2008): 44522–44614. [2008c].

Board of Governors of the Federal Reserve System. "Truth in Lending: Proposed rule; request for comment." *Federal Register* 73 (December 10, 2008): 74989–74999. [2008d].

Board of Governors of the Federal Reserve System and the Department of Housing and Urban Development. "Joint Report to the Congress Concerning Reform to the Truth in Lending Act and the Real Estate Settlement Procedures Act." July 1998. http://www.federalreserve.gov/boarddocs/rptcongress/tila.pdf.

Board of Governors of the Federal Reserve System et al. "Capital; Leverage and Risk-Based Capital Guidelines; Capital Adequacy Guidelines; Capital Maintenance: Residual Interests in Asset Securitizations or Other Transfers of Financial Assets. Notice of proposed rulemaking." *Federal Register* 65 (September 27, 2000): 57993–58011. [2000a].

Board of Governors of the Federal Reserve System et al. "Proposed Agency Information Collection Activities; Comment Request." *Federal Register* 65 (May 31, 2000): 34801–34819. [2000b].

Bookstaber, Richard. "Blowing up the Lab on Wall Street." *Time.* August 16, 2007.

Bookstaber, Richard. "Four Tasks for the Systemic Risk Regulator." *Seeking Alpha.* June 8, 2009. http://seekingalpha.com/article/141979-four-tasks-for-the-systemic-risk-regulator.

Borod, Ronald S., Steven B. Levine, Madeleine M. L. Tan, and Eugene Solomonov. "Reflections in plague time: perspectives on the subprime crisis." In *The Americas Restructuring and Insolvency Guide 2008–2009*, 47–55. London: Globe Business Publishing, 2008.

Bostic, Raphael, Kathleen C. Engel, Patricia A. McCoy, Anthony Pennington-Cross, and Susan Wachter. "State and Local Anti-Predatory Lending Laws: The Effect of Legal Enforcement Mechanisms." *Journal of Economics and Business* 60, nos. 1–2 (January-February 2008): 47–66. [2008a].

Bostic, Raphael, Kathleen C. Engel, Patricia A. McCoy, Anthony Pennington-Cross, and Susan Wachter. "The Impact of Predatory Lending Laws: Policy Implications and Insights." In *Borrowing to Live: Consumer and Mortgage Credit Revisited*, ed. Nicolas P. Retsinas and Eric S. Belsky, 138–169. Washington, D.C.: Brookings Institution Press, 2008. [2008b].

Bowley, Graham. "A Convert to Reform." *New York Times.* March 11, 2010.

Boyd, Roddy. "The Last Days of Bear Stearns." *Fortune.* March 31, 2008. http://money. cnn.com/2008/03/28/magazines/fortune/boyd_bear.fortune.

Boylon, Anthony Burke. "'Predatory' Practices: Chain Reaction; Neighborhoods Face Aftershocks of Foreclosure Wave." *Crain's Chicago Business.* May 21, 2002.

Bradley, Jeanette, and Peter Skillern. "Predatory Lending: Subprime Lenders Trick Homeowners into Expensive Loans." *Shelterforce.* January/February 2000. http://www.nhi. org/online/issues/109/bradley.html.

Brinkmann, Jay. "An Examination of Mortgage Foreclosures, Modifications, Repayment Plans and Other Loss Mitigation Activities in the Third Quarter of 2007." Mortgage Bankers Association. January 2008. http://www.mbaa.org/files/News/InternalResource/ 59454_LoanModificationsSurvey.pdf.

Brooks, Rick, and Ruth Simon. "Subprime Debacle Traps Even Very Credit-Worthy." *Wall Street Journal.* December 3, 2007.

Browning, Lynnley. "The Subprime Loan Machine." *New York Times.* March 23, 2007.

Budnitz, Mark. "The Development of Consumer Protection Law, The Institutionalization of Consumerism, and Future Prospects and Perils." *Georgia State Law Review* (2010) (forthcoming).

Bureau of Economic Analysis, Department of Commerce. "Gross Domestic Product: Third Quarter 2009 Second Estimate." News Release BEA 09–50. November 24, 2009.

Burrough, Bryan. "Bringing Down Bear Stearns." *Vanity Fair.* August 2008. http://www. vanityfair.com/politics/features/2008/08/bear_stearns200808?printable=true.

Burrows, Peter. "How Madoff Is Burning The SEC." *BusinessWeek.* December 31, 2008.

Business Wire. "Bear Stearns Launches Residential Mortgage Company." April 18, 2005. http://findarticles.com/p/articles/mi_m0EIN/is_2005_April_18/ai_n13627996/.

Cagan, Christopher L. "Mortgage Payment Reset: The Rumor and the Reality." White Paper, First American Real Estate Solutions. 2006. http://www.firstamres.com/pdf/ MPR_White_Paper_FINAL.pdf.

Calem, Paul S., Kevin Gillen, and Susan Wachter. "The Neighborhood Distribution of Subprime Mortgage Lending." *The Journal of Real Estate Finance and Economics* 29, no. 4 (December 2004): 393–410.

Calem, Paul S., Marsha J. Courchane, and Susan M. Wachter. "Sustainable Homeownership." Working paper. March 19, 2009.

*California v. Countrywide Financial Corp., et al.,* No. LC081846 (Cal. Sup. Ct., Los Angeles Co.). First Amended Complaint. July 17, 2008.

Calomiris, Charles W. "Subprime Turmoil: What's Old, What's New, and What's Next." *Resource Investor.* August 22, 2008. http://www.resourceinvestor.com/News/2008/8/ Pages/Subprime-Turmoil—What-s-Old—What-s-New—And.aspx.

Caniglia, John, and Timothy Heider. "83 Charged in Mortgage-Fraud Scheme Appraisers, Loan Officers among Those Indicted." *The Plain Dealer.* August 23, 2002.

Carr, Jim. National Community Reinvestment Coalition. "On the Subject of the Silent Depression." Testimony before the U.S. House of Representatives Committee on Oversight and Government Reform. September 23, 2009.

Carter, Matt. "Workouts Could Soften Impact of Subprime Lending Woes." *Inman News.* April 8, 2007.

Casey, Nicholas. "Banker: 'What'd I Do Wrong, Officer?' Cop: 'You've Got Algae in the Pool, Sir.'" *Wall Street Journal.* May 1, 2009.

Census Bureau, Center for Economic Studies. *Census Bureau Research Data: Center Research Proposal Guidelines.* 2007. http://www.ces.census.gov/index.php/ces/1.00/researchguidelines.

Center for Responsible Lending. "Subprime Lending: A Net Drain on Homeownership." Issue Paper No. 4, Center for Responsible Lending. March 2007.

Center for Responsive Politics. *Congressional Committees.* 2010. http://www.opensecrets.org/cmteprofiles/index.php.

Chan, Sewell. "Democrats Push Ahead on Finance Bill." *New York Times.* March 11, 2010.

Chang, Andrea, E. Scott Reckard, and Kathy M. Kristof. "Confusion at IndyMac Fuels Customers' Anger." *Los Angeles Times.* July 16, 2008.

Cho, David. "Pressure at Mortgage Firm Led To Mass Approval of Bad Loans." *Washington Post.* May 7, 2007.

Chomsisengphet, Souphala, and Anthony Pennington-Cross. "The Evolution of the Subprime Mortgage Market." *Federal Reserve Bank of St. Louis Review* 88, no. 1 (January/February 2006): 31–56.

Chomsisengphet, Souphala, Timothy Murphy, and Anthony Pennington-Cross. "Product Innovation & Mortgage Selection in the Subprime Era." Working paper. October 23, 2008.

Christie, Les. "Foreclosure Impact: Next Stop, Tax Drop." CNNMoney.com. November 29, 2007. http://money.cnn.com/2007/11/29/real_estate/foreclosure_tax_drop/.

Christie, Les. "Renewed HOPE for Homeowners." CNNMoney.com. May 21, 2009. http://money.cnn.com/2009/05/20/real_estate/new_hope_for_homeowners/index.htm.

Chung, Joanna, Michael Mackenzie, and Nicole Bullock. "Fed Adds $800bn to Boost Borrowing." *Financial Times.* November 25, 2008. http://www.ft.com/cms/s/0/e7411216-bafb-11dd-bc6c-0000779fd18c.html.

Citigroup Inc. "Annual Report Pursuant to Section 13 or 15(d) of the Securities Exchange Act of 1934 for the Fiscal Year Ended December 31, 2005." February 24, 2006. http://sec.gov/Archives/edgar/data/831001/000104746906002377/0001047469–06–002377-index.htm.

"Citigroup Inc., New York, New York et al." *Federal Reserve Bulletin* 87, no. 9 (September 2001): 600–612. [2001a].

"Citigroup Inc., New York, New York et al." *Federal Reserve Bulletin* 87, no. 9 (September 2001): 613–624. [2001b].

"Citigroup Inc., New York, New York: Order Approving the Acquisition of Savings Associations." Board of Governors of the Federal Reserve System. October 28, 2002. http://www.federalreserve.gov/BOARDDOCS/PRESS/orders/2002/20021028/attachment.pdf.

"Citigroup Inc. New York, New York and Citifinancial Credit Company Baltimore, Maryland: Order to Cease and Desist and Order of Assessment of a Civil Money Penalty Issued Upon Consent." Board of Governors of the Federal Reserve System. May 27, 2004. http://www.federalreserve.gov/boarddocs/press/enforcement/2004/20040527/attachment.pdf.

Citizens for Responsibility and Ethics in Washington. *Payday Lender$ Pay Up.* April 2009. http://www.citizensforethics.org/node/39053.

*Citizens United v. Federal Election Commission,* 558 U.S. 50 (2010).

Clark, Melanca, and Maggie Barron. "Foreclosures: A Crisis in Legal Representation." Report, Brennan Center for Justice, New York University School of Law. October 2009.

Clark, Nicola. "Mortgage Crisis Forces Sale of German Bank." *New York Times.* August 27, 2007.

CNN. "President-elect Obama Seeks Distance from Blagojevich Scandal; Record Low Interest Rate; $50 Billion Scam." *The Situation Room 4:00 PM EST.* December 16, 2008.

Cochrane, John H. *Testimony of John H. Cochrane, Professor of Finance, University of Chicago Booth School of Business, Before the United States House of Representatives Committee on Financial Services.* September 24, 2009.

Coffee, John C., Jr. "Analyzing the Credit Crisis: Was the SEC Missing in Action?" *New York Law Journal.* December 5, 2008.

Coffee, John C., Jr., and Hillary A. Sale. "Redesigning the SEC: Does the Treasury Have a Better Idea?" *Virginia Law Review* 95 (2009): 707–783.

Cohan, William D. *House of Cards.* New York: Doubleday, 2009.

Collins, Brian. "Subprime Lender Fails in California." *National Mortgage News.* November 29, 1999.

Committee on Capital Markets Regulation. "The Global Financial Crisis: A Plan for _Regulatory Reform." May 26, 2009. http://www.capmktsreg.org/pdfs/TGFC-CC-MR_Report_ 5–26–09.pdf.

Commodity Futures Trading Commission. "Over-the-Counter Derivatives: Concept Release." *Federal Register* 63 (May 12, 1998): 26114–26127.

Congressional Oversight Panel. "Foreclosure Crisis: Working toward a Solution." Report. March 6, 2009. http://cop.senate.gov/documents/cop-030609-report.pdf. [2009a].

Congressional Oversight Panel. "December Oversight Report. Taking Stock: What Has the Troubled Asset Relief Program Achieved?" Report. December 9, 2009. http://cop.senate.gov/documents/cop-120909-report.pdf. [2009b].

Congressional Research Service. "The Dodd-Frank Wall Street Reform and Consumer Protection Act: Regulations to be Issued by the Consumer Financial Protection Bureau." August 25, 2010.

Consumer Affairs. "Trailer Home Sales Collapse Repossessions Soar." November 25, 2001. http://www.consumeraffairs.com/news/trailer_homes.html.

Consumer Federation of America. "Lower-Income and Minority Consumers Most Likely to Prefer and Underestimate Risks of Adjustable Rate Mortgages." July 26, 2004. http://www.consumerfed.org/pdfs/072604_ARM_Survey_Release.pdf.

Cordell, Larry, Karen Dynan, Andreas Lehnert, Nellie Liang, and Eileen Mauskopf. "The Incentives of Mortgage Servicers: Myths and Realities." Working paper. 2008.

Corkery, Michael. "Mortgage Mess Hits Home for Nation's Small Builders." *Wall Street Journal.* March 21, 2008. [2008a].

Corkery, Michael. "Mortgage 'Cram-Downs' Loom as Foreclosures Mount." *Wall Street Journal.* December 31, 2008. [2008b].

Corkery, Michael. "A Florida Court's 'Rocket Docket' Blasts through Foreclosure Cases." *Wall Street Journal.* February 18, 2009.

Corkery, Michael, and Ruth Simon. "As Houses Empty, Cities Seek Ways to Fill the Void." *Wall Street Journal.* February 6, 2008.

Cornerstone Research. "Securities Class Action Filings, 2008: A Year in Review." 2009. http://securities.cornerstone.com/pdfs/YIR2008.pdf.

Coulton, Claudia, Michael Schramm, and April Hirsh. "BEYOND REO: Property Transfers at Extremely Distressed Prices in Cuyahoga County, 2005–2008." Center on Urban Poverty and Community Development. December 2008.

Cox, Christopher. Chairman, U.S. Securities and Exchange Commission. "Address at the Seniors Summit: Protecting Senior Investors in Today's Markets." September 22, 2008. www.sec.gov. [2008a].

Cox, Christopher. Chairman, U.S. Securities and Exchange Commission. "Turmoil in U.S. Credit Markets: Recent Actions Regarding Government Sponsored Entities, Investment

Banks and Other Financial Institutions." Testimony before the U.S. Senate Committee on Banking, Housing and Urban Affairs. September 23, 2008. www.sec.gov. [2008b].

Cox, James D., Robert W. Hillman, and Donald C. Langevoort. *Securities Regulation: Cases and Materials.* 6th ed. New York: Aspen Publishers, 2009.

Craig, Brenda. "Attorney Brian Maul wins Big for Sub Prime Mortgage Victim." LawyersandSettlements.com. August 13, 2008. http://www.lawyersandsettlements.com/articles/11075/Brian-Maul-Wins-Sub-Prime-Mortgage.html.

Craig, Susanne. "Merrill's $10 Million Men." *Wall Street Journal.* March 4, 2009.

Craig, Susanne, and Deborah Solomon. "Bank Bonus Tab: $33 Billion." *Wall Street Journal.* July 31, 2009.

Credit Suisse. "Subprime Loan Modifications Update." Fixed Income Research Report. October 1, 2008. [2008a].

Credit Suisse. "Foreclosure Update: Over 8 Million Foreclosures Expected." Fixed Income Research Report. December 4, 2008. [2008b].

*Credit Suisse Securities (USA) LLC v. Billing,* 551 U.S. 264 (2007).

Creswell, Julie. "Mortgage Lender New Century Financial Files for Bankruptcy." *New York Times.* April 2, 2007.

*Cuomo v. Clearing House Ass'n et al.,* 557 U.S. __, 129 S. Ct. 2710 (2009).

Curran, Rob. "WaMu Plunges 96% for the Week." *Wall Street Journal.* September 27, 2008.

Currie, Antony. "The Nine Lives of CDOs." *Wall Street Journal.* November 26, 2007.

Danis, Michelle A., and Anthony Pennington-Cross. "The Delinquency of Subprime Mortgages." *Journal of Economics and Business* 60, nos. 1–2 (January-February 2008): 67–90.

Dash, Eric. "Central Bank's Sudden Action Eases a Logjam in Corporate Borrowing." *New York Times.* August 18, 2007. [2007a].

Dash, Eric. "Four Major Banks Tap Federal Reserve for Financing." *New York Times.* August 23, 2007. [2007b].

Dash, Eric. "Bank Profits May Well Suffer, but Credit Crisis Hardly Leaves Them Defenseless." *New York Times.* August 27, 2007. [2007c].

Dash, Eric. "Citigroup Buys Parts of a Troubled Mortgage Lender." *New York Times.* September 1, 2007. [2007d].

Dash, Eric. "Citi Shakes Up Its Mortgage Business." *New York Times.* January 8, 2008. [2008a].

Dash, Eric. "Citigroup Combining Mortgage Operations Into One Unit." *New York Times.* January 9, 2008. [2008b].

Dash, Eric. "U.S. Approves Plan to Help Citigroup Cope With Losses." *New York Times.* November 24, 2008. [2008c].

Dash, Eric, and Julie Creswell. "Citigroup Pays for a Rush to Risk." *New York Times.* November 22, 2008. [2008a].

Dash, Eric, and Julie Creswell. "Citigroup Saw No Red Flags Even as it Made Bolder Bets." *New York Times.* November 23, 2008. [2008b].

Dash, Eric, and Andrew Ross Sorkin. "Throwing a Lifeline to a Troubled Giant." *New York Times.* September 18, 2008.

Davidson, D. A. "Washington Mutual, Inc." Analyst Report. October18, 2007.

Dell'Ariccia, Giovanni, Deniz Igan, and Luc Laeven. "Credit Booms and Lending Standards: Evidence From the Subprime Mortgage Market." European Banking Center Discussion Paper No. 2009–14S. 2008. www.ssrn.com.

DeMarco, Edward J. "The Future of the Mortgage Market and the Housing Enterprises." Statement of Edward J. DeMarco, Acting Director, Federal Housing Finance Agency, Before the U.S. Senate Committee on Banking, Housing and Urban Affairs. October 8, 2009.

DeMarco, Edward J. "Current State of the Government Sponsored Enterprises." Statement of Edward J. DeMarco, Acting Director, Federal Housing Finance Agency, Before the U.S. House of Representatives Subcommittee on Capital Markets, Insurance and Government Sponsored Enterprises. May 26, 2010.

Demyanyk, Yuliya S. "Quick Exits of Subprime Mortgages." *Federal Reserve Bank of St. Louis Review,* 91, no. 2 (March/April 2009): 79–93.

Demyanyk, Yuliya S., and Otto Van Hemert. "Understanding the Subprime Mortgage Crisis." Working paper. December 5, 2008.

Deng, Sheran. "SIVs, Bank Leverage and Subprime Mortgage Crisis." Working paper. 2008.

Dennis, Brady. "E-Mails Inside AIG Reveal Executives Struggling with Growing Crisis." *Washington Post.* December 30, 2009.

Dennis, Brady, and Robert O'Harrow. "A Crack in The System." *Washington Post.* December 30, 2008.

DeParle, Jason. "49 Million Americans Report a Lack of Food." *New York Times.* November 17, 2009.

DeParle, Jason, and Robert Gebeloff. "Food Stamp Use Soars, and Stigma Fades." *New York Times.* November 29, 2009.

Department of Housing and Urban Development. "Neighborhood Stabilization Program Data." March 19, 2009. http://www.huduser.org/Datasets/nsp.html. [2009a].

Department of Housing and Urban Development. "HUD Secretary Donovan Announces Expanded Eligibility for Making Home Affordable Refinancing." July 1, 2009. http://www.hud.gov/news/release.cfm?content=pr09–104.cfm. [2009b].

Department of Housing and Urban Development. "Secretary Donovan Announces New FHA-Making Home Affordable Loan Modification Guidelines." July 29, 2009. http://makinghomeaffordable.gov/pr_07302009.html. [2009c].

Department of Housing and Urban Development. "Administration Announces Initiative for State and Local Housing Finance Agencies." October 19, 2009. http://makinghomeaffordable.gov/pr_10192009.html. [2009d].

Department of Housing and Urban Development. "HOPE for Homeowners Program-Comprehensive Guidance." October 20, 2009. http://www.nls.gov/offices/adm/hudclips/letters/mortgagee/files/09–43ml.doc. [2009e].

Department of Housing and Urban Development. "Obama Administration Kicks Off Mortgage Modification Conversion Drive." November 30, 2009. http://makinghomeaffordable.gov/pr_11302009.html. [2009f].

Department of Justice, Civil Rights Division. "Fair Lending Enforcement Program." January 2001. http://www.justice.gov/crt/housing/bll_01.php.

Department of the Treasury. "The Department of the Treasury Blueprint for a Modernized Financial Regulatory Structure." March 2008. http://www.treas.gov/press/releases/reports/Blueprint.pdf.

Department of the Treasury. "Homeowner Affordability and Stability Plan." February 18, 2009. http://www.treas.gov/press/releases/tg33.htm. [2009a].

Department of the Treasury. "Making Home Affordable Updated Detailed Program Description." March 4, 2009. http://www.treas.gov/press/releases/reports/housing_fact_sheet.pdf. [2009b].

Department of the Treasury. "The Next Phase of Government Financial Stabilization and Rehabilitation Policies." September 2009. [2009c].

Department of the Treasury. "Making Home Affordable Program: Servicer Performance Report Through September 2009." October 8, 2009. [2009d].

Department of the Treasury et al. "Risk-Based Capital Guidelines; Capital Adequacy Guidelines, Capital Maintenance: Capital Treatment of Recourse, Direct Credit Substitutes and Residual Interests in Asset Securitizations. Final rule." *Federal Register* 66 (November 29, 2001): 59614–59667.

Department of the Treasury et al. "Interagency Guidance on Nontraditional Mortgage Product Risks; Final guidance." *Federal Register* 71 (October 4, 2006): 58609–58618.

Department of the Treasury et al. "Proposed Statement on Subprime Mortgage Lending." *Federal Register* 72 (March 8, 2007): 10533–10537. [2007a].

Department of the Treasury et al. "Statement on Subprime Mortgage Lending; Final guidance." *Federal Register* 72 (July 10, 2007): 37569–37575. [2007b].

Department of the Treasury et al. "Illustrations of Consumer Information for Nontraditional Mortgage Products; Final guidance." *Federal Register* 72 (June 8, 2007): 31825–31832. [2007c].

Department of the Treasury et al. "Illustrations of Consumer Information for Hybrid Adjustable Rate Mortgage Products; Final guidance." *Federal Register* 73 (May 29, 2008): 30997–31005.

Departments of the Treasury and Housing and Urban Development. "Curbing Predatory Home Mortgage Lending." June 20, 2000. http://www.huduser.org/publications/pdf/treasrpt.pdf.

DeSilver, Drew. "Where WaMu Went Wrong." *Seattle Times*. April 14, 2008.

deV. Frierson, Robert. Deputy Secretary of the Board of Governors of the Federal Reserve System. Letter to James E. Scott, Citigroup Inc. May 14, 2004. http://www.federalreserve.gov/boarddocs/legalint/federalreserveact/2004/20040514/.

Dietz, Diane. "Homeowners Face a Tangled Web: People Threatened with Losing their Homes Find it Nearly Impossible to Find Someone with the Authority to Help Them." *The Register-Guard*. May 4, 2009.

Dinallo, Eric R. Former Superintendent of the New York State Insurance Department. "Hearing on the Causes and Effects of the AIG Bailout." Testimony before the U.S. House of Representatives, Committee on Oversight and Government Reform. October 7, 2008. [2008a].

Dinallo, Eric R. Former Superintendent of the New York State Insurance Department. "Hearing to Review the Role of Credit Derivatives in the U.S. Economy." Testimony before the U.S. House of Representatives, Committee on Agriculture. November 20, 2008. [2008b].

Dodd, Ronald. "Subprime: Tentacles of Crisis Finance and Development." *Finance and Development* 44 (December 2007): 15–19.

Dodge & Cox. "Third Quarter Report, September 30, 2008, Stock Fund." September 30, 2008. http://www.dodgeandcox.com.

Donohue, Andrew J. U.S. Securities and Exchange Commission. "Testimony Concerning Investor Protection and Securities Fraud." Testimony before the U. S. House of Representatives, Committee on Financial Services, Subcommittee on Capital Markets, Insurance and Government-Sponsored Enterprises. February 4, 2009.

Donovan, Shaun. Secretary of the Department of Housing and Urban Development. "Helping Homeowners Avoid Foreclosure." Testimony before the U.S. Senate Committee on Banking, Housing and Urban Affairs Subcommittee on Housing, Transportation and Community Development. September 21, 2009.

Dough, Jim. "Equity Predators: Stripping, Flipping and Packing Their Way to Profits." Testimony before The U.S. Senate Special Committee on Aging. March 16, 1998.

Drew, Jill. "Frenzy." *Washington Post.* December 16, 2008.

Dugan, John C. Comptroller of the Currency. "Remarks before the American Bankers Association." September 26, 2005. [2005a].

Dugan, John C. Comptroller of the Currency. "Remarks before an OCC Credit Risk Conference." October 27, 2005. [2005b].

Dugan, John C. "Remarks Before the Consumer Federation of America." December 1, 2005. [2005c].

Dugan, John C. Comptroller of the Currency. "Remarks before the Greenlining Institute's 13th Annual Economic Summit." April 20, 2006. [2006a].

Dugan, John C. "Remarks Before the American Bankers Association, Phoenix, Arizona." October 16, 2006. [2006b].

Dugan, John C. Comptroller of the Currency. "Remarks before the America's Community Bankers." October 17, 2006. [2006c].

Dugan, John C. Comptroller of the Currency. "Remarks before the Exchequer Club and Women in Housing and Finance." January 17, 2007. [2007a].

Dugan, John C. Comptroller of the Currency. "Remarks before the Greenlining Coalition's 14th Annual Economic Summit." April 19, 2007. [2007b].

Dugan, John C. Comptroller of the Currency. "Remarks Before the Neighborhood Housing Services of New York." May 23, 2007. [2007c].

Dugan, John C. Comptroller of the Currency. Testimony before the Committee on Financial Services of the U.S. House of Representatives. September 5, 2007. [2007d].

Dugan, John C. Comptroller of the Currency. Testimony before the Senate Committee on Banking, Housing, and Urban Affairs. March 4, 2008.

Duhigg, Charles. "At Freddie Mac, Chief Discarded Warning Signs." *New York Times.* August 5, 2008. [2008a].

Duhigg, Charles. "Pressured to Take More Risk, Fannie Reached Tipping Point." *New York Times.* October 5, 2008. [2008b].

Duhigg, Charles. "Fighting Foreclosures, F.D.I.C. Chief Draws Fire." *New York Times.* December 11, 2008. [2008c].

Duhigg, Charles, and Carter Dougherty. "From the Midwest to M.T.A., Pain from Global Gamble." *New York Times.* November 11, 2008.

Duhigg, Charles, Stephen Labaton, and Andrew Ross Sorkin. "As Crisis Grew, A Few Options Shrank to One." *New York Times.* September 8, 2008.

Dunbar, John. "You Broke It, You Fix It?: Subprime Players Get Tax Money to Fix Subprime Mess." The Center for Public Integrity. August 25, 2009. http://www.publicintegrity.org/investigations/economic_meltdown/articles/entry/1629.

Dunbar, John, and David Donald. "The Roots of the Financial Crisis: Who Is to Blame?" May 6, 2009. http://www.publicintegrity.org/investigations/economic_meltdown/articles/entry/1286/.

Dungey, Doris ("Tanta"). "Mortgage Servicing for UberNerds." *Calculated Risk.* February 20, 2007. http://www.calculatedriskblog.com/2007/02/tanta-mortgage-servicing-for-ubernerds.html. [2007a].

Dungey, Doris ("Tanta"). "FICOs and UAS: We Will Add Your Distinctiveness to Our Collective." *Calculated Risk.* March 19, 2007. http://www.calculatedriskblog.com/2007/03/ficos-and-aus-we-will-add-your.html. [2007b].

*Dura Pharmaceuticals, Inc. v. Broudo*, 544 U.S. 336 (2005).

Eaton, Leslie, Ryan Knutson, and Philip Shishkin. "States Shut Down to Save Cash." *Wall Street Journal.* September 4, 2009.

Eavis, Peter. "Heard on the Street: Lehman Lurches into End Game." *Wall Street Journal.* September 10, 2008.

Eckholm, Erik. "Surge in Homeless Pupils Strains Schools." *New York Times.* September 5, 2009.

Edwards, John G. "U.S. regulators take over First National Bank." *Las Vegas Review-Journal (Nevada).* July 26, 2008.

Efrati, Amir. "U.S. Expands Scrutiny of Home Lenders." *Wall Street Journal.* December 3, 2007. [2007a].

Efrati, Amir. "SEC Probes WaMu on Appraisals." *Wall Street Journal.* December 21, 2007. [2007b].

Egan, Sean J. "Credit Rating Agencies and the Financial Crisis." Testimony before the U.S. House of Representatives, Committee on Oversight and Government Reform. October 22, 2008.

Eggert, Kurt. "The Great Collapse: How Securitization Caused the Subprime Meltdown." *Connecticut Law Review* 41, no. 4 (May 2009): 1257–1312.

ElBoghady, Dina. "HUD Chief Calls Aid on Mortgages a Failure." *Washington Post.* December 17, 2008.

ElBoghady, Dina. "Housing Agency's Cash Reserves will Drop below Requirement." *Washington Post.* September 18, 2009.

ElBoghdady, Dina, and Sarah Cohen. "The Growing Foreclosure Crisis." *Washington Post.* January 17, 2009.

ElBoghdady, Dina, and Renae Merle. "Struggling Mortgage Lender Taken Over by Regulators." *Washington Post.* July 12, 2008.

Eling, M., H. Schmeiser, and J. T. Schmit. "The Solvency II Process: Overview and Critical Analysis." *Risk Management and Insurance Review* 10, no. 1 (2007): 69–85.

Elliott, Douglas J. "Implications of the Bank Stress Tests." Working paper, Initiative on Business and Public Policy, The Brookings Institution. May 11, 2009.

Engel, Kathleen. "Do Cities Have Standing? Redressing the Externalities of Predatory Lending." *Connecticut Law Review* 38, no. 3 (2006): 355–391.

Engel, Kathleen C. "Mortgage Market Responses: Changing Markets, Changing Options." Working paper. April 17, 2009.

Engel, Kathleen C., and Thomas Fitzpatrick. "False Security: How Securitization Failed Wall Street." Working paper. 2010.

Engel, Kathleen C., and Patricia A. McCoy. "The Law and Economics of Remedies for Predatory Lending." In *Changing Financial Markets and Community Development,* edited by Jackson L. Blanton, Alicia Williams, and Sherrie L. W. Rhine, 155–169. Washington, D.C.: Board of Governors of the Federal Reserve System, 2001.

Engel, Kathleen C., and Patricia A. McCoy. "A Tale of Three Markets: The Law and Economics of Predatory Lending." *Texas Law Review* 80, no. 6 (2002): 1255–1381.

Engel, Kathleen C., and Patricia A. McCoy. "Predatory Lending: What Does Wall Street Have to Do with It?" *Housing Policy Debate* 15, no. 3 (2004): 715–751.

Engel, Kathleen C., and Patricia A. McCoy. "Turning a Blind Eye: Wall Street Finance of Predatory Lending." *Fordham Law Review* 75, no. 4 (2007): 2039–2103.

Engel, Kathleen C., and Patricia A. McCoy. "From Credit Denial to Predatory Lending: The Challenge of Sustaining Minority Homeownership." In *Segregation: The Rising Costs for America,* edited by James H. Carr and Nandinee K. Kutty, 81–123. New York: Routledge, 2008.

England, Robert Stowe. "Rebuilding the secondary market." *Mortgage Banking* 69, no. 7 (April 2009): 26–33.

Enrich, David. "WaMu, Wachovia Expect More Fallout." *Wall Street Journal.* September 11, 2007.

Enrich, David. "Banks Find New Ways To Ease Pain Of Bad Loans." *Wall Street Journal.* June 19, 2008.

Enrich, David. "Banks Load Up on Mortgages, in New Way." *Wall Street Journal.* September 10, 2009.

Enrich, David, Robin Sidel, and Deborah Solomon. "Fed Sees Up to $599 Billion in Bank Losses." *Wall Street Journal.* May 8, 2009.

Enrich, David, Dan Fitzpatrick, and Marshall Eckblad. "Banks Won Concessions on Tests." *Wall Street Journal.* May 9–10, 2009.

Ernst, Keith, Debbie Bocian, and Wei Li. "Steered Wrong: Brokers, Borrowers, and Subprime Loans." Report, Center for Responsible Lending. April 8, 2008.

Essene, Ren S., and William Apgar. "Understanding Mortgage Market Behavior: Creating Good Mortgage Options for All Americans." Working paper, Joint Center for Housing Studies, Harvard University. 2007.

Evans, Kelly. "Mortgage Turmoil Hits Renters." *Wall Street Journal.* October 11, 2007.

Faiola, Anthony, Ellen Nakashima, and Jill Drew. "What Went Wrong." *Washington Post.* October 15, 2008.

Fannie Mae. "Eligibility of Mortgages to Borrowers with Blemished Credit Records, Lender Letter No. 03–00." April 11, 2000. http://www.efanniemae.com/sf/guides/ssg/annltrs/pdf/2000/lendltrs2000.pdf.

Fannie Mae. "Understanding America's Homeownership Gaps: 2003 Fannie Mae National Housing Survey." 2004.

Fannie Mae. "An Introduction to Fannie Mae." July 2008. [2008a].

Fannie Mae. "Fannie Mae Announces Single National Down Payment Policy; Replaces Policy Regarding Markets where Home Prices are Declining." May 16, 2008. [2008b].

Fannie Mae. "National REO Rental Policy FAQs." January 13, 2009. http://www.fanniemae.com/newsreleases/2009/faq/FAQ_national_REO_rental_policy_010709.pdf.

"FDIC Says Banks Undercapitalized for Subprime Lending." *National Mortgage News.* February 14, 2000.

Federal Deposit Insurance Corporation. "FDIC Statistics on Depository Institutions." http://www2.fdic.gov/sdi/index.asp.

Federal Deposit Insurance Corporation. "Breaking New Ground in U.S. Mortgage Lending." *FDIC Outlook.* Summer 2006. http://www.fdic.gov/bank/analytical/regional/r020062q/na/2006_summer04.html.

Federal Deposit Insurance Corporation. *Quarterly Banking Profile* 3, no. 2 (March 31, 2009): 1–27. http://www2.fdic.gov/qbp/2009mar/qbp.pdf. [2009a].

Federal Deposit Insurance Corporation. "A Year in Bank Supervision: 2008 and a Few of Its Lessons." *Supervisory Insights* 6, no. 1 (Summer 2009): 3–18. http://www.fdic.gov/regulations/examinations/supervisory/insights/sisum09/si_sum09.pdf. [2009b].

Federal Deposit Insurance Corporation. "FDIC-Insured Institutions Earned $2.8 Billion in the Third Quarter of 2009." Press release PR-212–2009. November 24, 2009. [2009c].

Federal Housing Administration. "FHA Share of Home Purchase Activity." August 2009. http://www.hud.gov/offices/hsg/comp/rpts/fhamktsh/fhamkt.cfm.

Federal Housing Finance Agency. "U.S. Treasury Support for Fannie Mae and Freddie Mac." *Mortgage Market Note* 09–1A (July 9, 2009): 1–6. http://www.fhfa.gov/webfiles/14519/mmnote09–1A.pdf.

Federal Reserve System. "Monthly Report on Credit and Liquidity Programs and the Balance Sheet." October 2009. [2009a].

Federal Reserve System. "The October 2009 Senior Loan Officer Opinion Survey on Banking Lending Practices." 2009. [2009b].

Federal Trade Commission. "Prepared Statement of the Federal Trade Commission before the House Committee on Banking and Financial Services on Predatory Lending Practices in the Subprime Industry." May 24, 2000. http://www.ftc.gov/os/2000/05/predatorytestimony.htm.

Federal Trade Commission. "Citigroup Settles FTC Charges Against the Associates Record-Setting $215 Million for Subprime Lending Victims." September 19, 2002. http://www.ftc.gov/opa/2002/09/associates.shtm.

Federal Trade Commission. "Fairbanks Capital Settles FTC and HUD Charges." November 12, 2003. http://www.ftc.gov/opa/2003/11/fairbanks.shtm.

Federal Trade Commission. "Capital City Mortgage Settles FTC Charges." February 24, 2005. http://www.ftc.gov/opa/2005/02/capitalcity.shtm.

Federal Trade Commission. "Bear Stearns and EMC Mortgage to Pay $28 Million to Settle FTC Charges of Unlawful Mortgage Servicing and Debt Collection Practices." September 8, 2008. http://www.ftc.gov/opa/2008/09/emc.shtm.

*Federal Trade Commission v. Capital City Mortgage Corp.*, No. 1:98-CV-00237 (D.D.C.). Complaint. January 29, 1998.

Fettig, Dwight. "The History of a Powerful Paragraph." *The Region.* June 2008. http://www.minneapolisfed.org/publications_papers/pub_display.

*Fidelity Federal Savings & Loan Ass'n v. de la Cuesta*, 458 U.S. 141 (1982).

Financial Accounting Standards Board. "FASB Staff Position: Determining Fair Value When the Volume and Level of Activity for the Asset or Liability Have Significantly Decreased and Identifying Transactions That Are Not Orderly." FSP No. FAS 157–4. April 2, 2009. [2009a].

Financial Accounting Standards Board. "FASB Staff Position: Recognition and Presentation of Other-Than-Temporary Impairments." FSP Nos. FAS 115–2 and FAS 124–2. April 9, 2009. [2009b].

Financial Stability Board. "Report of the Financial Stability Forum on Enhancing Market and Institutional Resilience." April 7, 2008. http://www.financialstabilityboard.org/publications/r_0804.pdf.

Finkelstein, Brad. "OCC Takes Over 2 Banks." *Origination News.* August 2008.

Fishbein, Allen J., and Patrick Woodall. "Exotic or Toxic? An Examination of the Non-Traditional Mortgage Market for Consumers and Lenders." Consumer Federation of America. May 2006. http://www.consumerfed.org/pdfs/Exotic_Toxic_Mortgage_Report0506.pdf.

Fitch Ratings. "The Impact of Poor Underwriting Practices and Fraud in Subprime RMBS Performance." *Structured Finance Report.* November 28, 2007.

Fitzpatrick, Dan. "WaMu Fights to Win Over Wary Market." *Wall Street Journal.* September 12, 2008.

Fitzpatrick, Dan. "Calculating Merrill's Losses—A 'Wild A- Guess.'" *Wall Street Journal.* October 16, 2009.

Fitzpatrick, Dan, and Peter Lattman. "Washington Mutual Forces Out CEO." *Wall Street Journal.* September 8, 2008.

Fitzpatrick, Dan, and Damian Paletta. "GMAC Asks for Fresh Lifeline." *Wall Street Journal.* October 29, 2009.

Fitzpatrick, Dan, David Enrich, and Damian Paletta. "PNC Buys National City in Bank Shakeout." *Wall Street Journal.* October 25, 2008.

Fitzpatrick, Thomas J., IV, and Chris Sagers. "Faith-Based Financial Regulation: A Primer on Oversight of Credit Rating Organizations." *Administrative Law Review* 61, no. 3 (2009): 557–610.

Flitter, Emily. "Mortgage Brokerage Reform Measures Are Found Wanting." *American Banker.* August 13, 2008.

Foley, Stephen. "How Wall Street's Watchdog May Be Muzzled." *The Independent.* August 15, 2008.

*In Re Foreclosure Cases,* 2007 U.S. Dist. LEXIS 84011 (N. D. Ohio, October 31, 2007).

Fouché, Gladys. "Sub-prime Chill Reaches the Arctic." *The Guardian.* June 30, 2008. http://www.guardian.co.uk/business/2008/jun/30/subprimecrisis.creditcrunch.

Fox, Justin. "Congress Ready to Consider a Bolder Mortgage Fix." *Time.* December 23, 2008.

Fratantoni, Michael, et al. *Housing and Mortgage Markets: An Analysis.* Mortgage Bankers Association. 2005. http://www.mortgagebankers.org/files/Bulletin/InternalResource/38151_MBA_Monograph_N01.pdf.

Freddie Mac. "30-Year Fixed-Rate Mortgages Since 1971." http://www.freddiemac.com/pmms/pmms30.htm.

Freddie Mac. "Bulletin 2000–1." March 20, 2000. http://www.freddiemac.com/sell/guide/bulletins/pdf/b11001.pdf.

Freddie Mac. "Freddie Mac Extends Eviction Suspension Until March, Launches Rental Option for Foreclosed Borrowers, Tenants." January 30, 2009. http://www.freddiemac.com/news/archives/servicing/2009/20090130_reo-rental.html. [2009a].

Freddie Mac. "Freddie Mac Officially Launches REO Rental Initiative for Tenants, Owner-Occupants After Foreclosure." March 5, 2009. http://www.freddiemac.com/news/archives/servicing/2009/20090305_reo-rental-initiative.html. [2009b].

Fremont General Corporation. *Form 10-K—2005 Annual Report.* March 16, 2006. http://www.sec.gov/Archives/edgar/data/38984/000095012906002726/v18050e10vk.htm.

*In the Matter of Fremont Investment Advisors, Inc.* U.S. Securities and Exchange Commission Investment Adviser Act of 1940 Release No. 2317. November 4, 2004. http://www.sec.gov/litigation/admin/ia-2317.htm.

Fuld, Richard S., Jr. "The Causes and Effects of the Lehman Brothers Bankruptcy." Testimony before the U.S. House of Representatives, Committee on Oversight and Government Reform. October 6, 2008.

Gallagher, Dan. "Citi Plans to Absorb $49 Billion in SIV Assets onto Balance Sheet." *MarketWatch.* December 13, 2007. http://www.marketwatch.com/story/citi-plans-to-absorb-49-billion-in-siv-assets-onto-balance-sheet.

Garcia, Norma P. "Subprime Lending: Defining the Market and Its Customers." Testimony before the House Committee on Financial Services. March 30, 2004.

Geanakoplos, John D., and Susan P. Koniak. "Mortgage Justice is Blind." *New York Times.* October 30, 2008.

Geithner, Timothy F. President, Federal Reserve Bank of New York. "Reducing Systemic Risk in a Dynamic Financial System." Speech at the Economic Club of New York. June 9, 2008.

Geithner, Timothy F. Secretary of the Treasury. "Written Testimony before the Congressional Oversight Panel." U.S. Department of the Treasury press release TG-283. September 10, 2009.

Gensler, Gary. Chairman, Commodity Futures Trading Commission. Testimony before the House Committee on Financial Services. October 7, 2009.

Gensler, Gary. Chairman, Commodity Futures Trading Commission. "Remarks, OTC Derivatives Reform, FIA's Annual International Futures Industry Conference, Boca Raton, Florida." March 11, 2010.

Gerardi, Kristopher S., Andreas Lehnert, Shane M. Sherland, and Paul S. Willen. "Making Sense of the Subprime Crisis." Working Paper No. 2009-2, Federal Reserve Bank of Atlanta. February 2009.

Gerardi, Kristopher S., and Paul S. Willen. "Subprime Mortgages, Foreclosures, and Urban Neighborhoods." Public Policy Discussion Paper No. 2008-6, Federal Reserve Bank of Boston. December 2008.

Gerding, Erik F. "The Outsourcing of Financial Regulation to Risk Models and the Global Financial Crisis: Code, Crash, and Open Source." Working paper. March 1, 2009.

Gerth, Jeff. "Was AIG Watchdog Not Up To The Job?" *MSN Money.* November 10, 2008. http://articles.moneycentral.msn.com/Investing/Extra/was-aig-watchdog-not-up-to-the-job.aspx.

Gilleran, James Edward. Director, Office of Thrift Supervision. Remarks before the Exchequer Club. May 21, 2003.

Gilleran, James Edward. Director, Office of Thrift Supervision. Remarks before the Exchequer Club. January 21, 2004.

Gilleran, James Edward. Biography: James Gilleran, former Director, OTS: A brief summary of financial proposals filed with and actions by the SEC. November 18, 2008. http://sec.gov/spotlight/fairvalue/marktomarket/gilleranbio.pdf.

Gkonos, James, and Mark Cawley. "Current Developments in State and Federal Regulation of Swaps and Derivatives." *Emerging Issues, LexisNexis.* February 28, 2009. http://law.lexisnexis.com/practiceareas/Insights—Analysis/Business/Current-Developments-in-State-and-Federal-Regulation-of-Swaps-and-Derivatives.

Glacy, Anson J., Jr. "Against the Grain: The Wisdom of Countercyclical Capital." In *Risk Management: The Current Financial Crisis, Lessons Learned and Future Implications,* 38–39. Schaumburg, Illinois: The Society of Actuaries et al., 2008.

Glater, Jonathan D. "With Shares Battered, A.I.G. Ousts Its Leader." *New York Times.* June 16, 2008.

Goldfarb, Zachary A. "Fannie, Freddie Halt Foreclosures for Holidays." *Washington Post.* November 21, 2008. [2008a].

Goldfarb, Zachary A. "Modifying the Mortgage Giants." *Washington Post.* December 8, 2008. [2008b].

Goldfarb, Zachary A. "Schapiro's SEC Expected To Step Up Enforcement." *Washington Post.* February 4, 2009.

Goldfarb, Zachary A., and Alec Klein. "The Bubble: How Homeowners' Missed Mortgage Payments Set Off Widespread Problems and Woke Up the Fed." *Washington Post.* June 16, 2008.

Goldstein, Debbie, and Stacy Strohauer Son. "Why Prepayment Penalties Are Abusive in Subprime Loans." Policy Paper No. 4, Center for Responsible Lending. April 2, 2003.

Gomez, Amalia Nieto, et al. "Preying on Neighborhoods: Subprime Mortgage Lending and Chicagoland Foreclosures." National Training and Information Center. September 21, 1999.

Gomstyn, Alice. "Citigroup Bailout May Assist More Homeowners." ABC News. November 25, 2008. http://abcnews.go.com/Business/Economy/story?id=6325319&page=1&page=1.

González-Páramo, José Manuel. "The Response of the Eurosystem to the Financial Crisis: Keynote Speech at the European Parliament's Special Committee on the Financial, Economic and Social Crisis." November 10, 2009. http://www.ecb.int/press/key/date/2009/html/sp091110.en.html.

Goodman, Peter S. "Subprime Brokers Resurface as Dubious Loan Fixers." *New York Times.* July 20, 2009. [2009a].

Goodman, Peter S. "Lucrative Fees May Deter Efforts to Alter Troubled Loans." *New York Times.* July 30, 2009. [2009b].

Goodman, Peter S. "U.S. Will Push Mortgage Firms to Reduce More Loan Payments." *New York Times.* November 29, 2009. [2009c].

Goodman, Peter S., and Gretchen Morgenson. "By Saying Yes, WaMu Built Empire on Shaky Loans." *New York Times.* December 28, 2008.

Goodman, Peter S., and Jack Healy. "Job Losses Push Safer Mortgages to Foreclosure." *New York Times.* May 25, 2009.

Gosselin, Kenneth R. "Sub-Prime Lender Cutting Back." *Hartford Courant.* January 3, 2007.

Government Accountability Office. "Analysis of the Failure of Superior Bank, FSB, Hinsdale, Illinois." Report No. GAO-02–419T. February 7, 2002.

Government Accountability Office. "Consumer Protection: Federal and State Agencies Face Challenges in Combating Predatory Lending." Report No. GAO-04–280. January 2004.

Government Accountability Office. "OCC Consumer Assistance: Process Is Similar to That of Other Regulators but Could Be Improved by Enhanced Outreach." Report No. GAO-06–293. February 2006.

Government Accountability Office. "Troubled Asset Relief Program: Status of Efforts to Address Transparency and Accountability Issues." Report No. GAO-09–296. January 2009. [2009a].

Government Accountability Office. "Troubled Asset Relief Program: Status of Government Assistance Provided to AIG." Report No. GAO-09–975. September 2009. [2009b].

Government Accountability Office. "Troubled Asset Relief Program: Continued Stewardship Needed as Treasury Develops Strategies for Monitoring and Divesting Financial Interests in Chrysler and GM." Report No. GAO-10–151. November 2009. [2009c].

Government Accounting Office. "Loan Performance and Negative Home Equity in the Nonprime Mortgage Market." Report No. GAO-10–146R. December 16, 2009 [2009d].

Gramlich, Edward M. Governor, Board of Governors of the Federal Reserve System. "Remarks at Cleveland State University." March 23, 2001.

Gramlich, Edward M. Governor, Board of Governors of the Federal Reserve System. "Remarks at the Housing Bureau for Seniors Conference." January 18, 2002.

Gramlich, Edward M. Governor, Board of Governors of the Federal Reserve System. "Remarks at the Texas Association of Bank Counsel 27th Annual Convention." October 9, 2003.

Gramlich, Edward M. Governor, Board of Governors of the Federal Reserve System. "Remarks at the Financial Services Roundtable Annual Housing Policy Meeting." May 21, 2004.

Gramlich, Edward M. "Boom and Busts, The Case of Subprime Mortgages." Speech before the "Housing, Housing Finance & Monetary Policy" symposium sponsored by the Federal Reserve Bank of Kansas City. August 31, 2007. www.kansascityfed.org/publicat/sympos/2007/pdf/2007.09.04.gramlich.pdf. [2007a].

Gramlich, Edward M. *Subprime Mortgages: America's Latest Boom and Bust.* Washington, D.C.: The Urban Institute Press, 2007. [2007b].

Greenberger, Michael. "Our Confusing Economy, Explained." *Fresh Air.* Interview by Terry Gross. National Public Radio. April 3, 2008. http://www.npr.org/templates/story/story.php?storyId=89338743.

Greenspan, Alan. Chairman of the Board of Governors of the Federal Reserve System. "Remarks at the 37th Annual Conference on Bank Structure and Competition of the Federal Reserve Bank of Chicago." May 10, 2001. [2001a].

Greenspan, Alan. Chairman of the Board of Governors of the Federal Reserve System. "Remarks at the Conference of State Banking Supervisors." May 18, 2001. [2001b].

Greenspan, Alan. Chairman of the Board of Governors of the Federal Reserve System. "Remarks at the Conference on Bank Structure and Competition." May 10, 2002.

Greenspan, Alan. Chairman of the Board of Governors of the Federal Reserve System. "Remarks at the Annual Convention of the Independent Community Bankers of America, Orlando, Florida." March 4, 2003. [2003a].

Greenspan, Alan. Chairman of the Board of Governors of the Federal Reserve System. "Remarks at a Symposium Sponsored by the Federal Reserve Bank of Kansas City." August 29, 2003. [2003b].

Greenspan, Alan. Chairman of the Board of Governors of the Federal Reserve System. "Remarks at the 33rd Annual Legislative Conference of the Congressional Black Caucus." September 26, 2003. [2003c].

Greenspan, Alan. Chairman of the Board of Governors of the Federal Reserve System. "Remarks before the HM Treasury Enterprise Conference." January 26, 2004. [2004a].

Greenspan, Alan. Chairman of the Board of Governors of the Federal Reserve System. "Remarks at the Greater Omaha Chamber of Commerce 2004 Annual Meeting." February 20, 2004. [2004b].

Greenspan, Alan. Chairman of the Board of Governors of the Federal Reserve System. "Remarks at the Credit Union National Association 2004 Governmental Affairs Conference." February 23, 2004. [2004c].

Greenspan, Alan. Chairman of the Board of Governors of the Federal Reserve System. "Remarks at the Conference on Bank Structure and Competition." May 6, 2004. [2004d].

Greenspan, Alan. Chairman of the Board of Governors of the Federal Reserve System. "Remarks at the American Bankers Association Annual Convention." October 5, 2004. [2004e].

Greenspan, Alan. Chairman of the Board of Governors of the Federal Reserve System. "Remarks at America's Community Bankers Annual Convention." October 19, 2004. [2004f].

Greenspan, Alan. Chairman of the Board of Governors of the Federal Reserve System. "Remarks at the Federal Reserve System's Fourth Annual Community Affairs Research Conference." April 8, 2005. [2005a].

Greenspan, Alan. Chairman of the Board of Governors of the Federal Reserve System. "Risk Transfer and Financial Stability." Remarks to the Federal Reserve Bank of Chicago's Forty-First Annual Conference on Bank Structure. May 5, 2005. [2005b].

Greenspan, Alan. Chairman of the Board of Governors of the Federal Reserve System. "Remarks To the National Association for Business Economics Annual Meeting, Chicago, Illinois." September 27, 2005. [2005c].

Greenspan, Alan. *The Age of Turbulence: Adventures in a New World.* New York: The Penguin Press, 2007.

Gregory, Michael. "The Predatory Lending Fracas: Wall Street Comes under Scrutiny in the Subprime Market as Liquidity Suffers and Regulation Looms." *Investment Dealers Digest.* June 26, 2000.

Grim, Ryan. "Banks 'Frankly Own The Place.'" The Huffington Post. April 29, 2009. http://www.huffingtonpost.com/2009/04/29/dick-durbin-banks-frankly_n_193010. html.

Grim, Ryan. "Consumer Groups Rip Chris Dodd Over Financial Protection Agency Compromise." The Huffington Post. February 28, 2010. http://www.huffingtonpost. com/2010/02/28/consumer-groups-rip-chris_n_479983.html.

Grollmus, Denise. "All the President's Men: Meet the Biggest Predatory Lender in Cleveland—America's New Ambassador to the Netherlands." *Cleveland Scene.* October 19, 2005.

Group of Thirty. "Financial Reform: A Framework for Financial Stability." January 15, 2009. http://www.group30.0rg/pubs/reformreport.pdf.

Grow, Brian. "What's Holding Back Mortgage Modification?" *BusinessWeek.* February 12, 2009.

Grow, Brian, Keith Epstein, and Robert Berner. "How Banks are Worsening the Foreclosure Crisis." *BusinessWeek.* February 12, 2009.

Grynbaum, Michael M. "Ex-Fed Chairman Chides Current One." *New York Times.* April 9, 2008.

Guerrera, Francesco, and Ben White. "US groups tap capital markets for over Dollars 28bn." *Financial Times.* April 23, 2008.

Guerrera, Francesco, and Henny Sender. "JPMorgan to Buy Bear Stearns for $236m." *Financial Times.* March 16, 2008. http://www.ft.com/cms/s/0/e2206ed2-f380–11dc-b6bc-0000779fd2ac.html.

Guerrera, Francesco, Joanna Chung, and Aline van Duyn. "Citi and Merrill in $20bn ARS Agreements." *Financial Times.* August 7, 2008. http://www.ft.com/cms/s/0/a97b97ac-64a8–11dd-af61–0000779fd18c,dwp_uuid=4da69efc-1b8f-11dd-9e58–0000779fd2ac.html.

Guerrera, Francesco, and Nicole Bullock. "WaMu Reveals $10bn Capital Buffer." *Financial Times.* July 26, 2008. http://www.ft.com/cms/s/0/47d815de-5a9e-11dd-bf96–000077b07658.html.

Gunther, Marc. "The Power of Paulson." *Fortune.* September 16, 2008. http:// money.cnn.com/2008/09/13/news/newsmakers/gunther_paulson.fortune/?postversi on=2008091609.

Guttentag, Jack. *The Mortgage Encyclopedia.* New York: McGraw-Hill, 2004.

Hagerty, James R. "Fannie, Freddie Executives Knew of Risks." *Wall Street Journal.* December 10, 2008.

Hagerty, James R. "Banks Bite Bullet on Loans." *Wall Street Journal.* October 1, 2009. [2009a].

Hagerty, James R. "Fewer Catching Up On Lapsed Mortgages." *Wall Street Journal.* August 25, 2009. [2009b].

Hagerty, James R., and Jonathan Karp. "IndyMac Begins Dismantling Business As It Struggles to Keep Investors' Faith." *Wall Street Journal.* July 9, 2008.

Hagerty, James R., and Ruth Simon. "Option-ARMs Emerge As Home-Loan Worry." *Wall Street Journal.* April 18, 2007. [2007a].

Hagerty, James R., and Ruth Simon. "Mortgage Pain Hits Prudent Borrowers." *Wall Street Journal.* December 11, 2007. [2007b].

Hagerty, James R., and Ruth Simon. "Rates Fall, but Refinancings are Limited." *Wall Street Journal.* January 15, 2009.

Hansell, Saul. "How Wall Street Lied to Its Computers." *New York Times.* September 18, 2008.

Haughney, Christine. "Collateral Foreclosure Damage for Condo Owners." *New York Times.* May 15, 2008.

Haughwout, Andrew, Richard Peach, and Joseph Tracy. "Juvenile Delinquent Mortgages: Bad Credit or Bad Economy." Federal Reserve Bank of New York Staff Report. August 2008.

Haurin, Donald R., and Stuart S. Rosenthal. "The Growth Earnings of Low Income Households and the Sensitivity of Their Homeownership Choices to Economic and Socio-demographic Shocks." Working paper, U.S. Department of Housing and Urban Development. April 2005.

Haviv, Julie, and Emily Kaiser. "Web Lenders Woo Subprime Borrowers Despite Crisis." *Reuters.* April 22, 2007.

Hawke, John D., Jr. Comptroller of the Currency. "Remarks before the Federalist Society." July 24, 2003. [2003a].

Hawke, John D., Jr. Comptroller of the Currency. "Remarks before the American Bankers Association." September 22, 2003. [2003b].

Hawke, John D., Jr. Comptroller of the Currency. "Remarks before the American Bankers Association." October 4, 2004.

Heath, Thomas. "Freddie Mac, a Buffer against Crisis, Posts $2 Billion Loss." *Washington Post.* November 21, 2007.

Heisel, William. "Downey, Once Solid, Now at Risk." *Los Angeles Times.* July 24, 2008.

Heisel, William, and Tiffany Hsu. "Future Cloudy for Downey Savings." *Los Angeles Times.* October 23, 2008.

Heller, Michele. "DC Speaks: Seidman's OTS Hails Cavalry in Predator Fight." *American Banker.* July 14, 2000.

Heller, Michele. "LaFalce Rips OTS Exam Plan As 'a Complete Abrogation.'" *American Banker.* April 4, 2002.

Heller, Michele, and Rob Garver. "Gramm Takes Stand Against Predator Bills." *American Banker.* August 24, 2000.

Henriques, Diana B., and Lowell Bergman. "Mortgaged Lives: A Special Report; Profiting From Fine Print With Wall Street's Help." *New York Times.* March 15, 2000.

Hevesi, Dennis. "A Wider Loan Pool Draws More Sharks." *New York Times.* March 24, 2002.

Heyde, Frank, and Ulrike Neyer. "Credit Default Swaps and the Stability of the Banking Sector." Working paper. September 2008.

Hill, Claire A. "Regulating the Rating Agencies." *Washington University Law Quarterly* 82, no. 1 (2004): 43–94.

Hilsenrath, Jon, Damian Paletta, and Aaron Lucchetti. "Goldman, Morgan Scrap Wall Street Model, Become Banks in Bid to Ride Out Crisis—End of Traditional Investment Banking, as Storied Firms Face Closer Supervision and Stringent New Capital Requirements." *Wall Street Journal.* September 22, 2008.

Hilzenrath, David S. "Fannie's Perilous Pursuit of Subprime Loans." *Washington Post*. August 19, 2008.

Hoak, Amy. "Report: 20% of Home Mortgages were Underwater in December." *Wall Street Journal*. March 4, 2009.

Hogberg, David. "Ginnie Mae Grows as Freddie, Fannie Fade." *Investor's Business Daily*. January 14, 2009.

Holzer, Jessica. "Dispute with Banks Continues to Dog U.S. Mortgage Relief Program." *Wall Street Journal*. September 23, 2009. [2009a].

Holzer, Jessica. "Talks Stall on Mortgage Program." *Wall Street Journal*. September 23, 2009. [2009b].

HOPE NOW. "HOPE NOW: Industry Tops ONE MILLION Loan Workouts Since July '07." March 3, 2008. http://www.fsround.org/hope_now/pdfs/17–28FebruaryRelease.pdf.

Hopkins, Cheyenne. "Questions on Future of OTS." *American Banker*. January 14, 2008. [2008a].

Hopkins, Cheyenne. "When Mods Fail, What Next? Regulators Split on the Implications of Redefaults." *American Banker*. December 9, 2008. [2008b].

Hopkins, Cheyenne. "Untested Stress Tools At Center of New Debate." *American Banker*. February 17, 2009.

House of Representatives, Dodd-Frank Wall Street Reform and Consumer Protection Act: Conference Report to Accompany H.R. 4173. Report 111–517. June 29, 2010.

House of Representatives, Committee on Oversight and Government Reform. Hearing on the Financial Crisis and the Role of Federal Regulators. October 23, 2008. http://oversight.house.gov/images/stories/documents/20081024163819.pdf.

Hovakimian, Armen, Edward J. Kane, and Luc Laeven. How Country and Safety-Net Characteristics Affect Bank Risk-Shifting. Working paper. October 11, 2002.

Howley, Kathleen M. "Rating Subprime Investment Grade Made 'Joke' of Credit Experts." *Bloomberg*. December 20, 2007. http://www.bloomberg.com/apps/news?pid=newsarchive&sid=ajdL7eUHeUro.

HSBC Holdings plc. "2008 HSBC Holdings plc Annual Report and Accounts." March 2, 2009. http://www.hsbc.com/1/PA_1_1_S5/content/assets/investor_relations/hsbc2008ara0.pdf.

Hu, Henry T. C. "Misunderstood Derivatives: The Causes of Informational Failure and the Promise of Regulatory Incrementalism." *Yale Law Journal* 102 (1993): 1457–1513.

Hu, Joseph. *Basics of Mortgage-Backed Securities*. 2d ed. New Hope, Pennsylvania: Frank J. Fabozzi Associates, 2001.

Hudson, Michael. "Banking on Misery: Citigroup, Wall Street, and the Fleecing of the South." *Southern Exposure* 31, no. 2 (Summer 2003): 8.

Hudson, Michael. "How Wall Street Stoked the Mortgage Meltdown." *Wall Street Journal*. June 27, 2007.

Immergluck, Dan. "From the Subprime to the Exotic: Excessive Mortgage Market Risk and Foreclosures." *Journal of the American Planning Association* 74, no. 1 (Winter 2008): 59–76.

Insurance Information Institute. "The Financial Services Fact Book 2009." Report, The Financial Services Roundtable. December 18, 2008.

Internal Revenue Service. Revenue Procedure 2007-72. December 6, 2007.

International Financial Services London. "Securitisation 2009." April 2009. http://www.ifsl.org.uk/output/ReportItem.aspx?NewsID=25.

International Monetary Fund. "Global Financial Stability Report: Navigating the Financial Challenges Ahead." October 2009. http://www.imf.org/external/pubs/ft/gfsr/2009/02/pdf/text.pdf.

International Swaps and Derivatives Association, Inc. "ISDA Market Survey." 2007. http://www.isda.org/statistics/pdf/ISDA-Market-Survey-annual-data.pdf.

Investment Company Institute. Letter to Ms. Elizabeth M. Murphy, Secretary, U.S. Securities and Exchange Commission, on the Re-Proposed Rules for Nationally Recognized Statistical Ratings Organizations (File No. S7–04–09). March 26, 2009. http://www.ici.org/pdf/23359.pdf.

Ip, Greg. "Did Greenspan Add to Subprime Woes?" *Wall Street Journal.* June 9, 2007.

Irwin, Neil. "NBER: U.S. In Recession That Began Last December." *Washington Post.* December 1, 2008.

Ishmael, Stacy-Marie, Aline van Duyn, and Saskia Scholtes. "Bond Insurers Spark New Fears over Credit Crisis." *Financial Times.* January 18, 2008.

Ivry, Bob, and Linda Shen. "Washington Mutual Hobbled By Increasing Defaults on Options ARMs." *Bloomberg.* September 15, 2008. http://www.bloomberg.com/apps/ne ws?pid=20601087&sid=aNSwdt57nTBI.

Jackson, Howell E., and Jeremy Berry. "Kickbacks or Compensation: The Case of Yield Spread Premiums." Working paper. January 8, 2002.

Jackson, Paul. "Fremont's Subprime Platform Collapses; FDIC Steps In." *HousingWire Magazine.* March 2, 2007. http://www.housingwire.com/2007/03/02/fremont-collapses-will-exit-subprime-lending. [2007a].

Jackson, Paul. "National City Takes $200 Million Charge, Sees Fourth Quarter Earnings Pressure." *HousingWire Magazine.* December 17, 2007. http://www.housingwire.com/2007/12/17/national-city-takes-200-million-charge-sees-fourth-quarter-earnings-pressure. [2007b].

Jickling, Mark. "Averting Financial Crises." Congressional Research Service Report for Congress. March 21, 2008.

Johnson, Simon. "Systemic Risk: Are Some Institutions Too Big to Fail and If So, What Should We Do About It?" Testimony Submitted to the House Committee on Financial Services, Hearing on July 21, 2009.

"Judge Clears Deal for Enron Unit." *Washington Post.* January 19, 2002.

Kamalakaran, Ajay, and Mike Miller. "Fannie, Freddie Insolvent, Poole tells Bloomberg." Reuters. July 10, 2008. http://www.reuters.com/article/idUSBNG6370020080710.

Kane, Mary. "The Reach of Redlining." *Washington Independent.* August 21, 2008.

Kane, Mary. "Bank-Owned Homes Surge, Communities Stung." *Washington Independent.* March 3, 2009. [2009a].

Kane, Mary. "Loan Servicers Work the Fine Print in Obama Foreclosure Plan." *Washington Independent.* July 30, 2009. [2009b].

Kanef, Michael. Testimony before the House Subcommittee on Capital Markets, Insurance, and Government Sponsored Enterprises. September 27, 2007.

Kaper, Stacy, and Barbara A. Rehm. "Wachovia-Golden West: Sale Highlights an Agency's Challenge." *American Banker.* May 9, 2006.

Karmel, Roberta S. "The Future of the Securities and Exchange Commission as a Market Regulator." Working paper. 2009.

Karmin, Craig. "Pension Bills to Surge Nationwide." *Wall Street Journal.* March 16, 2009.

Karnitschig, Matthew, Deborah Solomon, Liam Pleven, and Jon E. Hilsenrath. "U.S. to Take Over AIG in $85 Billion Bailout; Central Banks Inject Cash as Credit Dries Up." *Wall Street Journal.* September 16, 2008.

Karp, Jonathan. "How the Subprime Mess Hit Poor Immigrant Groups." *Wall Street Journal.* December 6, 2007.

Kaufman, Henry. "Who's Watching the Big Banks?" *Wall Street Journal.* November 13, 2007.

Kelly, Kate, Amir Efrati, and Ruth Simon. "State Subprime Probe Takes a New Tack." *Wall Street Journal.* January 31, 2008.

Kennedy, Simon. "European Lenders Get Bailouts as U.S. Crisis Spreads—Update 3." *Bloomberg.* September 29, 2008. http://www.bloomberg.com/apps/news?pid=newsarch ive&sid=aX5CWTbg5Q2g.

Keoun, Brad. "Citi Agrees to Acquire SIV Assets for $17.4 Billion." *Bloomberg.* November 19, 2008. http://www.bloomberg.com/apps/news?sid=a4yl_7w1N9co&pid=20601087.

Keys, Benjamin J., Tanmoy K. Mukherjee, Amit Seru, and Vikrant Vig. "Did Securitization Lead to Lax Screening? Evidence from Subprime Loans." EFA 2008 Athens Meetings Paper. December 25, 2008.

Kimball-Stanley, Arthur. "Insurance and Credit Default Swaps: Should Like Things Be Treated Alike?" *Connecticut Insurance Law Journal* 15, no. 1 (2008–2009): 241–266.

Kirkpatrick, David D. "In a Message to Democrats, Wall St. Sends Cash to G.O.P." *New York Times.* February 8, 2010.

Krimminger, Michael. "Controlling Moral Hazard in Bank Resolutions: Comparative Policies & Considerations in System Design." Working paper. 2008.

Kristof, Kathy M., and Andrea Chang. "Federal regulators seize crippled IndyMac Bank." *Los Angeles Times.* July 12, 2008.

Kroszner, Randall S. Governor, Board of Governors of the Federal Reserve System. "Speech at the George Washington University School of Business, Financial Services Research Program Policy Forum." May 23, 2007.

Krueger, Alan B. "Statement for the Treasury Borrowing Advisory Committee of the Securities Industry and Financial Markets Association." U.S. Department of the Treasury press release TG-342. November 2, 2009.

Krugman, Paul. "The Fear Economy." *New York Times.* September 30, 2001.

Krugman, Paul. "The Dogbert Theory of the Debt." *New York Times.* November 30, 2009.

Krugman, Paul. "Fiscal Scare Tactics." *New York Times.* February 5, 2010.

Kulikowski, Laurie. "Banks' Foreclosure Pain Worsens with U.S. Job Losses." TheStreet. com. August 21, 2009. http://www.thestreet.com/story/10586042/banks-foreclosure-pain-worsens-with-us-job-losses.html.

Labaton, Stephen. "Agency's '04 Rule Let Banks Pile Up New Debt, and Risk." *New York Times.* October 3, 2008. [2008a].

Labaton, Stephen. "S.E.C. Knew Him as Foe and Friend." *New York Times.* December 18, 2008. [2008b].

Labaton, Stephen. "Unlikely Player Pulled into Madoff Swirl." *New York Times.* December 19, 2008. [2008c].

Labaton, Stephen. "S.E.C. Chief Pursues Reversal of Years of Lax Enforcement." *New York Times.* February 23, 2009. [2009a].

Labaton, Stephen. "Banks to Prepay Assessments to Rescue F.D.I.C." *New York Times.* September 29, 2009. [2009b].

Labaton, Stephen, and Steven R. Weisman. "U.S. Weighs Takeover of Two Mortgage Giants." *New York Times.* July 11, 2008.

Laby, Arthur B. "Reforming the Regulation of Broker-Dealers and Investment Advisors." Working paper. October 19, 2009.

Lacko, James M., and Janis K. Pappalardo. "The Effect of Mortgage Broker Compensation on Consumers and Competition: A Controlled Experiment." Report, Federal Trade Commission. 2004.

Laing, Jonathan R. "Aftershock of US Sub-Prime Debacle Will Be Felt on a Global Scale." *The Business.* July 14, 2007.

Landler, Mark. "U.S. Investing $250 Billion to Bolster Banks; Dow Surges 936 Points." *New York Times.* October 14, 2008.

Landler, Mark, and Eric Dash. "Drama Behind a $250 Billion Banking Deal." *New York Times.* October 14, 2008.

Lanman, Scott. "Fed Balance Sheet Jumps to $2.1 Trillion on Mortgages—Update 1." *Bloomberg.* March 19, 2009. http://www.bloomberg.com/apps/news?pid=20601068&sid=a2_HA_YKN7_k&refer=economy.

Lawder, David. "U.S. Agencies Pledge Crackdown on Mortgage Fraud." Reuters. September 17, 2009. http://www.reuters.com/article/GCA-Housing/idUSTRE58G3LM20090917.

Lee, C.K. Letter from C.K. Lee, Managing Director, Complex & International Organizations, OTS, to American International Group, Inc. March 10, 2008.

Lehman Brothers. Letter to the Office of Thrift Supervision Regarding the Acquisition of Delaware Savings Bank. June 30, 1999.

Leising, Matthew. "Fed Refuses Banks Request to Limit Credit-Default Swap Clearing." *Bloomberg.* December 12, 2008. http://www.bloomberg.com/apps/news?pid=newsarchive&sid=aaEvfvqK7zWs.

Leland, John. "Swindlers Find Growing Market in Foreclosures." *New York Times.* January 15, 2009.

Leonhardt, David, and Vikas Bajaj. "Drop Foreseen in Median Price of U.S. Homes." *New York Times.* August 26, 2007.

Leonnig, Carol D. "How HUD Mortgage Policy Fed the Crisis." *Washington Post.* June 10, 2008.

Levine, Jeffrey M. "The Vertical-Integration Strategy." *Mortgage Banking* 67, no. 5 (February 2007): 58–65.

Levitan, Adam. "Hydraulic Regulation: Regulating Credit Markets Upstream." *Yale Journal on Regulation* 26, no. 2 (July 2009): 143–227.

Levitz, Jennifer. "Fremont General Settles Deceptive-Loans Case." *Wall Street Journal.* June 10, 2009.

Levy, Ari. "Ranieri Becomes Victim of Crisis as Franklin Seized." *Bloomberg.* November 8, 2008. http://www.bloomberg.com/apps/news?sid=aX4BbAxqP7gc&pid=20601109.

Lewis, Al. "Not Being Aware Is a Bear." *Denver Post.* March 21, 2008.

Lewis, Michael, and David Einhorn. "The End of the Financial World as We Know It." *New York Times.* January 3, 2009.

Lichtblau, Eric. "Ex-Regulators get set to Lobby on New Financial Rules." *New York Times.* July 27, 2010.

Linder, Craig. "Though It's Sound for Now, Clouds Hanging Over OTS." *American Banker.* October 1, 2003.

Lipton, Eric, and Stephen Labaton. "Deregulator Looks Back, Unswayed." *New York Times.* November 17, 2008.

Livingston, Sandra. "Bank 'Walkaways' From Foreclosed Homes Are a Growing, Troubling Trend." *Plain Dealer.* July 18, 2009.

Lord, Rich. "Penalizing Homeowners." *Pittsburgh City Paper.* January 6, 2005.

Lovell, Phillip, and Laura Isaacs. "The Impact of the Mortgage Crisis on Children and Their Education." Report, First Focus. April 2008.

Lowenstein, Roger. "Triple-A Failure." *New York Times.* April 27, 2008.

Lubove, Seth. "Bust and Boom in the Subprime Market Wall Street Overhyped It a Few Years Ago and Underrates It Now: The Business of Lending to Iffy Consumers." *Forbes.* December 27, 1999.

Lucchetti, Aaron. "Rating Game: As Housing Boomed, Moody's Opened Up." *Wall Street Journal.* April 11, 2008. [2008a].

Lucchetti, Aaron. "S&P Email: 'We Should Not be Rating It.'" *Wall Street Journal.* August 2, 2008. [2008b].

Lucchetti, Aaron, David Enrich, and Joann S. Lublin. "Fed Hits Banks With Sweeping Pay Limits." *Wall Street Journal.* October 23, 2009.

Lucchetti, Aaron, and Serena Ng. "How Rating Firms' Calls Fueled Subprime Mess." *Wall Street Journal.* August 15, 2007.

Lucchetti, Aaron, and Serena Ng. "S&P Ramps Up Mortgage Downgrades." *Wall Street Journal.* January 31, 2008.

Lueck, Sarah. "Mortgage Market Turmoil: Schumer Deflects Blame to IndyMac, Regulator." *Wall Street Journal.* July 14, 2008.

Luhby, Tami. "FDIC's Bair Pushes Aggressive Mortgage Plan." CNNMoney.com. November 14, 2008. http://money.cnn.com/2008/11/14/news/economy/fdic_bair/index.htm. [2008a].

Luhby, Tami. "Washington Mutual Tries to Soothe Anxiety." CNNMoney.com. September 12, 2008. http://money.cnn.com/2008/09/11/news/companies/wamu_3Q_update/index.htm. [2008b].

Luo, Michael, and Megan Thee-Brenan. "Poll Reveals Trauma of Joblessness in U.S." *Wall Street Journal.* December 15, 2009.

Macro International. "Summary of Findings: Consumer Testing of Mortgage Broker Disclosures." July 10, 2008. http://www.federalreserve.gov/newsevents/press/bcreg/20080714regzconstest.pdf.

Manning, Jeff. "Chase mortgage memo pushes 'Beats & Tricks.'" *Oregonian.* March 27, 2008.

Maremont, Mark. "FDIC Faces Mortgage Mess after Running Failed Bank—Subprime Lender Made Problem Loans on Regulators' Watch." *Wall Street Journal.* July 21, 2008.

Margolies, Dan. "Kansas City Presses Lenders as Wave of Foreclosed Homes Adds to Vacant Housing Blight." *Kansas City Star.* November 21, 2008.

Markon, Jerry. "$33 Million Fraud." *Washington Post.* November 14, 2008.

Markopolos, Harry. "Assessing the Madoff Ponzi Scheme and Regulatory Failures." Testimony before the U.S. House of Representatives Committee on Financial Services. February 4, 2009.

Marsh, Bill. "A Tally of Federal Rescues." *New York Times.* September 28, 2008.

Mason, Joseph R. "Turmoil in U.S. Credit Markets: Examining the Securities Underwriting Practices at Investment Banks." Testimony before the U.S. Senate Committee on Banking, Housing, and Urban Affairs. June 10, 2008.

Mason, Joseph R., and Josh Rosner. "How Resilient Are Mortgage Backed Securities to Collateralized Debt Obligation Market Disruptions?" Working paper. February 15, 2007. [2007a].

Mason, Joseph R., and Josh Rosner. "Where Did the Risk Go? How Misapplied Bond Ratings Cause Mortgage Backed Securities and Collateralized Debt Obligation Market Disruptions." Working paper. May 14, 2007. [2007b].

Mayer, Christopher, and Karen Pence. "Subprime Mortgages: What, Where, and Whom?" Working Paper No. 14083, National Bureau of Economic Research. June 2008.

Maynard, Nick, Timothy Flacke, and Christina Kasica. "Prize-Linked Savings: The Save to Win Project." Report, Doorways to Dreams Fund. September 11, 2009. http://www.d2dfund.org/http%3A/%252Fd2dfund.org/savetowinreport.

*Mayor and City Council of Baltimore v. Wells Fargo Bank, N.A.,* No. 1:08-cv-00062-BEL (D. Md.). Declaration of Elizabeth M. Jacobson. June 1, 2009. [2009a].

*Mayor and City Council of Baltimore v. Wells Fargo Bank, N.A.,* No. 1:08-cv-00062-BEL (D. Md.). Declaration of Tony Paschal. April 9, 2009. [2009b].

*Mayor of the City of New York v. Council of the City of New York,* 4 Misc. 3d 151 (N.Y. Sup. Ct. 2004).

McCoy, Patricia A. *Banking Law Manual: Federal Regulation of Financial Holding Companies, Banks and Thrifts.* 2d ed. Newark: Lexis, 2000 & cumulative supplements.

McCoy, Patricia A. "A Behavioral Analysis of Predatory Lending." *Akron Law Review* 38, no. 4 (2004–2005): 725–739. http://www.uakron.edu/law/lawreview/v38/docs/McCoy384.pdf.

McCoy, Patricia A. "The Home Mortgage Disclosure Act: A Synopsis and Recent Legislative History." *Journal of Real Estate Research* 29, no. 4 (2007): 381–397. http://aux.zicklin.baruch.cuny.edu/jrer/papers/pdf/past/v0129n04/03.381_398.pdf. [2007a].

McCoy, Patricia A. "Rethinking Disclosure in a World of Risk-Based Pricing." *Harvard Journal on Legislation* 44 (Winter 2007): 123–166. [2007b].

McCoy, Patricia A. "The Moral Hazard Implications of Deposit Insurance: Theory and Practice." In Vol. 5, *Current Developments in Financial and Monetary Law,* 417–441. Washington, D.C.: International Monetary Fund, 2008.

McCoy, Patricia A., Andrey D. Pavlov, and Susan Wachter. "Systemic Risk Through Securitization: The Result of Deregulation and Regulatory Failure." *Connecticut Law Review* 41, no. 4 (2009): 1327–1375.

McCoy, Patricia A., and Elizabeth Renuart. "The Legal Infrastructure of Subprime and Nontraditional Mortgage Lending." In *Borrowing to Live: Consumer and Mortgage Credit Revisited,* ed. Nicolas P. Retsinas and Eric S. Belsky, 110–137. Washington, D.C.: Brookings Institution Press, 2008.

McCracken, Jeffrey, and Gregory Zuckerman. "Surge in Auto-Loan Delinquencies Is Latest Trouble for the Economy." *Wall Street Journal.* December 6, 2007.

McDaniel, Raymond. "Credit Policy Issues at Moody.doc." October 21, 2007. http://oversight.house.gov/images/stories/Hearings/Committee_on_Oversight/Confidential_Presentation_to_Moodys_Board_of_Directors_October_2007.pdf.

McGreer, Bonnie. "Reich to Resign as OTS Director." *American Banker.* November 11, 2008.

McKay, Betsy, and Damian Paletta. "Fremont Sells Unit, Easing Pressure." *Wall Street Journal.* April 15, 2008.

Meinero, Mark M., and Ben Rooney. "Gas Price Record Reaches $4 a Gallon." *CNNMoney.com.* June 8, 2008. http://money.cnn.com/2008/06/08/news/economy/gas_prices/index.htm?cnn=yes.

Mendales, Richard E. "Collateralized Explosive Devices: Why Securities Regulation Failed to Prevent the CDO Meltdown, and How to Fix It." Working paper. 2009.

Merle, Renae. "Foreclosure Relief Is Getting Lost in Fine Print of Loans." *Washington Post.* November 13, 2008.

Merle, Renae. "Just a Band-Aid on the Foreclosure Problem?" *Washington Post.* February 3, 2009. [2009a].

Merle, Renae. "Aid to Borrowers not Preventing Rising Delinquency." *Washington Post.* April 4, 2009. [2009b].

Merle, Renae. "Face-Lift for Foreclosure Prevention." *Washington Post.* May 26, 2009. [2009c].

Merle, Renae. "Not Paying the Mortgage, Yet Stuck With the Keys: Foreclosure Backlog Imperils Recovery." *Washington Post.* June 24, 2009. [2009d].

Merle, Renae. "Racing the Clock to Avoid Foreclosures." *Washington Post.* October 12, 2009. [2009e].

Merriam-Webster. "Securitization." In *Merriam-Webster's Online Dictionary*. 2010. http://www.merriam-webster.com/dictionary/securitization.

"MetLife Buys Residential Mortgage Assets." TheStreet.com. June 4, 2008. http://www.thestreet.com/s/metlife-buys-residential-mortgage-assets/newsanalysis/financial-services/10419700.html?puc=_tscrss. January 24, 2010.

Mian, Atif, and Amir Sufi. "The Consequences of Mortgage Credit Expansion: Evidence from the 2007 Mortgage Default Crisis." Working paper. October 2008.

Mildenberg, David, and Karen Freifeld. "Countrywide's Underwriters Sued for Fraud by New York—Update 2." *Bloomberg*. January 25, 2008. http://www.bloomberg.com/apps/news?pid=20601208&sid=axRMZutUG2BQ&refer=finance.

Miller, Jay. "Foreclosure Class Action Could Spark Copycats." *Crain's Business Journal*. February 18, 2008.

Millman, Joel. "Sawdust Shock: A Shortage Looms as the Economy Slows." *Wall Street Journal*. March 3, 2008.

Miroff, Nick. "Foreclosure Epidemic Infecting Rental Market." *Washington Post*. December 9, 2008.

Mishel, Lawrence, and Jared Bernstein. "Economy's Gains Fail to Reach Most Workers' Paychecks." Economic Policy Institute. August 30, 2007. http://www.epi.org/publications/entry/bp195/.

Mishkin, Frederic S. Governor, Board of Governors of the Federal Reserve System. "Speech at the Forecaster's Club of New York." January 17, 2007. [2007a].

Mishkin, Frederic S. Governor, Board of Governors of the Federal Reserve System. "Speech at the Levy Economics Institute of Bard College." April 20, 2007. [2007b].

Mollenkamp, Carrick. "Citigroup cuts credit to some in U.K." *Wall Street Journal*. February 4, 2008.

Mollenkamp, Carrick. "Subprime Resurfaces as Housing-Market Woe." *Wall Street Journal*. July 9, 2009.

Moody's Investors Service. Letter to Ms. Elizabeth M. Murphy, Secretary, Securities and Exchange Commission, Regarding Re-proposed Rules for Nationally Recognized Statistical Rating Organizations, Release No. 34–59343; File No. S7–04–09. March 28, 2009. http://www.sec.gov/comments/s7–04–09/s70409–20.pdf.

Moore, Heidi N. "Fannie and Freddie: Another Bailout That Leaves Shareholders Starving." *Wall Street Journal*. July 14, 2008. [2008a].

Moore, Heidi N. "Bailout Arbitrage: The Sale of National City." *Wall Street Journal*. November 20, 2008. [2008b].

Morgan Stanley ABS Capital I, Inc. Trust 2007-HE7. "Prospectus Supplement and Prospectus Filed September 28, 2007." September 28, 2007. http://www.sec.gov/Archives/edgar/data/1030442/000091412107002180/p10401463–424b5.txt.

Morgenson, Gretchen. "Home Loans: A Nightmare Grows Darker." *New York Times*. April 8, 2007. [2007a].

Morgenson, Gretchen. "Inside the Countrywide Lending Spree." *New York Times*. August 26, 2007. [2007b].

Morgenson, Gretchen. "Borrowers Face Dubious Charges in Foreclosures." *New York Times*. November 6, 2007. [2007c].

Morgenson, Gretchen. "Creative Loans, Creative Compensation." *New York Times*. November 18, 2007. [2007d].

Morgenson, Gretchen. "Given a Shovel, Americans Dig Deeper Into Debt." *New York Times*. July 20, 2008. [2008a].

Morgenson, Gretchen. "Behind Biggest Insurer's Crisis, a Blind Eye to a Web of Risk." *New York Times.* September 28, 2008. [2008b].

Morgenson, Gretchen. "Countrywide to Set Aside $8.4 Billion in Loan Aid." *New York Times.* October 6, 2008. [2008c].

Morgenson, Gretchen. "Was There A Loan It Didn't Like?" *New York Times.* November 2, 2008. [2008d].

Morgenson, Gretchen. "How the Thundering Herd Faltered and Fell." *New York Times.* November 9, 2008. [2008e].

Morgenson, Gretchen. "That Money Isn't Leaving the Vault." *New York Times.* November 21, 2008. [2008f].

Morgenson, Gretchen. "Debt Watchdogs: Tamed or Caught Napping?" *New York Times.* December 7, 2008. [2008g].

Morgenson, Gretchen. "Top Enforcer at the S.E.C. Steps Down." *New York Times.* February 10, 2009. [2009a].

Morgenson, Gretchen. "Why Treasury Needs a Plan B for Mortgages." *New York Times.* December 6, 2009. [2009b].

Morgenson, Gretchen, and Charles Duhigg. "Mortgage Giant Overstates the Size of Its Capital Base." *New York Times.* September 6, 2008.

Morgenson, Gretchen, and Geraldine Fabricant. "Countrywide's Chief Salesman and Defender." *New York Times.* November 11, 2007.

Morgenson, Gretchen, and Jenny Anderson. "New Part of Credit Market Hit by Home-Loan Jitters." *New York Times.* August 15, 2007.

Mortgage Bankers Association. "MBA National Delinquency Survey." 2005–2010. http://www.mortgagebankers.org.

Morton, David. "Predatory Lenders: How They Can Steal Your House—Legally." *Cleveland Free Times.* June 28, 2000.

Muir, Jennifer, and John Gittelsohn. "Downey bank customers stay calm despite takeover." *Orange County Register.* November 22, 2008.

Murawski, Carsten. "The Impact of Clearing on the Credit Risk of a Derivatives Portfolio." Working paper. October 2002.

Murray, Brendan. "Paulson Backs Fannie, Freddie in Their 'Current Form'—Update 8." *Bloomberg.* July 11, 2008. http://www.bloomberg.com/apps/news?pid=20601103&refer=us&sid=aZAHrlJZ1snM.

Murray, Teresa Dixon. "National City will retain control after $7 billion infusion." *Plain Dealer.* April 21, 2008. [2008a].

Murray, Teresa Dixon. "National City's Fall: A Post-Mortem." *Plain Dealer.* October 27, 2008. [2008b].

Murray, Teresa Dixon. "Problem Mortgage Rate Loan Worsens in Ohio, but Not as Much as in Some Other States." *Plain Dealer.* November 19, 2009.

Naughton, Keith. "Ford May Add $4 Billion to Pensions, Spurring Aid Bid—Update 4." *Bloomberg.* February 6, 2009. http://www.bloomberg.com/apps/news?pid=20601087&sid=ayUQrdXHM_kk.

*In Re New Century TRS Holdings, Inc., et al.*, No. 07–10416 KJC (Bkrtcy. D. Del.). Final Report of Michael J. Missal, Bankruptcy Court Examiner. February 29, 2008.

New York Insurance Department. *Circular Letter No. 19.* September 22, 2008. [2008a].

New York Insurance Department. *First Supplement to Circular Letter No. 19.* November 20, 2008. [2008b].

Ng, Serena, and Carrick Mollenkamp. "Goldman Fueled AIG Gambles." *Wall Street Journal.* December 12, 2009.

Ng, Serena, Carrick Mollenkamp, and Scott Patterson. "A 'Subprime' Gauge, in Many Ways?" *Wall Street Journal.* December 12, 2007.

Ng, Serena, and Susanne Craig. "How Lehman Opened the Fed's Spigot—Deal Takes Advantage of New Lending Facility." *Wall Street Journal.* April 11, 2008.

Nocera, Joe. "Risk Mismanagement." *New York Times.* January 4, 2009. [2009a].

Nocera, Joe. "From Treasury to Banks, an Ultimatum on Mortgage Relief." *New York Times.* July 11, 2009. [2009b].

Norris, Floyd. "As Bank Profits Grew, Warning Signs Went Unheeded." *New York Times.* November 16, 2007.

Norris, Floyd. "Customers, Not Brokers, Profited in an Odd 2007." *New York Times.* January 2, 2008. [2008a].

Norris, Floyd. "Reckless? You're in Luck." *New York Times.* September 19, 2008. [2008b].

Norris, Floyd. "The Deal That Fueled Subprime." *New York Times.* March 6, 2009. [2009a].

Norris, Floyd. "A Lack of Rigor Costs MBIA." *New York Times.* November 13, 2009. [2009b].

Norris, Floyd, and Alex Berenson. "Conseco Files for Bankruptcy Protection." *New York Times.* December 19, 2002.

Norris, Floyd, and Eric Dash. "In a Spiraling Credit Crisis, Large Mortgages Grow Costly." *New York Times.* August 12, 2007.

Northedge, Richard. "AIG London unit not regulated by FSA." *Independent.* March 15, 2009.

"NPA Members Give OTS Chairman the Pink Slip." *U.S. Newswire.* June 3, 2002.

Office of the Attorney General of California. "Attorney General Brown Announces Landmark $8.68 Billion Settlement with Countrywide." October 6, 2008. http://ag.ca.gov/newsalerts/release.php?id=1618&year=2008.

Office of the Attorney General of Illinois. "Press Release: Madigan Continues Fight Against Mortgage Foreclosure Crisis." November 26, 2007. http://www.illinoisattorneygeneral.gov/pressroom/2007_11/20071126.html.

Office of the Attorney General of Massachusetts. "Attorney General Martha Coakley Reaches $10 Million Settlement with Subprime Lender Fremont Investment and Loan." June 9, 2009. http://www.mass.gov/?pageID=cagopressrelease&L=1&L0=Home&sid=Cago&b=pressrelease&f=2009_06_09_fremont_agreement&csid=Cago.

Office of the Attorney General of the State of New York. *In re Countrywide Home Loans, Inc., Assurance of Discontinuance Pursuant to Executive Law 63 15.* November 22, 2006. [2006a].

Office of the Attorney General of the State of New York. "Countrywide Agrees to New Measures to Combat Racial and Ethnic Disparities in Mortgage Loan Pricing." December 6, 2006. http://www.oag.state.ny.us/media_center/2006/dec/dec05a_06.html. [2006b].

Office of the Comptroller of the Currency. "Advisory Letter 2000–7: Abusive Lending Practices." July 26, 2000. http://www.occ.treas.gov/ftp/advisory/2000–7.txt.

Office of the Comptroller of the Currency. "Advisory Letter 2002–3: Guidance on Unfair or Deceptive Acts or Practices." March 22, 2002. http://www.occ.treas.gov/ftp/advisory/2002–3.txt. [2002a].

Office of the Comptroller of the Currency. "News Release NR 2002–40: Comptroller Welcomes Growing Consensus that Fee Disparity Problem Must Be Fixed." May 9, 2002. http://www.occ.treas.gov/ftp/release/2002–40.txt. [2002b].

Office of the Comptroller of the Currency. "Advisory Letter 2003–2: Guidelines for National Banks to Guard Against Predatory and Abusive Lending Practices." February 21, 2003. http://www.occ.treas.gov/ftp/advisory/2003–2.pdf.

Office of the Comptroller of the Currency. "Bank Activities and Operations; Final rule." *Federal Register* 69 (January 13, 2004): 1895–1904. [2004a].

Office of the Comptroller of the Currency. "Bank Activities and Operations; Real Estate Lending and Appraisals; Final rule." *Federal Register* 69 (January 13, 2004): 1904–1917. [2004b].

Office of the Comptroller of the Currency. *OCC Bulletin 2004–20*. 2004. [2004c].

Office of the Comptroller of the Currency. "OCC Guidelines Establishing Standards for Residential Mortgage Lending Practices." *Federal Register* 70 (February 7, 2005): 6329–6334.

Office of the Comptroller of the Currency. "Application Filed By JPMorgan Chase Bank, N.A., Columbus, Ohio to Acquire Certain Assets and Assume Certain Deposits from the Bank of New York: CRA Decision # 136." September 15, 2006. [2006a].

Office of the Comptroller of the Currency. "2006 Survey of Credit Underwriting Practices." Report, National Credit Committee. October 2006. [2006b].

Office of the Comptroller of the Currency. "OCC's Quarterly Report on Bank Trading and Derivatives Activities, Third Quarter 2009." December 18, 2009. http://www.occ.treas.gov/ftp/release/2009–161a.pdf.

Office of the Comptroller of the Currency and Office of Thrift Supervision. "OCC and OTS Mortgage Metrics Report: Disclosure of National Bank and Federal Thrift Mortgage Loan Data October 2007—March 2008." Report, OCC and OTS Mortgage Metrics. June 2008. [2008a].

Office of the Comptroller of the Currency and Office of Thrift Supervision. "OCC and OTS Mortgage Metrics Report: January-June 2008." Report, OCC and OTS Mortgage Metrics. September 2008. [2008b].

Office of the Comptroller of the Currency and Office of Thrift Supervision. "OCC and OTS Mortgage Metrics Report: Disclosure of National Bank and Federal Thrift Mortgage Loan Data, Second Quarter 2009." Report, OCC and OTS Mortgage Metrics. September 2009.

Office of Federal Housing Enterprise Oversight. "Portfolio Caps and Conforming Loan Limits." *Mortgage Market Note 07–1*. September 6, 2007. http://www.fhfa.gov/webfiles/1246/MMNOTE9607.pdf.

Office of the General Counsel, New York Insurance Department. Opinion Letter. June 16, 2000.

Office of the Inspector General, Department of Housing and Urban Development. "Controls Over FHA's Single-Family Lender Approval Process Need Improvement." Audit Report 2009-SE-0004. September 30, 2009. http://www.hud.gov/offices/oig/reports/files/ig0900004.pdf.

Office of the Inspector General, Department of the Treasury. "Material Loss Review of The First National Bank of Keystone." Report, OIG-00-067. March 10, 2000.

Office of Inspector General, Department of the Treasury. "Safety and Soundness: Material Loss Review of NetBank, FSB." Report, OIG-08–032. April 23, 2008. [2008a].

Office of Inspector General, Department of the Treasury. "Safety and Soundness: Material Loss Review of ANB Financial, National Association." Report, OIG-09-013. November 25, 2008. [2008b].

Office of Inspector General, Department of the Treasury. "Safety and Soundness: Material Loss Review of IndyMac Bank, FSB." Report, OIG-09–032. February 26, 2009. [2009a].

Office of Inspector General, Department of the Treasury. "Safety and Soundness: Material Loss Review of Downey Savings and Loan, FA." Report, OIG-09-039. June 15, 2009. [2009b].

Office of the Inspector General, FDIC. "Material Loss Review—The Failure of Pacific Thrift and Loan Company, Woodland Hills, California." Report, Audit No. 00–022. June 7, 2000.

Office of the Inspector General, FDIC. "Material Loss Review of Franklin Bank, S.S.B., Houston, Texas." Report No. AUD-09–014. July 2009. http://www.fdicoig.gov/reports09/09–014–508.shtml.

Office of Inspector General, U.S. Securities and Exchange Commission. "SEC's Oversight of Bear Stearns and Related Entities: The Consolidated Supervised Entity Program." Report No. 446-A. September 25, 2008. http://finance.senate.gov/press/Gpress/2008/prg092608i.pdf (unredacted) and http://www.sec-oig.gov/Reports/AuditsInspections/2008/446-a.pdf (redacted).

Office of Inspector General, U.S. Securities and Exchange Commission. "Practices Related to Naked Short Selling Complaints and Referrals." Report No. 450. March 18, 2009. http://www.sec-oig.gov/Reports/AuditsInspections/2009/450.pdf.

Office of Thrift Supervision. "Lending and Investment: Final rule." *Federal Register* 61 (September 30, 1996): 50951–50984. [1996a].

Office of Thrift Supervision. "Subsidiaries and Equity Investments: Final rule." *Federal Register* 61 (December 18, 1996): 66561–66579. [1996b].

Office of Thrift Supervision. "Proposed Agency Information Collection Activities." *Federal Register* 65 (August 4, 2000): 48049–48056. [2000a].

Office of Thrift Supervision. "Responsible Alternative Mortgage Lending: Advance notice of proposed rulemaking." *Federal Register* 65 (April 5, 2000): 17811–17818. [2000b].

Office of Thrift Supervision. "OTS Tests 'Mystery Shopping' to Help Check Thrifts' Fair Lending Compliance." July 27, 2000. [2000c].

Office of Thrift Supervision. "OTS Receives EU Equivalency Designation for Supervision of AIG." OTS 07–011. February 22, 2007. [2007a].

Office of Thrift Supervision. "Supervisory Agreement between OTS and AIG Federal Savings Bank." June 7, 2007. http://www.ots.treas.gov. [2007b].

Olson, Dan, and Sasha Aslanian. "From 35th Street to Wall Street: Anatomy of a Foreclosure." Minnesota Public Radio. May 5, 2008. http://minnesota.publicradio.org/display/web/2008/05/02/foreclosureanatomy/.

Onaran, Yalman. "Bear Stearns Halts Redemptions on Third Hedge Fund." *Bloomberg.* July 31, 2007. http://www.bloomberg.com/apps/news?pid=20601087&refer=home&sid=as4Ljb0FH2kY.

Onaran, Yalman. "Lehman Brothers to Cut 1,300 Jobs in Mortgage Unit." *Bloomberg.* January 17, 2008. http://www.bloomberg.com/apps/news?pid=20601208&sid=aywW10qoZsys&refer=finance.

Onaran, Yalman, and Dave Pierson. "Banks' Subprime Market-Related Losses Reach $506 Billion: Table." *Bloomberg.* August 27, 2008. http://www.bloomberg.com/apps/news?pid=newsarchive&sid=aDmQ660oJbfw.

"Online Bank Fails, and Regulators Shut It." *New York Times.* September 29, 2007.

Osinski, Michael. "My Manhattan Project: How I Helped Build the Bomb that Blew up Wall Street." *New York Magazine.* March 26, 2009.

Osterman, Cynthia. "Eviction Can Come Suddenly for Renters." Reuters. February 14, 2008.

Overbye, Dennis. "They Tried to Outsmart Wall Street." *New York Times*. March 10, 2009.

Overdahl, James A. Testimony Regarding Reducing Risks and Improving Oversight in the OTS Derivatives Market, Before the Senate Subcommittee on Securities, Insurance, and Investment. July 9, 2008.

Padilla, Matthew. "Fremont General Files for Bankruptcy." *MortgageInsider*. June 19, 2008.

Paletta, Damian. "National City Is Under U.S. Scrutiny—Memorandum Agreement With Regulators Effectively Puts Banking Unit on Probation." *Wall Street Journal*. June 6, 2008. [2008a].

Paletta, Damian. "FDIC Banked Significant Savings in Brokering WaMu Sale." *Wall Street Journal*. September 27, 2008. [2008b].

Paletta, Damian. "Banks Die Too Fast for the Regulators." *Wall Street Journal*. January 23, 2009.

Paletta, Damian, and David Enrich. "Regulators Step Up Bank Actions." *Wall Street Journal*. August 26, 2008.

Palmeri, Chris. "Over One Million People Lost Their Home in 2008." *BusinessWeek*. January 14, 2008.

Parlour, Christine A., and Andrew Winton. "Laying off Credit Risk: Loan Sales versus Credit Default Swaps." Working paper. August 29, 2008.

Partnoy, Frank. "How and Why Credit Rating Agencies Are Not Like Other Gatekeepers." University of San Diego Legal Studies Research Paper no. 07–46. May 2006.

Partnoy, Frank. *F.I.A.S.C.O.: Blood in the Water on Wall Street*. New York: W.W. Norton & Co., 2009.

Partnoy, Frank, and David A. Skeel, Jr. "The Promises and Perils of Credit Derivatives." *University of Cincinnati Law Review* 75 (2007): 1019–1051.

Pate, R. Carter, Michael C. Buenzow, and Rishi Sadarangani. "Subprime Auto Finance: The Year of the Bankruptcies." *American Bankruptcy Institute Journal* 17, no. 4 (May 1998): 30.

Patterson, Scott. "Housing Cycle is Caught in Vicious Circle." *Wall Street Journal*. February 20, 2008.

Paul, Peralte C. "NetBank Future in Doubt." *Atlanta Journal-Constitution*. September 19, 2007.

Paulson, Henry M., Jr. "Remarks on Recommendations from the President's Working Group on Financial Markets." U.S. Treasury Document No. HP-872. March 2008. [2008a].

Paulson, Henry M., Jr. "GSE Initiatives": Testimony before the U.S. Senate Banking Committee. July 15, 2008. [2008b].

Paulson, Henry M., Jr. "Statement by Secretary Henry M. Paulson, Jr. on Treasury and Federal Housing Finance Agency Action to Protect Financial Markets and Taxpayers." Department of the Treasury Press Release HP-1129. September 7, 2008. [2008c].

Paulson, Henry M., Jr. "Remarks by Secretary Henry M. Paulson, Jr. on Financial Rescue Package and Economic Update." Department of the Treasury Press Release HP-1265. November 12, 2008. [2008d].

Pavlov, Andrey D., and Susan M. Wachter. "Mortgage Put Options and Real Estate Markets." *Journal of Real Estate Finance and Economics* 38, no. 1 (2009): 89–103.

Pelley, Scott. "World of Trouble." CBS News. February 15, 2009. http://www.cbsnews.com/stories/2009/02/13/60minutes/main4801309.shtml.

Peterson, Christopher L. "Federalism and Predatory Lending: Unmasking the Deregulatory Agenda." *Temple Law Review* 78 (2007): 1–98.

Petruno, Tom, and William Heisel. "Downey Stops Cash Loss but Warns on Liquidity." *Los Angeles Times.* August 12, 2008.

The PEW Charitable Trust. "Defaulting on the Dream: States Respond to America's Fore-closure Crisis." April 2008.

Pew Health Group. "Still Waiting: 'Unfair or Deceptive' Credit Card Practices Continued as Americans Wait for New Reforms to Take Effect." October 2009.

Philips, Matthew. "The Monster That Ate Wall Street." *Newsweek.* October 6, 2008.

Phillips, Michael M. "Fed Chief's Boyhood Home Is Sold after Foreclosure." *Wall Street Journal.* February 14, 2009.

Pilling, David, Jonathan Soble, and Gillian Tett. "Subprime Credit Loss Heading for Dollars 400bn, Say G7 Finance Chiefs." *Financial Times.* February 11, 2008.

Pinedo, Anna T., and Amy Moorhus Baumgardner. "Federal Mortgage Modification and Foreclosure Prevention Efforts." *Uniform Commercial Code Law Journal* 41 (Spring 2009): 319–345.

Pittman, Mark, Elliot Blair Smith, and Jesse Westbrook. "Cox's SEC Censors Report on Bear Stearns Collapse." *Bloomberg.* October 7, 2008. http://www.bloomberg.com/apps/news?pid=20601109&sid=av2fpp3blAgY.

Podelco, Mary. "Hearing on Predatory Mortgage Lending: The Problem, Impact and Responses." Testimony before the U.S. Senate Committee on Banking, Housing, and Urban Affairs. July 26, 2001.

Pollock, Lauren. "Downey Curtails Some Lending." *Wall Street Journal.* October 16, 2008.

Poser, Norman S. "Why the SEC Failed: Regulators Against Regulation." Brooklyn Law School Legal Studies Research Paper No. 132. February 2009.

Pouliot, Karlie. "Foreclosure-Related Stress, Suicide on the Rise?" Fox News. July 25, 2008. http://www.foxnews.com/story/0,2933,391448,00.html.

"Predatory Lending Laws Neutered." *Atlanta Journal-Constitution.* August 6, 2003.

The President's Working Group on Financial Market Developments. "Policy Statement on Financial Market Developments." March 13, 2008. https://treas.gov/press/releases/reports/pwgpolicystatemktturmoil_03122008.pdf.

Pressley, James. "U.S. Homeowners Will Lose up to $10 Trillion, Talbott Estimates." *Bloomberg.* February 12, 2009. http://www.bloomberg.com/apps/news?pid=20601088&sid=ahOc6ZN_3HE0&refer=patrick.net.

"Professionally Gloomy." *Economist.* May 15, 2008.

Pulliam, Susan, Serena Ng, and Randall Smith. "Merrill Upped Ante as Boom in Mort-gage Bonds Fizzled." *Wall Street Journal.* April 16, 2008.

Purnanandam, Amiyatosh. "Originate-to-Distribute Model and the Subprime Mortgage Crisis." Working paper, University of Michigan, Stephen M. Ross School of Business. April 27, 2009.

Quercia, Roberto G., Michael A. Stegman, and Walter R. Davis. "The Impact of Preda-tory Loan Terms on Subprime Foreclosures: The Special Case of Prepayment Penalties and Balloon Payments." Report, Center for Community Capitalism, January 25, 2005.

Raiter, Frank L. "Credit Rating Agencies and the Financial Crisis." Testimony before the U.S. House of Representatives, Committee on Oversight and Government Reform. October 22, 2008.

Rath, Molly. "Swimming With Sharks: Subprime Lenders Put the Bite in Baltimore's Poorest Homeowners." *Baltimore City Paper.* March 29, 2000.

Razzi, Elizabeth. "'Hope for Homeowners' Still Long in Coming." *Washington Post.* September 28, 2008.

Read, Madien. "Citigroup Puts SIVs on Balance Sheet." *USA Today.* December 15, 2009.

Reagan, Ronald. "Remarks at the Annual Meeting of the Boards of Governors of the World Bank Group and International Monetary Fund." September 29, 1981. http://www.reagan.utexas.edu/archives/speeches/1981/92981a.htm.

Reagor, Catherine. "Lawsuits Targeting Mortgage Schemes." *Arizona Republic.* March 4, 2007.

Reckard, E. Scott. "Refinance Pitches in Sub-Prime Tone." *Los Angeles Times.* October 29, 2007.

Reckard, E. Scott, and Andrea Chang. "Banks Hit by Fallout from the Crisis at Indymac." *Los Angeles Times.* July 15, 2008.

Reckard, E. Scott, and Mike Hudson. "Workers Say Lender Ran 'Boiler Rooms.'" *Los Angeles Times.* February 4, 2005.

Reddy, Anitha. "Lending Case to Cost Citigroup $215 Million." *Washington Post.* September 20, 2002.

Reddy, Sudeep. "Lenders to Home Buyers Tighten Further." *Wall Street Journal.* November 6, 2007.

Reich, John M. Director, Office of Thrift Supervision. "Remarks before the Community Bankers Association of New York State." November 18, 2005.

Reich, John M. Director, Office of Thrift Supervision. "Remarks to the Exchequer Club." February 15, 2006. [2006a].

Reich, John M. Director, Office of Thrift Supervision. "Remarks to Women in Housing Finance." March 22, 2006. [2006b].

Reich, John M. "Remarks to the New York Bankers Association, New York, NY." April 6, 2006. [2006c].

Reich, John M. "Remarks to the Joint Conference of the Ohio Bankers League & Illinois League of Financial Institutions, Colorado Springs, Colorado." September 22, 2006. [2006d].

Reich, John M. Director, Office of Thrift Supervision. "Remarks to the America's Community Bankers Annual Conference." October 15, 2006. [2006e].

Reich, John M. Director, Office of Thrift Supervision. "Remarks to the New York Bankers Association." November 9, 2006. [2006f].

Reich, John M. Director, Office of Thrift Supervision. "Remarks to the Independent Community Bankers of America." March 6, 2007. [2007a].

Reich, John M. Director, Office of Thrift Supervision. "Remarks to the California Bankers Association." April 10, 2007. [2007b].

Reich, John M. Director, Office of Thrift Supervision. "Remarks to the Pittsburgh Community Reinvestment Group, Regulatory Speaker Series." April 18, 2007. [2007c].

Reich, John M. Director, Office of Thrift Supervision. "Remarks to the New Jersey League of Community Bankers." May 3, 2007. [2007d].

Reich, John M. Director, Office of Thrift Supervision. "Remarks to the Financial Services Roundtable Housing Policy Council." May 17, 2007. [2007e].

Reich, John M. Director, Office of Thrift Supervision. "Remarks to the Exchequer Club." September 19, 2007. [2007f].

Reich, John M. Director, Office of Thrift Supervision. "Remarks to the British Bankers' Association." October 3, 2007. [2007g].

Reich, John M. Director, Office of Thrift Supervision. "Remarks to the New York Bankers Association." October 26, 2007. [2007h].

Reich, John M. Director, Office of Thrift Supervision. "Remarks to the American Bankers Association Summer Meeting." July 21, 2008.

Reichman, Deb. "Bush Unveils Help to Homeowners with Risky Mortgages." *Detroit Free Press.* August 31, 2007.

Renuart, Elizabeth, and Diane E. Thompson. "The Truth, the Whole Truth, and Nothing but the Truth: Fulfilling the Promise of Truth in Lending." *Yale Journal on Regulation* 25, no. 2 (2008): 181–244.

Reuters. "Big Mortgage Lender in Chapter 11 Filing." *New York Times.* August 22, 2007.

Reuters. "A Losing Year at Countrywide, but not for Chief." *New York Times.* April 25, 2008.

*Ricci, et al. v. Ameriquest Mortgage Co., et al.,* No. 05–1214 JRT/FLN (D. Minn.). Declaration of Mark Bomchill. January 2007.

Richardson, Karen, and Aaron Lucchetti. "Bond Insurers Weather Hit to Ratings." *Wall Street Journal.* January 19, 2008.

Rivlin, Alice M. "Reducing Systemic Risk in the Financial Sector." Testimony before the House Committee on Financial Services. July 21, 2009.

Ropp, James B. Testimony before the House Financial Services Committee. March 20, 2009.

Rucker, Patrick. "Wall Street Often Shelved Damaging Subprime Reports." Reuters. July 27, 2007. http://www.reuters.com/articlePrint?articleId=USN2743515820070727.

Rudolf, John Collins. "Judges' Frustration Grows with Mortgage Servicers." *New York Times.* September 4, 2009.

"Ruptured Credit." *Economist.* May 15, 2008.

Rushton, Emory W. Senior Deputy Comptroller and Chief National Bank Examiner, OCC. Testimony before the U.S. House of Representatives, Committee on Financial Services, Subcommittee on Financial Institutions and Consumer Credit. March 27, 2007.

Saulny, Susan. "Banks Starting to Walk Away on Foreclosures." *New York Times.* March 29, 2009.

Scannell, Kara. "Crisis Highlights SEC's Limits: Agency's Lack of Tools To Stem Financial Woes May Rekindle Debate." *Wall Street Journal.* March 18, 2008.

Scannell, Kara, and Deborah Solomon. "Unraveling the Subprime Mess." *Wall Street Journal.* September 4, 2007.

Scannell, Kara, and Susanne Craig. "SEC Chief Under Fire as Fed Seeks Bigger Wall Street Role." *Wall Street Journal.* June 23, 2008.

Schapiro, Mary L. Chairman, U.S. Securities and Exchange Commission. "Address to Practising Law Institute's 'SEC Speaks in 2009' Program." February 6, 2009.

Schloemer, Ellen. "Losing Ground: Foreclosures in the Subprime Market and Their Cost to Homeowners." Center for Responsible Lending. December 28, 2006. http://www.responsiblelending.org/mortgage-lending/research-analysis/foreclosure-paper-report-2–17.pdf.

Schmitt, Richard B. "Regulator Takes Heat over IndyMac." *Los Angeles Times.* October 6, 2008.

Schoen, John. "Regulators Struggle to Contain Foreclosure Fraud." MSNBC.com. April 6, 2009. http://www.msnbc.msn.com/id/30070957.

Scholtes, Saskia. "Fannie and Freddie Slide." *Financial Times.* July 8, 2008. http://www.ft.com/cms/s/0/69066b72–4c87–11dd-96bb-000077b07658.html.

Schumer, Charles E., and Carolyn B. Maloney. "The Subprime Lending Crisis: The Economic Impact on Wealth, Property Values and Tax Revenues, and How We Got Here." Report, Joint Economic Committee of Congress. October 25, 2007.

Schwarcz, Steven L. "Protecting Financial Markets: Lessons from the Subprime Mortgage Meltdown." *Minnesota Law Review* 93 (December 2008): 373–406.

Schwartz, Nelson D. "Beware of the Housing Fallout." *New York Times.* October 28, 2007.

Securities and Exchange Commission. "Statement of the Securities and Exchange Commission Concerning Financial Penalties." January 4, 2006. http://www.sec.gov/news/press/2006–4.htm.

Securities and Exchange Commission. "Oversight of Credit Rating Agencies Registered as Nationally Recognized Statistical Rating Organizations." *Federal Register* 72 (June 18, 2007): 33564–33636. [2007a].

Securities and Exchange Commission. "Case Closing Recommendation, Case No. NY 07563." November 21, 2007. [2007b].

Securities and Exchange Commission. "Summary Report of Issues Identified in the Commission Staff's Examinations of Select Credit Rating Agencies." July 2008.

Securities and Exchange Commission. "Amendments to Rules for Nationally Recognized Statistical Rating Organizations: Final rule." *Federal Register* 74 (February 9, 2009): 6456–6484. [2009a].

Securities and Exchange Commission. "Amendments to Rules for Nationally Recognized Statistical Rating Organizations: Part II; Final rules." *Federal Register* 74 (December 4, 2009): 63832-63865. [2009b].

*Securities and Exchange Commission v. Mozilo et al.*, No. CV-09–3994 (C.D. Cal.). Complaint and Demand for Jury Trial. June 4, 2009.

Seebach, Mary Jane M. Letter to Jennifer Johnson, Secretary, Board of Governors of the Federal Reserve System. March 27, 2006. http://www.federalreserve.gov/SECRS/2006/April/20060411/OP-1246/OP-1246_45_1.pdf.

Seebach, Mary Jane M. Letter to Regulation Comments, Chief Counsel's Office, Office of Thrift Supervision. May 7, 2007. http://files.ots.treas.gov/comments/0dbce609–691d-456b-9b30–867f922c1b65.pdf.

Seidenberg, Steven. "Salvage Plan: Beleaguered Homeowners Hope the Administration's New Program Will Break the Logjam Over Mortgage Loan Workouts." *ABA Journal* (May 2009). http://www.abajournal.com/magazine/article/salvage_plan/.

Seidman, Ellen. "CRA in the 21st Century." *Mortgage Banking* 60 (October 1, 1999): 6.

"Senate Confirms Geithner to Head Treasury." *Washington Independent.* January 26, 2009.

Sengupta, Rajdeep, and Yu Man Tam. "The LIBOR-OIS Spread as a Summary Indicator." *Economic Synopses* no. 25 (2008). Federal Reserve Bank of St. Louis. http://research.stlouisfed.org/publications/es/08/ES0825.pdf.

Sharick, Merle, Erin E. Omba, Nick Larson, and James D. Croft. "Eighth Periodic Mortgage Fraud Case Report to Mortgage Bankers Association." Mortgage Asset Research Institute. April 2006.

Shear, William B. "Characteristics and Performance of Nonprime Mortgages." Government Accountability Office Report No. GAO-09-848R. July 2009. http://www.gao.gov/new.items/d09848r.pdf.

*Shearson/American Express, Inc. v. McMahon*, 482 U.S. 220 (1987).

Shenn, Jody. "ARM Lenders Prep for Wave Of Teaser-Rate Expirations." *American Banker.* January 18, 2006.

Shenn, Jody. "Fannie, Freddie Subprime Spree May Add to Bailout." *Bloomberg.* September 22, 2008. http://www.bloomberg.com/apps/news?pid=20601109&sid=ay0Kkt47a3s4.

Shepard, Bill. "Perils and Phantasms." *Investment Dealers' Digest* (February 3, 2003): 2.

Shepard, Bill. "The Synthetic CDO Shell Game." *Investment Dealers' Digest* (May 16, 2005): 1–10.

Shrivastava, Anusha. "Commercial Paper Isn't As Healthy As It Seems." *Wall Street Journal.* October 9, 2009.

"Shutting up Shop: The Long-feared Surge in Bankruptcies in America Is Now Under Way." *Economist.* October 9, 2008.

Sidel, Robin. "Latest Trouble Spot for Banks: Souring Home-Equity Loans." *Wall Street Journal.* March 12, 2008. [2008a].

Sidel, Robin. "Charge-Offs Start to Shred Card Issuers." *Wall Street Journal.* December 11, 2008. [2008b].

Sidel, Robin, and Damian Paletta. "Overextension behind Latest U.S. Bank Closings." *Globe and Mail.* July 28, 2008.

Sidel, Robin, David Enrich, and Dan Fitzpatrick. "WaMu Is Seized, Sold Off to J.P. Morgan, in Largest Failure in U.S. Banking History." *Wall Street Journal.* September 26, 2008.

Simon, Ruth. "Home Rundown: A Look at the Pros and Cons of Different Types of Mortgages—and Which One May Be the Best for You Now." *Wall Street Journal.* January 16, 2006.

Simon, Ruth. "Lenders Rethink Home-Equity Loans." *Wall Street Journal.* January 16, 2008. [2008a].

Simon, Ruth. "Defaults Rising Rapidly For 'Pick-a-Pay' Option Mortgages." *Wall Street Journal.* April 30, 2008. [2008b].

Simon, Ruth. "Mortgages Made in 2007 Go Bad at Rapid Clip." *Wall Street Journal.* August 7, 2008. [2008c].

Simon, Ruth. "Modified Loans Do Little to Help Homeowners." *Wall Street Journal.* December 8, 2008. [2008d].

Simon, Ruth. "Easing Mortgages Isn't a Panacea." *Wall Street Journal.* December 9, 2008. [2008e].

Simon, Ruth. "Option ARMs See Rising Defaults." *Wall Street Journal.* January 30, 2009. [2009a].

Simon, Ruth. "Loan-Modification Plan Revised to Address Second Mortgages." *Wall Street Journal.* April 29, 2009. [2009b].

Simon, Ruth. "Guidelines Aim to Ease Short Sales." *Wall Street Journal.* December 1, 2009. [2009c].

Simon, Ruth. "Some Borrowers Find Little Relief." *Wall Street Journal.* December 1, 2009. [2009d].

Simon, Ruth. "Redefault Rate Decreases for Restructured Mortgages." *Wall Street Journal.* December 22, 2009. [2009e].

Simon, Ruth, and James R. Hagerty. "One in Four Borrowers Under Water." *Wall Street Journal.* November 24, 2009.

Simpson, Glenn R. "Loan Data Focus of Probe—Countrywide Files May Have Included Dubious Information." *Wall Street Journal.* March 11, 2008.

Simpson, Glenn R., and James R. Hagerty. "Countrywide Loss Focuses Attention on Underwriting." *Wall Street Journal.* April 30, 2008.

Sirri, Erik. Director, Division of Trading and Markets, U.S. Securities and Exchange Commission. "Testimony Concerning Credit Default Swaps." Testimony before the House Committee on Agriculture. October 15, 2008.

Sloan, Allan. "Chaos on Wall Street." *Fortune.* March 31, 2008. http://money.cnn.com/2008/03/28/news/economy/disaster_sloan.fortune/index.htm.

Smith, Adam. *An Inquiry into the Nature and Causes of the Wealth of Nations.* London: W. Strahan and T. Cadell, 1776.

Smith, Geoff, and Sara Duda. "Roadblock to Recovery: Examining the Disparate Impact of Vacant Lender-owned Properties in Chicago." Report, Woodstock Institute. September 2009.

Smith, Randall, and Kara Scannell. "Regulator Schapiro To Run SEC For Obama." *Wall Street Journal.* December 18, 2008.

Smith, Valerie L., Forrest Pafenberg, and Laura Goren. "Mortgage Markets and the Enterprises in 2005." Report, Office of Federal Housing Enterprises Oversight. September 2006.

Somerville, Glenn, and David Lawder. "Treasury Sees Millions More Foreclosures." Reuters. September 9, 2009.

Sorkin, Andrew Ross. "The Race to Save Lehman Brothers." *New York Times.* October 20, 2009.

"SOS—'Save Our Stocks:' A Look Back at a Year of Bailouts, Underwater Investors and Sunken Hopes." *Wall Street Journal.* January 2, 2009.

Soundview Home Loan Trust 2006–3. Prospectus Supplement. August 10, 2006.

Stango, Victor, and Jonathan Zinman. "How a Cognitive Bias Shapes Competition: Evidence from Consumer Credit Markets." Working paper. 2006.

Stecklow, Steve. "Banks Doubted a Lender, but Still Propped It Up." *Wall Street Journal.* November 9, 2009.

Stein, Eric. Testimony before the Senate Committee on Banking, Housing and Urban Affairs. October 16, 2008.

Stein, Gabrielle. "Cram-Downs Confuse ABS Prospects." *SourceMedia.* January 26, 2009.

Stempel, Jonathan. "Moody's to Cut 275 Jobs, Take 4th Quarter Charge." Reuters. January 7, 2008. http://www.reuters.com/article/governmentFilingsNews/idUSN0728259920080107. [2008a].

Stempel, Jonathan. "WaMu Has $3.33bln Loss, May Be Cut To 'Junk.'" Reuters. July 22, 2008. http://www.reuters.com/article/idUSN2232254820080722. [2008b].

Stempel, Jonathan. "National City has $1.76 Billion Loss on Loan Write-Offs." Reuters. July 24, 2008. http://www.reuters.com/article/idUSN2446228320080724. [2008c].

Stern, Gary H. Chief Executive of the Federal Reserve Bank of Minneapolis. "Better Late Than Never: Addressing Too-Big-To-Fail." Remarks before the Brookings Institution. March 31, 2009.

Stern, Gary H., and Ron H. Feldman. *Too Big to Fail: The Hazards of Bank Bailouts.* 1st paperback ed. Washington, D.C.: Brookings Institution Press, 2009.

Stevens, Paul Schott. "Statement before the U.S. Securities and Exchange Commission Roundtable on Oversight of Credit Rating Agencies." April 15, 2009.

Stewart, Amy. "Federal Home Loan Bank of San Francisco Announces Board of Directors Appointment." *Reuters Business Wire.* January 22, 2008.

Stoll, John D. "GMAC Slashing Jobs in Auto-Finance Area." *Wall Street Journal.* February 21, 2008.

Stone, Brad. "Banks Mine Data and Woo Troubled Borrowers." *New York Times.* October 22, 2008.

Story, Louise. "Making Trouble for Lehman." *New York Times.* June 4, 2008. [2008a].

Story, Louise. "Home Equity Frenzy Was a Bank Ad Come True." *New York Times.* August 15, 2008. [2008b].

Story, Louise. "For Bank of America, the Pressure Mounts Over Merrill Deal." *New York Times.* January 16, 2009. [2009a].

Story, Louise. "Wall St. Finds Profits by Reducing Mortgages." *New York Times*. November 22, 2009. [2009b].

Stout, David. "Fannie Mae to Allow Borrowers to Lease Homes." *New York Times*. November 6, 2009. [Stout, D. 2009].

Stout, Lynn. "Regulate OTC Derivatives by Deregulating Them." *Regulation* (Fall 2009): 30–33. [Stout, L. 2009].

Streitfeld, David. "A Town Drowns in Debt as Home Values Plunge." *New York Times*. November 11, 2008.

Streitfeld, David. "As an Exotic Mortgage Resets, Payments Skyrocket." *New York Times*. September 9, 2009. [2009a].

Streitfeld, David. "Interest Rates are Low, but Banks Balk at Refinancing." *New York Times*. December 13, 2009. [2009b].

Streitfeld, David. "Defaults Rise in Loan Modification Program." *New York Times*. April 14, 2010.

Streitfeld, David, and Gretchen Morgenson. "Building Flawed American Dreams." *New York Times*. October 19, 2008.

Streitfeld, David, and Louise Story. "F.H.A. Problems Raising Concerns of Policy Makers." *New York Times*. October 9, 2009.

Strott, Elizabeth. "Citi Faces $11 Billion Writedown." MSN.com. November 5, 2007. http://articles.moneycentral.msn.com/Investing/Dispatch/CitiFacesHugeWriteDown.aspx.

Stulz, René M. "Over-the-Counter Derivatives Markets Act of 2009." Testimony before the House Committee on Financial Services. October 7, 2009.

Stutt, Amanda. "Fighting Foreclosure: Subprime Borrowers Battle (and Beat) Lenders in Court." *Village Voice*. September 3, 2008.

"Subprime and Predatory Lending: New Regulatory Guidance, Current Market Conditions, and Effects on Regulated Financial Institutions, Hearing before the Subcommittee on Financial Institutions and Consumer Credit of the House Committee on Financial Services." 110th Cong., 1st Sess. March 27, 2007. http://frwebgate.access.gpo.gov/cgi-bin/getdoc.cgi?dbname=110_house_hearings&docid=f:35410.pdf.

Swecker, Chris. Assistant Director, Criminal Investigation Division, FBI. "Mortgage Fraud and its Impact on Mortgage Lenders." Testimony before the House Financial Services Subcommittee on Housing and Community Opportunity. October 7, 2004.

Sword, Doug, and Anthony Cormier. "New Trend in Homes: Appeal Tax Values." *International Herald Tribune*. September 12, 2007.

Sylvan, Louise. Deputy Chair, Australian Competition and Consumer Commission. "20 Years On: What Will Fair Trading Look Like in 2027?" Lecture on the occasion of the 20th anniversary celebration of the NSW Fair Trading Act. November 22, 2007.

T2 Partners, LLC. "An Overview of the Housing/Credit Crisis and Why There Is More Pain to Come." Report. January 27, 2009.

Tanoue, Donna. "Open Forum Risk and Subprime Lending." *National Mortgage News*. October 25, 1999.

Tanoue, Donna. Chairman, Federal Deposit Insurance Corporation. Testimony on Recent Bank Failures and Regulatory Initiatives before the House Committee on Banking and Financial Services. February 8, 2000. [2000a].

Tanoue, Donna. Chairman, Federal Deposit Insurance Corporation. "Remarks before the Annual Conference, National Congress for Community Economic Development." October 13, 2000. [2000b].

Taylor, Charles. "Making the Biggest Firms Hold More Capital." *American Banker.* March 13, 2009.

Technical Committee of the International Organization of Securities Commissions. "Report of the Task Force on the Subprime Crisis: Final Report." May 2008. http://www.iasplus.com/iosco/0805ioscosubprimereport.pdf.

*Tellabs v. Makor Issues & Rights, Ltd.,* 551 U.S. 308 (2007).

Terris, Harry. "ARM Workout Calls Trigger Fierce Debate." *American Banker.* October 9, 2007.

Terris, Harry. "Servicer-Held Mortgages Less Likely to Go Bad after Mod." *American Banker.* December 23, 2008.

Thomas, Kenneth H. "Megathrifts Like Wamu Now Too Big for OTS to Regulate." *American Banker.* August 16, 2002.

Thompson, Diane. "Why Servicers Foreclose When They Should Modify and Other Puzzles of Servicer Behavior: Servicer Compensation and its Consequences." Working paper. October 2009.

Thompson, James R. "Counterparty Risk in Financial Contracts: Should the Insured Worry about the Insurer?" Working paper. November 2008.

Thorson, Eric M. Inspector General, Department of the Treasury. Letter to Hon. Charles Grassley. December 22, 2008. http://grassley.senate.gov/news/Article.cfm?customel_dataPageID_1502=18591.

Tillman, Vickie A. Testimony before the House Subcommittee on Capital Markets, Insurance and Government Sponsored Enterprises. September 27, 2007.

Timiraos, Nick. "Borrowers Miss Out on Billions in Savings." *Wall Street Journal.* March 3, 2010.

Timiraos, Nick, and Deborah Solomon. "Loan Losses Spark Concern over FHA." *Wall Street Journal.* September 4, 2009.

Tomsho, Robert. "U.S. Aims to Buoy Student-Loan Market." *Wall Street Journal.* May 21, 2008.

Tomsho, Robert, and John Hechinger. "Lenders Predict Harsher Climate for Student Loans." *Wall Street Journal.* February 14, 2008.

Trexler, Phil. "Foreclosure Victim, 90, Apparently Shoots Self." *Akron Beacon Journal.* October 3, 2008.

Trickey, Erick. "Welcome to Foreclosure Central." *Cleveland Magazine.* July 2007.

Tully, Shawn. "Meet the 23,000% Stock For 20 Years, Countrywide Financial Has Been on a Tear with the Housing Boom Winding Down, Can This Mortgage Star Keep from Falling?" *Fortune.* August 15, 2003.

Turner, Lynn E. Former Chief Accountant, U.S. Securities and Exchange Commission. Testimony before the U.S. House of Representatives, Committee on Oversight and Government Reform. October 7, 2008.

Uchitelle, Louis. "Fearing Slide in Economy, Fed Cuts Its Discount Rate." *New York Times.* August 18, 2007.

Uchitelle, Louis. "Unemployment Hits 7.2%, 16-Year High." *New York Times.* January 10, 2009.

United States Senate Committee on Banking, Housing, and Urban Affairs. "Brief Summary of the Dodd-Frank Wall Street Reform and Consumer Protection Act." 2010. http://banking.senate.gov.

Vekshin, Allison. "FDIC Failed to Limit Commercial Real-Estate Loans." *Bloomberg.* October 19, 2009. http://www.bloomberg.com/apps/news?pid=20601087&sid=ay69xSKX9MM8.

Volcker, Paul A. Former Chairman of the Federal Reserve. Statement before the House Committee on Banking and Financial Services. September 24, 2009.

"Wachovia Corporation at Citigroup 2007 Financial Services Conference—Final." *FD (Fair Disclosure) Wire.* January 30, 2007.

Walsh, John G. Chief of Staff and Public Affairs, Office of the Comptroller of the Currency. "Remarks before the Mossavar-Rahmani Center for Business and Government." October 24, 2007.

Walter, Elisse B. Commissioner, U.S. Securities and Exchange Commission. "Testimony before the House Financial Services Committee." March 20, 2009.

Warsh, Kevin. Memorandum to Chairman Ben S. Bernanke Regarding BofA. December 29, 2008.

*In re Washington Mutual, Inc.*, No. 2:08-md-1919 MJP (W.D. Wash.). Class Action Complaint. 2008.

*Watters v. Wachovia Bank, N.A.*, 550 U.S. 1 (2007).

Waxman, Henry A. Opening Statement of Rep. Henry A. Waxman, Chairman, Committee on Oversight and Government Reform, Credit Rating Agencies and the Financial Crisis. October 22, 2008.

Wessel, David. "Lessons From the Housing Bubble." *Wall Street Journal.* May 29, 2008.

Whalen, Christopher. Statement before the U.S. Senate, Committee on Banking, Housing, and Urban Affairs, Subcommittee on Securities, Insurance, and Investment. June 22, 2009.

White, Alan. "Deleveraging the American Homeowner: The Failure of the 2008 Voluntary Mortgage Contract Modifications." Working paper. August 7, 2009.

White, Ben, and Francesco Guerrera. "JPMorgan Lifts Bear Offer Fivefold." *Financial Times.* March 24, 2008. http://www.ft.com/cms/s/0/35054692-f9a6–11dc-9b7c-000077b07658.html.

White, Lawrence J. *The S&L Debacle.* New York: Oxford University Press, 1991.

White, Patricia. Associate Director, Division of Research and Statistics, Board of Governors of the Federal Reserve System. Statement before the U.S. Senate, Committee on Banking, Housing, and Urban Affairs, Subcommittee on Securities, Insurance, and Investment. June 22, 2009.

Whiteman, Louis. "FDIC Chief Talks Tough On Subprime Loan Business." *American Banker.* November 3, 1999.

Wighton, David. "Morgan Stanley Taps China for $5bn." *Financial Times.* December 19, 2007.

Wilczek, Yin. "SEC Proposes Rule Changes to Beef Up Regulatory Framework for Money Funds." *BNA Banking Report* 92 (2009): 1470.

Williams, Julie L. Chief Counsel and First Senior Deputy Comptroller. "Remarks before the Risk Management Association's Retail Risk Management Conference." June 3, 2003. [2003a].

Williams, Julie L. Chief Counsel and First Senior Deputy Comptroller. "Remarks before the Consumer Federation of America, 15th Annual Consumer Financial Services Conference." December 5, 2003. [2003b].

Williams, Julie L. Chief Counsel and First Senior Deputy Comptroller. "Remarks before America's Community Bankers, Government Affairs Conference." March 9, 2004. [2004a].

Williams, Julie L. First Senior Deputy Comptroller and Chief Counsel. "Remarks before the Annual Meeting of the Cleveland Neighborhood Housing Services." June 15, 2004. [2004b].

Williams, Julie L. Acting Deputy Comptroller of the Currency. "Remarks before the Independent Community Bankers of America." March 11, 2005. [2005a].

Williams, Julie L. Acting Deputy Comptroller of the Currency. "Remarks before the BAI National Loan Review Conference." March 21, 2005. [2005b].

Williams, Julie L. Acting Deputy Comptroller of the Currency. "Remarks before the Regional Interagency Committee." May 3, 2005. [2005c].

Williamson, Elizabeth, and Kara Scannell. "Family Filled Posts at Industry Groups." *Wall Street Journal.* December 18, 2008.

Williamson, Elizabeth, and Ruth Simon. "Plan to Cut Foreclosure Rate Clears Key Hurdle." *Wall Street Journal.* January 9, 2009.

Wilmarth, Arthur E., Jr. "The OCC's Preemption Rules Exceed the Agency's Authority and Present a Serious Threat to the Dual Banking System." *Annual Review of Banking & Financial Law* 23 (2004): 225–364.

Wilmarth, Arthur E., Jr. Testimony before the House Committee on Financial Services, Subcommittee on Financial Institutions and Consumer Credit. April 26, 2007.

Wilmott, Paul. "For Wall Street, Greed Wasn't Good Enough." *New York Times.* September 18, 2008.

Woellert, Lorraine, and Dawn Kopecki. "Credit-Rating Companies 'Sold Soul,' Employees Said." *Bloomberg.* October 22, 2008. http://www.bloomberg.com/apps/news?pid=2 0601087&sid=ac8Bkp_7F4Rc.

Woodward, Susan E. "A Study of Closing Costs for FHA Mortgages." Report, U.S. Department of Housing and Urban Development, Office of Policy Development and Research. May 2008.

Yoon, Al. "Chase to Tackle Modifying Investor-Owned Mortgages." Reuters. January 16, 2009. http://www.reuters.com/article/regulatoryNewsFinancialServicesAndRealEstate/idUSN162841212009011.

Zandi, Mark. Testimony before the U.S. House Financial Services Committee. July 21, 2009.

STATUTES, BILLS, AND REGULATIONS

*Statutes*

7 U.S.C. § 1a
7 U.S.C. § 2
7 U.S.C. §§ 27a-27f
12 U.S.C. § 1464
12 U.S.C. § 1467a
12 U.S.C. § 1820
12 U.S.C. § 1831f
15 U.S.C. § 57a
15 U.S.C. § 77q
15 U.S.C. § 78c
15 U.S.C. § 78i
15 U.S.C. § 78j
15 U.S.C. § 78o
15 U.S.C. § 78o-7
15 U.S.C. § 78p
15 U.S.C. § 78t

15 U.S.C. §§ 1601–1693r

15 U.S.C. § 1602

15 U.S.C. § 1639

Alternative Mortgage Transactions Parity Act of 1982, Pub. L. No. 97–320.

American Recovery and Reinvestment Act of 2009, Pub. L. No. 111–5.

Commodity Exchange Act, 7 U.S.C. §§ 1 et seq.

Council Directive 2002/87 of the European Parliament and of the Council of December 16, 2002 (Financial Conglomerates Directive). 2002 O. J. L. 35, February 2, 2003, p. 1.

Cranston-Gonzalez National Affordable Housing Act, Pub. L. No. 101–625.

Credit Card Accountability, Responsibility, and Disclosure Act of 2009, Pub. L. No. 111–24.

Credit Rating Agency Reform Act of 2006, Pub. L. No. 109–291.

Depository Institutions Deregulation and Monetary Control Act of 1980, Pub. L. No. 96–221.

Dodd-Frank Wall Street Reform and Consumer Protection Act of 2010, Pub. L. No. 111–203.

Economic Stimulus Act of 2008, Pub. L. No. 110–185.

Emergency Economic Stabilization Act of 2008, Pub. L. No. 110–343.

Ensuring Continued Access to Student Loans Act of 2008, Pub. L. No. 110–227.

Federal Deposit Insurance Corporation Improvement Act of 1991, Pub. L. No. 102–242.

Financial Services Regulatory Relief Act of 2006, Pub. L. No. 109-473.

Ga. Code Ann. § 7-6A-12.

Gramm-Leach-Bliley Act of 1999, Pub. L. No. 106–102.

Helping Families Save Their Homes Act of 2009, Pub. L. No. 111–22.

Home Owners Loan Act of 1933, Pub. L. No. 101-73.

Housing and Economic Recovery Act of 2008, Pub. L. No. 110–289.

Magnuson-Moss Warranty—Federal Trade Commission Improvement Act, Pub. L. No. 93–637.

N.Y. Ins. Law § 6901.

Real Estate Settlement Procedures Act, 12 U.S.C. §§ 2601–2617.

Riegle-Neal Community Development and Regulatory Improvement Act of 1994, Pub. L. No. 103-325.

Secure and Fair Enforcement Mortgage Licensing (SAFE) Act of 2008, Pub. L. No. 110–289.

Securities Act of 1933, 15 U.S.C. §§ 77a et seq.

Securities Exchange Act of 1934, 15 U.S.C. §§ 78a et seq.

Truth in Lending Act, 15 U.S.C. §§ 1601–1667f.


*Bills*

Anti-Predatory Lending Act of 2000, H.R. 3901.

Consumer Mortgage Protection Act of 2000, H.R. 4213.

Predatory Lending Consumer Protection Act of 2000, H.R. 4250 and S. 2415.

Predatory Lending Deterrence Act, S. 2405.

The Wall Street Reform and Consumer Protection Act, H.R. 4173.


*Regulations*

12 C.F.R. § 7.4000

12 C.F.R. §§ 7.4007–7.4009

12 C.F.R. § 34.4

12 C.F.R. §§ 204.17g-2 through 204.17g-6
12 C.F.R. § 226.1
12 C.F.R. § 226.19
12 C.F.R. § 226.32
12 C.F.R. § 226.34
12 C.F.R. § 303.207
12 C.F.R. § 337.6
12 C.F.R. § 559.3
12 C.F.R. § 560.2
17 C.F.R. § 40.2
17 C.F.R. pt. 200
17 C.F.R. §§ 229.1100—229.1123
17 C.F.R. pt. 240
17 C.F.R. § 240.15c3–1

# Index

Note: Page numbers followed by "*f*" and "*t*" denote figures and tables, respectively.

Volcker, Paul, 89, 123, 245

Wachovia Bank, 79, 92, 93, 108, 111, 167, 171
Wachovia Corporation, 36, 237, 238
  acquisition of Golden West and World Savings, 180–83
  response to crisis, 183–84
Wachovia Mortgage Corporation, 171
Wagoner, Rick, 125
walkaways, 144
*Wall Street Journal*, 26, 29, 50, 62, 74, 86, 93, 96, 103, 178, 179, 186
Walsh, John, 77
warehouse lending, 21, 45, 69
Warsh, Kevin, 114, 119
Washington Mutual Bank (WaMu), 27, 31, 37, 38, 92, 94, 96, 104, 108, 110, 178–79, 181, 182

*Washington Post*, 73, 160
Watterson-Prime, 46
Waxman, Henry, 193–94
Wells Fargo Bank, 30, 70, 79, 84, 111, 116, 131, 134, 137, 171, 238
Whalen, Christopher, 250
White, Alan, 127
Whitefish Bay, 61
wholesale lending, 27
Williams, Julie, 21, 158, 168, 169, 173
Willumstad, Robert, 106
WMC Mortgage Corporation, 26
World Savings Bank, 36, 180
write-downs, assets, 73

yield spread premiums (YSPs), 32, 231

zombie banks, 117

31901050393638